Global Finance Series

Edited by
John Kirton, University of Toronto, Canada,
Michele Fratianni, Indiana University, United States and
Paolo Savona, University of Rome Guglielmo Marconi, Italy

The intensifying globalization of the twenty-first century has brought a myriad of new managerial and political challenges for governing international finance. The return of synchronous global slowdown, mounting developed country debt, and new economy volatility have overturned established economic certainties. Proliferating financial crises, transnational terrorism, currency consolidation, and increasing demands that international finance should better serve public goods such as social and environmental security have all arisen to compound the problem.

The new public and private international institutions that are emerging to govern global finance have only just begun to comprehend and respond to this new world. Embracing international financial flows and foreign direct investment, in both the private and public sector dimensions, this series focuses on the challenges and opportunities faced by firms, national governments, and international institutions, and their roles in creating a new system of global finance.

Also in the series

Sovereign Wealth Funds and International Political Economy
Manda Shemirani
ISBN 978-1-4094-2207-5

Securing the Global Economy
G8 Global Governance for a Post-Crisis World
Andreas Freytag, John J. Kirton, Razeen Sally and Paolo Savona
ISBN 978-0-7546-7673-7

Debt Relief Initiatives
Policy Design and Outcomes
Marco Arnone and Andrea F. Presbitero
ISBN 978-0-7546-7742-0

Full series listing at the back of the book

Global Financial Crisis
Global Impact and Solutions

Edited by

PAOLO SAVONA
Gugliemo Marconi University, Italy

JOHN J. KIRTON
University of Toronto, Canada

CHIARA OLDANI
University of Viterbo 'La Tuscia, Italy

ASHGATE

Published by
Ashgate Publishing Limited
Wey Court East
Union Road
Farnham
Surrey, GU9 7PT
England

Ashgate Publishing Company
Suite 420
101 Cherry Street
Burlington
VT 05401-4405
USA

www.ashgate.com

British Library Cataloguing in Publication Data
Global financial crisis : global impact and solutions. --
(Global finance series)
1. Global Financial Crisis, 2008-2009. 2. Economic policy.
3. International economic relations.
I. Series II. Savona, Paolo, 1936- III. Kirton, John J.
IV. Oldani, Chiara.
330.9'0511-dc22

Library of Congress Cataloging-in-Publication Data
Savona, Paolo, 1936-
Global financial crisis : global impact and solutions / by Paolo Savona, John Kirton and Chiara Oldani.
    p. cm.
Includes index.
ISBN 978-1-4094-0271-8 (hardback) -- ISBN 978-1-4094-0272-5
(ebook) 1. Financial crises. 2. Global financial crisis, 2008-2009. 3. International economic relations. 4. Economic policy--International cooperation. I. Kirton, John J. II. Oldani, Chiara. III. Title.
HB3722.S328 2011
330.9'0511--dc22

2010053686

ISBN 978 1 4094 0271 8 (hbk)
ISBN 978 1 4094 0272 5 (ebk)

Printed and bound in Great Britain by the
MPG Books Group, UK

Contents

PART I: INTRODUCTION

PART II: SOLUTIONS IN AMERICA AND ASIA

PART III: SOLUTIONS IN EUROPE

PART IV: IMPACTS AND RESPONSES IN THE BRICS

PART V: IMPACTS AND RESPONSES IN DEVELOPING COUNTRIES

PART VI: INNOVATION IN GLOBAL ECONOMIC GOVERNANCE

PART VII: FROM G8 TO G20

List of Figures

List of Tables

List of Contributors

Pietro Alessandrini is a professor of monetary economics at the Faculty of Economics of the Università Politecnica delle Marche in Ancona.

Carlo A. Bollino is a professor of economics at the Faculty of Economics of the University of Perugia and is the former chair of the Italian energy system.

Gregory Chin is a professor in the Department of Political Science and Faculty of Graduate Studies at York University and a Senior Fellow of The Centre for International Governance Innovation in Waterloo, Canada.

Andrew F. Cooper is associate director of The Centre for International Governance Innovation in Waterloo, Canada, and a professor in the Department of Political Science at the University of Waterloo.

Hugo Dobson is a professor of the Japanese international relations at the National Institute of Japanese Studies and the School of East Asian Studies at the University of Sheffield.

Robert C. Fauver is a former G7 sherpa and former U.S. Undersecretary of State for Economic Affairs, and president of Fauver Associates.

Michele Fratianni is a professor emeritus at the Kelley School of Business at Indiana University, professor of international finance at the Faculty of Economics of the University of Ancona in Italy, and a member of MoFiR (Money and Finance Research Group).

Raffaele Galano is a professor of finance and risk management and the chair of the Latin American Observatory of Economics and Law (Osservatorio Economico Giuridico Latino America—OEGLA).

John J. Kirton is director of the G8 Research Group, co-director of the G20 Research Group, and a professor of political science at Trinity College at the Munk School of Global Affairs at the University of Toronto.

Giorgio La Malfa has retired from a chair in economics at the Università di Catania. A former minister of budget and of European affairs, he is member of the Italian Parliament.

Domenico Lombardi is a non-resident fellow in global economy and development at the Brookings Institution and the president of Oxonia, the Oxford Institute for Economic Policy.

Juan Carlos Martinez Oliva is a principal director of the Research Department of the Bank of Italy.

Libero Monteforte is a researcher at the Bank of Italy on secondment to the Italian Treasury.

Chiara Oldani is a lecturer in economics at the University of Viterbo 'La Tuscia' and director of research of the Association for the Encyclopaedia of Banking and Finance (Asso.n.e.b.b.) in Rome.

Victoria Panova is director of the Moscow office of the G8 Research Group and a senior lecturer at the Moscow State Institute on International Relations (MGIMO).

Sara Savastano is lecturer at the Faculty of Economics at the University of Rome 'Tor Vergata'.

Paolo Savona is a professor emeritus of economic policy at Gugliemo Marconi University in Rome.

Andrew Schrumm is a partnerships manager at The Centre for International Governance Innovation in Waterloo, Canada.

Diéry Seck is director of the Centre for Research on Political Economy in Dakar.

Paola Subacchi is research director of international economics at Chatham House in London.

Naoki Tanaka is the president of the Centre for International Public Policy Studies in Tokyo.

George M. von Furstenberg is a professor emeritus of economics at Indiana University.

Preface

This book continues the tradition of Ashgate's Global Finance Series of using the annual G8 summit as a catalyst to explore the central themes in the emerging dynamic of global governance, as shaped by summit itself. It continues the series' central concern with core finance issues. It focuses on the impacts of the financial crisis that peaked in the United States in the fall of 2008 and spread around the world over the following year, and the policy responses in North America, Asia, Europe, the emerging BRIC countries of Brazil, Russia, India, and China, and the developing world beyond.

This volume reports the results of research conducted by the Research Group on Global Financial Governance and the G8 Research Group, with support from The Centre for International Governance Innovation (CIGI), the Review of Economic Conditions in Italy, and the Centre for International Public Policy Studies in Japan. These strands of research were brought together at authors' workshops in Rome in the summer of 2008. They were subsequently revised, updated, supplemented by other contributions, and integrated into a common framework for their presentation here.

This book draws its contributors from North America, Europe, and Africa. It involves scholars and practitioners who bring first-hand professional experience with the G8, central banking, government, and multilateral economic organizations. These contributors come largely from the disciplines of economics and the international political economy and international organization fields of political science. With this variety of perspectives, analytical approaches, and judgements, the collection combines the insights of experts who draw on a rich assortment of regional experiences, theoretical traditions, interpretative frameworks, and concluding convictions, on a G8-wide and broader global scale.

Acknowledgements

In producing this volume, we have enjoyed the exceptional support of those who have contributed in many different ways. Our first debt is to the *Review of Economic Conditions in Italy* and the *Journal of European Economic History* and its editorial staff guided by Michele Barbato, which provided part of the funding that made our research and authors' workshop possible, and to the Unicredit Bank, the Aspen Institute Italia, and the Istituto Affari Internazionali. Our second debt is to CIGI as well as Canada's Department of Foreign Affairs and International Trade (DFAIT) and the Jackman Foundation for their essential financial contributions. We are also most grateful to Chatham House. We also owe much to the outstanding leaders and scholars—including DFAIT's Leonard Edwards, Ron Garson, and John Sloan, to Paola Subacchi and Ruth Davis at Chatham House, and to Marta Dassù, Paolo Guerreri, Roberto Menotti, and Josef Schluttenhofer at Aspen Institute Italia, who saw the exceptional opportunity that such a project offered, provided essential support, rich collegiality, and warm hospitality, and mobilised superb intellectual resources to make this project a success.

We very much appreciate the efficient help from the many talented staff that made our venture possible. In Rome, we are as always grateful to Francesca Camilli. In Toronto, we owe a special word of thanks to Madeline Koch, whose managerial and editorial skills were essential in helping organise the contributions and ensuring that initial thoughts and rough drafts were transformed into a polished integrated book. We are also grateful to Zaria Shaw, who with help from Kaitlin Leeder, provided editorial assistance in the final stages. More broadly, we note with deep appreciation the indispensable contributions of Jenilee Guebert, Ella Kokotsis, and many others.

At the University of Toronto, we are grateful for the continuing support of our colleagues at the Munk School of Global Affairs and Trinity College in the University of Toronto, in particular Louis Pauly, who oversees our research activities, and Peter Hajnal, who assisted with the vital task of securing the anonymous referees who reviewed our draft manuscript and who collectively approved it for publication. We owe much to the comments of our referees, whose keen insights and suggestions have, we hope, made this a better book. At Trinity College, we acknowledge the critical support of Andrew Orchard, Geoffrey Seaborn, Linda Corman and Robert Bothwell. At the Department of Political Science, Robert Vipond and David Cameron provided encouragement and support. At the University of Toronto Library, Carole Moore, supported by Marc Lalonde and Richard Hydal, has been consistently supportive.

As always, we reserve a special word of thanks for Kirstin Howgate and Margaret Younger, and their colleagues at Ashgate, for recognising the virtue of producing this volume and for working so effectively and patiently to ensure the smooth adoption and publication of the manuscript. Finally, we acknowledge the understanding, patience, and support of our families as we laboured to convert raw drafts into published text. We are also indebted to our alumni and students at universities throughout the world. They provide a constant source of inspiration and constructive criticism as we pursue our work.

Paolo Savona, John J. Kirton, and Chiara Oldani

List of Abbreviations and Acronyms

ACA	Aid Council for Africa
AfDB	African Development Bank
AFSI	L'Aquila Food Security Initiative
AIG	American International Group, Inc.
AU	African Union
BIS	Bank for International Settlements
BRIC	Brazil, Russia, India, and China
CCP	central counterparty
CDS	credit default swaps
CIGI	The Centre for International Governance Innovation
DAC	Development Assistance Committee (of the Organisation for Economic Co-operation and Development)
DSGE	dynamic stochastic general equilibrium
EBRD	European Bank for Reconstruction and Development
ECB	European Central Bank
ECLAC	Economic Commission for Latin America and the Caribbean
ECU	European currency unit
EMU	European Monetary Union
EPU	European Payments Union
ESFS	European System of Financial Supervision
ESRC	European Systemic Risk Council
FAO	Food and Agriculture Organization
FCL	flexible credit line
FDI	foreign direct investment
FDIC	Federal Deposit Insurance Corporation (United States)
FHA	United States Federal Housing Administration
FSB	Financial Stability Board
G5	Group of Five (Brazil, China, India, Mexico, and South Africa)
G7	Group of Seven (Canada, France, Germany, Italy, Japan, the United Kingdom, the United States, and the European Union)
G8	Group of Eight (G7 plus Russia)
G10	Group of Ten central bank governors (Belgium, Canada, France, Germany, Italy, Japan, the Netherlands, Sweden, Switzerland, the United Kingdom, and the United States)
G20	Group of Twenty (G8 plus Argentina, Australia, Brazil, China, India, Indonesia, Korea, Mexico, Saudi Arabia, South Africa, and Turkey)

GCAP	Global Call to Action Against Poverty
GDP	gross domestic product
GNI	gross national income
GNP	gross national product
HAP	Heiligendamm-L'Aquila Process
HDP	Heiligendamm Dialogue Process
HIPC	heavily indebted poor country
IBSA	India-Brazil-South Africa Dialogue Forum
IDA	International Development Association
IEA	International Energy Agency
ILO	International Labour Organization
IMFC	International Monetary and Financial Committee (of the International Monetary Fund)
IMF	International Monetary Fund
IPCC	Intergovernmental Panel on Climate Change
J8	Junior Eight
LIBOR	London interbank offered rate
LTCM	Long-Term Capital Management
MDG	Millennium Development Goal
MEF	Major Economies Forum on Energy and Climate
NAB	New Arrangements to Borrow
NAM	Non-Aligned Movement
NEPAD	New Partnership for Africa's Development
NGO	nongovernmental organization
ODA	official development assistance
OECD	Organisation for Economic Co-operation and Development
OEEC	Organisation for European Economic Co-operation
OTC	over-the-counter
OTD	originate-to-distribute
P5	Permanent Five members of the United Nations Security Council (China, France, Russia, the United Kingdom, and the United States)
PAC	Programma de Aceleracion de Crecimiento
PASOK	Panhellenic Socialist Movement
PCL	precautionary credit line
PIGS	Portugal, Ireland, Greece, and Spain
PPP	purchasing power parity
PRSP	poverty reduction strategy paper
PT	Partito de Trabajadores
RBI	Reserve Bank of India
REC	regional economic community
SAP	structural adjustment programme
SCO	Shanghai Cooperation Organisation
SDR	special drawing right

SEC	Securities and Exchange Commission (United States)
SME	small and medium-sized enterprise
TARP	Troubled Asset Relief Program (United States)
UNCTAD	United Nations Conference on Trade and Development
UNDP	United Nations Development Programme
UNECA	United Nations Economic Commission for Africa
UNESCO	United Nations Educational, Social, and Cultural Organization
UNFCCC	United Nations Framework Convention on Climate Change
UNICEF	United Nations Children's Fund
UNSC	United Nations Security Council
WTO	World Trade Organization

PART I
Introduction

Chapter 1
Introduction and Analysis

John J. Kirton, Chiara Oldani, and Paolo Savona

The Challenge

As 2010 unfolded and a new decade began, the global community remained scarred by the destructive grip of the worst global recession in 60 years. In the speed, scope, and scale of its impact, the financial and economic crisis—which began in America, then crossed the Atlantic before going global—far surpassed that of the Asian-turned-global one a decade before. Indeed, this crisis was worse than any since the one in the 1930s, whose haunting memory lives on vividly in the minds of policy makers and their citizens today. While the contemporary crisis clearly began in the mortgage markets of the United States and erupted through financial markets connecting America and key European countries, its complexity and surrounding uncertainty have meant there remains little convincing consensus on its causes, contagion mechanisms, and consequences for major countries and regions around the world. There is also ongoing debate on the effectiveness and innovativeness of the specific policy responses by leading governments, their international institutions, and major firms as well as the effectiveness and innovativeness of the global governance that international institutions offered as a global public good.

What is clear, however, is that the crisis, while deeply affecting all, had distinctive impacts on North America, Asia, Europe, the emerging countries of Brazil, Russia, India, and China (BRIC), and the developing world beyond. It thus evoked in each key country and region varying policy responses and innovations in the instruments and institutions employed to restore stability and growth and to reduce the chance of similar crises erupting again. These differences have compounded the challenge of forging international consensus on the innovations in global economic governance required of today's globalized financial and economic system. At the same time, the unprecedented crisis provides the economic, social, and political demand and perhaps also the supply of political will to fundamentally alter the international economic institutional architecture first constructed in 1944–45.

Yet as the crisis recedes in reality and memory, more than two years after the collapse of Lehman Brothers in New York on 15 September 2008, it remains unclear what lies ahead. Will the aftermath resemble the collapse of the stock market in New York City in October 1929, when ensuing bouts of recovery and confidence proved brief while the real economy receded to new lows that led to social fragmentation, the death of democracy in leading countries, and world war? Or will it be more like the imminent collapse of a bankrupt New York in 1975, when the predicted global financial devastation was met by the leaders of the new G7 successfully convincing a reluctant American president to act in order prevent a destructive cycle of the new financial instability that already had the established economic powers in its grips?

The Purpose

This volume explores these dynamics of economic crisis and impact, policy response, and innovation in global governance. It examines the nature of the crisis, its consequences in major regions and countries, the innovations in the ideas, instruments, and institutions that constitute their national and regional policy responses—particularly in the context of the 2009 G8 L'Aquila Summit—and the implications of their responses for international cooperation, coordination, and institutional change in global economic governance. On this foundation, it identifies appropriate ways to reform and even replace the architecture created in the mid 20th century in order to meet the global challenges of the 21st.

The Framework

To guide this exploration, this book employs and develops a crisis-response-innovation framework first created to explore the way national governments and global governance institutions cope with acute crises in the field of health (Cooper et al. 2007; Cooper and Kirton 2009).

Crisis

This framework begins, as its first component, with the crisis itself. Many still see the 2007–09 crisis and ensuing 'great recession' as unprecedented on most dimensions, since at least the stock market crash in 1929 and the subsequent Great Depression. Such novelty arises in the complex interplay of financial, economic, business practices, and government policies that created the crisis, in the speed and scope of its contagion, and its continuation in crisis sectors, notably its apparent epicentre in the housing market of the United States.

The framework thus starts by identifying the crisis catalysts and causes, ranging from long-term structural ones to more proximate ones in the policy and practices of business, professional communities, consumers, national governments, and international institutions. It next considers its characteristics, notably its depth and duration of the crisis. It then assesses its course, including its particular contagious spread and path across sectors, regions, and countries, and when it was contained and came to a close. It finally asks if this was primarily the latest instalment of financial crises that have regularly come during the many centuries in the past, or one that is genuinely novel, flowing from the complex adaptive system that the global economy has now become. If it is the latter, then the challenge for firms, governments, and international institutions will be much greater, requiring innovations on a scale never seen before in order to provide an appropriate, adequate, and effective response.

Consequences

The second component identifies the consequences, or impacts of the crisis, over the short, medium, and longer terms. From the start there was a debate about who would be hit hardest and fastest, as the former belief in the decoupling of major regions from America broke down. There was another debate, which still continues, about whether the road to recovery would resemble those of market meltdowns and recessions past, and which letter of the alphabet or symbol would best graph its course. It extended to who would recover soonest, to enjoy the greatest growth over the long term.

There was also a debate about the geopolitical impacts of the crisis on a hard-hit America soon sporting a popular new president, on a China with massive amounts of money to stimulate but with serious institutional, ecological, social, and political vulnerabilities, and on many other consequential countries and regions of the world. The crisis gave new life to the old and ongoing debates about America's imperial decline, the emergence of Asia or the rise of the rest (Zakaria 2008; Joffe 2009; Arrighi and Silver 1999). But it added new dimensions, notably a power shift brought by a financial collapse rather than victory or defeat in a system-wide war, or one that reversed the long-term trend toward democratization and openness in the world, with the emerging democracies in Central and Eastern Europe, the recent democracies such as Spain, and the democratic pioneers in Britain, America, and France being hit hardest of all.

The assessment of consequences thus begins with the economy, at the levels of the firm, marketplace, national economies, and the global economy as a whole. But it extends to embrace the geopolitical changes that a crisis of the magnitude of the great meltdown and great recession of 2007–09 brought in its wake. It focuses on who won and who lost, and whether the different and common impacts provided the structural foundation for competition or collaboration among states.

Capabilities

The consequences of the crisis depended importantly on the capabilities and vulnerabilities that the relevant actors and institutions had at the time it arrived. In sharp contrast to the 1997–99 Asian-turned-global financial crisis, this time it was those with the greatest overall financial and economic capabilities that seemed most surprised by the crisis and were poorly equipped to cope, while those that had suffered most from the previous global financial crisis in 1997–99 and even poorer countries had the ability to endure at limited cost. It was America as the single superpower in the post-Cold War period, Anglo-American market capitalism as the model, and New York and London as the leading global financial centres that suffered most. In sharp contrast, the leading victims of the 1997–99 crisis—Korea, Indonesia, and Brazil—this time seemed to have the strengths to insulate them from the worst consequences, in large part because they had learned from the last time how to ensure that they would never again be consumed when the subsequent crises came. Yet even with this searing lesson and policy response from less than a decade earlier, they might have had lucky escapes with good insurance policies, rather than having been global leaders with capacities for prescience, prediction, and prevention. Indeed, few beyond the Bank for International Settlements (BIS) seemed able and willing clearly to predict and warn of the crisis to come.

The third component thus concentrates on the capabilities and vulnerabilities with which firms, countries, and international institutions started the crisis. It considers the size and capacity of the material resources these actors had, as well as their vulnerabilities and resilience. It also considers their predictive and policy capacities, asking how well actors foresaw the crisis and implemented preventive measures or insurance policies in response. It asks how and how well their capabilities were mobilized and deployed in response after the crisis struck. On this basis, it considers which capabilities count the most in the 21st-century world: the depth and sophistication of financial markets still concentrated in the G7 countries; governments' foreign exchange reserves where China, Japan, and Russia led the pack; governments' debt and deficit positions and resulting ability for long-term stimulus, policy, or regulatory sophistication; and other capabilities that can be brought to bear.

Response

Crises and their consequences create the conditions for actors, with their particular configuration of capabilities, to recalculate their preferences and strategies or even redefine their interests and identities in potentially transformational ways. But crises merely create an opportunity that can be wasted, rather than dictate the details and degree of the response (Finnemore and Sikkink 1998). Indeed, by 2010, as the crisis receded in reality and thus in memory, many felt that the old ways were returning, that the opportunity had been lost, that the window for transformational change was rapidly closing, or that some had seized the moment much better than many had.

The fourth component of the framework thus deals with the policy response, primarily from national governments but also from firms, international institutions, and other actors. It identifies how timely and well tailored the policy response was, and how well it matched the particular content, course, causes, and consequences of the crisis, whether or not these were well understood. This component of the book charts the repertories of standard responses deployed, and assesses how well they worked, behind the rediscovery, new respectability, and deployment of

Keynesian monetary and policy stimulus. It explores the causes of these responses and their consequences in making the crisis better or worse. It identifies whether these crisis-bred responses were divergent or convergent, unilateral or coordinated, and whether they were appropriate in each case. It asks whether and why policy choices were made for competition or cooperation, in the short and longer terms.

Innovation

The fifth component addresses innovation. It focuses on the new instruments, ideas, and institutions that were invented in response to the crisis, from quantitative easing in monetary policy through direct financial support to endangered sectors on to detailed regulations during peacetime of how much firms could pay senior staff. It considers how effective they were in comprehending and containing the crisis, its harmful consequences, and the likelihood that such a crisis would erupt again. It further asks how the repertoire of old and new instruments, ideas, and institutions helped bring the crisis to a conclusion, in a way that created the structural conditions for a better economy, society, and policy for the years ahead. In short, was the opportunity for innovation that the crisis opened wasted or not?

Governance

The sixth component is governance, at the global level above all. Just as the crisis of the Great Depression helped create and shape the pillars of the old international financial architecture and order—based on the Bretton Woods bodies founded largely on the classic formula for intergovernmental organizations—so the 2007–09 crisis inspired calls for a new Bretton Woods order, with strong, supranational new multilateral organizations to preside authoritatively over the sovereign states of old (Ikenberry 2001). While such calls were not taken up in the short run, the crisis did lead to stronger powers, resources, and reform of the old institutions, notably the International Monetary Fund (IMF) and the European Union. It also catalysed the creation of several new, innovative plurilateral institutions—the G20 summit, the Financial Stability Board (FSB), and even BRIC summits. How well these were designed and operated is an important cause of how well the crisis has been dealt with and how the global geo-economic and geopolitical order will unfold in the years ahead.

Recommendations

The seventh and final component consists of policy recommendations, aimed at firms, national governments, and international institutions alike. It considers the adequacy, given the characteristics of the crisis and its consequences, of the existing responses, innovations, and governance arrangements. On this basis it offers policy recommendations, ranging from feasible ones for the short term aimed at critical components through to fundamental changes required over the long term for the global system as a whole.

The Contributions

Part II of the book, 'Solutions in America and Asia', begins the examination of how individual regions and countries have created the crisis, contributed to it, and tried to cure it. It begins with its epicentre in America and extends to the closely connected Asian region, with a focus on Japan.

In Chapter 2, 'Crisis, Response and Innovation in America and Abroad', Robert Fauver examines the financial and broader economic crisis confronting the global community, suffering from the first synchronized recession since the first oil shock of 1973–74. In the big three countries outside of Europe, the macroeconomic responses to the crisis have been a combination of classic policy moves and a few new, innovative ideas. All three countries have relied heavily on monetary policy easing. On the fiscal front some new ideas are being tried. Clearly the macroeconomic situation requires a large-scale global stimulus that is transferred from the domestic to the international economy.

In Chapter 3, 'Crisis, Response, and Innovation in Japan', Naoki Tanaka notes that even though the economic and financial crisis originated in the U.S., because of the distinct integration of global markets, East Asian countries faced equal challenges in response. In Japan, the crisis revealed an inherent defect in the financial system—a lack of securitization in its credit market. In contrast to American and European markets, Japan's securitization market remained underdeveloped due to credit default swaps not having been fully utilized and due to the procyclicality of the banking sector in general. The credibility of Japan's financial institutions was questioned as non-performing loans increased and measures to maintain balance sheets often meant selling assets and contracting credit lines. Measures to ensure micro-level functionality have destabilized macroeconomic management, mainly because Japan's economy is so tied to that of the United States. Japan holds the second highest amount of U.S. foreign exchange reserves in the world. This poses a structural constraint—in having to adapt to excessive American consumption—on achieving the right production factors in Japan's domestic economy and the creation of new domestic markets. The global shortage of demand will continue unless countries such as Japan are able to activate the expansion mechanism of net payments effectively. A Japanese-tailored structural reform to increase government spending to improve the supply side is paramount in helping the country recover and maintain equilibrium. The Japanese labour force should be redistributed to emphasize high value-added productivity. In so doing, the Japanese government should work toward developing networks of goods and services conducive to global environmental objectives. In these ways, Japan can realize productive and sustainable growth.

In Chapter 4, 'The Macroeconomics of the Global Financial and Economic Crisis', Libero Monteforte looks beyond the American banking system and mortgage market to identify broader causes of the crisis. These include technical financial issues such as banking procyclicality, macroeconomic imbalances multiplied by insufficient governance in international finance, and policy mistakes resulting from fiscal and monetary policy designed to postpone the crisis. These causes can be combined in a common microeconomic framework that focuses on incentives for excessive risk taking. This structural reduction of risk aversion, due to government policy, summarizes the variety of causes of the crisis. Moreover, the technical difficulties in monitoring risk aversion in real time can explain the large errors and revisions in the forecasts released in the last quarter of 2008. Although the crisis started in the U.S., it was Germany and Japan that suffered the most, due to factors in both demand and supply. Commercial trade contracted much more than world gross domestic product (GDP), perhaps because of protectionism measures. In regard to economic policy, it is almost impossible to use fiscal policy to counter the cycle. An evaluation of the stimulus plans should therefore look at the medium-run effect. Innovative monetary policy such as quantitative easing, while important in the short term, risks fuelling inflation in the longer term. There are no unique indicators to signal when such dangers—and the necessary need for policy adjustment—will arise.

Part III, 'Solutions in Europe', turns to the European region. In Chapter 5, 'Crisis, Response, and Innovation in Europe', Paolo Savona and Chiara Oldani emphasize that the close economic connection between America and Europe and London's status as a global financial and monetary centre spread the American-created crisis instantly to Europe, where it had very different effects on the countries within. Overall, the European banking and financial sectors were able to manage the shock from across the Atlantic, despite a decline in manufacturing and exports due to deflated demand. Savona and Oldani examine these impacts and discuss the ineffectiveness of Europe's regionally uncoordinated and late policy response. The European Commission and parliament addressed the financial crisis by creating an ad hoc technical working group to analyse the roots of the meltdown and suggest the main modifications to the present financial architecture needed to restore confidence and to create the basis for stronger financial markets. However, the suggested modifications did not consider the limited rationality of investors and markets, which formed the basis of the crisis itself. New regulatory improvements are recommended to alter the present shape of the European financial system and its incentives, to the detriment of speculative operators.

In Chapter 6, 'Europe: From One Crisis to the Other', Paola Subacchi examines the consequences of the spread of the financial crisis to Europe. She describes how the 2010 sovereign debt crisis exposed deficiencies in governance and policy coordination in the European Monetary Union (EMU) and changed the role Europe would play in rebalancing the world economy. When the U.S. crisis hit, as a result of government stimulus packages, lower tax revenues, and the impact of automatic stabilizers, Europe's debt-to-GDP ratios rose from 61 percent to 74 percent in 2009, with the greatest gaps in states that had experienced fast but unsustainable growth or critical fiscal positions before the crisis—mostly in southern Europe. Subacchi asserts that widening regional differences and modest economic performance overall make policy coordination more urgent in Europe. She offers policy recommendations required to prepare the region against future crises, including strengthening the role of the European Commission to speak as a strong, unified voice for Europe, seeking fiscal consolidation and structural reforms to remain competitive and achieve growth, and coordinating policy tools such as improved peer-monitoring systems among states. Subacchi maintains that admission to the EMU should require strict due diligence and reliable macroeconomic indicators. To this she adds that the consequences of a situation such as happened in Greece in 2010 only exacerbated Europe's growth problems and arguably decreased the region's potential output. Overall, Subacchi believes the governance framework of the EMU should have a common fiscal policy for all countries with better fiscal redistribution. In the future, she expects exports will drive the European economy and will play a neutral role in rebalancing the world economy.

In Chapter 7, 'Europe's Institutional, Inflation, Investment, and Incentive Challenges', Carlo A. Bollino focuses on European policy choices. These choices have emphasized social cohesion and the need for institutions to keep a significant portion of the risk of securities they sell. Since 1600, there has been an economic and financial crisis every nine years: the 2008 crisis was not among the worst. In Europe, the absence of a common fiscal and monetary policy deprived the region of the possibility of using a proper policy mix for long-term solutions. Output prices fell more than supply prices and underlying employment. Global warming also presented new macroeconomic and microeconomic challenges that must be addressed, because the amount of investment needed to achieve announced targets adds pressure to the financial system. Management incentives with high leverage and the underlying causes of this crisis must also be addressed. Moreover, old-style exit strategies must be employed quickly to avoid serious inflation. This risk is increased because the inflation of wages and goods is the only assured way to correct imbalances in asset prices rapidly, and because, outside Germany, inflation is not seen as bad. The prospect of inflation arising soon is strengthened by the fact that stock markets in the U.S., Italy, and elsewhere were showing signs of a V-shaped recovery by the summer of 2009. The real risk is too much government and regulation in Europe, rather than public spending, as the latter represents intergenerational solidarity rather than burden shifting. As for the causes and character of this crisis, there are two types of crisis: a sudden shift in the system, which causes a shipwreck and requires the lower class passengers to be rescued, or a mountain-climbing crisis where all cling to a rope that slips, requiring everyone to be raised from the very top. The proper policy response depends critically on the kind of crisis it is.

Part IV, 'Impacts and Responses in the BRICs', widens the focus to embrace the multifaceted effects on and the policy response of the major emerging economies of Brazil, Russia, India, and China. This group is united not by geography but by its members' simultaneous if uneven rise as economic powers, their labelling as such by Jim O'Neill of Goldman Sachs in 2001, and their subsequent institutional status by 2009 as a summit-level club of their own.

In Chapter 8, 'Mediating Financial Instability: China, the BRICs, and Continuing Rise', Gregory Chin explores the direct impact of the financial crisis on the BRICs' financial systems, currencies, exports and imports, interest rates, industrial output, remittances, employment, credit sources, and foreign direct investment (FDI). The perspective of the BRICs is relevant because they are emerging as a nexus where the traditional North and South can either learn to cooperate or compete for global economic power and influence. He outlines the effects in each country, maintaining that Russia has been affected most directly and severely: FDI, stock markets, and industrial output plunged over the first six months of 2009, and GDP was forecast to contract by between 6 percent and 8 percent that year. India has been affected more than anticipated due to its increased integration in the world economy. Brazil fell into a technical recession, with unemployment at 9 percent. Although demand for exports decreased considerably, China was affected less directly by the crisis due to its less liberalized financial system, and due to the banking reforms that it has undertaken since the 1997–99 Asian financial crisis. In all BRIC members, the state intervened through interest rate adjustments, monetary and exchange rate policy, and industrial and employment policy.

In Chapter 9, 'Russia: Impact and Response', Victoria Panova focuses on Russia, a critical country as a member of both the developed country G8 and the emerging economy BRICs. It is the country hit hardest by the crisis in both groups, and plays a critical role in bringing both groups together for the greater global good. The potential capability that remains within Russia after the crisis will allow it to rise back and continue its interrupted development, making it to the top of the world economic powers in the medium term.

In Chapter 10, 'Brazil and Latin America: Impact and Response', Raffaele Galano examines Brazil and Latin America. In a world long divided between a rich core and a poor periphery, with exchange rates favouring the former, the BRICs are eroding this dichotomy, as some approach and enter the rich world. Latin America's countries, growing strongly between 2003 and 2008, were less affected by the financial crisis than many others. But they still suffered from declining purchasing power and contracting international trade. Brazil's long expansion, at 6.8 percent a year, dropped to 3.5 percent by the third quarter of 2008. In the summer of 2009, the IMF forecast 0.3 percent of growth for Latin America, 1 percent for Brazil, and –0.2 percent for Mexico for the year. Brazil, with ample foreign exchange reserves, surplus in the balance of payments, and controllable public debt, responded to the crisis with stimulative fiscal policy. Optimistic forecasts showed a V-shaped recovery for Brazil in 2010, although its presidential elections that year could affect the outcome if spending expands while tax receipts decline. Interest rates in Brazil remained high. The state used four state-owned banks as policy instruments for specific sectors, making Brazilian monetary policy more like the Chinese. Brazil's growth plan to stimulate domestic demand and finance firms was also similar to China's. While the BRICs play an important role, the four countries differ culturally, politically, and economically, as well as in their interests, and China could be considered in a class of its own with regard to exports and foreign exchange reserves..

Part V, 'Impacts and Responses in Developing Countries', widens the vista still further to include the majority of countries that belong to the developing world, with the poorest continent and countries of Africa at the core. In Chapter 11, 'Sub-Saharan Africa: Impact and Response', Diéry Seck explores the effects and policy reactions of sub-Saharan Africa in its individual countries and as a region. He first notes the inherited and self-made unfavourable and capabilities conditions in Africa prior to the crisis, and the resulting need to transform the region into one where development is similar to other poor regions of the world. He then examines the impact of the crisis, assesses the adequacy of currency current development strategies—with a focus on finance—and then proposes policy solutions to make such strategies more effective in Africa.

In Chapter 12, 'Africa in the Face of the Crisis', George M. von Furstenberg suggests that protracted aid failure in sub-Saharan Africa reduces the potential benefits of building on existing aid mechanisms as long as those in power in the region, along with their western 'development' partners, serve themselves first. He sees no crisis-driven emergency rationale for more aid. Partly by reason of the lack of financial development outside South Africa, sub-Saharan Africa was touched only relatively lightly and briefly by the global financial and economic crisis. Its real GDP growth rate was cut in half in 2009 before returning to more than 5 percent growth in 2010 according to IMF forecasts. Furthermore, because most of the strikes against sub-Saharan Africa are human made rather than due to natural conditions, bribery, long delays, and insecurity along the trade corridors contribute significantly to the isolation of land-locked African countries. Volatile export proceeds have been a fact of life in all countries at low levels of development that rely on exports of natural resources, particularly metals and minerals, for which export volume and price tend to vary. High volatility of export proceeds, then, is a consequence of low and undiversified development and not its cause. Most troubling to the case for more aid 'by right' and without credible accountability is that aid has much more powerful advocates and friends than aid effectiveness: those who stand to benefit most from aid are those who can render it ineffective for their own account.

In Chapter 13, 'The Broader Impacts on the Developing World', Sara Savastano looks at coordination among the international institutions involved in development. Contrary to previous economic downturns, the 2009 crisis spread into developing countries from industrialized countries through higher interest rates, sharp changes in commodity prices, and impacts on investment, trade, migration, and remittances. The actions undertaken by less developed countries varied among countries and across regions. The main policy response to the crisis was a vigorous fiscal stimulus together with an aggressive easing of monetary policy. Government and international and regional organizations convened in L'Aquila for the 2009

G8 summit and agreed on strong procyclical political support for food security and for agriculture. Additional political support should be considered a priority for overall investment in education, health, and infrastructure as well as to protect government spending on programmes that target the poor. There are grounds for hope, as poverty rates declined between 1985 and 2005, even if Africa was largely left out.

Part VI, 'Innovation in Global Economic Governance', leaps further to the international level to examine the impact of the crisis on the ideas, instruments, and institutions at the centre of global governance, in both established and emerging forms.

In Chapter 14, 'From the Dollar Standard to a Supernational Money', Pietro Alessandrini and Michelle Fratianni argue that the crisis, starting in America at the centre of the international monetary system, raised issues not only of immediate financial response, regulation, and reform but also of longer-term, structural monetary reform. They argue that the current international monetary system remains fragile because America's net indebtedness is rising and the dollar standard is deteriorating. The resulting trends, reminiscent of those in the traumatic period between the first and second world wars, demand fundamental reform. This goes beyond a greater reliance on special drawing rights (SDR), as proposed by China and mandated by the G20 London Summit in April 2009, to the creation of a full-scale supernational money. It would be institutionally managed within a clearing union where central banks agree on the size and duration of overdrafts, which bears the burden of external adjustment, and on the coordination of monetary policy. The IMF is best positioned to monitor and enforce these rules. Both a declining America and rising China have rational incentives to move toward such a truly innovative and transformational international monetary regime. To develop their argument, the authors look first at the history of international money, with its hierarchical structure and long transition time between dominant currencies. They then examine the basic weakness of an international money that is also a national money, and where the national goals will win over global public goods. They next explore the deteriorating dollar standard, and why and how long it can continue, the defects of the SDR scheme, and their supernational bank money alternatives. They conclude with policy recommendations aimed at a feasible but fundamental policy reform.

In Chapter 15, 'The Role of International Money', Juan Carlos Martinez Oliva assesses the concept of an international money by looking first at the dual external and internal role that an international money must play. This dilemma is apparent today, with the U.S. aimed at preserving its role of key currency country in spite of its huge payments imbalances and China interested at maintaining its competitive advantage in the trade field while possibly avoiding substantial capital losses in its dollar-denominated securities. But is the era of the dollar really about to end? Even at the end of 2009, foreign investors were still buying large amounts of U.S. treasuries. Nonetheless, the idea of an international money for world payments often emerges in the debate, with an emphasis on enhancing the role of SDR, or creating an international clearing union. The European Payments Union, in the 1950s, is the only case of practical implementation of Keynes's concept of a clearinghouse. Its success relied on factors such as members' clear commitments, Europe's economic need, U.S. political pressure, and a temporary nature. A similar move to a global cognate now could help to cope with the problem of global imbalances, but resistance is likely on the U.S. side, as America has no incentive to erode the U.S. dollar's status as the only international money, with all the benefits involved.

In Chapter 16, 'Asymmetries in the International Monetary System', Domenico Lombardi examines the international monetary system and the traditional and new sources of asymmetry therein. He argues that the current international monetary system exhibits deep-seated sources of instability that, in the absence of corrective measures, may affect the long-run sustainability of the financial globalization that has occurred in the past few decades. Lombardi reviews the historical foundations of the current monetary system, highlighting early attempts to analyse and control its potential sources of instability. He elaborates on the increasing sources of asymmetry exhibited by the system in the recent decades, following the increasing waves of trade and financial liberalization in several developing countries, and concludes by assessing options for strengthening the role of SDRs as global reserve assets and for reforming the institutional anchor of the system as provided by the IMF.

Part VII, 'From G8 to G20', examines the elite, exclusive plurilateral clubs that will do much to determine the direction and shape of the domestic and international reform efforts and that will occupy a central place in providing stability, growth, development, and crisis response when the next crisis comes.

In Chapter 17, 'Reconciling the Gs: The G8, the G5, and the G20 in a World of Crisis', Andrew F. Cooper and Andrew Schrumm address the argument that the G8 is fading in relevance, especially when its well-known flaws in legitimacy have been exacerbated by its failures in the face of the financial crisis and by competition from a new G20 summit system in response. They first examine the G8 to determine why it is vulnerable to competition. They then consider whether its flaws are so fatal that the G8 will be not just be down but also out of the global economic governance game. They conclude that the G8 has considerable accumulated strengths that mean it will live on. But the current financial crisis, coming on top of the G8's legitimacy and efficiency crisis, means it is endangered, and may even die, as the hub of global economic decision making in the years ahead.

In Chapter 18, 'The G8, the G20, and Civil Society', Hugo Dobson looks at the limitations of the G8 and the G20 in their social foundations, especially in their ability and willingness to respond to and involve the citizens whom they claim to represent, whose needs they claim to meet, and whose understanding and approval are vital if the necessary reforms are to be put into effect. He concludes that both institutions have much to do to acquire the popular legitimacy and thus their citizens' contribution, to enable them to serve as a stable, assured hub of global economic governance in a crisis-ridden but individually empowered world.

In Chapter 19, 'The G8 and the G20: Rejuvenated by the Crisis', Giorgio La Malfa begins with the paradox that the current crisis has revived both the G8 and G20 summits, making them of interest to more than just the demonstrators who always attend the G8. The crisis has also focused the agendas of both on economics and finance. Because this crisis is global and not just internal to the G8, the G8 Plus Five (Brazil, China, India, Mexico, and South Africa) at least—and even the G20—would be a better forum than the G8 to respond. But the problem of who to invite for which discussion is shown by Italy's experience in hosting the G8 in 2009. It is thus hard to see how the G8's variable geometry at L'Aquila can be institutionalized. Meanwhile, the G20 maintains the focus on economic subjects, and the G8 will cover political-security issues, even if they are also dealt with in wider forums, as well as some specific issues such as climate change or aid for Africa. The G8 has not, however, analysed the deeper causes of the crisis, which relate to excessive reliance on the working of markets. Nor has the analysis touched on the heavy and growing disequilibrium in the U.S. balance of payments. But neither the G8 nor the G20 will likely accept proposals for an international money, especially as many wonder whether SDRs can be debased more rapidly than the U.S. dollar. Neither the U.S. nor the Chinese currently contemplate a future where their currency is similarly destined to fade away, the way that sterling receded from centre stage in the 20th century.

In Chapter 20, 'The Contribution of the G8's 2009 L'Aquila Summit', John J. Kirton argues that the summit was a 'solid success'. It brought together an unprecedented number of leaders and produced concrete results in the areas of finance, climate change, food security, nuclear non-proliferation and disarmament, trade, and summit architecture. Furthermore, the legitimacy of the G8 was enhanced even with the presence of the G20 summit. L'Aquila proved that the G8 remains relevant and capable of detailed, flexible, and effective action in an innovative, inclusive, and sustainable way. It is thus well positioned to provide global governance in several domains. By Kirton's assessment, the L'Aquila Summit achieved adequate results, and future G8 summitry will remain a proven, subject-driven, and inclusive forum for effective global governance.

Part VIII, 'Conclusion', contains Chapter 21, 'Conclusion and Recommendations'. Here John J. Kirton synthesizes the consensus, debates, and recommendations among the authors with regard to all elements of the analytical framework discussed in this volume—the crisis, its consequences, the capabilities of the actors it affected, their policy responses, the innovations in these responses, governance at the international levels, and recommendations for policy and institutional reform.

References

Arrighi, Giovanni and Beverly Silver (1999). *Chaos and Governance in the Modern World System* (Minneapolis: University of Minnesota Press).

Cooper, Andrew F. and John J. Kirton, eds. (2009). *Innovation in Global Health Governance: Critical Cases* (Farnham: Ashgate).

Cooper, Andrew F., John J. Kirton, and Ted Schrecker, eds. (2007). *Governing Global Health: Challenge, Response, Innovation* (Aldershot: Ashgate).

Finnemore, Martha and Kathryn Sikkink (1998). 'International Norm Dynamics and Political Change.' *International Organization*, vol. 52, no. 4, pp. 887–917.

Ikenberry, G. John (2001). *After Victory: Institutions, Strategic Restraint, and the Rebuilding of Order after Major Wars* (Princeton: Princeton University Press).

Joffe, Josef (2009). 'The Default Power: The False Prophecy of America's Decline.' *Foreign Affairs*, September/October <www.foreignaffairs.com/articles/65225/josef-joffe/the-default-power> (August 2010).

Zakaria, Fareed (2008). *The Post-American World* (New York: W.W. Norton).

PART II
Solutions in America and Asia

Chapter 2

Crisis, Response, and Innovation in America and Abroad

Robert C. Fauver

A close study of the 2008–09 global financial crisis is critical to understanding its implications for future policy makers. At that time, the world faced much more than a financial crisis. Moreover, the broad implications or side effects of the financial crisis must be considered in order to understand fully the consequences of the policy decisions that led to the global financial crisis in the first place.

The 2008–09 crisis significantly changed the world's economic and financial landscape. It created two basic types of costs for investors and consumers: economic costs and financial costs. Both are interrelated and tend to feed off each other. Difficulties in one area create additional problems for the other.

The world economy experienced its deepest downturn in decades—and the first synchronized recession in the industrial world since the first oil crisis of 1973–74. As the macroeconomic implications of the financial crisis became better understood, and as the depth of the financial crisis itself became apparent, the International Monetary Fund ([IMF] 2009, 10) significantly reduced its forecasts for global 2009 real growth from 2.2 percent to 0.5 percent. This reduction occurred only three months after the IMF's earlier forecast. The industrialized countries were the hit hardest with the forecasts of their real growth dropping to a decline of 2 percent—down from the October estimate of a modest –0.5 percent. Hardest hit was the United States, where growth was expected to decline by 1.6 percent—from the earlier estimate of zero. The forecast reduction in global growth since October 2008 amounted to a loss of global gross national product (GNP) on the order of $1.2 trillion—simply from the downward revision.

This deteriorating economic outlook hit financial firms hard. The worsening credit conditions affecting a broader range of markets over the winter months caused the IMF to raise its October estimate of the potential deterioration in U.S.-originated credit assets held by banks and others from $1.4 trillion to $2.2 trillion. Much of this deterioration occurred in the mark-to-market portion of their estimates (mostly securities), especially in corporate and commercial real estate securities. But degradation also occurred in the loan books of banks, reflecting the weakening outlook for the economy (IMF 2009, 2).

The IMF's rough estimates expected that write-downs for European and U.S. banks during 2009 and 2010 (offset partly by the anticipated revenues over the same period) would result in a net capital shortfall of at least $0.5 trillion. This implied that for U.S. and European banks taken together approximately $500 billion of new capital was necessary just to prevent their capital position from deteriorating further (IMF 2009, 2).

Global equity markets lost more than 50 percent—roughly $31 000 billion of market capitalization in one year. According to the survey of consumer finances produced by the U.S. Federal Reserve released on 12 February 2009, average net worth was estimated to have fallen 22.7 percent from 2007 until October 2008 (Bucks et al. 2009). The drop in wealth likely hit affluent pre-retirement baby boomers and the newly retired the worst, since it is those demographic groups that tend to have the highest net worth.

These results were the product of many years of economic policy decisions undertaken in the major industrialized countries. But it is also important to recognize the role of decisions taken in the leading emerging market economies. There is plenty of blame to spread among economic policy makers in both industrialized countries and emerging markets.

The financial crisis was long in the making. It was the result of numerous policy choices primarily in the United States, but the crisis was magnified and lengthened and deepened by the policy choices outside the U.S.—both those taken before the crisis and those taken in response to it.

The Crisis

Most analysts believe that the financial crisis started with problems in the U.S. subprime mortgage market. For nearly 20 years, Congress and various administrations pushed the concept of widespread home ownership. Special attention was paid to the ability of minorities and low-income families to join the ranks of home owners. From the 1970s onward, policy efforts focused on reducing down payment requirements for home buyers.

A couple starting out in the 1950s would have been required to come up with 20 percent of the purchase price as a down payment. That was a lot of money. In the 1970s Congress pushed the Federal Housing Administration (FHA) to devise programmes aimed at lowering down payment requirements—first to 10 percent down. Then the FHA developed the 'magic' money plan requiring only 5 percent down. By the 1990s, the FHA and commercial lenders were financing 'no money down' new home purchases for qualified borrowers.

In the 1990s banks and other lenders were identifying some low-income neighbourhoods as being ineligible for mortgage loans. The Clinton administration, supported by the Congress, moved to make such 'redlining' of neighbourhoods illegal. Congress decided that this practice amounted to discrimination against minorities. Regulations were changed to make this form of credit allocation illegal. Political pressure was put on lenders to increase mortgage lending to low-income borrowers significantly.

After a time, lenders complained that their balance sheets could not take any more risky loans. They threatened to stop lending to low-income borrowers. Congress reacted by pushing the Federal National Mortgage Association (Fannie Mae) and the Federal Home Loan Mortgage Corporation (Freddie Mac) to increase substantially their purchases of low-income mortgages. The resulting purchases freed up lending by banks and other mortgage lenders. They could essentially give endless new loans and sell them off quickly to Freddie Mac and Fannie Mae. Huge profits came from the service fees associated with the new loans. Lenders faced virtually zero risk as they immediately sold off the risky loans.

By 2005, lenders were making loans without verifying the income of borrowers or their ability to make the required payments. And the use of adjustable interest rate loans became increasingly widespread. Artificially low initial interest rates were essentially 'bait and switch' rates for uninformed borrowers. Unqualified borrowers increasingly became first-time home owners. And the flood of new buyers pushed housing prices sky high.

As is always the case, the housing bubble eventually popped. The initial stages of the housing crisis appeared to be a normal kind of market adjustment. But regulators and financial institutions were unaware of the wide extent to which sub-prime mortgages had been securitized and that these securitized instruments had, in turn, been used to back other financial products ranging from insurance products to derivatives. The fall in value of securitized sub-prime loans quickly spread to other financial assets. The financial crisis became full blown.

Near the end of the Bush administration, U.S. treasury secretary Henry Paulson worked with Congress to pass the Troubled Asset Relief Program (TARP), with some $700 billion in relief. The original purpose of the TARP was to fund the purchase of troubled or toxic assets of banks in order to strengthen their capital positions. Stronger balance sheets were supposed to enable banks to resume providing credit to the economy (Moses 2008).

But Paulson changed his mind. Instead of buying troubled assets, he decided that banks needed straight injections of capital—so he provided loans. A significant problem with the TARP was the establishment of prices for the assets. Given that the market for securitized mortgage paper had essentially dried up with little trading taking place, it became impossible to determine the market value of the assets. When the U.S. Treasury decided to purchase a troubled asset it faced a difficult decision in making its purchase proposal—if the price was significantly below book value, then banks would face serious losses. But if the assets were bought at book value, then the government would inevitably lose money on the transactions since a substantial number of the mortgages underlying the securitized assets were likely to be foreclosed on.

While all of this was taking place in the United States, much was happening elsewhere. In Europe, banks were also engaged in the sub-prime market both directly through investments in securitized sub-prime mortgages and indirectly through the various derivative products based on the sub-prime securities. Significant balance sheet losses were taking place in Europe. British banks were hard hit. British authorities similarly rejected a policy of fully nationalizing banks, except in rare individual cases such as Northern Rock. The British government took also a controlling share in other instances, such as with Lloyds Halifax Bank of Scotland. Germany also moved forward with new legislative authority to nationalize financial firms.

For Europe, the financial crisis quickly turned into a real growth problem. Dramatic slowdowns occurred across Europe and the recession widened into a global problem. For years, Europe had relied on exports to the U.S. to underpin domestic growth. With the falloff in the U.S. economy, European production declined and the underlying weakness of domestic demand became apparent.

In Asia, the two key countries—Japan and China—largely escaped the financial aspects of the sub-prime crisis. In Japan, the experience of regulators and financial firms with their own financial bubble, which had started in 1989, led to relatively cautious engagement of Japanese banks in the wide range of sub-prime based instruments. Some would argue that Japan's timid participation in the sub-prime market was based not on foresight, but rather on fear of repeating their earlier problems.

China's lack of a mature, integrated financial market helped it to escape the global problems. But for a decade or so both China and Japan formulated their growth strategies based on growing exports to the U.S. market. Exports were to provide the stimulus to their domestic growth and employment creation. Obviously the sharp growth slowdown in the U.S. produced a dramatic decline in exports to the United States. Japan's economy shifted sharply into recession. China's growth rate slowed significantly—roughly by half from the 12 percent growth rate of earlier in the decade. Since for some time the second driver of Japan's growth had been rising exports to China, the Chinese slowdown added to the reduction in Japan's exports. Most of the exports to China could be called indirect exports to the United States. These exports largely went to China's export sector. They were not consumer goods for the domestic Chinese market. Hence the derivative effect of the U.S. slowdown was to slow Japan's exports to China.

The Response

The stage was now set for the incoming Obama administration in January 2008. Bank lending had plummeted, the stock market had dropped billions of dollars in asset value, the largest insurance firm—AIG—had been essentially nationalized, several securities firms had been merged with commercial banks, the stock market crash and the freezing up of credit markets had driven the economy into recession, and the Treasury had already spent roughly $350 billion of the $700 billion of TARP money (Lawder 2009).

In addition to the financial market turmoil, the new administration faced a widening recession in the domestic economy, with rising unemployment levels, a declining real estate market, a near bankrupt American automobile industry, and an investor public that had watched billions of dollars of financial assets disappear. Older Americans saw their retirement savings decline dramatically.

During the transition period, Barack Obama's team decided that it needed a fiscal stimulus package passed by the Congress early in the new term. So the Democratic leadership was informed that Obama wanted a stimulus package of between $500 billion and $700 billion.

Nancy Pelosi, the Democratic speaker of the House of Representatives, moved quickly to draft the stimulus package. She ignored the views of Republicans and some Democrats by drafting the legislation in her office instead of in a committee. The final House bill received no Republican votes. The Senate also moved relatively quickly, with majority leader Harry Reed controlling the process. The Senate, however, needed a few Republican votes to secure passage of the legislation. Hence a few small compromises were made. The final bill reconciled by the House and Senate was passed on 13 February 2008. A few days later, on 17 February, Obama signed the *American Recovery and Reinvestment Act*. Proposed new spending totalled $787 billion. This was a historic stimulus package, either in dollar terms or as a share of gross domestic product (GDP) (BBC 2009).

Many commentators suggested that a significant portion of the spending would not take place in either 2009 or 2010. The Congressional Budget Office estimated that only $185 billion of the total spending would take place in 2009—roughly 23 percent. By the end of 2010 roughly one half of the total package would be spent. This would not be a straightforward stimulus bill and unfortunately, as a result, the direct impact on the current recession would be considerably smaller than suggested by the overall package. In early June, Obama called for faster release of the stimulus money, noting that only 5 percent had been spent so far.

The second major effort by the new administration aimed at the domestic economy was the submission of Obama's first budget on 26 February 2009. The proposed budget looked out over a 10-year period. It foresaw government spending jumping from 21 percent of GDP in 2008 to 27.7 percent in 2009 and 24 percent in 2010. This indicated a sharp rise in spending levels by the federal government. Moreover, the level of federal debt would rise from $5.8 trillion to $15.4 trillion over the next 10 years—triple the level of national debt. Most analysts argued that the assumptions underlying the budget were very optimistic. The debt level could thus easily exceed these projections (Elmendorf 2009).

Summing up the macroeconomic efforts, the Obama administration signed into law a very large fiscal stimulus package and submitted an expansionary budget to be reviewed by Congress. The administration simultaneously aimed at strengthening financial markets. But little success was recorded. The administration did not purchase any troubled assets from the banking system. The Treasury then seemed to decide that there was no chance for Congress to authorize additional TARP money so it considered the swap of loans to financial institutions for common stock. This swap would strengthen balance sheets without requiring new congressional authority. It would represent a major federal ownership in financial institutions.

But the Obama administration did not appear averse to partial nationalization of financial institutions.

The Federal Reserve System continuously provided liquidity to markets. Staggering amounts of reserves were added to the system; yet most commercial banks did not use the injections to promote new lending. The reserves were deposited by banks. Of some concern was the ability of the Federal Reserve to remove the liquidity injections when the economy began to turn around. Some observers worried that there would be inflation concerns when the recovery got underway (Dudley 2009).

The Obama administration reviewed the regulatory environment for financial firms. There were clear gaps in the pre-crisis regulatory structure. Little oversight existed for hedge funds and off-balance sheet transactions. The administration sought to overhaul financial market regulations completely, with an aim of consolidating the oversight functions into a single agency—most likely the Treasury Department. While there would continue to be a role for agencies such as the Securities and Exchange Commission (SEC) and the Federal Deposit Insurance Corporation (FDIC), the Treasury would assume overall regulatory responsibility for assuring that all products were covered and that any risky activities in one sector or product would be shared with other product regulators. Given the role of various congressional committees in this oversight process, regulatory reforms would be slow to come.

At first glance, responses to the macroeconomic problems in Asia looked strong. Japan quickly passed a supplemental bill, then a second, and then focused on a third. China announced a large stimulus package. But as the details became more clear, the package largely consisted of subsidized credit, not new spending from the central government. Local and regional governments were been slow to use the credits.

By early 2009, the global recession was well entrenched and deep seated. Europe continued to postpone hard domestic spending decisions. European leaders saw little they could do by themselves to correct their domestic recessions. Instead they waited for the U.S. recovery to once again provide growing export markets for their products. They seemed to believe that their recovery would take place after the U.S. expansion began. The discussions among the G7/8 members leading up to the April G20 London Summit proved futile regarding joint stimulus efforts (G20 2009). The G8 L'Aquila Summit did little better three months later.

In Asia, Japan continued to work toward a new supplemental budget, which had some unique aspects never tried before. The supplemental package announced in April was roughly ¥15.4 trillion ($154 billion), equal to about 2 percent of GDP (Harding 2009). This doubled Japan's earlier stimulus effort. The stimulus package focused on health care and medical services, subsidies to local governments, a new social safety net for non-regular workers, and more use of government financial institutions to ease the credit crunch and solar energy. While the use of energy credits was innovative, over the previous five years real growth in Japan had depended on exports. The outlook for recovery continued to depend on the external sector.

China's budget showed that a plan to run a deficit of only 3 percent of GDP. The stimulus programme announce in the fall was 4 trillion renminbi ($586 billion). Estimates suggested that over two years the infrastructure package would be worth 14 percent of GDP (Chien 2008). The government's commitment to domestic structural spending—roads, bridges, and so on—might produce domestic demand growth above what would have been the case. However, the effects of China's domestic growth on the world economy were very small. While Chinese imports are sensitive to Chinese exports—largely commodities, parts, and components—consumer demand does not focus on imported products. So without a renewal of Chinese exports, the rest of Asia would not benefit from modest stimulus to domestic demand in China.

So once again, the global economy seemed to be waiting for Godot—and Godot was the U.S. recovery. Many analysts expected the recovery to come late in 2009 or early in 2010. But no one suggested it would be strong. A classic V-shaped cycle was not in the offing. Rather, there would likely to be a slow pickup.

Innovations in Policy Responses

The macroeconomic responses of Japan, the U.S., and China to the current crisis were a combination of classic policy moves and a few innovative ideas.

All three countries relied heavily on monetary policy easing. In Japan and the U.S., interest rates were very low and liquidity provisions were significant. In China, monetary policy did ease, but the lack of a sophisticated domestic capital market continued to hamper the effectiveness of classic monetary policy responses to weakening domestic demand. Credit rationing remained the primary tool for monetary policy.

On the fiscal front, some new ideas were tried. In the U.S. the very large stimulus package was not front loaded. Instead, new spending during the first year would amount to only some 20 percent of the total package; even during the second year only roughly 50 percent of the spending would occur. Most of the spending was not of the classic pump-priming variety. The stimulus package focused more on policy changes by the Democratic Party. It remained to be seen if this approach would result in similar multiplier effects experienced historically in conjunction with fiscal stimulus packages.

In Japan a significant portion of the stimulus package relied on energy credits rather than direct spending. The consumer responses to this new concept were impossible to predict.

Furthermore, in China, there was no historical experience with efforts to stimulate domestic demand. For example, what is the marginal propensity to import from consumption increases likely to be? Good data exist on the relationship between export manufacturing sector growth and import propensities.

But there is no information on the relationship between domestic consumption and imports. Thus, from a global perspective, the effect of China's attempt to shift to consumption-led economic growth on the world economy was unknown. Evidence suggested that the global effect would be quite small.

Clearly, the macroeconomic situation required global stimulus that was transferred from domestic to the international economy. Time will tell whether these responses from the U.S., China and Japan were successful on a longer term basis. In the short run, growth in 2009 in China exceeded expectations of even the most optimistic. China's stimulus strengthened domestic demand significantly during 2009. In Japan, growth was disappointing by the end of the year, and preliminary estimates for 2010 suggested that the stimulus policies did not foster sustained expansion. The picture in the United States was less clear. Real growth rose strongly in the third quarter of 2009, but subsequent data revisions portrayed a weaker-than-expected recovery path. Most analysts expected an expansion between 2 percent and 3 percent in 2010, which suggested that the fiscal stimulus was not as large as hoped for.

References

BBC (2009). 'Q&A: Obama Stimulus Plan.' 17 February. <news.bbc.co.uk/2/hi/business/7874407.stm> (August 2010).

Bucks, Brian, Arthur Kennickell, Traci Mach, et al. (2009). 'Changes in U.S. Family Finances from 2004 to 2007: Evidence from the Survey of Consumer Finances.' *Federal Reserve Bulletin*, vol. 95. <www.federalreserve.gov/pubs/bulletin/2009/articles/scf/default.htm> (August 2010).

Chien, Kirby (2008). 'China Okays $586 Billion Stimulus to Boost Economy.' 9 November, Reuters. <www.reuters.com/article/idUSTRE4A816L20081109> (August 2010).

Dudley, William (2009). 'The Federal Reserve's Liquidity Facilities.' 18 April, speech to the Vanderbilt University Conference on Financial Markets and Financial Policy Honouring Dewey Daane, Nashville, TN. <www.bis.org/review/r090422c.pdf> (August 2010).

Elmendorf, Douglas W. (2009). 'Letter to the Honorable Judd Gregg.' 27 July. <www.cbo.gov/doc.cfm?index=10295&type=1> (August 2010).

G20 (2009). 'Global Plan for Recovery and Reform.' 2 April, London. <www.g20.utoronto.ca/2009/2009communique0402.html> (August 2010).

Harding, Robin (2009). 'Aso Launches $154 Billion Japan Stimulus.' *Financial Times*, 10 April.

International Monetary Fund (2009). *World Economic Outlook: Crisis and Recovery.* April. <www.imf.org/external/pubs/ft/weo/2009/01/> (August 2010).

Lawder, David (2009). 'Paulson: TARP Still Needed for Bank Capital.' 16 January, Reuters. <www.reuters.com/article/idUSTRE50F4YY20090116> (August 2010).

Moses, Abigail (2008). 'Paulson's TARP Reform Spells Return of Systemic Risk, BNP Says.' 13 November, Bloomberg. <www.bloomberg.com/apps/news?pid=newsarchive&sid=aouifFqWYy0M&refer=home> (August 2010).

Chapter 3
Crisis, Response, and Innovation in Japan

Naoki Tanaka

In assessments of the global economic system, some views draw on hegemonic models. However, the real function of the globalized economy lies in the mutual interactions among groups of subjects that determine their positions in accordance with the environments surrounding them, and that are reflected in their own looking glasses. Individual domestic disequilibria among groups of sovereign states have already been pictured in their mirrors, and they have adapted to determine their respective positions in the globalized economy.

However, in 2008, when a systemic risk hit Japan's economy, a defect—inherent in its indirect financing-oriented financial system—came to light. The defect relates to the risks that should otherwise be taken broadly so that resources for ensuring the country's future could be distributed optimally. Due to the nature of Japan's financial system, such risks had to be concentrated in banks' loan assets. In contrast, it was believed that in the financial system in the United States, which revolved around direct financing, socially needed risks were borne broadly by households. It was believed that even if a process of risk materialization began with losses, it would not lead to the destabilization of the financial system. In other words, the conventional wisdom found Japan's financial system inferior to America's.

However, liquidity dried up as markets for securitized instruments lost their pricing functions. In Japan, the credibility of financial institutions was called into question as they piled up nonperforming loans. In the U.S., however, the loss of discipline at the time of creating securitized instruments upended the original theme of risk diversification.

The U.S. markets failed to rein in the accumulation of sub-prime loans as mortgage-backed securities were created. This failure also dealt a blow to consumer loans and to the market mechanism for providing student loans.

In Japan, a mechanism had become all too familiar for financial institutions. They obtained loan claims using borrowers' land holdings as collateral. In recognition of the situation, efforts were made to reform the system fundamentally. Those efforts were targeted specifically at setting lending rates at levels in accordance with a probability distribution of risk—that is, shifting to a practice of determining loan margin rates. In actuality, however, such a practice did not take root easily.

Meanwhile, a completely new phenomenon emerged. When risks began surfacing, they set in motion a mechanism to press corporate borrowers to honour their financial covenants, under which they promised to maintain certain balance sheet requirements. In reality, however, compliance in times of recession often meant forced sell-offs of assets and shrunken credit lines. This was the phenomenon of procyclicality: once there is a deviation from equilibrium, worse disequilibrium results. It thus became evident that a contradiction existed between banks' efforts to create a new formula for credit extension—a search for micro-level optimum behaviour—and the design of built-in stabilizers at the level of macroeconomic management.

After the Great Depression, the U.S. adopted a mechanism that prioritized housing construction. Its tax code and financial system were made to fit this mechanism. Premised on the configuration of such a system, a consumer-finance framework was implemented. Households were now able to take out home-equity loans based on the continued increase in the value of their homes, also known as cashing out housing assets. This is the background to phenomena later observed in the U.S., such as the decline in the savings rate and excessive consumption habits.

The securitization of finance became common in the U.S. after mortgage-backed securities took root as a standardized instrument. As the pricing function was lost in the markets for securitized products, however, major job adjustments inevitably ensued for those working at financial institutions. Yet from a long-term perspective, adjustments of household consumption have an important bearing on the economy. The U.S. economy has lived with the excess spending habits of households, along with the twin deficits of the current account and the budget, for more than a quarter of a century—a situation some term as the triple deficit. All three must be corrected now as a result of the 2008–09 financial crisis.

In Asia, in past years some key developments have represented an adaptation to the excess consumption habits of the American economy, which have been reflected in the Asian mirrors. Those developments included 'East Asia's miracle' that occurred in the 1980s and afterward, China's switch to an open economy policy, and the spread of supply chain management throughout the Asia-Pacific region. In determining their positions in the global economy, the countries and regions of East Asia, including Japan, accepted as a given the images of the U.S. economy that were reflected in their respective mirrors. Indeed, those East Asian economies, heavily dependent on external demand, looked into the mirrors for various images of the American economy, picked the image that they thought most suited themselves, and tailored their economies to match the selected U.S. image.

In light of this background to the continued balance-of-payments disequilibrium, East Asian countries face difficulties with an intensity almost equal to those accompanying the adjustment process of the U.S. economy.

China, Japan, and Russia hold the most foreign exchange reserves. These countries are financing the U.S. current account deficits with their reserves. At the same time, those hefty reserves mean that the three countries are having difficulty stimulating domestic demand in such a way as to adapt to the American market. The massive accumulation of foreign exchange reserves is evidence that structural obstacles are impeding a desirable combination of production factors in the domestic economy as well as the creation of new domestic markets.

The 2008 global financial crisis triggered the adjustment of the U.S. economy. This points to a strong possibility of a global shortage of demand unless the expansion mechanism of absorption (net payments) is activated in East Asia. Consequently, there has been growing concern that a deflationary trend will likely take root around the world.

When it comes to stimulating domestic demand, China is focusing anew on developing its western regions. Japan, for its part, needs to put in place innovative initiatives for structural reform so that it will be able to expand domestic demand on a sustainable basis in the 21st century.

In pursuing structural reform, Japan will need to address specific targets, which will include enhancing the roles of labour as a production factor, agriculture on the supply side, and health care and a range of other services. Also important will be stepped-up efforts to tackle environmental conservation through innovative production systems and products. Japan would do well by producing reforms through incentive mechanisms conducted in Japan as well as in the rest of Asia. Such reforms will have to be as comprehensive as the supply management system in the Asia-Pacific region.

Bank Lending Procyclicality

A search for answers to two fundamental questions could offer clues about what Japan should do to return to a growth track.

First, why did the Japanese economy shrink so fast, even though securitization never took off there as it did in the United States? Second, how did an economic crisis that originated outside of Japan so directly sap domestic demand, given the relatively small share of exports in the country's gross domestic product (GDP)?

Before these answers can be explored, the characteristics of Japan's banking system must be clarified and the phenomenon of procyclicality elucidated. These analyses take on particular importance because Japan's banking mechanism clearly differs from that of the U.S. and Europe.

The Japanese securitization market has remained underdeveloped, primarily because credit default swaps (CDS)—which can be bought as protection for buyers of securitized debt—are not popular there. Japan has no equivalent to the American International Group, Inc. (AIG), the U.S. insurance giant that sold tens of billions of dollars' worth of these quasi-insurance products and was at the forefront of the economic meltdown.

Japanese banks have preferred to pursue the common policy of improving profit margins by lending, while choosing not to rely on profits earned through the shadow banking system, seen as the prime culprit behind the credit crisis. The banks' average profit margins—the gap between lending and deposit rates—was about one third the average 3 percent spread of their western peers.

Unlike their U.S. counterparts, Japanese banks largely steered clear of aggressive securitization in which banks' loan assets, as part of management resources, are bundled into securities for sale to investors. This securitization process transfers the credit risk of assets to other institutions and enables banks to remove the value of assets from their balance sheets.

Instead, Japanese banks sought to deepen their ties with corporate borrowers by increasing their cross-shareholdings, although the ceiling on such ownership by a financial institution was set at 5 percent.

During Japan's recovery phase following the 'Lost Decade' of the 1990s, which began in 2003, major banks tried to boost profitability by maximizing their lending-deposit rate spread, but their efforts produced negligible results. The primary reason behind their moderate margin growth is Japan's 'overbanking'. Simply put, the country has too many banks competing for too few borrowers. The situation has prevented banks from setting lending rates according to the level of credit risk.

Since the collapse of the bubble economy in 1991, there has been no significant change in banks' behaviour. The practice of cross-shareholding regained momentum during Japan's latest recovery phase, following the Asian-turned-global financial crisis of 1997–99, indicating that firms grew worried about being targeted by mergers and acquisitions.

A typical case is Nippon Steel Corp., Japan's top steelmaker. It forged stronger capital ties with two domestic rivals so they could defend themselves against the increased takeover threat of steel giant ArcelorMittal SA of Luxembourg. Japanese firms' obsession with retaining stable shareholders caused them to desperately ask banks to buy more shares.

The country's overnight interbank rates remained relatively stable, even as the credit crisis that started in 2007 spread across the world. This was a sharp contrast to western rivals, which were swamped by liquidity shortages in the securitized markets.

However, a different form of credit squeeze occurred in Japan. The collapse of stocks and other financial assets proved a serious blow for Japanese banks, which are subject to accounting rules that require them to write down the value of assets, including their shareholdings, if their market prices fall sharply.

The ensuing huge write-downs discouraged banks from extending more loans to corporate borrowers. The banks instead were concerned with whether they could meet the revised capital-adequacy requirements of the Basel II formula issued by the Basel Committee on Banking Supervision.

Taken together, the procyclicality of banks' lending behaviour became progressively evident in Japan. The phenomenon was exemplified by the fact that banks have grown reluctant to lend money now that they are under the pressure of falling financial asset values. This development further amplifies downward swings in the real economy.

Consequently, the role of banks as lenders, not to mention companies' governance systems, has been called into question. When the Japanese financial sector plunged into the abyss of systemic risk between 1997 and 2002, top executives at large businesses were inclined to believe that risky financial institutions should be separated from healthy industrial operations. In 2007–08, however, no business leaders brought up the subject, probably because they felt qualms about having asked banks to increase cross-shareholdings.

Rather, there was an argument that Japanese firms' weak profits came on the heels of shrinking foreign demand. This was followed by a freeze of money among financial institutions. In that sense, it is no wonder that almost no one complained loudly about bank executives in Japan, although this kind of criticism intensified in western countries.

Given that exports constitute significantly large shares of GDP in East Asian countries—notably China, Korea, Taiwan, and Singapore—these countries were deeply upset by disappearing foreign demand.

Meanwhile, some wondered why faltering foreign demand exerted an unexpectedly great effect on Japan's domestic demand, even though Japan's export-to-GDP ratio remained relatively low. The answer lies in how the leadership of major manufacturers influences the inner aspects of economic and social systems.

The development of Japan's economy and society has been driven by the corporate policies of high-profile firms such as Toyota Motor Corp., Honda Motor Co., Panasonic Corp., Canon Inc., Sony Corp., and Hitachi Ltd. These companies' policies are the backbone of highly productive allocations of resources.

Japan's economic recovery, which began in 2003, received a boost from an increase in private-sector capital investment. Given Japan's comparatively expensive labour costs, manufacturers' renewed commitment to investing in plant and equipment was made possible by their overwhelming advantage in technological innovation. Moreover, a new wave of capital spending came after manufacturers shifted production to low-wage countries, offering a vision of the path to be followed by Japan in the 21st century.

Until recently, expectations were running high for the Japanese economy to enter a propitious cycle of higher capital spending, a brighter job outlook, and demand growth. But this rosy scenario suddenly fell apart when the global slowdown was triggered by the U.S. sub-prime loan turmoil in 2007–08.

Management at Japanese manufacturers is typically capable of making bold decisions. Manufacturers have been involved in drastic inventory cuts since October 2008 in anticipation of worldwide final durable demand falling by half. Full-scale inventory control is the primary cause of steep decreases in GDP in the period from October to December 2008. Manufacturers also extensively adjusted stockpiles in the following quarter.

But after April 2009, their activities were pushed to new levels of inventory control based on achievements in each industry and at individual firms, forcing management to change their mindset to concentrate resources on providing high value to consumers and developing eco-products, as well as to respond swiftly to burgeoning business trends in emerging economies.

Japanese firms that completed the deepest inventory cuts should thus be among the first group of challengers for innovative projects under the leadership of new management teams.

Japanese Companies and China

A considerable proportion of Japanese companies has been pulled along by China's economy. As this dynamic plays out, a division has arisen among Japanese companies for the first time since World War II.

In 2003 China began to exert an enormous influence on the global economy. Since the fall of that year, foreign direct investment (FDI) in China has grown tremendously. Why did it start then?

At the end of 1999, China officially decided to join the World Trade Organization (WTO). In 2000, FDI in China came alive at a single stroke. Labour-intensive industries began to think of using China as a base to supply the world. China's farming villages mapped out the position of sending workers to urban centres along the country's coast. With regard to resource distribution within China, the country became a net importer of agricultural products. Within large cities the direction pointed toward generating huge demand for construction materials used in homes and commercial buildings.

Throughout China, more than 250 large cities sprang up. Large quantities of cement, aluminium and steel were in demand, and electricity shortages became a constant occurrence. This continual expansion of investment caused a roller coaster for energy and mineral resource procurement from China. For the five years from 2003 through 2008, trade conditions for not only oil-producing countries but also those rich in resources such as coal, iron ore, and natural gas thus suddenly changed for the better.

Japanese companies continued to improve their corporate performance through exports to China as well as to other resource-rich countries. General trading firms continued to invest in raw-material industries such as steel, petrochemicals, pulp and paper, and non-ferrous materials; the shipping industry, including container ships for transporting products, tankers for shipping crude oil, and bulk carriers for transporting coal and iron ore; construction machinery such as large cranes; and resource excavation companies for procuring natural resources. Corporate results improved, dragged along by the economy of China with its WTO membership.

However, at some point an adjustment was inevitable. As an indication, the market capitalization of companies in these industries underwent a massive correction beginning in May 2008. Would Japan's corporate groups prostrate themselves before China's economic adjustment? While there were certainly corporate groups that wished China's economy would maintain its high growth rate over the medium- to long-term future, there were also a large number of corporate groups in Japan that thought that the weaknesses in China's economy should be overcome. This is a characteristic of Japan, which has matured on both the manufacturing front and the technology front.

Research and development companies exploring energy conservation, resource conservation, and improvement of the environment, along with companies that hold commercial technologies for improving the quality of water, air, and land, are becoming significant in supporting Japanese industry. As long as the Chinese economy, being driven to make adjustments, can enjoy sustainable growth, interest in this new area of Japanese industry must be pursued. A representative opinion is that maintaining a real growth rate in excess of 8 percent will keep the employment situation in China from deteriorating. However, the approach of expanding investment to that end as in the past must be abandoned. What is needed is economic reform from inside. To that end, China must move toward policies that give the highest priority to environmental protection and resource conservation. Thus the economic leaders of China have never been as interested in Japanese companies as they are today.

While there is a growing recognition that Anglo-American economic management is becoming blocked even in China, interest in the developing power of Japanese industry and technology partially compensates. That is not to say that Japan's business world will remain in a split state regarding interest in China. Even inside Japan, new industrial integration should be examined.

Japan's Supply Side for a Low-Carbon Society

Increased government spending needs to be linked to medium- to long-term improvement of the supply side. The Japanese government faces a test of whether it is wise enough to use expenditure expansion to prompt the supply side of the national economy to increase employment and heighten the value-added productivity.

The Japanese government has responded to economic downturns since 1965, when it began relying on the new issuance of government bonds, by almost automatically cranking up public works projects. As this Japanese-style Keynesian approach has taken hold, it has eroded the function of the government.

The labour force should have been redistributed to enhance high value-added productivity. To this end, the government should have intervened to ensure that appropriate job retraining and lifelong education were available while taking into account the aptitudes of individual workers.

In reality, however, the government did no more than attempt simply to increase the number of jobs, which has in turn compelled it to boost public works spending in supplementary budgets each fiscal year.

The worsening employment situation since 2008 has highlighted the Japanese government's lack of a scheme to match job supply with demand on a long-term basis. Social efforts are needed to accumulate know-how for matching contacts with individual workers. Public-private partnerships will likely produce results on an individual basis.

Medium-term efforts to improve the supply side are also required in fields other than the labour market. Capital equipment must be examined from a similar perspective. To overcome the 2008–09 economic crisis, investment in research and development must stimulated and capital equipment must be created for the future economy.

In developing the supply side to realize a low-carbon society, a 'coalition of the willing' is required. Goods and services demanded in such a society must exert a minimal adverse impact on the global environment. To build a network of suppliers of these goods and services, there must be leaders and new combinations of fundamental technologies.

Corporate research-and-development investment is also essential to overcoming technological obstacles blocking the realization of a low-carbon society. Setting up a coalition of the willing to deal with each project would seem a desirable course. The government does not have to get involved if the market can realize the matching function required by society. But asymmetries in information would be inevitable when it comes to a challenge of the unknown future. Public-private partnerships are significant here as well.

The Japanese government has long been reluctant to study how it should engage in such fields as the labour and capital markets, the two basic factors that should shore up the future supply side. This is fully demonstrated by the present state of affairs in which the economic crisis led to a governmental crisis.

Chapter 4

The Macroeconomics of the Global Financial and Economic Crisis

Libero Monteforte[1]

It is probably still too early for a thorough assessment of the causes and effects of the 2008–09 financial crisis. Since 2007 there have been a number of unprecedented economic events, both in the financial sector and in the real economy. How far the consequences of these events will go and how the world economy will change once order has been restored to market conditions remains uncertain.

Several scholars have started to study the crisis from different points of view. Andrew Rose and Mark Spiegel (2009) have tried to verify if an early warning system of macro and micro indicators could have predicted it. Carmen Reinhart and Kenneth Rogoff (2009) and Barry Eichengreen and Kevin O'Rourke (2010) have compared the crisis to other similar historical events, trying to shed light on the near future. The crisis was such a huge event that a number of economists have also started to think how economic theory should be reinterpreted (see Acemoglu 2009; Economist 2009; Wyplosz 2009).

This chapter examines the causes and consequences of the crisis from a broad macroeconomic perspective, which potentially encompasses alternative explanations. It considers the short-term indicators and forecasts to detect signals of structural changes that the crisis may bring about. Finally, it gives some caveats regarding the economic policy response adopted in reaction to the crisis.

A Bubble with Wide and Deep Roots

Regarding the causes of the crisis, several authors focus on the banking system and housing market in the United States.[2] It is certainly true that the U.S. mortgage

---

1 The opinions expressed here are personal and do not necessarily reflect those of the institutions to which the author is affiliated. The author is grateful to Paolo Savona for continuous encouragement in his research and to Lorenzo Codogno, Francesco Nucci, and Jules Leichter for helpful discussions and comments. He thanks in particular Sara Minelli and Elisa Scambelloni for excellent help in editing the text. All errors and shortcomings are the author's.

2 See Chapter 2 by Robert Fauver for a description of the failures of the mortgage market in the United States in recent years.

market was the epicentre of the process. But other complementary factors were also critical.

One school of thought concentrates on technical microeconomic factors, mainly related to the financial sector. These factors include accounting standards, conflicts of interest in the rating agencies, uneven financial market regulation between commercial banks and investment banks, the procyclicality in the Basel II accord set out by the Basel Committee on Banking Supervision (BCBS) and the new originate-to-distribute (OTD) model of lending. These factors are certainly important. However, they are not at the heart of recent events.

More importantly, a second school of international analysts offers explanations related to global imbalances and the corresponding flows of saving from newly industrialized to advanced countries. This has been a hazardous process in itself. But derivatives and an inadequate governance of the international monetary system exacerbated these imbalances.

A third school, less frequently cited, focuses on economic policy, particularly in the United States. Following 11 September 2001, a strong expansionary monetary and fiscal policy stance acted to postpone a crisis that should have closed a decade of excess and illusions such as the so-called 'new economy paradigm'. This delay was

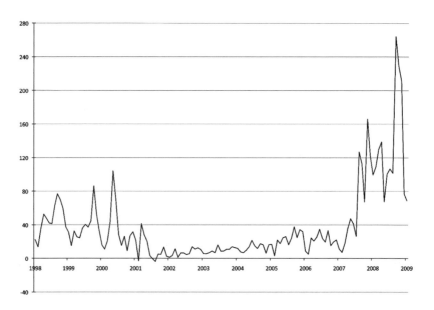

Figure 4.1   Spreads on corporate liabilities

Note: Commercial paper spread (spread between yields on 90-day investment-grade commercial paper and on three-month U.S. treasury bill).

Source: International Monetary Fund (2009, 164).

the basis for a greater 'future' crisis that brought about the biggest downturn since 1929.

To summarize, the crisis exploded in the U.S. banking sector. The reasons for the strong and fast contagion in financial markets and around the world stand in the accumulation of large domestic and global imbalances, as well as ineffective coordination in financial supervision and regulation.

These different explanations can be put into a single macroeconomic framework. Since 1999 substantial mistakes have been made in economic policy and financial regulation in advanced countries, and those mistakes have resulted in incentives for excessive risk taking.[3] The domestic result has been the increase of household debt. At the international level, there have been substantial trade imbalances and cross-border debts. The measure of the reduction in risk aversion in financial markets has been the compression of all interest rate spreads. In the years before the crisis, spreads appeared smaller than what would be consistent with fundamentals (see Figure 4.1). The spread compressions should have been interpreted as an early warning signal of the crash.

Low real interest rates pushed investments but also pushed private consumption. In addition, in particular in the U.S., an increasing share of the expenses for durable goods was paid with consumer credit. Similarly, U.S. bills created adverse incentives to give access to mortgage markets to households with small disposable income and thus to risky borrowers. This contributed to increasing house prices and to inflating the bubble in the real estate sector. The increase of both consumer credit and unsustainable mortgages was an indication of the structural underestimation of future risk.

How is it possible that such risky behaviour continued for so long? Economic policy acted as a lender of last resort in times and in circumstances that in the past should have induced prudence. Households and bankers realized that buying a house and making profits on risky borrowers was in fact a biased gamble. If things were right, the result was an increase for banks and landlords, but not for the whole economy. Otherwise, the government would cover the losses. This interpretation can appear overstated but it is consistent with the previous actions of governments and regulators. The bail-out of Long-Term Capital Management (LTCM) in 1998 is probably a representative case. LTCM was a hedge fund, so an operator known to work with high leverage and without the strict regulation that applied to commercial banks. The bankruptcy could have been considered a normal event, but public authorities organized a bail-out. Following these kind of interventions, markets and, in particular, investments banks increased their risky contracts and profitability. It is questionable whether this behaviour was rational; if such behaviour is rational, it is conditional on the policy stance. According to this interpretation, what happened in the aftermath of the Lehman Brothers

---

3   The view that the deep roots of the crisis lie in bad policies is shared with Chiara Oldani, Rainer Masera, and Paolo Savona (2008) who, analogously to this chapter, examine the three families of explanations cited above.

bankruptcy in September 2008 was simply an overshooting of the risk aversion of private agents, both in the real and in the financial sectors. Markets, households, and firms realized that the government was no longer in a condition be able to save everyone. Financial markets started to penalize all risky assets, with a sharp drop in stock market prices and a dramatic decrease in bank lending (for a while banks lent only to central banks, the safest borrower in the system). Consistent with this increase in risk aversion, households raised their savings rate and business confidence collapsed, resulting in a dramatic fall in investment.

These events can be summarized in terms of a sharp increase in the risk aversion, from the low levels of the pre-crisis era. Risk aversion is an unobservable parameter, which became popular in macroeconomics following the Lucas critique (Lucas 1976). Today it is widely used in econometric models labelled dynamic stochastic general equilibrium models (DSGE), while it was not explicitly considered in the previous generation of Keynesian models. In DSGE modelling it is included as a structural 'deep' parameter; therefore it is difficult to identify and to assess their changes in real time. Moreover, the crisis could be considered the result not only of a shift in the parameter that drives the consumer behaviour but also of biased expectations. A fully fledged econometric analysis on these issues has not been provided yet and is left for future research.

As of the last quarter of 2008, a jump in risk aversion could have been considered reasonable, but it was almost impossible to estimate the size of this change. Thus in October 2008 all forecasters began to revise their growth expectations down gradually, but only after a semester was the size of this revision completed.[4] Now forecasters and the economic theory are blamed as they were unable to predict the crash. Most of the allegations seem overstated. It was an unprecedented event and the size of the shock was so large that non-linearities strongly affected any model-based prediction. Economics and econometrics should, and probably will, learn from this crisis, but there are no guarantees that other similar events will be predictable in the future. The debate has started and interesting points have been made by Ignazio Visco (2009) and *The Economist* (2009).

The Aftermath of the Crisis

Within three quarters after the Lehman Brothers bankruptcy, several peculiar effects appeared at the global level. Two international puzzles concerning the economic downturn are discussed herein.

First, the crisis originated in the financial sectors of the United States and the United Kingdom, but quickly transferred to the real economy all over the world.

---

4   In June 2009 the forecasts of gross domestic product (GDP) issued by the Organisation for Economic Co-operation and Development ([OECD] 2009) were revised upward for the first time since June 2007.

Table 4.1   International macroeconomic forecasts: Growth in gross domestic product

	2007	2008	2009	2010	2011
Consensus Forecasts[a]					
United States	2.1	0.4	−2.4	3.2	3.1
Japan	2.3	−1.2	−5.2	2.2	1.6
France	2.3	0.3	−2.2	1.4	1.6
United Kingdom	2.6	0.5	−4.9	1.3	2.3
Italy	1.4	−1.2	−5.0	0.8	1.1
Germany	2.5	1.3	−5.0	1.6	1.7
International Monetary Fund					
United States	2.1	0.4	−2.4	3.1	2.6
Japan	2.4	−1.2	−5.2	1.9	2.0
France	2.3	0.3	−2.2	1.5	1.8
United Kingdom	2.6	0.5	−4.9	1.3	2.5
China	13.0	9.6	8.7	10.0	9.9
India	9.4	7.3	5.7	8.8	8.4
Italy	1.5	−1.3	−5.0	0.8	1.2
Germany	2.5	1.2	−5.0	1.2	1.7
Euro area	2.8	0.6	−4.1	1.0	1.5
Organisation for Economic Co-operation and Development					
United States	2.1	0.4	−2.4	3.2	3.2
Japan	2.4	−1.2	−5.2	3.0	2.0
France	2.3	0.3	−2.5	1.7	2.1
United Kingdom	2.6	0.5	−4.9	1.3	2.5
China	14.2	9.6	8.7	11.1	9.7
India	9.6	5.1	6.6	8.3	8.5
Italy	1.4	−1.3	−5.1	1.1	1.5
Germany	2.6	1.0	−4.9	1.9	2.1
Euro area	2.7	0.5	−4.1	1.2	1.8
Member countries	2.8	0.5	−3.3	2.7	2.8
World Trade[c]					
International Monetary Fund[b]	7.2	2.8	−10.7	7.0	6.1
Organisation for Economic Co-operation and Development	7.3	3.2	−11	10.6	8.4
Oil					
Consensus forecasts[a,d]			65.07[e]	81.90[f]	84.50[g]
International Monetary Fund[h]	71.13	97.03	61.78	80.00	83.00
Organisation for Economic Co-operation and Development[i]	72.50	97.00	61.50	78.90	80.00

Sources: Consensus Economics (2010), International Monetary Fund (2010), Organisation for Economic Co-operation and Development (2010).

Notes: [a] Mean of projections for March 2010, April 2010, and May 2010. [b] Volume (goods and services). [c] Average of world merchandise import and export volumes seasonally and working-day (except inflation) adjusted. [d] West Texas Intermediate (U.S. dollars per barrel) [e] End of November 2009. [f] End of August 2010. [g] End of May 2011. [h] Simple average of prices of UK Brent, Dubai, and West Texas Intermediate crude oil. [i] Brent crude oil price (U.S. dollar per barrel). Indices through 2009 are based on data compiled by International Energy Agency for oil and by Hamburg Institute of International Economics for the prices of other primary commodities; estimates and projections for 2010 and 2011 are from the Organisation for Economic Co-operation and Development.

In autumn 2008 the common wisdom, as stated in the *World Economic Outlook* published by the International Monetary Fund (IMF), was that 'the likelihood that financial stress will be followed by a downturn appears to be associated with the extent to which house prices and aggregate credit rise in the period before the financial stress' (IMF 2008, 131). The following quarters revealed quite a different pattern. In 2009 the most adversely affected economies, Germany and Japan, had no major imbalances or housing bubbles. In these economies gross domestic product (GDP) fell at a rate of about 5 percent, while the U.S. contracted at a rate of 2.4 percent. The prediction was, on the contrary, true for countries such as China (on the up side) and the UK (on the low side). A fragmented picture is also today predicted by the main forecasters, sharing the view of a slightly weaker recovery for Japan and the euro area than for the U.S. in the two-year period of 2010–11 (see Table 4.1). How can this be explained?

This crisis can be considered as a laboratory experiment, acting as a simultaneous stress test for all economies. It produced an unsurprising result: economies with resilient private sectors and strong governments were able to better absorb a large shock. On the other hand, economies that built their competitiveness on rigid production factors suffered the most. This is a supply-side explanation.

The demand-side explanation could be that both Germany and Japan were in trouble because they were exporting countries, and trade was in free fall. This explanation should be associated with the previous one—otherwise how can China's good performance be explained? But this raises a second puzzle. The Organisation for Economic Co-operation and Development (OECD) and the IMF reported a drop in commercial trade in 2009 of more than 10 percent, compared with a much smaller contraction in GDP in the same period (see Table 4.1). How can such a collapse be interpreted? Several explanations have been proposed. An intuitive hypothesis refers to the trade credit, as banking conditions are known to affect firms' trading volumes (Amiti and Weinstein 2009). A different explanation considers the recent increase of delocalization of firms and the compositional effect due to the fact that the decrease in trade was concentrated in durable and intermediate goods (see Berms et al. 2010; Eaton et al. 2010).[5] However, a new generation of protectionism could have played a role, and some authors have indeed talked about a 'murky protectionism' (Baldwin and Evenett 2009).

Trying to solve these puzzles is important in order to understand the strength and persistence of the current recovery. But, more importantly, these issues are relevant to comprehending what the world economy will be in the decade to come. In particular, questions arise about potential output in the post-crisis period. As underlined by Olivier Blanchard (2009), chief economist of the IMF,

---

5   On one hand, the large diffusion of delocalization could have multiplied the decrease in imports from advanced countries. On the other hand, durable and intermediate goods are the most volatile components of the international flows, and therefore were largely affected by such a large global shock.

some parts of the economic system have broken. Some firms went bankrupt that would not have in a normal recession. In advanced countries, the financial systems are partly dysfunctional, and will take a long time to find their new shape. Meanwhile, financial intermediation—and, by implication, the process of reallocation of resources that is central to growth—will be impaired. In emerging market countries, capital inflows, which decreased dramatically during the crisis, may not fully come back in the next few years. Changes in the composition of world demand, as consumption shifts from advanced to emerging economies, may require changes in the structure of production. In nearly all countries, the costs of the crisis have added to the fiscal burden, and higher taxation is inevitable.

All this means that we may not go back to the old growth path, that potential output may be lower than it was before the crisis.

How much has potential output decreased? It is difficult to tell: we do not see potential output, only actual output. The historical evidence is worrisome, however. The IMF's forthcoming *World Economic Outlook* presents evidence from 88 banking crises over the past four decades in a wide range of countries. While there is large variation across countries, the conclusion is that, on average, output does not go back to its old trend path, but remains permanently below it. The possible good news is that the trend itself appears to be unaffected: on average, crises permanently decrease the level of output, but not its growth rate. So, if past is prologue, the world economy likely will return to its past growth rate. But, especially in advanced countries, the period of above-average growth, characteristic of normal recoveries, may be short-lived or nonexistent.

Policy Innovations

Thanks to the experience of the Great Depression, economic policy was extremely fast in response to the downturn in 2007–09. The advantages of these actions are important and well known. But perhaps not all the costs are equally understood.

In the period of 2008–09 all the major countries introduced strongly expansionary fiscal policies. Support for stimulus plans was innovative with respect to the pre-crisis era. Up to 2008 it was considered blasphemy to affirm the need of fiscal policy to counterbalance economic downturns, but during the recession the international institutions changed their minds and blamed governments for not running large enough deficits. In 2010 they finally returned to the orthodoxy, under the pressure of capital markets and the European financial turmoil.

Asking governments to use fiscal policy to counteract the cycle is poor advice, unless in extreme recessions such as the one just experienced.[6] This is mainly because of implementation delays and the difficulties of matching the future timing of macro effects with the accuracy of quarterly forecasts. What the government can undoubtedly do is foster medium- to long-run growth, and to do so not only by changing the borrowing requirement, but also by using budget-neutral measures and regulatory instruments. This orientation would require analyses of the structural effects of the crisis on potential output growth. These studies are still in their initial stages.

Furthermore, official claims regarding the size of the stimuli plans were somewhat suspect, as they often referred to net amounts rather than the gross amounts. Also, it was often unclear who benefited from them. For example, the plan proposed by U.S. treasury secretary Henry Paulson was announced in 2008 as a relief to address toxic assets of banks, but *ex post* was also used to finance the automotive industry.

To summarize, the fiscal packages were like huge black boxes that would require detailed and proper assessments of their single components. More in-depth studies are probably needed to assess the medium-term effects of these plans.

With regard to monetary policy, a number of new measures were adopted by central banks. These interventions are called 'quantitative easing' and 'credit easing'. These terms always indicate a sizeable increase in the balance sheet of central banks (see Figure 4.2).

Such interventions can take the form of purchases of firms' stocks or other private (and even public) liabilities. There seems to be broad agreement among national and international institutions on the need for these instruments given current conditions. Certainly in the short term these operations are useful to increase liquidity and moderate asset prices, but they also can be hazardous. Central banks' balance sheets are taking on risky assets. Doing so can pose unprecedented problems over the medium term. These problems are larger where the public debt is increasing a lot. Extreme events in the future due to these risks cannot be ruled out. Monetary authorities are fully aware of these issues and the European Central Bank has been particularly prudent in the use of these tools. But can central banks be sure to withdraw these operations with the right forward-looking timing? For these reasons the conditions of the exit strategies will be at the heart of the policy debate in the following years.

Conclusions

This chapter considers several causes of the crisis, which have been separately identified by many authors. All these factors point to a change in the behaviour

---

6   See Lorenzo Forni, Libero Monteforte, and Luca Sessa (2009) and the references cited therein for an updated description of the empirical estimates on fiscal policy multipliers.

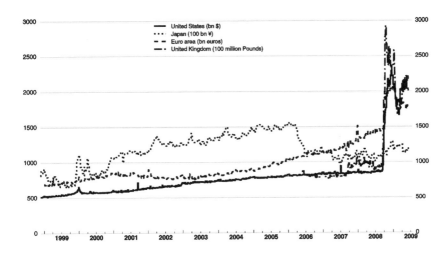

Figure 4.2   Central banks' balance sheets

Note: Latest available date: 11 June 2009.

Source: Organisation for Economic Co-operation and Development (2009).

of private sector operators toward risky (and profitable) operations. This change was probably supported by earlier economic policy mistakes and inadequate financial supervision.

Economic models and forecasts were unable to assess the magnitude of the recession on a timely basis because of both the size of the shock and the features of econometric models, which do not take into account changes in 'deep parameters', such as risk aversion, and biased expectations.

How economies changed because of the crisis is still unknown, but it is urgent to study this issue, in order to guide current economic policies. Governments and monetary authorities reacted to the downturn with aggressive and unprecedented measures. In the short term this provided a good signal to restore confidence. But in the medium term there are a number of risks that should not be underestimated.

References

Acemoglu, Daron (2009). *The Crisis of 2008: Structural Lessons for and from Economics.* CEPR Policy Insight No. 28, January. Centre for Economic Policy Research, London. <www.cepr.org/pubs/policyinsights/CEPR_Policy_ Insight_028.asp> (August 2010).

Amiti, Mary and David E. Weinstein (2009). *Exports and Financial Shocks.* Working Paper 15556. National Bureau of Economic Research, Cambridge MA. <www.nber.org/papers/w15556.pdf> (August 2010).

Baldwin, Richard and Simon Evenett, eds. (2009). *The Collapse of Global Trade, Murky Protectionism, and the Crisis: Recommendations for the G20* (London: VoxEU). <www.voxeu.org/index.php?q=node/3199> (August 2010).

Berms, Rudolfs, Robert C. Johnson, and Kei-Mu Yi (2010). *Demand Spillovers and the Collapse of Trade in the Global Recession.* Working Paper No. 10/142, June. International Monetary Fund, Washington DC. <www.imf.org/external/pubs/ft/wp/2010/wp10142.pdf> (August 2010).

Blanchard, Olivier (2009). 'Sustaining a Global Recovery.' *Finance and Development*, vol. 46, no. 3 (September), <www.imf.org/external/pubs/ft/fandd/2009/09/blanchardindex.htm> (August 2010).

Consensus Economics (2010). *Consensus Forecasts*, March (London: Consensus Economics).

Eaton, Jonathan, Sam Kortum, Brent Neiman, et al. (2010). *Trade and the Global Recession.* Paper prepared for the EFIGE Scientific Workshop and Policy Conference, Banca d'Italia, Rome, 16–18 June.

Economist (2009). 'The Other-Worldly Philosophers.' 16 June.

Eichengreen, Barry J. and Kevin H. O'Rourke (2010). 'What Do the New Data Tell Us?' 8 March, VoxEU. <www.voxeu.org/index.php?q=node/3421> (August 2010).

Forni, Lorenzo, Libero Monteforte, and Luca Lessa (2009). 'The General Equilibrium Effects of Fiscal Policy: Estimates for the Euro Area.' *Journal of Public Economics*, vol. 93, no. 3–4, pp. 559–585.

International Monetary Fund (2008). *World Economic Outlook: Financial Stress, Downturns, and Recoveries.* October. <www.imf.org/external/pubs/ft/weo/2008/02> (August 2010).

International Monetary Fund (2009). 'Global Financial Stability Report: Responding to the Financial Crisis and Measuring Systemic Risks.' April. <www.imf.org/External/Pubs/FT/GFSR/2009/01> (August 2010).

International Monetary Fund (2010). *World Economic Outlook: Rebalancing Growth.* April. <www.imf.org/external/pubs/ft/weo/2010/01/> (August 2010).

Lucas, Robert (1976). 'Econometric Policy Evaluation: A Critique.' In K. Brunner and A.H. Meltzer, eds., *The Phillips Curve and Labor Markets* (New York: American Elsevier).

Oldani, Chiara, Rainer Masera, and Paolo Savona (2008). 'Subprime Credits or Subprime Policies?' 19 September Paper prepared for the Sixth Colloquium on "Derivatives, Risk Return and Subprime," Associazione Luiss-Guido Carli, Fondazione Cesifin Alberto Predieri in collaboration with the Journal of Financial Stability, Lucca, Italy.

Organisation for Economic Co-operation and Development (2009). *OECD Economic Outlook.* No. 85, June. Paris.

Organisation for Economic Co-operation and Development (2010). *OECD Economic Outlook.* No. 87, May. Paris.

Reinhart, Carmen M. and Kenneth Rogoff (2009). *The Aftermath of Financial Crises*. NBER Working Paper No. 14656, January. National Bureau of Economic Research, Washington DC. <www.nber.org/papers/w14656> (August 2010).

Rose, Andrew K. and Mark M. Spiegel (2009). *Cross-Country Causes and Consequences of the 2008 Crisis: Early Warning*. Working Paper Series 2009–17. Federal Reserve Bank of San Francisco. <www.frbsf.org/publications/economics/papers/2009/wp09-17bk.pdf> (August 2010).

Visco, Ignazio (2009). *La crisi finanziaria e le previsioni degli economisti*. Faculty of Economics, University of Rome 'La Sapienza', Bank of Italy, Rome, 4 March. <www.bancaditalia.it/interventi/intaltri_mdir/visco_040309/Visco_040309.pdf> (August 2010).

Wyplosz, Charles (2009). *Macroeconomics after the Crisis: Dealing with the Tobin Curse*. The Walter-Adolf-Joehr Lecture, 15 May.

PART III
Solutions in Europe

Chapter 5

Crisis, Response, and Innovation in Europe

Paolo Savona and Chiara Oldani

The Impact of the Crisis on Europe

The close economic ties between Europe and the United States and the crucial global monetary and financial role played by the City of London were the conduits for the lightning-fast spread of the crisis triggered by the sub-prime mortgage defaults in the U.S. and the consequent fall in global real aggregate demand in 2008. The effects of this crisis differed among euro area countries, among non-euro European Union countries, and among such neighbouring non-members as Turkey and Russia. The differences appear to have been sharpest within the euro group.

It is well known that the euro area is not an optimal currency area, and the consequences of this condition are manifold.[1] Banking and financial arrangements remain differentiated within the euro area, and national supervisory authorities differ in vigour and efficacy. Some analysts hold that certain countries, Italy among them, lack a truly modern financial system, which is why their banking and securities markets were less exposed to the global financial crisis of 2007–08. This analysis has been presented as a criticism, but, by comparison with the consequences of the more 'modern' American and British systems, it may not be such. Some members of the European Union have not completed a return to a market economy after their experiences of central planning and being 'governed by outside' (i.e., by Soviet Russia). Turkey is torn between modernism in the broad sense and Islamic revival. Post-communist Russia is a case apart for a few reasons, including its large territory outside of physical Europe.

It is also well known that although the euro was created in the hopes that it would bring political union in its wake ('money first', in the famous slogan of former European Commission president Roy Jenkins, although his own country opted out of the EU single currency), no such union has ever come about. Rather, the goal may have receded, leaving a legacy of lame institutional arrangements in the EU in which the rules of competition apply to all countries but are concentrated on industry (which represents no more than a quarter of European gross domestic product [GDP]), while the single currency (with its irrevocably fixed exchange rates) applies to only half the members. Meanwhile, fiscal policy remains in the

---

1   Robert Mundell (1961), the author of the optimal currency area theory, won the Nobel Prize in 1999 at the start of the euro.

hands of the single member states, but under the constraints of the Stability and Growth Pact agreed to in Amsterdam in 1997, which has at its heart a ceiling on the general government deficit of 3 percent of national GDP. Given these patchwork arrangements, more than anything else the financial crisis has eaten up the stock of household savings, in all its various forms, and taken a huge bite out of banks' capital and reserves.

European banking and financial systems have withstood the trans-Atlantic tidal wave. There were a few instances of nationalization. Some cases were sizeable (such as the Royal Bank of Scotland in the United Kingdom and Fortis in Belgium), but they were extremely modest in comparison with those undertaken in America. In any case, the institutional and economic set-up of the EU was not altered. In the real economy, by contrast, the crisis struck the only sector exposed to competition, namely industry. Agriculture was sheltered and services were semi-sheltered, due to the amendment of the Directive on Services in the Internal Market (the Bolkestein directive) to prevent firms doing business in any EU country from applying home-country labour contracts.

In short, in Europe the impact on real economic activity was more severe in manufacturing given its growth model based on exports. It suffered because of the decline in global demand, which was due to decreased domestic consumption. Consequently the most vulnerable countries, apart from the United Kingdom, were Spain, Austria, and Ireland in the euro area, Poland among the other EU member states, and Turkey and Russia outside the EU. The initial drop of financial wealth in the euro area was half the value of European stocks. The decline in real economic activity averaged 5.8 percent in 2008 alone, with spikes of 8.2 percent in Germany and 7.5 percent in Italy, while the French economy contracted by 4.6 percent. The average drop in the GDP becomes less significant because of differences among the three main sectors of the economy as well as within each sector in terms of dependence on world trade. The true cost of the crisis will be increased public debt as a result of lower revenues and higher public expenditures.

Europe's Macroeconomic Policy Response

Historically, the euro area's monetary policy has been shaped by powerful monetarist orthodoxy. The Treaty of Maastricht assigns the single mandate of price stability to the European Central Bank (ECB). The French economist Jean-Paul Fitoussi aptly summed up this policy approach in his description of the U.S. as a producer of ideas that has no intention of consuming domestically, but produces exports because there is someone willing to import them. The main buyer, in this case, is the German Bundesbank. EU fiscal policy is equally orthodox—'not flexible' is perhaps a more appropriate term—under the old principle that to inculcate a particular type of behaviour, prohibition beats toleration.

The current crisis has dispelled this twofold orthodoxy. The growth rate of M3—the broadest measure of money supply—followed a peculiar trend from the middle of 2004 to the end of 2008, rising from 5 percent to 12 percent and then, in the first quarter of 2009, dropping to 6 percent as a result of a small increase in credit and portfolio reallocation, both domestic and foreign.[2] Since March 2009 official interest rates have been kept relatively high (with respect to inflation and the comparative rates in the U.S. and in the rest of the world) to permit the 'non-conventional' creation of a monetary base serving all the market demand and accepting a large and unusual number of financial assets. In the meantime the average EU government deficit soared to 4.6 percent of GDP in 2008: for the first time since the Stability and Growth Pact was signed, no country has been subjected to an excessive deficit procedure for violating the 3 percent ceiling.

These policy choices were late in coming, so that the doses of monetary and fiscal stimulus were larger than would have been necessary had the moves had been timely. The efficacy of the measures, inevitably, suffered. Except for providing the indispensable liquidity eliminated by the paralysis of the interbank market and the withdrawal of bank deposits, most of the decisions, especially on the fiscal policy front, did not come until nearly the end of 2008, almost two years after the crisis began. Those decisions took effect in 2009 and continued into 2010. Late in 2008 British prime minister Gordon Brown budgeted a deficit of 8 percent of the UK's GDP, after the Bank of England—as stated by governor Mervyn King in October 2008 'created a monetary base to an extent unprecedented in its 340 years of life'. The British pound fell below parity with the euro—at the height of 'irrational exuberance' in the British financial market, it had been worth more than twice the continental currency. Germany budgeted a deficit of 3.3 percent, after giving guarantees of €400 billion on new bond issues; France had a GDP deficit of 8.75 percent plus a very large number of guarantees and much recapitalization of financial intermediaries. Other European countries experienced a soaring deficit, in particular overall economic conditions in Portugal, Ireland, Greece, and Spain (unpleasantly referred to as the PIGS) were poor in terms of production, employment, and consumption. In particular, Greece reached an unexpected deficit of 12.5 percent of GDP in 2009 and remains close to bankruptcy. European countries and the International Monetary Fund (IMF) intervened to rescue the country, which was unable to raise funds in the international market.[3]

It was not only monetary and fiscal orthodoxy that suffered, but the fundamental principles of political economy also dissolved as consequences of the American-based crisis. Rescue packages everywhere shifted the burden onto future generations in the form of public debt.

A further constraint came from the Maastricht Treaty. It left sovereignty over foreign exchange rates to the 27 member states of the EU, even though they are divided into the 16 eurozone-members and 11 non-members. This relegation of sovereignty essentially had the effect of negating the existence of the common

---

2   The ECB discloses the entire data set on money and interest rates on its website.

3   The spread between Greek and German bonds reached 600 basis points in the spring of 2010.

market. Moreover, after the introduction of the euro in 1999, its market value went down by one third and then climbed up nearly two times the minimum reached before.[4] The situation has been reinforced by the ECB's interest rate policy, which sets the euro systematically higher than the dollar, strengthening the euro's appreciation. The official reaction was that the exchange rate was irrelevant in determining the level of exports, but that would not be true without the exceptional growth of world trade in that period. When the situation reversed following the sub-prime crisis and exports dropped, most authorities started to be concerned about the effects on exports, admitting that the euro exchange rate plays a role. But the appreciation of the dollar reduced pressure on governments to take political decisions on the subject. Things stayed as they were 10 years before. Over the same period, unlike Europe the UK manoeuvred its interest rates, quantity of money, fiscal deficit, and exchange rate according to its needs without any strong reaction from any other EU state.

The EU exists within an incomplete institutional framework, which precludes any future possibility of regaining a satisfactory level of income and employment. The slowness of decision making and the absence of all but sporadic coordination in response to the financial crisis stemmed from the lack of will to proceed like a political union and from the constraints of European institutions, which had been designed for stability, even at the cost of deflation, rather than for growth. This approach has been criticized by international organizations. But differences in economic structure have also been a factor. Saving, as reflected in national balances of payments, still has sharply divergent characteristics. Germany has a current account surplus that rivals China's and the Netherlands and Austria also exhibit surpluses; Spain, Greece, and Ireland above all—but also Italy and France, albeit to a much lesser extent—went into deficit. Rationally, the surplus countries should take up the burden of stimulating internal demand within the euro area, while the deficit countries should benefit from this impulse. But in practice all euro area countries—regardless of whether their foreign accounts show a deficit or a surplus—found themselves struggling to comply with the limit on public budget deficits.

This institutional, political, and economic stalemate is the cause for the EU's protracted inaction. In rational terms, such a stance could be justified by the fact that the EU has an export-led model of growth, and that trade with the rest of the world is so massive that its decline could never be made up for by domestic demand. This approach remains valid if trade within the euro area is considered as external trade, as it actually is conducted by euro members, instead of being considered as consumption or investment—an approach that creates persistent differences in the institutional framework. This consideration is especially powerful in a country such as Italy, where the public debt is enormous and trade plays a relevant role. So 'political' Europe chose to concentrate on the social costs of the crisis, investing

---

4   The exchange rate between the euro and the U.S. dollar was fixed at 1.11 on 1 January 1999; its minimum value since then has been 0.82 and its maximum 1.60.

resources in assistance to the most disadvantaged, awaiting impulses from the rest of the world. However, since the countries running large external deficits, such as the U.S. and the UK, did not hesitate to reflate their domestic demand by relying on their neighbours' savings, the inactive European policy could not prevent the crisis from worsening—it could not prevent social costs much higher than what public intervention could alleviate.

The world now faces the classical problem in economics, the search for the right measure, which can be tested only after the fact. Given the circumstances, not even European-wide coordination would have sufficed to overcome the crisis. As the final communiqué of the G20 London Summit succinctly observed: 'a global crisis requires a global solution' (G20 2009). Disunity in action increases the cost of the crisis and, together with the time delay, decreases the efficacy of the antirecession measures taken. This is what actually happened. The only initiatives that suggest that economic geopolitics is moving in the right direction—if not on the right track—are those managed by the IMF. The obstacle to the efficacy of this coordination still lies in having no uniformity in the foreign exchange regimes among members of the World Trade Organization (WTO): some are allowed to peg and some have flexible exchange rates. Nor is there a single global monetary standard that can be managed independently of any national currency. The sooner the G20 (or G8) faces these institutional weaknesses, the better the coordinated decision will be in pushing sustainable world growth. The later it acts, the higher the probability of a dollar crisis.

Despite this sad scenario, European Commission economic commissioner Joaquín Almunia immediately rejected the proposal of Zhou Xiaochuan, the governor of the People's Bank of China, to expand the use of special drawing rights (SDRs) and toward a coordinated management of international reserves at the IMF. Almunia's reaction underestimated the relevance of the problem for the future of the European economy in facing America's growing indebtedness. It reflects the strong attraction of the European ruling class to the idea of the euro as an international reserve currency. This was suggested by the ECB, not for the welfare of Europe but as an expression of good monetary policy management.

The management of reserve currencies by official authorities interferes with the basic requirement for fair competition and trade, and influences the terms of trade. Monetary and financial flaws prevail on them. European growth is subject to the fate of the dollar as an international monetary standard. China's initiative to free Europe's economic future from the U.S. dollar would be in the EU's interest. It would create a new standard or would improve the current agreement on SDRs, pushing the international monetary system away from the uncertainties of managing a national currency, including obviously the euro.

The idea of pushing the euro as a new international monetary standard would preserve the possibility of continued instability because of imbalances in the foreign accounts financed by growing international indebtedness. The system would remain vulnerable because of the risk of collapse of the standard and because of an unequal distribution of international labour and incomes. It is the old dilemma that the use of national money cannot perform the two tasks of internal and external stability. With respect to Europe's currency, it is not supported by any state leader. The dollar keeps its strong position as the world's primary standard for the exchange of goods and financial assets because the U.S. remains the international leader despite the weakness of the economic factors behind its money. But for how long?

Europe's Financial Regulatory Response

The European Commission and Parliament began addressing the financial crisis in 2008 by creating an ad hoc technical working group to analyse the roots of the meltdown. It suggested the main modifications to the present financial architecture in order to restore confidence and create the basis for stronger financial markets. In February 2009, the High-Level Group on Financial Supervision in the EU (2009), chaired Jacques de Larosière, produced a report that proposed a new regulatory agenda, stronger coordination of supervision, and more effective procedures for crisis management. With respect to the global financial architecture, the group issued 31 recommendations aimed at dealing with the institutional, regulatory, and business practices of the global financial system that has contact with Europe. In particular, the recommendations address key points of policy and regulation reform, supervisory reform, and global reform.

The report considered the main issues in the regulatory system and stressed the weaknesses of capital requirements rules set out by the Basel Committee on Banking Supervision (BCBS). As a first point, it called for the procyclicality of Basel II rules to be diminished, since they were in part responsible for the European credit crunch and recession. European countries should adopt a common definition of capital requirements for banks, in order for the homogeneous application of the Basel rules without causing asymmetric effects among countries. A gradual increase of capital from 2007 levels should be imposed on all financial intermediaries, especially those not considered banks.

With respect to regulation, the report recognized the 'parallel banking system', such as hedge funds and other financial intermediaries, as a weak link in the financial web, since, without any deposit base or liquidity, they are more exposed to liquidity problems. As a result, their maximum size and freedom should be reduced, to limit their potentially negative influence on the global banking and financial system.

The key role of credit rating was affirmed by the need to consider the evolution of financial markets and practice and to stop the application of standard practices to structured and exotic financial products, which have non-standardized payoffs.

With respect to financial derivatives, the report recommended a higher level of simplification and standardization for over-the-counter (OTC) transactions. This is, however, just one side of the coin.[5] The European Commission stated in July 2009 that in order to ensure a safe, efficient, and sound derivatives market the chosen model was the central counterparty (CCP). This model of a centralized body was to be introduced in Europe by the end of that year by means of proper regulation. It would differ from the bilateral netting system where the two parties involved bear the risk of the operation. The CCP could be implemented by financial institutions purchasing only standardized OTC contracts. It would be 'effectively a mutual insurance with mutual defences. It makes collateral management simpler, as it is the CCP that collects and manages collateral. It is also safer, as the CCP is the central guarantor and is an institution solely focused on managing risks with several layers of protection' (Commission of the European Communities 2009, 6). Incentives to 'dismantle any commercial hesitation to take up CCP clearing wherever possible' would be introduced at a European regulatory level (11). These advantages would come at a cost for participants, and could not be used for non-standardized contracts, where bilateral clearing applies. The use of a CCP in this manner represents the first step toward better market disclosure and enhanced transparency of OTC transactions, which constitute more than two thirds of the global derivatives market. These principles should be applied at the global level. If European OTC securities are subject to heavier rules, monitoring, and control, there is a clear incentive to trade OTC contracts outside the EU.

In June 2009, the G8 finance ministers (2009) adopted the 'Lecce Framework: Common Principles and Standards for Propriety, Integrity, and Transparency', proposed by Giulio Tremonti, the minister responsible for the Italian treasury. The Lecce Framework moves in the direction of the recommendations contained in the de Larosière report. The necessary financial rules should be global, rather than European in nature, as should the authorities that deal with the weaknesses of the global financial system.

Furthermore, standardization should not apply to the security's payoff, risks, and settlement procedures, as the situation can change after the rule takes effect. Rather, it should apply to the counterparty (at any stage of the transaction). The counterparties involved in OTC transactions should be registered. Sufficient capitalization and liquidity should be a prerequisite to trade OTC.

The de Larosière report also sought simplification, which is a very vague term: if it refers to the pay-off of derivatives, it does not mean a smaller risk is involved. If it refers to contractual rules (which are absent at present), then any proper and effective rule would represent an improvement with respect to the present 'anarchy' of OTC transactions by non-banking institutions. The report encourages the introduction of a central clearing house for European credit default swaps (CDS), following risks and losses observed during the sub-prime crisis and the September 2008 Lehman Brothers bankruptcy. However, it can become an empty house. If the clearing house is compulsory only for European-based transactions,

---

5　See Chiara Oldani (2008) for further analysis of the contribution of derivatives to global instability.

the above-mentioned criticisms basically apply. It would be not very difficult for traders to settle transactions outside European markets to avoid the regulatory constraint. Nevertheless, any derivative surfing in the global financial system—not only credit default types of contracts—should be collateralized. Otherwise market players will find a way to exchange the credit risk without calling it a credit default, shifting any risk out of control.

The de Larosière report recommends '[guaranteeing] that issuers of securitized products retain on their books for the life of the instrument a meaningful amount of the underlying risk (non-hedged)' (High-Level Group 2009, 25). This guarantee is highly welcome. If applied to the global financial system, it would break the fundamentals of the originate-to-distribute (OTD) model, which is at the root of the global financial crisis. However, the OTD model is also at the base of European domestic banking and financial systems. An alternative structure needs to be clearly identified before the old one is cancelled.

From the domestic institutional point of view, the report suggests that Europe set up the European Systemic Risk Council (ESRC) and the European System for Financial Supervision (ESFS). The ESRC would have macroeconomic duties, while the ESFS microeconomic ones. The EU adopted these proposals in September 2009 and, in July 2010, moved to make it possible for the ESRC to be up and running by 1 January 2011.

The ESRC will be chaired by the ECB president and will be composed of members of the boards of the ECB, the European Commission, and other European supervising and monitoring bodies. The ESRC will pool and analyse relevant information, prioritize, and issue macroprudential risk warnings. There should be mandatory follow-up and, where appropriate, action will be taken by the relevant authorities in the EU. At the global level, the ESRC will warn the IMF, the Bank of International Settlements (BIS), and the Financial Stability Board (FSB) in case of global dysfunction of the monetary and financial system. The establishment of such an institution to deal with risk management is certainly positive. This institutional design has various good points, such as the coordination of European procedures and authorities for financial risk management. But it could be stronger. The European Commission and Parliament should issue directives and laws to impose these changes, which a technical body cannot introduce. Moreover, some international financial institutions, such as the IMF, have been unable to deal with the financial crisis and its effects. It is unclear how the global warning system can be successful if it involves the Bretton Woods institutions.

The ESFS should be independent from industry and politics. It is a centralized body to coordinate local vigilance and supervision. The European Commission, Parliament, and Council should appoint managers and staff of the ESFS for a period of eight years. The ESFS should be established in Europe gradually, after harmonizing local financial rules and practices. Its microprudential supervision task with respect to European banks, insurance companies, and financial intermediaries is closely connected to global regulation, especially the American and British regulation.

The Achilles' heel in the new European institutional design is that the European institutions involved in the ESRC have no authority over the European exchange rate. This flaw undermines the accountability and reputation of the ESRC itself in the medium and long terms. Exchange rate risk is a financial risk. It must be managed as with other risks, and not left to the market, if the other countries do not leave it alone. At present the euro is unmanaged, while the American and Chinese exchange rates and reserves drive the foreign exchange market.

The new European financial architecture, as depicted in the de Larosière report, would restore confidence and stabilize the financial system. But cross-border interactions and gaps in the global financial system can remain and diminish the effectiveness of the reform.

The Need for Behavioural Finance Theory

The 2007–08 crisis underlined the limited rationality of financial operators and regulators. Standard finance theory is based on the efficient markets hypothesis, which states that financial markets are 'informationally efficient', or that prices on traded assets, such as stocks, bonds, or property, already reflect all known information. Agents are utility maximizers, have perfect information, and have rational expectations.

Nevertheless, the sub-prime crisis was the result of a chain of interlinked securities, which were sensitive to house prices, through which risk was distributed, as well as the result of the asymmetry of information that was created via complexity and the opaque way that risks were spread though the financial system (Gorton 2009). Such a framework cannot be operated by purely rational operators, utility maximizers players, perfect financial markets, and rational regulators.

The limited rationality is ignored in most analysis, but most dangerously in most policy responses to the crisis. The European de Larosière report was not immune from this criticism. The effectiveness of its recommendations will be heavily reduced.

One alternative stream of finance theory, behavioural finance, does not support the efficient markets hypothesis (Thaler 1993). It tries to explain finance theory puzzles, such as the equity premium puzzle, the earnings forecast bias, or the overconfidence of investors. The hypotheses at the base of behavioural analysis are those of psychology. Players have limited rationality, use the information available in a biased way, and follow the market in a very irrational manner.

Behavioural finance can be particularly helpful in analysing crisis and turbulence, since they are the products of irrational behaviour and inefficient markets and rules. The shadow banking system (or parallel banking system, in the words of the de Larosière report) contaminated the savings sector, and the absence of a global regulatory framework for international investment funds played a massive role in amplifying the crisis (Avgouleas 2009, 26). The 'system failed to provide rational actors with suitable incentives to conduct appropriate credit controls and disclose borrower information' (39). The overconfidence of investors and falling risk premium were assumed as though credit risk was reduced. Following the principles of behavioural finance, Emilios Avgouleas suggests several regulatory reforms that explicitly consider the limited rationality of financial agents as observed in financial markets. These reforms include the following:

- *Containing homogenization:* The segregation in the financial business is the only policy tool to lead the global financial system to decouple and diversify the activity. The universal bank model, together with the OTD model, should be radically revised.
- *Choosing suitable policy tools:* Containing liquidity risk is as crucial as avoiding bank bankruptcies. The massive injection of liquidity by central banks is an expensive policy, and is probably more expensive than limiting *ex ante* the credit ability of unregulated financial operators.
- *Restricting deposit insurance and moral hazard:* Limiting the size of the insurance scheme limits the moral hazard.
- *Protecting public funds and preventing free riding on the public guarantee:* Segregation limits the possibility of banks to access public funds, but should be consistent with the major role played by the banking sector. Rescue plans of banks should not produce a mispricing of banking risks.
- *Reducing complexity and ensuring effective supervision:* External limits on securitization of assets would reduce complexity and make supervision more effective.
- *Lowering leverage:* Imposing a limit on leverage also limits the tendency to focus on short-term profit. The effective definition of such a limit is, however, quite difficult.

These regulatory improvements would change the present shape of the financial system and its incentives' scheme, to the detriment of speculative operators, who earned enormous fees thanks to free securitization and the lack of transparency. Although the de Larosière report did not consider this alternative approach and philosophy of financial markets, they should be considered in the effective implementation of the new European financial system.

Financial derivatives were responsible for spreading the crisis throughout the global financial system; credit derivatives, especially swaps and options contracts, gained tremendous popularity after 2004. The IMF's *Global Financial Stability Report* devoted its attention to them in 2007 (IMF 2007). With respect to the global OTC market, credit default contracts now represent less than 6 percent of the notional amount (see Table 5.1). The U.S. Securities and Exchange Commission (SEC) has imposed a centralized compensation mechanism (i.e., clearing house) for such contracts to improve market liquidity practice and transparency. This regulatory decision and the global attention paid to credit derivatives is the result of a misleading interpretation of the phenomenon. Credit defaults are different types of transactions from mortgage-related debt and structured debt securities.

The payoff of the two types of financial products can be radically different. The excessive loss in mortgage-related debt securities was the result of a lack of transparency and full information and of the inability to price the risk that caused a drop in the credit multiplier with a liquidity scarcity. The loss in credit defaults is basically the result of losses in the underlying market, but does not reflect a weakness in the market infrastructure or risk management procedures (Shadab 2010). This awareness was not translated into any recent regulatory improvements, in either the U.S. or Europe. Both believe that a stronger regulation of derivatives will simply diminish existing risks. In the absence of proper capitalization and liquidity, any traditional security, and not only financial derivatives, can represent a danger to financial stability.

Table 5.1   Amount outstanding of OTC derivatives

Risk category/instrument	Notional amount	Gross market value
Foreign exchange	49 196	2069
Interest rate	449 793	14 018
Equity linked	6591	710
Commodity	2944	545
Credit default	32 693	1801

Note: End December 2009 (billions of U.S. dollars).

Source: Bank for International Settlements (2010).

The G8 and the Crisis

After the Japanese-hosted G8 Toyako-Hokkaido Summit in 2008, most countries applied the same exit strategy: heavy public spending. The Italian-hosted G8 L'Aquila Summit in 2009 pointed out the urgent need for a common legal standard for financial markets and players.

Central banks started to supply any amount of monetary base to cover the drastic reduction of the velocity of money. After September 2008, when the slowdown turned into recession, G20 countries decided to spend $1 trillion in rescue plans for banks, financial institutions, and public firms and tried to alleviate the worse effects in the labour market. U.S. president Barack Obama reinforced the intervention in the banking system and rescued banks, which were heavily involved in the crisis; this decision did not come without a cost, since the industrial sector was in crisis too, but it left no money on the floor. The EU failed to take decisions and Greece is paying a huge cost for this inaction. Britain, France, and, to a lesser extent, Italy adopted rescue plans. The abundant liquidity injected into the global financial system and the zero or quasi-zero interest rates policy adopted by central banks alleviated the worse effects in the short run. But they created the conditions for inflationary effects in the medium term. The negative effects in the medium and long terms need to be reduced by clearly stating the exit strategy, for which central banks are responsible.

Some estimates presented in the G20 London communiqué stated that the fiscal stimulus reached about 10 percent of global GDP in 2009 (G20 2009). The same amount came in the form of monetary base. However, the small amount of coordination among G20 countries with respect to the quality of their intervention (i.e., social security for some, consumption for others) diminished the efficacy of the interventions. Different speeds of recovery and asymmetric effects of globalization can modify the efficacy and success of rescue plans.

The loss of confidence in 2007–09 caused the credit market to dry up and led to the massive selling in stock exchanges, together with the drop in the real estate prices. Consequently the effects spread to the real sector, mainly to that part of it driven by exports. More liquidity and more public expenditure in 2009 helped restore confidence. The first signs of recovery appeared in 2009, thanks also to emerging economies. If recovery means a positive sign in macro-data rather than a return to the economic conditions that existed before the crisis, indications were already evident by the second quarter of 2009. By August 2010, of the 42 countries monitored by the Economist Intelligence Unit nine showed negative figures; in the first quarter of 2009 there had been 28. If this exit strategy were true, the recovery was the result of the 'old' model, with a significant difference in a more cautious behaviour of banks and financial institutions, and a renewed attention of supervisory authorities.

A recovery process relying on massive public spending and liquidity looks much like those policies that brought the global financial system into crisis. They allowed global imbalances, free but asymmetric exchange rate regimes under WTO agreements, and massive foreign exchange reserves accumulation irrespective of current account surplus and national savings. The world thus needs new global rules for the financial and banking system, and also for foreign exchange management. It is no longer sustainable to have a global currency system with the fixed and artificially devalued exchange rate of the Chinese renminbi and a euro left free— or more correctly unmanaged—to float, like a lonely child in a swimming pool.

If the G8—or, perhaps more appropriately, the G20—focuses only on the financial conditions, regardless of regulating securities, forgetting about counterparties, and without considering the entire global financial architecture, there will be large costs to pay in the future.

References

Avgouleas, Emilios (2009). 'The Global Financial Crisis, Behavioural Finance and Financial Regulation: In Search of a New Orthodoxy.' *Journal of Corporate Law Studies*, vol. 9, no. 1, pp. 23–59.

Bank for International Settlements (2010). 'Table 19: Amounts Outstanding of Over-the-Counter (OTC) Derivatives.' *BIS Quarterly Review,* June, <bis.org/statistics/otcder/dt1920a.pdf> (August 2010).

Commission of the European Communities (2009). *Ensuring Efficient, Safe, and Sound Derivatives Markets.* COM(2009) 332 final, 3 July. Brussels. <eur-lex.europa.eu/LexUriServ/LexUriServ.do?uri=COM:2009:0332:FIN:EN:PDF> (August 2010).

G8 Finance Ministers (2009). 'The Lecce Framework: Common Principles and Standards for Propriety, Integrity, and Transparency.' 13 June, Lecce, Italy. <www.g8.utoronto.ca/finance/fm090613.htm#framework> (August 2010).

G20 (2009). 'Global Plan for Recovery and Reform.' 2 April, London. <www.g20.utoronto.ca/2009/2009communique0402.html> (August 2010).

Gorton, Gary (2009). 'The Subprime Panic.' *European Financial Management*, vol. 15, no. 1, pp. 10–36.

High-Level Group on Financial Supervision (2009). *The High-Level Group on Financial Supervision in the EU.* Chaired by Jacques de Larosière, 25 February. Brussels. <ec.europa.eu/internal_market/finances/docs/de_larosiere_report_en.pdf> (August 2010).

International Monetary Fund (2007). *Global Financial Stability Report: Market Developments and Issues.* April. Washington DC. <www.imf.org/External/Pubs/FT/GFSR/2007/01/pdf/text.pdf> (August 2010).

Mundell, Robert A. (1961). 'A Theory of Optimal Currency Areas.' *American Economic Review*, vol. 51, no. 4, pp. 657–665.

Oldani, Chiara (2008). *Governing Global Derivatives* (Farnham: Ashgate).

Shadab, Houman (2010). 'Guilty by Association? Regulating Credit Default Swaps.' *Entrepreneurial Business Law Journal*, vol. 4, no. 2, pp. 407–466. <papers.ssrn.com/sol3/papers.cfm?abstract_id=1368026> (August 2010).

Thaler, Richard H., ed. (1993). *Advances in Behavioral Finance* (New York: Russell Sage).

Chapter 6

Europe: From One Crisis to the Other

Paola Subacchi[1]

The financial and economic crisis that had as its zenith the collapse of Lehman Brothers in September 2008, and the United States at its epicentre, is still too close for a proper assessment of its causes and, most of all, long-term consequences. If Zhou Enlai felt entitled to suspend his judgement on the French Revolution 200 years after the event, one must surely be careful not to jump to definite conclusions only a few years after the crisis.

Having seen the crisis transform from a financial and banking crisis in late 2008 to a sovereign debt crisis in 2010, Europe illustrates this point well. At the end of 2008 it looked as though the crisis had had a selective impact on the region, with some countries more exposed than others through their banking and financial system. For instance, the United Kingdom, Ireland, and Spain, owing to substantial housing booms, suffered from the credit crunch and its adverse impacts. These countries saw the earliest and sharpest contractions in investment and private consumption as businesses and consumers were starved of credit. Gross investment declined by 12 percent in Spain and almost 20 percent in the UK in the final quarter of 2008; in Ireland the corresponding figure was a staggering 37 percent. These countries also witnessed a deceleration in private consumption from the beginning of 2008: from the peak of the crisis in 2008 to its trough, private consumption fell by 34 percent in Ireland, 21 percent in Spain, and 15 percent in the UK. For comparison, the figures for France and Germany were 0.7 percent and 2.8 percent respectively. In the final quarter of 2008, Irish gross domestic product (GDP) had contracted by almost 10 percent year on year—the most serious recession in the European Union.

Countries with a more traditional, not to say backward, banking and financial system felt vindicated. Commenting at the end of September 2008, Peer Steinbrück, Germany's finance minister, referred to 'reckless Anglo-Saxon financial engineering' and the failure of the American model of economic liberalism, while he praised the more regulated, long-term–oriented, and industry-based German economy that had proven more resilient.[2] In Italy,

[1] The author thanks Rodrigo Delgado Aguilera and William Jackson for their research help.

[2] 'This "laisser faire" ideology', Steinbrück said, 'was as simplistic as it was dangerous ... This largely underregulated system is collapsing today' (Benoit and Thornhill 2008).

finance minister Giulio Tremonti expressed a similar concept, describing the financial crisis as 'the collapse of paper pyramids' (Cazzullo 2010).

Then, in late 2008 the crisis that up to that point had paralyzed global financial markets began to affect the real economy through the trade system. It dragged the world economy into the worst recession since 1929. Countries with a large export sector, such as Germany and Japan, which up to then had been almost unscathed by the crisis, were severely hit by a sudden sharp drop in their exports. Although the severity of the downturn varied considerably within the region, in 2009 the world economy in aggregate recorded the worst contraction since the Great Depression, with GDP falling by 0.6 percent. In Europe the recession was even worse, with a contraction in GDP of 4.1 percent.

The third, and possibly last, stage of the transformation of the crisis had its critical point in May 2010 when the European Commission's Ecofin Council, in concert with the International Monetary Fund (IMF), approved a €750 billion emergency funding facility. By then Greece's spiralling public debt had generated a serious crisis in confidence. What had been mistakenly thought to be an isolated episode, given Greece's relatively small weight, was sending shockwaves through the banking and financial system. Once again, interdependencies within the European economy had been underestimated, and there was a risk of contagion from Greece to other countries with critical fiscal positions. Investors quickly became wary of the spread to other European economies of the risks to the financial system from holdings of sovereign debt.[3] Bond yields spiked in Portugal, Ireland, Spain, and Italy.

If dealing with and responding to the 2008–09 financial and economic crisis posed a huge policy challenge, the sovereign debt crisis that began in January 2010 and erupted in April and May of the same year, completely changed the nature of Europe's crisis and its impact on the economies of the region. It was the sovereign debt crisis that exposed the deficiencies in the governance and in the framework of policy cooperation within the European Monetary Union (EMU). Most of all, it was the sovereign debt crisis that changed the role that Europe would play in rebalancing the world economy. The weakness of all the southern European economies, coupled with the need to rebalance the economy of the eurozone, the constraints imposed by a fixed exchange rate regime within the EMU, and the need for some EMU member states to structurally reform their economies, has shifted the burden of adjustment to the external sector. Exports will drive the European economy in the coming years. As a result, if until late 2009 Europe could be expected to play a substantially neutral role in rebalancing the world economy, it must now focus on export-led policies in order to engineer the rebalancing of its own economy.

Such a shift will likely create tensions with the United States, which is more and more concerned about its own growth given the ongoing deleveraging.

---

[3]   For instance, French banks were believed to be exposed to €75 billion of Greek government debt.

Because of its own constraints, the U.S. seems decreasingly able to provide much growth to the world economy. And the U.S. new political emphasis on the manufacturing sector and exports and an increasingly aggressive stance toward China's exchange rate suggest that going forward the U.S. will also be less likely to be the main engine of growth for the world economy and the consumer of the last resort.

Europe, the U.S., and China have increasingly conflicting goals. Indeed, Europe aims to rebalance its economy through exports—rather than rely mainly on intra trade—while the U.S. plans to increase exports to counterbalance domestic deleveraging and to push job creation. China, in turn, continues its export-driven growth. In the future, tensions will surface over the exchange rate. This is already evident in the aggressive stance of the U.S. Congress toward China.[4] And euro area countries may repeat their concerns made in mid 2008 about the strength of the euro *vis-à-vis* the dollar if the euro returns to the territory of $1.50 to $1.60.[5] Given the now huge interdependencies in the world economy at the levels of trade and of capital flows, the exchange rate is regarded as the main mechanism for adjustment. It is therefore the area where a framework for policy cooperation is needed as are more effective tools for cooperation and enforcement mechanisms.

This chapter argues that the crisis has caught Europe off guard, exposed the limits of its policy framework, exacerbated the structural weaknesses of its model of growth—even with the possibility that the region's potential output has been permanently downshifted—and emphasized the regional differences and called for a reform of its governance model.

The chapter is organized as follows. The first section assesses the impact of the financial crisis on the European economies and looks at the policy response. It also discusses the different models of growth prevailing in different countries before the crisis and how structural weaknesses enhanced the impact of the crisis. The discussion then turns to the sovereign debt crisis that erupted in the first months of 2010 and argues that this was the crisis, rather than the financial and economic one in 2008–09, that exposed the shortfalls in euro area governance. It concludes by looking at measures to reform Europe's governance. Widening regional differences and, more generally, a modest economic performance going forward make policy coordination in Europe more urgently needed than ever.

---

[4]   These tensions may be somewhat defused by recent policies in China to allow the renminbi to appreciate against the dollar. From June 2010 to the end of the year, it strengthened against the dollar by 3.5 percent.

[5]   Although the fall of the euro against the dollar of 20–25 percent between mid 2008 and mid 2009 allayed these concerns for the time being, it has provided a significant stimulus to euro area exporters.

On the Verge of Collapse: Credit Growth and Bubbles

Europe has a problem with economic growth that predates the crisis. During the 1990s, when the U.S. was experiencing its productivity miracle and China was beginning to flex its economic muscles, the European economy was growing on average around 2 percent per year (although this rose closer to 3 percent by the later part of the decade) (see Table 6.1).

Table 6.1   Gross domestic product growth rates (%) in Europe, the United States, and China

	Average gross domestic product growth (%)					
	1990–94	**1995–99**	**2000–04**	**2005–08**	**2009**	**2010**
European Union	1.3	2.8	2.3	2.4	–4.1	1.8
Euro area	–	–	1.9	2.0	–4.1	1.8
United States	2.4	4.0	2.6	2.1	–2.6	2.8
China	10.9	9.1	9.2	11.2	9.2	10.3

Source: International Monetary Fund (2010, 2011).

Neither the creation of the monetary union in 1999 nor the inclusion in the EU of new member states from Eastern and Central Europe in 2004 resulted in a substantial acceleration in Europe's GDP growth.[6] If Europe's overall performance was disappointing in the pre-crisis years, there were, however, cases of strong growth. Spain from 1997 to 2007 managed to grow at an average rate of 3.8 percent. Similar examples of high growth were registered in Central and Eastern Europe. The Polish economy grew at an average rate of 4.5 percent over the same period, while the three Baltic economies grew at 6.5–8 percent (reaching around 10 percent in 2005–06).

But this outstanding performance proved to be unbalanced, either because growth tended to concentrate in a few sectors or because it was fuelled by strong foreign capital inflows. In the case of Spain, nearly 20 percent of GDP was in some way related to real estate or construction, and one sixth of the workforce was employed in it (Martin Torres 2009). In the years preceding the crisis, Spain had the largest housing market in the EU, with 900 000 new houses recorded in 2006;

---

[6]   In 2004, the EU expanded to include eight Central and Eastern European countries of the Czech Republic, Estonia, Hungary, Latvia, Lithuania, Poland, Slovakia, and Slovenia, as well as Cyprus and Malta. Bulgaria and Romania joined in 2007. On average the new member states have been performing better than their Western European neighbours for a number of reasons, including strong capital inflows in the years preceding the EU membership. However, given the size of their economies, the impact on the average for the whole EU is not particularly significant.

between 2000 and 2007, the average house price grew by 134 percent (an annual average rate of 13 percent).

As for the new member states, foreign capital inflows contributed to a domestic credit boom on the back of loans denominated in foreign currencies, such as euros or Swiss francs. Furthermore, the high levels of foreign bank ownership, which in some countries reached 100 percent, gave a false impression of security that in the unlikely event of major a financial shock, parent banks would stand by to rescue their local affiliates.

Excessive credit growth fuelled by foreign capital flows not only created imbalances that became unsustainable in the aftermath of the collapse of Lehman Brothers, but also facilitated the transmission of the crisis from the United States to Europe. When the U.S. financial and banking system clogged up, foreign capital flows dried up. Struggling parent banks constrained funding to their local subsidiaries through tightened credit or higher costs of borrowing. The pressure on local currencies took its toll, regardless of whether countries had floating exchange rates or currency pegs to the euro.[7] Fortunately, loans came from a few Western European banks that had a particularly high percentage of loans to Eastern Europe and funded much of the Baltics' credit-fuelled growth.

For some of the most exposed countries, including Sweden and Belgium, loans to emerging European markets represented as much as 30 percent of GDP—in the particular case of Austria, this figure was a staggering 70 percent, including more than 30 percent of the country's total banking assets (IMF 2009b, 14–15; Árvai et al. 2009, 38).

Policy Response No. 1

On the whole, Europe's policy response to the crisis was swift and appropriate given the timeframe and the available tools.[8] In August 2007, when the credit crunch started rippling through global financial markets, the European Central Bank (ECB) provided an initial emergency injection of €94.8 billion into the euro area's money markets, the largest of its kind up to then (and the first since 11 September 2001). The Bank of England followed a similar strategy, including a £50 billion provision to the banking sector in April 2008.

The Bank of England set the pace for bringing interest rates almost down to zero and for introducing alternative tools such as quantitative easing. It brought down interest rates by 450 basis points from the Lehman collapse to March 2009. In March 2009 it also took the bold decision of using quantitative easing as a

---

[7] Of all the new Central and Eastern European countries, only Estonia, Slovenia and Slovakia have adopted the euro.

[8] However, the actual issue was the appropriateness and the effectiveness of the existing tools. See William White (2009).

further tool for providing monetary stimulus, as interest rates were already too close to zero (0.5 percent). For this purpose it created £75 billion of new money.[9]

The ECB followed the Bank of England although somewhat more timidly, at least in the aftermath of the crisis (see Figure 6.1). Its base rate was still a percentage point higher than the UK's at the time of Lehman collapse, but it later dropped to a historic low of 1 percent, the lowest rate since the euro was adopted.

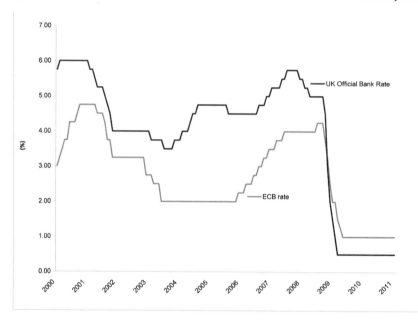

Figure 6.1   Bank of England and European Central Bank interest rates
Source: Bank of England (2011); European Central Bank (2011).

Monetary policy interventions, however, had to be supplemented with fiscal polices both in the form of government bail-outs to troubled companies and measures in support of weakening economies (see Table 6.2). The banking sector was the main recipient of government and central bank money. This was to ensure that credit flows were not frozen and so to avoid a possible collapse.[10]

---

[9]   This asset purchase scheme increased to £200 billion until it was put on hold in February 2010.

[10]   For instance, the European Bank for Reconstruction and Development and the ECB helped negotiate assurances between parent banks and affiliates. Direct capital assistance was offered, notably a €3 billion loan to Sweden's Riksbank in June 2009 to help it support its banking sector. This complemented an earlier €10 billion currency swap, given that a significant amount of bank funding was provided in foreign currency.

Table 6.2   Support for the European banking sector (as of May 2009)

	($ billion)			(% of 2008 gross domestic product)		
	Upfront	Guarantee	Total	Upfront	Guarantee	Total
Austria	37	110	147	8.9	26.5	35.4
Belgium	24	133	157	4.8	26.3	31.1
France	46	504	550	1.6	17.6	19.2
Germany	136	678	814	3.7	18.5	22.2
Italy	19	58	76	0.8	2.5	3.3
Netherlands	54	295	348	6.2	33.9	40.1
Spain	84	284	367	5.2	17.6	22.8
Sweden	25	313	338	5.1	64.6	69.7
United Kingdom	505	1677	2182	18.9	62.7	81.6
United States	1070	10 484	11 554	7.5	73.5	81.0

Source: International Monetary Fund (2009a).

More than $2 trillion was spent between 2007 and 2009 in the U.S. and Europe to support ailing financial institutions through capital injections, guarantees, or partial nationalizations. The UK was one of the earliest to respond, nationalizing troubled mortgage lender Northern Rock in September 2007 after it suffered a bank run (the first in the UK since the 19th century). As the crisis deepened in 2008, additional support was provided to other major banks and building societies; in fact, the scale of the UK government's upfront financing of the financial sector was proportionally higher than that of any other country, including the United States. Continental European authorities were also pressed to support their troubled banks, with the major recipients being UBS (Switzerland), Fortis (Benelux), and ING (the Netherlands).

A more severe crisis was fortunately contained, yet spiralling bad debts from the east could remain a headache for some time (a major Austrian bank that was heavily exposed in the region was nationalized as late as December 2009).

When the crisis finally hit the real economy, intervention in support of growth became necessary even if some governments, notably that of Germany, were reluctant to risk a further deterioration of their fiscal position. The size of the stimulus packagaes varied across Europe from 3.8 percent of GDP in Spain to 0.2 percent of GDP in Sweden. As a result of fiscal stimulus packages, alongside falling tax revenues and the impact of automatic stabilisers, debt-to-GDP ratios among European economies increased from a pre-crisis average of around 61 percent to as much as 74 percent in 2009. For some countries, the fiscal position deteriorated more rapidly and widely than for others, on the back of a number of factors including large current spending with little scope for 'easy' cuts and efficiency gains (Greece), a rapid drop in GDP growth and consequent impact on fiscal revenues (Spain and Portugal), and a large bail-out (Ireland). Given the pattern of public indebtedness, problems seemed to be concentrated in countries that had fast but unsustainable growth in the pre-crisis years or had pre-existing critical fiscal positions, or both (see Table 6.3). With the exception of Ireland, these countries were concentrated in southern Europe.

Table 6.3   Public indebtedness problems in Europe

	Fiscal deficit (% of GDP)	Debt (% of GDP)	External debt (% of GDP)	Short-term debt[a] (% of GDP)	Current account deficit (% of GDP)
Greece	−9.6	136.6	74.0	0.9	−10.8
Portugal	−7.3	85.1	48.4	7.7	−10.0
Ireland	−32.3	98.7	48.1	4.2	−2.7
Spain	−9.3	63.6	26.4	3.7	−5.2
Italy	−5.0	118.6	50.5	4.4	−2.9
United Kingdom	−10.5	78.8	20.5	2.1	−2.2
United States	−11.1	92.7	27.5	5.0	−3.2

Notes: GDP = gross domestic product. [a] All figures for 2010. Includes debt from monetary authorities due in one year or less.

Source: European Commission (2010); Bank for International Settlements, International Monetary Fund, Organisation for Economic Co-operation and Development, and World Bank (2010).

This unprecedented and fast accumulation of debt almost inevitably led to a vicious cycle of widening spreads, differentials in credit rates, difficulties for refinancing, and the worst case scenario of sovereign default.

Euro Imbalances and the Sovereign Debt Crisis

Concerns over sovereign debt in Europe surfaced in 2010 and centred on Greece— by far the most precarious of the indebted euro area states. For most of 2009, Greece was perceived to be weathering the global recession fairly well. Yet when the government of the Panhellenic Socialist Movement (PASOK) came to power in October 2009, the scale of the unreliable reporting of economic statistics was unveiled. Government deficit figures were revised upward: the forecast deficit for 2009 submitted to the European Commission in the autumn was 12.7 percent of GDP, skyrocketing from the 5.1 percent submitted in spring. Although upward revisions to debt and deficit figures in 2009 have been common throughout the eurozone, the scale of the Greek revisions was exceptional. Given already high government debt, private investors swiftly lost confidence and the risk premium on government bonds markedly increased.

A first attempt to quell market fears was made in January when Greece outlined a stability and growth programme. However, this did little to settle markets' nerves. By March, the eurozone and the IMF had hammered out a deal designed to provide Greece with funds if requested. The original package was expected by most analysts to be around €30 billion. Yet when Greece actually requested funds in April—prompted by a looming debt rollover on 19 May—€110 billion had to be put on the table to offer funding for three years ahead, highlighting how little progress Greece was expected to make in this period.

Despite this demonstration of commitment to supporting Greece's financing requirements, debt projections pointed to delayed restructuring rather than a convincing solution (government debt is projected to reach around 150 percent of GDP by 2012). Perceived risk continued to rise and spread to other peripheral eurozone countries, especially Portugal. Staring crisis in the face, the eurozone and the IMF announced the €750 billion European Stabilization Mechanism in May.

Policy Response No. 2

The European Stabilization Mechanism shifted the onus for restoring confidence to all countries with severe fiscal shortfalls as well as competitiveness problems. But some of these countries, Greece in particular, had no track record of successfully managing a debt reduction programme. The odds of being able to keep the debt under control while, at the same, restoring competitiveness were not high enough to inject confidence among international investors. However, the national government's policies managed to win the support of the IMF and Ecofin, permitting the release of the second tranche of its financial assistance package (a total of €9 billion) in mid September 2010. By that time, even though structural reforms seemed to be running ahead of schedule, Greece still faced the challenge of restoring growth and, as a result, of increasing tax revenues.

The Greek crisis acted as an alarm bell for other indebted euro area states to bring their public finances under control. Following Greece, Portugal was in the spotlight because of the rate-to-GDP of its indebtedness at 77 percent in 2009 and the necessary large cuts to its budget deficit (amounting to roughly €9 billion, or around 5.5 percent of GDP) in order to stabilize the already high government debt. But certain factors were working in its favour: GDP growth (1.0 percent in the first quarter of 2010) was encouraging, while a political coalition agreed on extra austerity measures during May whereby value-added tax income and corporate taxes were increased to reduce the deficit by an extra €2.1 billion (1.3 percent of GDP) in 2010.

Ireland and Spain both have high budget deficits but relatively low historic debt levels. Ireland, despite pushing through front-loaded spending cuts, became the second eurozone member to request EU-IMF financial assistance (of around €85 billion) as financial markets became sceptical that the Irish government could support ailing banks. The collapse of a property bubble with the onset of recession had serious knock on effects into the domestic banking sector. In September, the cost of recapitalizing the banks was announced at around €45 billion, up to €34 billion of which was to be used to recapitalize Anglo-Irish bank, pushing the fiscal deficit for 2010 to around 30 percent of GDP.

Meanwhile, Spain's parliament narrowly approved an extra €15 billion of spending cuts in May (including cutting civil servants' pay and reducing public investment). The Spanish authorities also took a transparent and constructive approach to the Europe-wide bank stress tests in July 2010. These were expected to—and duly did—find heavy exposure among Spanish *cajas* to risky sovereign debt. However, the government's approach alongside the existence of the Fund for Orderly Bank Restructuring, authorized to use €99 billion to recapitalize ailing banks and fund mergers (around €15 billion of which has already been used), has restored a degree of confidence in the Spanish economy and has brought down the cost of issuing debt.

The Challenges for Policies

The sovereign debt crisis—a development of the financial and economic crisis unique to Europe—not only exposed the limitation of the eurozone's governance and policy framework, but also intrinsically threatened the political fundamentals of the currency union. It is perhaps too early for an objective assessment of the situation and for drawing well-rounded policy recommendations. There are, however, a number of issues about the future governance of the euro area and, to some extent, of the EU as a whole that need to be addressed—and are indeed being addressed (see Subacchi 2010).

First of all, the European Stabilization Mechanism has raised the issues of credibility and moral hazard. Despite their repeated commitment to the Lisbon Treaty's 'no bail-out' clause, European governments—and the IMF—eventually provided a safety net for countries at risk of default. Will this affect the euro area's credibility in the future? Probably not. Financial markets never believed the 'no bail-out' clause. Nor was confidence boosted by the eurozone's clumsy attempts to avoid anything that looked remotely like a concession to lax fiscal policies. If, at the beginning of the Greek crisis, the euro area had come out with a credible plan and a confidence message delivered with one voice, this would have proved more effective and, in the long run, less costly, to reassure investors, tame volatility, and reduce uncertainty. So speaking with one voice should become one of Europe's priorities.

The second issue is Europe's ability and willingness to coordinate and cooperate on number of policy issues and have the right policy tools in place to, ideally, prevent crises and, failing this, resolve crises. So far, Europe has been able to coordinate a policy response only to avert the currency union's collapse. Indeed, the stabilization scheme in May 2010 was a case of last-minute intervention to avert disaster (see Barber 2010).

As a third lesson from the crisis, and going forward, fiscal consolidation should be supported by plans to improve competitiveness and increase productivity, trying to achieve the right balance between fiscal measures and growth-oriented policies, between fiscal coordination and structural reforms. These plans should be credible and there should be no room for complacency. Furthermore, with the public opinion in most vulnerable countries uncommitted at best, or hostile to any austerity measure at worst, reaching out and building support are critical. Thus fiscal measures and plans for reforms should be clearly communicated, while the adjustment burden should be distributed in a transparent and fair way so that people in those countries do not feel unjustly hit.

Finally, policy tools are needed to identify potential emergencies. Greece was the tip of the iceberg, rather than an isolated case. Clearly, surveillance at the EU level was not strong enough to prevent countries from building up unsustainable debt positions. As has been proposed, member states should have the right to review other member states' annual budgets. Such reviews would also act as a means of monitoring compliance with agreed objectives. And surveillance should not be confined to budgetary matters, but should be extended to the main economic indicators, such as GDP growth, productivity growth, and balance of payment.

Greece's problems have also demonstrated that there was a lack of due diligence when the country was admitted to the currency union. Greater thoroughness as well as fuller scrutiny of its figures would have revealed Greece's structural shortfalls. Bids for membership of the eurozone should be more rigorous. Estonia, whose application the European Commission was approved in May, may provide a test case. The release of timely, reliable, and comparable series of macroeconomic indicators—Greece's statistics were not—should become part of the requirements for members-to-be. The criteria for membership should be changed: the Maastricht criteria assume 'one size fits all'. Cyclical as well as structural indicators should be considered. A currency union requires accurate statistics, a full exchange of information, cooperation on policy, and peer pressure. The survival of the single currency union depends on them.

Conclusions: The Crisis Legacy

How will Europe come out of the crisis? Again, enough time needs to pass in order to achieve perspective. One thing, however, seems clear: the crisis may have exacerbated Europe's growth problem and may have caused a permanent downshift in the region's potential output.

Already before the crisis, the euro area's potential output lagged compared to that of the United States—approximately 2 percent potential GDP growth versus nearly 3 percent for the United States. These figures are roughly in line with the average growth rates over the course of the previous decade. Most of this lag was due to Europe's lower population growth as well as its lower levels of productivity. In contrast, the U.S. had enjoyed a productivity boom during the 1990s thanks to the adoption of information technologies in critical sectors of the economy, mainly in services.

Based on past experience the most likely scenario for Europe is one where its GDP recovers its pre-crisis growth rates, albeit at a lower level owing to the losses incurred by the crisis; that is, the output gap will never recover and the economy will grow below potential.[11] This will inevitably have an adverse impact on long-term growth prospects and prosperity. Regional gaps are likely to widen and, indeed, by the third quarter of 2010 had already showing signs of doing so (see Figure 6.2).

Indeed, Germany's economy has been doing relatively well, thanks to robust emerging market growth in the first half of 2010 and a weaker euro on the back of Europe's sovereign debt woes. This has been supporting exports (up by almost 25 percent in the second quarter of 2010, with exports to China growing at almost 60 percent). It spurred growth of 2.3 percent (quarter on quarter) in the second quarter of 2010. The situation compares with a modest 1.0 percent (quarter on

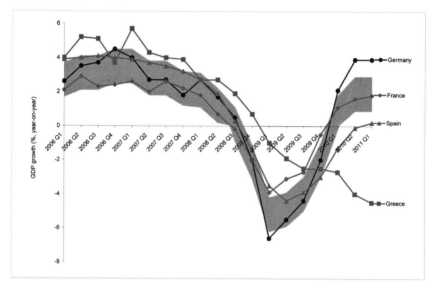

Figure 6.2   Divergence of gross domestic product growth within the Euro area

Source: European Commission (2011).

---

[11]   A less likely scenario is one in which growth surges above trend levels after 2010 because of better-than-expected GDP growth. In this case the output gap may close, losses may be made up, and the region would return to pre-crisis growth rates, maintaining in any case the GDP gap relative to the United States.

quarter) in the same period in the euro area as a whole. Clearly benefits have been unevenly distributed and fundamental problems of competitiveness among the highly indebted states have not been solved. As a result growth has begun to diverge within the euro area. The economic recovery in Spain, Greece, and Ireland remains weak. Despite the favourable external conditions, exports have failed to contribute to economic growth in Greece. Indeed, the contraction of the Greek economy is, at the moment, accelerating.[12] And although rising in Spain and Ireland, exports have been offset by rising imports. At the same time investment remains feeble (around 20 percent lower than the previous year in Greece and Ireland) and consumers remain reluctant to spend. Widening regional differences and uneven performances within the euro area need to be addressed before they trigger the next crisis. The current governance framework is unsatisfactory with regard to fiscal redistribution within a currency area with no common fiscal policy. But if the problem is clear, how to solve it remains to be seen.

References

Árvai, Zsófia, Karl Driessen, and İnci Ötker-Robe (2009). *Regional Financial Interlinkages and Financial Contagion Within Europe.* IMF Working Paper WP/09/6. International Monetary Fund, Washington DC. <www.imf.org/external/pubs/ft/wp/2009/wp0906.pdf> (August 2010).

Bank for International Settlements, International Monetary Fund, Organisation for Economic Co-operation and Development, et al. (2010). 'Joint External Debt Hub.' <www.jedh.org> (December 2010).

Bank of England (2011). 'Statistical Interactive Database: Official Bank Rate History.' <www.bankofengland.co.uk/mfsd/iadb/Repo.asp?Travel=NIxIRx> (January 2011).

Barber, Tony (2010). 'Saving the Euro: Bound Towards a Tense Future.' *Financial Times*, 12 October. <www.ft.com/cms/s/0/c5fcc1e4-d643-11df-81f0-00144feabdc0.html#axzz15f9L8Mo9> (August 2010).

Benoit, Bertrand and John Thornhill (2008). 'Sarkozy Says Era of Laissez-Faire Ideology Is Finished.' *Financial Times*, 26 September.

Cazzullo, Aldo (2010). 'Una manovra per la stabilità fedele al governo Berlusconi.' *Corriere della Serra*, 31 May. <www.corriere.it/politica/10_maggio_31/cazzullo_tremonti_ac263ebc-6c85-11df-b7b4-00144f02aabe.shtml> (August 2010).

European Central Bank (2011). 'Statistical Data Warehouse.' <sdw.ecb.europa.eu/browse.do?node=bbn131> (January 2011).

European Commission (2010). 'General Government Data: General Government Revenue, Expenditure, Balances, and Gross Debt.' Autumn 2010, Part I: Tables

---

[12] Greek GDP growth was –4.5 percent in the third quarter of 2010, a fall from –4.0 in the second quarter and –2.7 in the first.

by Country. <ec.europa.eu/economy_finance/db_indicators/gen_gov_data/documents/2010/autumn2010_country_en.pdf> (December 2010).

European Commission (2011). 'Eurostat.' National Accounts Database. <epp.eurostat.ec.europa.eu/portal/page/portal/national_accounts/data/database> (January 2011).

International Monetary Fund (2009a). *Fiscal Implications of the Global Economic and Financial Crisis*. IMF Staff Position Note, SPN/09/13, 9 June. Washington DC. <www.imf.org/external/pubs/ft/spn/2009/spn0913.pdf> (August 2010).

International Monetary Fund (2009b). 'Global Financial Stability Report: Responding to the Financial Crisis and Measuring Systemic Risks.' April. <www.imf.org/External/Pubs/FT/GFSR/2009/01> (August 2010).

International Monetary Fund (2010). *World Economic Outlook: Recovery, Risk, and Rebalancing*. October. <www.imf.org/external/pubs/ft/weo/2010/02> (October 2010).

International Monetary Fund (2011). *World Economic Outlook Update: Global Recovery Advances but Remains Uneven*. January. <www.imf.org/external/pubs/ft/weo/2011/update/01/index.htm> (January 2011).

Martin Torres, Angel (2009). 'Boom to Bust: Lessons from the Spanish Property Crisis.' *Frontiers in Finance*, March, pp. 22–24. KPMG). <www.kpmg.com/Global/en/IssuesAndInsights/ArticlesPublications/Frontiers-in-Finance/Documents/frontiers-in-finance-2009-Mar.pdf> (August 2010).

Subacchi, Paola (2010). 'Emerging from the Emergency.' *European Voice*, (Brussels: Carnegie Endowment for International Peace). <carnegieendowment.org/publications/index.cfm?fa=view&id=40884> (August 2010).

White, William R. (2009). *Should Monetary Policy 'Lean or Clean'?* Globalization and Monetary Policy Institute Working Paper No. 34, August. Federal Reserve Bank of Dallas, Dallas. <www.dallasfed.org/institute/wpapers/2009/0034.pdf> (August 2010).

Chapter 7

Europe's Institutional, Inflation, Investment, and Incentive Challenges

Carlo A. Bollino

The surprising aspect of Europe's poor policy response to the 2007–09 crisis is that history shows that there have been numerous crises in the past, an ample sample from which it should be possible to learn appropriate lessons. In *Manias, Panics, and Crashes: A History of Financial Crises*, Charles Kindleberger (1978) stated that there were 39 big crises between 1622 and 1998. If one adds the most recent ones, this means an average of one crisis every nine years. Why, given such evidence, have politicians not learned from the past? This chapter seeks to understand why policy makers have taken ambiguous responses to the crisis.

Institutional Imbalance

The absence of a fiscal policy, coordinated with a common monetary policy has deprived Europe of the possibility of using a proper policy mix for a long time (see Gerbet 1989). The ineffectiveness of uncoordinated policies undertaken in Europe is really not a surprise for critics of the construction of a monetary union in Europe without an institutional setup aimed at a common fiscal policy.

During normal times of relatively small but reasonably positive growth, this issue has been confined to the economics classroom. The entire theoretical macroeconomic framework, inspired by Keynes, was not well suited to describe the European economic system: an economic area, which is not an 'optimal currency area' where there is a unique monetary policy and several different fiscal policies, namely as many as member states in the EU (Persson and Tabellini 1991).[1] Indeed, in recent times, with 27 member states, there were 28 fiscal policies, the last one being the recommendation of the European Commission to promote fiscal competition among member states. In this respect, even if fiscal competition is a pragmatic hint to curb politicians' appetite for heavy taxation, it cannot be taken as a reference paradigm for the common fiscal policy of Europe. The reason is that it can work only downward, when public intervention can be reduced. One country

---

1   Torsten Persson and Guido Tabellini (1991) explain the differences in fiscal policies among the European countries due to differences in their political and economic structure. They believe that fiscal policy coordination is unrealistic unless the environment changes.

reduces taxes and others will follow such a virtuous example. As a consequence, fiscal competition becomes another form of a beggar-thy-neighbour policy within Europe, because it has the effect only to move headquarters of multinationals from one capital to another. But what if there is a need for more public intervention in Europe to stimulate the economy? In this case, the simple paradigm of competition among institutional systems cannot work, for it ignores the public good dimension of a coordinated effort. And indeed, the lack of coordination among national fiscal policies has exerted the most severe effects, during the 2007–08 crisis.

The suggested technical reform of the European financial architecture in the de Larosière Report explicitly introduces a coordinating power by two technical bodies, the European Systemic Risk Council (ESRC) and the European System of Financial Supervision (ESFS) (High-Level Group on Financial Supervision 2009). These organizations should be supported by the European Parliament and Commission issuing directives and laws to impose the new institutional set-up, with the ultimate goal of '[guaranteeing] that issuers of securitized products retain on their books for the life of the instrument a meaningful amount of the underlying risk (non-hedged)' (25).

In this respect, the classical view according to Tobin argues that stronger regulation will firstly constitute 'the sand in the wheel', i.e., a break, or at least a brake, in the perverse and endless mechanism of the originate-to-distribute (OTD) model, which was at the root of the recent global financial crisis. Financial innovation will continue to develop, but checked by those new and more effective rules. Unfortunately, rather than issuing new common rules at the European level, governments have individually issued new debt to solve domestic emergencies and contingencies. Moreover, they have done so in an uncoordinated fashion.

In addition, in terms of macroeconomic stabilization, there was a clear mismanagement by the European Central Bank (ECB), when it announced an inflationary risk as the reason for increasing the interest rate exactly in the midst of the worst period of the crisis in July 2008. This action was taken after a period of an unchanged interest rate since June 2007 (a 13-month period). Although the United States Federal Reserve changed its policy rate five times in the same period, eventually increasing the policy rate in the wrong way, ECB appeared not to realize what was happening. Apparently, it was blind to the cues of the new crisis and was only able to mechanically read consumer price statistics.[2]

As a result of this incomprehensible monetary action and of uncoordinated individual government interventions, there was more direct state intervention and less inter-generational solidarity. These responses were the opposite of what would

---

2   There were, nonetheless, some interesting research papers produced at the ECB, such as the one by Marcel Fratzscher (2009), who explains the appreciation of the dollar during the financial crisis. However, there should not have been any fear of imported inflation, by way of the euro exchange rate depreciation, and therefore there was no reason to fear inflation at that time.

be needed by Europe to prevent historical decline, as long argued in the economic literature (Dixit and Lambertini 2001).[3]

Which is the way forward? The big issues confronting the future of Europe in a new post-industrial globalized society are the promotion of individual talent, new human capital, technological innovation, and a new climate and energy paradigm. These ambitious goals need lean state regulation and not massive direct government intervention. They call for more cohesion and solidarity among generations. An aggressive and forward-looking Europe should define a common and effectively shared set of binding principles and rules. Individual states should not extend public intervention in the financial market.

Inflation

One possible explanation of Europe's poor policy response is indecisiveness about the appropriate strategy to use. Given that a crucial feature of the crisis was a stronger and faster decrease in asset and output prices than the reduction in output quantity or employment, a classical Keynesian expansionary policy may not find the immediate favour. The policy maker might wonder why it would be necessary to intervene by increasing real demand with public expenditure, while the crisis is affecting the financial side of the economy.

An alternative strategy is the old exit out of crisis: inflation. This has always been used in emergencies (Barro and Gordon 1984). The positive consequence of such unpopular medicine is that the inflation of wages and goods prices helps to correct asset price imbalances faster. A massive injection of money supply might help push up wage earners' income and therefore, via consumer demand, goods' prices. An increase in monetary income, coupled with an output price increase, should lead unequivocally to an increase in savings (at least in monetary terms, not necessarily in percentage of gross domestic product [GDP]). But even if the proportion of savings to GDP does not increase, as long as the savings increase is a positive quantity, the aggregate effect will be that households can repay a higher proportion of defaulted sub-prime loans. This should unequivocally reduce the toxicity of existing assets. It therefore proves the conjecture that inflation helps correct asset price imbalances.

However, there is also a negative consequence of inflation in this context. In the classical economics textbook, the consequence of inflation is typically described as a benefit for the debt holder, who pays less in real terms in the future. This is also a cost for the debt issuer, namely financial institutions. Given the new anti-inflationary institutional framework set by the ECB statute, Basle II rules, and so on, inflation is not a policy option anymore. At least it is not an option that can be

---

3   Avinash Dixit and Luisa Lambertini (2001) show that if the fiscal or monetary policies of the ECB and member countries are decided separately, the Nash equilibrium output or inflation, or both, are beyond the optimal equilibrium level.

explicitly stated in an official communiqué of a G8 or G20 meeting. In Germany one still cannot mention inflation. Statistical data supporting a V-shaped recovery of stock markets have suggested that markets may expect that inflation may burst soon. By 2010 private markets were predicting a fast way out of the crisis. Such a pervasive desire for real activity acceleration could bring about some robust price increase. On the contrary, policy makers remained over-cautious and sceptical about a robust recovery, aware of the inflationary potential of such increases in money supply and hopeful that a slow recovery would not fuel inflation.

Energy and Climate Investment

Two problems help explain Europe's undecided policy stance. First, this crisis occurred in the middle of an energy and climate change crisis (Nordhaus 2007). Even if macroeconomists dismissed the problem of an oil price peak at almost $150 as minor, compared to the size of the financial crisis, in the summer of 2008 the price of oil in real terms reached the historical record of the second oil shock of 1980–81. Moreover, Europe's environmental policy envisaged massive investment to satisfy binding targets, coupled with severe sanctions for non-compliant member states.[4] In this context, policy options became more uncertain and the political debate, especially in Europe, became bitter. This was only a preview of what happened in December 2009 at the United Nations climate change conference in Copenhagen.

The issue of climate change is relevant, because the amount of investment needed to achieve the announced targets adds pressure to the financial system (Cremer et al. 2004). As the simple Keynesian lesson shows, savings must equal investment, and such additional capital requirement must come out of savings. Precise calculations about the size of such required investment to cope with carbon dioxide emissions are difficult to assess. But the order of magnitude is around one or two percentage points of GDP for the next few decades (Stern 2008). Such a sustained drain of resources has a public good dimension for both world environmental quality and the network infrastructure in the energy sector. These are formidable decisions to be taken in terms of new policy and investment allocation, requiring strong and coordinated decision making. The ultimate conclusion is that either today's consumers save more to ensure a cleaner world for future generations or a financial strain shall occur in capital markets and energy markets. The global warming problem is sending a global warning to the financial community.

---

4   The so-called '20-20-20' package developed in 2007 envisaged setting goals by 2020 in terms of a 20 percent target of renewable energy sources shares in European fuel mix; a 20 percent target of energy savings, introducing investment in new and better technologies and inducing more responsible consumer behaviour; and a 20 percent target of reduced carbon dioxide emissions.

Management Incentives

The second problem is that the management incentives of the financial institutions were poorly designed, as evident in the literature (Bantel and Jackson 1989). Incentives were not too high, but the uncertainty reward structure proved wrong.[5] As an illustration, there are two lotteries, one where the prizes are zero dollars with 50 percent probability and $10 million with 50 percent probability, and the other where the prizes are $3 million with 50 percent probability and $7 million with 50 percent probability. Both lotteries have a fair value of $5 million. The winning probability depends on the individual's ability as a bank manager, who must enter in the lottery paying with his or her professional reputation, which is worth, say, $1 million.

In the first lottery, if the manager is reputable and the bank loses, the value of the manager's reputation is lost. All efforts should be devoted to making the bank gain, to win the stock option bonus, and to maintain or possibly augment professional reputation. In the second lottery, regardless of the management effort, the winner gains more than just reputation, even in the worst case.

This pedagogical example shows why the OTD model and all its disastrous consequences were morally unacceptable: it was not so much because the model shifted risk, but because it rendered managers unaccountable for their behaviour (John et al. 2000). Moreover, in the framework of an agency problem, it remains to ascertain why the 'principal' allowed such behaviour by its 'agent'.

Unfortunately, policy makers, who want to cap bank managers' salaries seem to continue to assume a moralist posture. If, for example, the lottery value is capped at $2 million but prizes in the second lottery are reduced to $1 million and $3 million respectively, with 50 percent probability each, it will not solve the problem: there will continue to be a perverse incentive structure for bank management to walk away with a substantial positive reward even in the worst case.

The right reform should reintroduce for the individual incentive the risk of winning zero in the lottery. This means the manager is at risk of being fired if unsuccessful.

Uncertainty

Another possible explanation of the weak response of policy makers is that an effective policy response depends on the type of crisis. A severe problem for policy makers with the 2007–08 crisis was the uncertainty of which policies to adopt to cope with the crisis because of the uncertainty about the type of the crisis itself.

At the macroeconomic level, the perception of the crisis in the U.S. and in Europe was different. Two dramatic images evoke a crisis situation: a passenger

---

5   Teresa John and Kose John (John and John 1993) analysed the agency problem of pay-to-performance sensitivity.

ship develops a large hole in its hull and the last man in a group climbing a cliff suddenly loses his grip. Both constitute an emergency that must be dealt with promptly.

In the case of a flooded vessel, it is imperative to attempt to rescue first those passengers below deck. The spectacular image of the *Titanic* shows that masses of third class passengers packed in the bottom of the hold were the first to risk death. It is for the mass of these passengers that adequate number of lifeboats are to be provided. This is the case for welfare policies, low-income support, unemployment benefits, healthcare policies extending benefits to low-income recipients—in short, anything that can help the most disadvantaged groups, those trapped at the low end of the income distribution scale.

To save the whole group of rock climbers, however, action must first take place from above: by pulling the top people up the entire group can be rescued. It is the rescue procedure from the peak (the search party moves down the cliff, or the rescue hoist is lowered from above). So rescuing the climber at the top of the rope allows the rescue of all the others. Economic policy measures thus need to be selective: scarce public resources should be concentrated on the most innovative companies—businesses that are doing research and development, are the most successful in international markets, and have better productivity. Policy action is geared to selective intervention to spur technology, innovation, and investment and create incentives to help the top end of income distribution. The stimulus to investment in new technologies pulls all the rest of the economy.

These two extreme images suffice to show that different economic structural crises call for different policy responses. There are evident differences between the U.S. and Europe. In the U.S. the growth of the economy is sensitive to household consumption growth. When families spend, the economy recovers, but for them to spend, income support is required. In contrast, European economic growth is based largely on an export-led model; the economic cycle in Europe is sensitive to exports, and especially the manufacturing sector, as in Italy and Germany (Barrell and Pain 1997). To make exports competitive, there should be support for investment and scientific research.

In both economic areas, there is thus a need for the appropriate policy action, but no single policy can simultaneously fit Europe and the United States. A common stance cannot come out of a G8 or G20 summit. Diverse interests around the table prevent a common commitment. And neither the Americans nor the Europeans will admit that only one action is right for each of them. They will be tempted to argue that they need everything. Political opportunism will prevail, so as to please every constituency, both at the bottom end and at the top end of the income distribution. U.S. and European leaders will be tempted to say that, of course, welfare policies for workers are necessary, as are innovation policies for business.

However, the attempt to please large political constituencies will appear not to be plausible, given resource scarcity and government budget constraint. The ultimate result is that final statements shall be void of real content.

References

Bantel, K.A. and S.E. Jackson (1989). 'Top Management and Innovations in Banking: Does the Composition of the Top Team Make a Difference.' *Strategic Management Journal*, vol. 10, no. 51, pp. 107–124.

Barrell, Ray and Nigel Pain (1997). 'Foreign Direct Investment, Technological Change, and Economic Growth within Europe.' *Economic Journal*, vol. 107, no. 445, pp. 1770–1786.

Barro, Robert J. and David B. Gordon (1984). *Rules, Discretion, and Reputation in a Model of Monetary Policy.* Working Paper No. 1079, February. National Bureau of Economic Reearch. <www.nber.org/papers/w1079> (August 2010).

Cremer, Helmuth, Philippe De Donder, and Firouz Gahvari (2004). 'Political Sustainability and the Design of Environmental Taxes.' *International Tax and Public Finance*, vol. 11, no. 6, pp. 703–719.

Dixit, Avinash K. and Luisa Lambertini (2001). 'Monetary-Fiscal Policy Interactions and Commitment versus Discretion in a Monetary Union.' *European Economic Review*, vol. 45, no. 4–6, pp. 977–987.

Fratzscher, Marcel (2009). *What Explains Global Exchange Rate Movements during the Financial Crisis?* Working Paper Series No. 1060, June. European Central Bank, Brussels. <www.ecb.int/pub/pdf/scpwps/ecbwp1060.pdf> (August 2010).

Gerbet, Pierre (1989). 'The Delors Report.' Centre Virtuel de la Connaissance sur l'Europe. <www.ena.lu/the_delors_report-02-10827> (August 2010).

High-Level Group on Financial Supervision (2009). *The High-Level Group on Financial Supervision in the EU.* Chaired by Jacques de Larosière, 25 February. Brussels. <ec.europa.eu/internal_market/finances/docs/de_larosiere_report_en.pdf> (August 2010).

John, Kose, Anthony Saunders, and Lemma W. Senbet (2000). 'A Theory of Bank Regulation and Management Compensation.' *Review of Financial Studies*, vol. 13, no. 1, pp. 95–125.

John, Teresa A. and Kose John (1993). 'Top-Management Compensation and Capital Structure.' *Journal of Finance*, vol. 48, no. 3, pp. 949–974.

Kindleberger, Charles P. (1978). *Manias, Panics, and Crashes: A History of Financial Crises.* 5th ed. (Hoboken: John Wiley and Sons).

Nordhaus, William (2007). *The Challenge of Global Warming: Economic Models and Environmental Policy* (New Haven: Yale University Press).

Persson, Torsten and Guido Tabellini (1991). *The Politics of 1992: Fiscal Policy and European Integration.* CEPR Discussion Paper No. 501. Centre for Economic Policy Research.

Stern, Nicholas (2008). 'The Economics of Climate Change.' *American Economic Review*, vol. 98, no. 2, pp. 1–37. <pubs.aeaweb.org/doi/pdfplus/10.1257/aer.98.2.1> (August 2010).

PART IV
Impacts and Responses in the BRICs

Chapter 8

Mediating Financial Instability: China, the BRICs, and Continuing Rise

Gregory Chin[1]

This chapter offers an initial assessment of the impact of the global financial crisis on Brazil, Russia, India, and China, often referred to as the BRIC group of emerging economies, focussing on the period between the summer of 2008 and the summer of 2009. The BRIC perspective on the global economic crisis is important because the simultaneous rise of these countries, occurring in the same phase of world history, and their performance during the crisis suggest significant shifts in the world economy and in the international hierarchy of states (Hurrell 2006; Chin 2008). Despite continuing American predominance and its enduring capacity for international leadership, the sustained rise of the BRICs suggests that a reorganization of the world order is underway, constituting a transition of broader significance than the cumulative investment potential of these four 'emerging markets' as originally envisioned by Goldman Sachs.[2]

The substantive concern of this chapter is to analyse the impact of the global crisis, comparatively, on the individual BRIC countries; the effects of their state mediation; and the ensuing international implications at the (global) systemic level.[3] The first section below offers a brief overview of the global crisis: the origins and the effects on the advanced economies as it spread to the developing world, with a focus on the BRIC countries. The second section discusses the varied impact of the crisis on each BRIC country. The third section examines

1   The author thanks Kathryn Hochstetler, Victoria Panova, and the anonymous reviewers for their comments; Andrew F. Cooper, John Kirton, and Paolo Savona for the opportunity to present these ideas in Rome in June 2009; Madeline Koch and Chiara Oldani for their editorial guidance; and The Centre for International Governance Innovation, York University, Chatham House, and the G8 and G20 Research Groups at the University of Toronto for supporting the research.

2   On the continuing predominance of the United States in international affairs see, for example, Richard N. Haass (2005) Joseph Nye (2009), Robin Niblett (2010). On the significance of the BRICs beyond their potential as emerging markets see Timothy M. Shaw, Andrew F. Cooper, and Gregory T. Chin (2009). For the original BRIC formulation see Dominic Wilson and Roopa Purushothaman (2003).

3   A similar interest in analysing state mediation of international economic integration can be found in Linda Weiss (2003). Earlier versions of such analysis are found in Peter Katzenstein (1978).

the differing responses of the respective BRIC countries and outlines the main factors that account for these differences. The central finding is that the crises of world finance and liquidity had a more direct effect in the Russian case, and more indirect effects on Brazil, India, and China. In Russia, the crisis affected the financial sector and foreign reserve holdings quite severely, and then spread to dramatic declines in industrial output and exports. The indirect effects of the crisis on China, India, and Brazil were seen mainly in declining export revenues and rising layoffs in export-oriented sectors.

What is most striking, however, is the way that each of the BRIC countries was able to counter the negative effects of the crisis, including resisting currency devaluation and fending off related external financial pressures. Governments in each country actively stimulated their national economies through expansionary monetary and fiscal policy. In all four BRIC countries, the state mediated the effects through adjustments in interest rates, monetary policy, exchange rates, industrial policy, and employment policy. This chapter suggests that the main lesson to be drawn is that the capacity of the BRIC countries to respond effectively to the crisis was determined in part by their healthy foreign currency reserves, as well as by the relatively strong macro fundamentals going into the crisis, including their favourable fiscal and balance-of-payments positions. In contrast to outcomes in the United States, Britain, and parts of Europe, what was crucial in crisis management among the BRICs was the regulatory capacity of the state to intervene to manage market conditions and international economic integration. These two factors insulated the BRIC governments from external economic shocks. China, Brazil, and India had the strongest insulation going into the crisis. As the BRICs emerged from the crisis, they took further measures to maintain growth, including encouraging deeper ties of trade and finance among one another, as demand from the advanced economies was expected to remain low for some time. China's particularly high level of savings could play a unique and important role in supporting more of such trade and investment among emerging countries and within the developing world.

The Origins of the Crisis

Whereas there has been considerable debate about the specific causes of the global crisis, the origins of the global financial-turned-economic crisis lay in the combination of worldwide financial excesses and a lack of appropriate regulation, which was a growing problem over the past few decades and especially in the last decade, and also the bursting of the housing and oil price bubbles, excessively low interest rates in key countries of the world economy, massive trade surpluses in some countries and trade deficits in others, and savings rates that were too low in some parts of the world economy and too high in other areas.[4] World leaders and

---

    4   This section draws on Marcelo de Paiva Abreu, Manmohan Agarwal, Sergey Kadochnikov, John Whalley, and Yu Yongding (2009, 1–6).

top economists had to focus on the financial and liquidity crisis, which turned into a global economic recession, characterized by slumping world economic growth over two or three years, spikes in unemployment, pressures on public revenues, and deflation.

What has been understudied to date has been how the financial crises in the rich world spread globally to the emerging market economies—including the actual channels through which the crisis in the advanced economies radiated outward to the rest. Prior to 2008, the hypothesis of the 'decoupling' of the emerging economies from the advanced economies was, in fact, a hot topic. It led some analysts to defend the idea that the emerging countries might not feel the effects of the deepening crisis that had taken hold in the advanced economies by 2008. The spread of the crisis beyond the trans-Atlantic world showed, however, that the major emerging economies were more integrated than some had been suggesting. Nonetheless, the differentiated effects of the crisis—as it spread from the rich countries to the emerging—suggests that the emerging countries are actually integrated into the global economy in the realms of finance, trade, and investment in ways that differ than the advanced economies. The exact pattern of the integration of the major emerging countries, their particular forms of state regulation, and the implications in relation to crisis management all require more thorough scholarly attention.

The crisis started in the United States and Europe, and then radiated globally, with implications for the developing world. It evolved as it spread, with effects varying not only from developed to developing countries, but also within the different parts of developing world where there is further segmentation. In the advanced economies, the crisis resulted in the drying up of credit as vulnerable financial institutions became highly risk adverse and very cautious in assessing the creditworthiness of other companies. Even with massive government bail-outs to the biggest lending institutions in the United States, the United Kingdom, and Europe, companies and households were often unable to obtain credit. The lack of supply of credit resulted in companies shutting down or curtailing their production and sales activities, and households being compelled to increase their savings. The cumulative effect was a fall in consumption in the advanced economies.

In the developing world, the crisis affected the credit availability for a large number of low-income and highly vulnerable countries, as well as demand for the exports of developing countries from the advanced economies. It did not immediately affect developing and transition economies, as the crisis did not start in their financial systems. However, as global liquidity began to dry up and as demand fell in the mature markets, trade volumes and the price of exports from the developing countries also declined. Contraction in output and employment in the export industries of the developing countries worsened and, in turn, spread to other industries inside the countries, causing further losses in output and employment. In brief, the crisis started in the 'virtual economy' of the advanced economies and spread into the 'real economy' both inside the developed world and across the global South.

The extent of the impact of the global crisis on the BRIC economies depended on the varying importance of external financial inflows and exports to their national economies and on their specific approaches to regulating the linkages to the global economy. The increased integration of these major developing countries into the global financial and economic system since the beginning of the 21st century meant that the crisis seriously affected investment in these major developing countries. Foreign direct investment (FDI) did decline in developing economies more broadly, and in some of the major emerging economies, as foreign financial institutions and financial investors withdrew their investments in developing countries' stock markets, which, in turn, resulted in sharp declines in stock prices (of sometimes 50 percent or more) and large currency devaluations (of more than 25 percent). The drop in stock prices had a contagion effect on other investment flows to developing countries. However, the specific effects of currency devaluation depended on the share of imports in production or in the consumption basket of workers. The latter varies from country to country among the BRIC countries. In terms of trade, in 2009 exports of goods and services as a proportion of gross domestic product (GDP) was 15 percent for Brazil, 23 percent for India, 34 percent for Russia, and 40 percent for China (Abreu et al. 2009, 3). For the regions of the respective BRIC countries, exports averaged 26 percent of GDP for Latin America and the Caribbean, 22 percent for South Asia, 40 percent in Eastern Europe and Central Asia, and almost 50 percent for East Asia. Countries heavily dependent on exports were therefore more affected when the global financial crisis turned into a broader global economic one.

A Spreading Crisis

The global financial crisis had varied impacts on the BRIC countries as it spread beyond the U.S. and Europe. Considerable variation was also evident in the responses of the individual states to the crisis. Both impact and crisis management response were shaped by path-dependent variables. The impacts were most dramatic and direct in the case of Russia, and less severe and less direct for Brazil, India, and China. The crisis turned out to be a critical phase for each of the BRIC countries in defining or altering the trajectory of their development. In terms of shared or common experience, the direct and indirect impacts of the global crisis on the BRIC countries can be seen in the following: availability of international and domestic credit; foreign investment, including portfolio investment and FDI; exports and imports; exchange rates; interest rates; industrial output; remittances; employment; and social welfare provision. An area of uncertainty was in the impact of the global crisis on foreign aid flows from the G7 and the emerging BRIC donors to other parts of the developing world.

Russia

The immediate or short-term impact of the global financial crisis on Russia was dramatic. The problems for the Russian economy started in July 2008, when a combination of political concern about the war in Georgia and plummeting crude oil prices caused a currency crisis for Russia. As the effects of the global financial crisis and economic recession took hold in the summer of 2008, Russia saw the severe effects in its financial markets, and then spreading into a broader economic recession. Russia's two stock markets plunged twice in late 2008, wiping out close to $1 trillion in the value of Russian shares and leading to Prime Minister Vladimir Putin's decision to close the stock exchanges and suspend trading for periods in September and October (Faulconbridge 2008). Russia's banks saw panic withdrawals from growing fear of a financial collapse. By October, the Russian central bank was spending $600 million a day to buy rubles to support its exchange rate (Vasilyeva and Birch 2008). From July 2008 to January 2009, Russia's foreign exchange reserves fell $210 billion, from a peak of higher a than half trillion, to $386 billion, as the central bank adopted a policy of gradual devaluation to combat the fall in the value of the ruble. From August 2008 to January 2009, the ruble had weakened 35 percent against the dollar (Maternovsky 2009). However, the effects of currency devaluation 'on the ground' were somewhat muted by the fact that imported items do not figure prominently in the daily consumption of a large part of the Russian population. There was a substantial decline in Russia's currency reserves as the government had to use close to half of its reserve to defend the value of the ruble.[5] Nonetheless, by mid December 2008, Russian officials acknowledged that the country was entering into a recession, as economic growth had declined in the preceding two months (BBC 2008).

By the first half of 2009, incoming FDI, which had reached a record $28 billion in 2007, had dried up to a few billion. Foreign trade volume had slid down to 45.3 percent. In May 2009, Russia's Federal Statistics Service reported that the country's industrial output was down 14.9 percent year on year between January and April (Russia Today 2009). The downturn accelerated in April. The data showed the magnitude of Russia's economic woes, even as global commodity prices began to rebound in the first four months of the year. The drop was driven by falls in manufacturing output, which was down 25.1 percent year on year in April as those sectors exposed to the crisis bore the brunt of the downturn. Steel production, cement, and construction materials recorded more than 30 percent falls year on year. Automotive production declined more than 60 percent. Mitigating the losses, to a limited extent were gains in food production, with cereal production up more than 23 percent, meat up 12.7 percent, and dairy up 4 percent. Layoffs

---

5   Some Russian economists have questioned whether the currency devaluation brought on by the global crisis was a negative outcome, suggesting that the ruble may have been significantly overvalued prior to crisis. As such, the currency devaluation caused by the crisis could be seen as an unintended positive outcome.

linked to the crisis were mainly in metallurgy and financial services. However, Russia did not see a major spike in job losses despite the industrial declines, as Russian enterprises were able to exercise a range of flexible employment practices to respond to the crisis.[6]

In April 2009, the Russian economy was still some distance from recovery. Further declines in output could be expected, with tentative steps to recovery emerging much later in the year. In May 2009, Russia's industrial production fell a further 17 percent, suggesting that the economy was still far from stabilizing, let alone recovering. GDP contracted nearly 10 percent in the first quarter and was expected to decline by as much as 8 percent in 2009. The global financial crisis dampened demand for oil and other commodities, greatly affecting the world's largest energy supplier. The drop in oil prices, the drying-up credit markets, and the decrease in the ruble produced the worst national economic crisis for Russia in a decade. The government's policy interventions (namely ruble devaluation and capital injections into the banking sector) proved inefficient and failed to stimulate domestic demand. But Russia's central bank was expected to be able to keep the ruble stable, keeping the national currency rate at 35 rubles per dollar until the end of 2009.

India and Brazil

The impacts of the global crisis on India and Brazil were less dramatic than on Russia, but evident nonetheless. Many in India (and to a lesser extent in Brazil) hoped that the real economy would escape relatively unscathed, would continue to grow, and would even help to buoy the world economy at a time of overall global downturn. However, it became evident during the crisis that India had become much more integrated into the world economy, and, consequently, experienced an impact. Indian exports decreased and growth slowed, which had the potential to touch hundreds of millions of people living on less than a dollar a day. The reduction in Indian exports affected not only export-oriented value-added industries, but also industries across the entire value chain (Kuroda 2009).

According to the Reserve Bank of India (RBI), the effects extended along three dimensions: financial, real economy, and confidence (Subbarao 2009). India's financial markets—equity markets, money markets, foreign exchange markets, and credit markets—all came under pressure due to the global liquidity squeeze, as overseas financing dried up. This shifted the pressure of credit demand from Indian companies to the domestic banking sector and put pressure on domestic

---

6   The flexible employment options and adjustment measures for temporarily trimming the workforce in periods of declining demand draw on work arrangements that evolved out of the Soviet period. The latent potential of Russian industry to adapt to a major decrease in demand, through employment adjustments, may not have been appreciated prior to the crisis.

money markets and credit markets. The foreign exchange market was affected because of the reversal of capital flows due to the global deleveraging process. Corporations converted locally raised funds into foreign currency to meet their external obligations. This combination exerted downward pressure on the rupee. Further liquidity tightening resulted when the RBI intervened in the foreign exchange market to manage the volatility of the rupee.

Although Indian financial markets continued to function in an orderly fashion, despite the seizure in global financial markets, the tightening of global liquidity that followed the failure of Lehman Brothers in September 2008 caused risk aversion in the Indian financial system. Indian banks became more cautious about lending. This crisis of confidence in the banking sector came despite the fact that Indian banks had strong balance sheets, were capitalized at high levels, and were well regulated. The capital adequacy ratio of Indian banks was well above the norms set by the Basel Committee on Banking Supervision (BCBS) and those stipulated by the RBI. No Indian banks had to be rescued.

The global financial crisis of 2008–09 was the first in more than 30 years that was not exacerbated by Brazil. The country's strong external balance sheet—that is, a public sector that is a net creditor to the outside world—and its sound macro policy framework and well-capitalized banks helped moderate the shocks coming from the United States (John Prideaux, quoted in Economist 2009). Brazil's financial and monetary reforms since the beginning of the 21st century helped position the country to weather the global crisis and allowed it to maintain access to capital markets at a relatively advantageous rate (PRNewswire 2009). The benefits of the Real Plan of the 1990s, which came with the introduction of the real in 1994, and the commodities booms of the 2000s left Brazil with record stocks of hard currency. It became a net exporter of capital for the first time in 2006, which, along with the growing buying power of the expanding Brazilian middle class, provided the country with a financial cushion.

The Real Plan plus the requirement to run a primary surplus (before interest payments are made on the public debt) allowed the government to eliminate most of its dollar-denominated debt. These measures strengthened Brazil's external account position and curbed price rises, keeping inflation under control. The steady demand for commodities—especially from the BRIC partners China and India—helped Brazil to create a large cushion of foreign exchange reserves and allowed it to pay down its public debt. Brazil received an investment-grade ranking for the first time in 2008. In short, the years between 2005 and 2008 were very good for Brazil. It came through the crisis rather well in good part because it went into the crisis flush.

For India's real economy, the effects of the global crisis were indirect, and were transferred mainly via a slump in international demand for Indian exports. The United States, the European Union and the Middle East, which account for three quarters of India's goods and services trade were in a synchronized downturn. The contraction of overseas migrant employment opportunities caused a slowdown in remittances as the Middle East had to adjust to lower crude prices, and as advanced economies went into recession. These dynamics resulted in a crisis of confidence.

While the effects of the global crisis on Brazil were not as severe as they were for Russia, Brazil did fall into technical recession in early to mid 2009 (Xinhua 2009). However, after the economy shrank for these two quarters, it started growing again (John Prideaux, quoted in Economist 2009).

During the crisis, Brazil's unemployment rate rose to a two-year high of 9 percent, although most of the job losses were confined to the export sectors. The growth in manufacturing and service sectors facilitated economic diversification. Brazil's relatively strong macroeconomic fundamentals, built painstakingly after a decade of reform, provided stability and resiliency, and institutional investors continued to positive investment opportunities in Brazil.

The Indian government emphasized that the country was not a source of the global financial crisis and was negatively affected by the crisis through 'pernicious feedback loops' between external shocks and domestic vulnerabilities, but, on the whole, demonstrated resiliency in weathering the crisis (Subbarao 2009).

China

The Chinese case is not straightforward. China was less directly affected by the financial crisis than other countries, due to its more closed financial system and the banking reforms it had undertaken since the 1997–99 Asian financial crisis. In this period, the Chinese government took concerted measures to address structural weaknesses in the financial sector, especially the high level of non-performing loans that were threatening Chinese financial institutions. China's low level of foreign debt relative to its huge store of foreign currency reserves also provided a cushioning effect. Limits to currency convertability (especially on capital accounts) and exchange rate controls also provided China with another layer of insulation. The combination of Beijing's new-found strengths and Washington's problems led other countries, including some G7 members, to urge Beijing to provide a greater financial hand in this crisis, by increasing its contributions to the Bretton Woods institutions, to provide more bilateral international financing to countries in need, and to increase its imports (Chin 2008).

However, Chinese exports declined dramatically as demand slowed in the developed countries. China's leaders and citizens alike were concerned about the ripple effects of the global financial crisis, both on the Chinese economy and on the global economy. Worldwide demand for Chinese exports fell, leading to slowdowns in industrial production and a wave of factory closures and layoffs in export-oriented southern coastal China. The job losses led to growing frustration, especially among the migrant labour populations, which constitute a large percentage of the workforce in the labour-intensive export-processing sectors. The potential for rising unemployment and labour unrest was a cause for concern for Chinese authorities. This anxiety was reflected in the edict issued by central authorities in Beijing in late 2008 that enterprise managers at local factories in the coastal zones would have to seek permission from local Chinese Communist Party authorities if they wanted to release (fire) large numbers of workers. During the first half-year of the global crisis, contractions in the Chinese growth rate, consecutive drops in housing prices, and losses in industrial sectors ranging from electricity production, textiles, non-ferrous metals and information technology raised further concerns. However, the slowdown and factory closures were not only the result of global downturn: some of these 'negative' trends, specifically the transfer of a portion of the workforce out of labour-intensive, low-technology sectors, actually preceded the global financial meltdown, and had been encouraged by Beijing as part of its efforts to push China's exports up the technology ladder.

State Responses

As a short-term response to the global financial crisis, governments in many of the developing countries, similar to governments in all developed countries, undertook measures to shore up their large financial institutions and financial systems. To counter the economic decline, governments implemented expansionary monetary policy with sharp falls in the interest rates of central banks (often very close to zero), supplemented by expansionary fiscal policy. The result was ballooning deficits, most notably in the advanced economies that traditionally provided international liquidity. In the BRIC and developing countries, the policy response to the current global crisis depended on each country's fiscal and balance-of-payments positions (Abreu et al. 2009, 5).

In all four BRIC countries, the state mediated the effects through adjustments in interest rates, monetary policy, exchange rates, industrial policy, and employment policy. Unlike the less developed countries in the global South, the BRICs had built up public financial cushions for weathering external financial storms. In many of those other developing countries, the balance of payments is more precarious and reserves are inadequate, but—this time—the BRIC countries did not have to rely on financing from either the International Monetary Fund (IMF) or the World Bank to finance expansionary fiscal policy. The BRICs went into the crisis with stronger macro fundamentals than many of the traditional G7 members (the Russian case was an exception because of its reliance on energy exports).

Among these commonalities, there have been subtle differences in the policy responses of the BRIC countries (Abreu et al. 2009, 5). China, with its small fiscal deficit and massive foreign currency reserves, could respond with robust expansionary fiscal policy. India and Brazil, with sizeable reserves but larger fiscal deficits, relied more on monetary policy to ease access to capital for manufacturers and entrepreneurs. Russia, heavily dependent on oil and natural gas exports and energy revenues, experienced a rapidly worsening government fiscal position when energy prices fell dramatically at the start of the global crisis. However, as energy prices began to rose as of mid 2009, the Russian government experienced a turn-around in its fiscal situation, and followed the other BRICs in taking measures to stimulate the domestic economy through public spending, targeting strategic industries, and scientific and industrial innovation. In the summer of 2009, all four countries were at the stage in the policy cycle of analysing the feedback and effects of their initial policy interventions and gauging next steps. The details of the four BRIC country cases are examined below, focusing first on immediate-term responses and then on projected mid- to longer-range objectives.

China

On 10 November 2008, the Chinese government announced an historic $586 billion stimulus package aimed at encouraging growth and domestic consumption in 10 areas, with new investment for housing, rural infrastructure, transportation, health, education, environmental protection, industry, post-disaster reconstruction, incomes, taxes, and finance. These measures were aimed at loosening the credit supply for major projects that helped rural areas, reducing taxes to help small businesses and offer rebates to exporters, and starting massive infrastructure spending to aid cement, iron, and steel producers. Chinese authorities preceded these changes by reducing interest rates, in coordination with the major G7 economies. The Chinese measures were aimed at stimulating domestic demand. At the same time, China maintained a favourable balance of payments by curtailing imports in coordination with the downturn in exports, thereby protecting its huge foreign exchange reserves. Chinese authorities maintained the value of the renminbi throughout the crisis period, continuing to fend off pressure from the G7 to revalue its currency.

In June 2009, the World Bank revised its forecast of China's economic growth rate to 7.2 percent in 2009, from its earlier forecast of 6.5 percent, as the government's expansionary fiscal and monetary policies had kept the economy growing at a respectable pace (Zhang Xiang 2009b). The World Bank further projected GDP growth to reach 7.7 percent for 2010. Ardo Hansson, lead economist for China at the World Bank, said that 'it is too early to say a robust recovery is on the way' (Zhang Xiang 2009b). The positive signs were the result of the half-trillion dollar fiscal stimulus plan, while the monetary stimulus led to a surge in new bank lending. More positive signs emerged in the real estate sector, and consumption held up well. However, weak exports continued to be the main drag on growth, while imports recovered as raw material imports rebounded. Liu Mingkang, chair of China's banking regulatory agency, forecasted that economic growth would be around 8 percent for 2009 (Zhang Xiang 2009b). China's domestic demand was recovering steadily and credit growth remained high. At the same time, Liu cautioned that China still faces severe challenges including sluggish overseas demand, rising unemployment, and an unstable international economic and financial situation.

Brazil and India

In response to the crisis, the Brazilian government introduced a series of macro control measures, implemented a domestic stimulus package, and sought additional international cooperation with other countries, especially China, India, and Russia. Brazil moved swiftly to adjust its economic policies and ease the impact of the global slump. In February 2009, the central bank cut its basic annual interest rate by 1 percentage point to 9.25 percent. The rate had been 13.75 percent a month earlier. The Central Bank of Brazil sold millions of dollars in repurchase agreements and dollar swaps and increased the amount of money for lending in order to stabilize the value of the real, which had lost more than 30 percent against the U.S. dollar since the start of the crisis.

President Luis Inácio Lula da Silva signed a law creating a sovereign wealth fund worth 14.2 billion reals ($6.4 billion). The government granted tax breaks to banks, automakers, construction firms, and airlines late in 2008. These tax cuts on industrial products helped to trigger record auto sales of 271 494 new vehicles in March 2009, up 17 percent from the same period in 2008. Production levels in the Brazilian auto industry rebounded during the first quarter of 2009.[7] To help farmers and the agricultural sector, the government encouraged banks to provide more loans to farmers and agricultural companies. According to the finance ministry, the agricultural sector would receive loans totalling at least 15.8 billion reals ($6.79 billion) by the end of 2009.

Brazil did suffer from fiscal vulnerability, in which government debt would amount to about 70 percent of GDP in 2009. Although most of this debt was domestic, which helped to limit the country's exposure to currency shocks, Brazil's public debt was still high among the emerging economy group. In contrast, China and Russia carried much lower government debt burdens. To protect Brazil from external shocks, especially the high levels of dollar-denominated foreign debt that caused instability each time it had wobbled in the past, and to preserve the 'investment grade' credit rating that it received from Moody's rating agency in September 2009 for government bonds, Lula sought international support, especially from the other BRICs. The Brazilian president's efforts to advance South-South cooperation were particularly evident in the spring to summer months of 2009, including signing a large-scale currency swap agreement with China. The deal would lubricate trade further between the two countries and would free up a portion of Brazil's U.S. foreign exchange holdings in case the value of the real needed to be defended.

The Indian government, similar to the Brazilian government, took steps to maintain the stability of its currency, to augment foreign exchange liquidity, and to keep credit delivery on track so as to avoid dampening growth. As in China, this marked a reversal of the RBI's policy stance prior to the onset of the global crisis from monetary tightening in response to heightened inflationary pressures of the previous period to monetary easing to ease inflationary pressures and growth slowdown. Among the non-conventional measures taken, the RBI established a rupee-dollar swap facility for Indian banks to assist in managing their short-

---

7   Overall car sales for the first quarter of 2009 also reached record high levels as well, with 668 314 registered sales.

term foreign funding requirements. The Indian government invoked emergency provisions of the *Fiscal Responsibility and Budget Management Act* to relax fiscal targets and launched two stimulus packages in December 2008 and January 2009. These combined efforts amounted to about 3 percent of GDP. They included additional public spending (capital expenditure), spending on infrastructure, cuts in indirect taxes, expanded guaranteed cover for credit to small and micro enterprises, and additional support to exporters.

The Indian government's domestic stimulus measures came on top of already announced additional spending on the social safety net for the rural poor, a farm loan waiver package, and salary increases for government staff, which were intended also to stimulate demand. Indian political analyst Ajay Singh noted that, despite the lingering world economic recession, the economic sectors of the BRICs, especially India and China, were showing optimism on growth, income and employment (cited in Deng Shasha 2009). He added that the Indian government was confidently expecting GDP growth of above 7 percent for 2009, rising from 6.7 percent the previous year. Moreover, the re-election of the Congress Party in the spring of 2009 further contributed to maintaining stability and growth.

Russia

The Russian government took a number of bold and concerted measures to respond to the crisis between September and December 2008. On 18 September, Russian president Dmitry Medvedev instructed ministers to inject 500 billion rubles into the markets and $150 billion for banks, pledging that the financial system would receive 'all necessary support' (Halpin 2008). On 29 September, Prime Minister Vladimir Putin announced a government policy of $50 billion in state loans (8 percent of Russia's foreign currency assets) to refinance Russian corporations that had been relying on foreign loans. On 7 October, Medvedev announced an additional $36 billion for banks, bringing a total of $200 billion for the banks (Mauldin 2008). By mid November, the Russian government had spent $222 billion to respond to the crisis, which was 13.9 percent of its GDP; in the same month, the state spent an average of $22 billion a week of its reserves (Kommersant 2008b; Stott 2008). To aid the economic turn-around further, on 20 November Putin announced a package of tax reforms (reductions in corporate profit tax and value-added tax), to help stimulate corporate growth, and in December, the government lifted import tariffs on industrial equipment that was needed in the metallurgy, construction, forestry, and textile industries, and increased tariffs on imported cars (Kommersant 2008a).

The Russian government's domestic stimulus and crisis management measures started taking effect in January 2009. Although the country fell into two quarters of record negative growth in first two quarters of 2009, by the third quarter, the Russian economy had emerged from recession (Nicholson 2009b). Already by May 2009, the unemployment rate had declined to 9.9 percent from 10.2 percent in April, the first fall since September 2008. Inflation for the first six months of

2009 fell to 7.1 percent. However, in June 2009, the Russian government used the context of the crisis to launch a new anti-crisis programme, drawing another 1.4 trillion rubles ($46.7 billion) from the state budget. Medvedev emphasized that it was necessary for Russia to 'begin the process of modernization without delay' (Nicholson 2009a). He pledged to implement 'responsible macroeconomic policy' that was aimed at maintaining economic stability and creating incentives for the growth, using the 'public's savings' (Yu Maofeng and Zhao Jialin 2009). The crisis programme was aided by the fact that the ruble had begun to stabilize in January 2009. As energy prices started to rise again, Russia's reserves began to grow again and reached a high of $452 billion by the end of the year. Russian stocks also rebounded in 2009. The anti-crisis plan called for increased investment in the economy and the formation of an entirely new model of economic growth that stressed innovation, departing from heavy dependence on energy exports and overseas borrowing. The programme aimed to modernize the Russian economy and optimize the economic structure by helping the commodity economy evolve into an innovative economy. It covered five priorities of development: energy saving, nuclear technology, space technology, health care, and information technology. Of the total stimulus, 17.5 percent would be spent on the real economy, with priority given to education, health care, and pensions. The high tech sectors of space and nuclear industries would receive 300 billion roubles ($9.66 billion).

Although the Russia government's intervention in response to the effects of the global crisis on the Russian economy had achieved the desired effect, finance minister Alexei Kudrin warned that Russia must reduce its greatly expanded budget deficit before 2011, noting Russia's 'vulnerability to the crisis is higher than that of the countries with more diversified economies' (Babich 2009). He set a goal of reducing the budget deficit to 3 percent by 2011. Kudrin's comments speak to the fact that despite the ultimate objectives of the new anti-crisis modernization programme, the Russian government—especially the Economic Development Ministry—had been relying on government assistance programmes and rising oil prices to export their way out of the recession. If innovative industries are to play a greater role in Russia's national growth in the future, Russia will need to raise its productivity much higher than its current rate, which is currently one fourth the level of the United States.

Geostrategic Implications

From the perspective of the shifting world order, the more interesting but less precise predictions are about the medium-term and longer-term impacts of the current crisis on the BRICs. Here there is no consensus among the pundits. The Allianz Group hedged its predictions, or, to be less generous, offered a rather confusing picture. According to Karine Berger at Euler Hermes, a subsidiary of Allianz, 'the most likely scenario is that the emerging economies will exit the crisis weak and impoverished' (quoted in Kahn 2009). This was because the emerging economies had not created enough wealth and had not sufficiently developed their domestic markets over the past decade of globalization to allow them to recover from the crisis on their own. However, Michael Konstantinov, a fund manager at Allianz Global Investors UK, predicted the emerging powers would come out of the crisis sooner. He counted on the resiliency and fundamentals of the BRIC economies and considered 'the recession as primarily a developed world phenomenon' (quoted in Ng 2009). He noted that the BRICs were still growing and driven increasingly by higher domestic demand and lower export reliance. Kostantinov noted the surge in trade among the BRIC and their international currency moves.

Jim O'Neill, the chief economist of Goldman Sachs, who first coined the term 'BRIC', re-evaluated the situation yet remained steadfast. He predicted that the BRIC countries would come out earlier and stronger than the G7. The global crisis, according to O'Neill, meant China and the other emerging economies would overtake developed economies even more quickly (Faulconbridge and Stott 2009). Some argued that China's recovery did not represent a sustainable upturn because it was driven mainly by state stimulus and that the high level of banking lending since the start of 2009 fuelled a new round of non-performing loans in China's state banks, putting them back into a position of longer-term fragility. Albert Edwards, a strategist at the Société Générale, predicted that the 'bubble of belief' in China was about to burst (Wilson 2009). Others noted that the level of new state spending for social welfare and the social safety net for the rural poor in China was not sufficient, that serious constraints on increased domestic consumption remain, and that Beijing's moves would be unsuccessful in helping the country to reduce its export dependency.

Defying the nay-sayers, O'Neill estimated that China's economy will overtake the United States in under 20 years, by which time the four BRICs could dwarf the G7. Challenging those who predicted that the 'BRICs dream' would be shattered by the crisis, O'Neill saw China challenging the U.S. for the top position in the world economy by 2027, and the combined BRIC countries being bigger than the G7 within 20 years (Faulconbridge and Stott 2009). That would be 10 years ahead of his earlier predictions about the BRICs. Goldman Sachs predicted that the world economy would contract by 1.1 percent in 2009, and that the BRICs would average 4.8 percent growth, allowing them to 'dominate the world growth picture even more than when the world economy was booming'. This included Russia, which was still forecasted as weak for 2009.

The view of the somewhat embattled but still influential U.S. investment firm is that the BRICs actually dominated world growth even more during the crisis than when the global economy was booming—despite Russia having been hit hard by the crisis. O'Neill suggested that China had a 'good crisis', in the sense that the crisis forced it to adjust its role in the world and to realize that its next stage of growth cannot be driven only by exports (Faulconbridge and Stott 2009; see also Wang Yong 2008). The Goldman Sachs forecast for Chinese growth was 8.3 percent for 2009 and 10.9 percent for 2010, with the world economy growing by only 3.3 percent in 2010. These numbers were somewhat higher than the World

Bank's revised estimates. Goldman Sachs estimated that India would grow at an average rate of 6.3 percent between 2011 and 2050, China at a rate of 5.2 percent, Brazil at a rate of 4.3 percent, and Russia at a rate of 2.8 percent because of its forecast population decline.

Part of the challenge in making sense of the mid- to long-range impact of the crisis on the BRICs is that most analysts stuck to a relatively short time frame and, more importantly, because there is no logical theory for longer-term prediction of historical contingencies.[8] For China, as the primary example, most economists focused on asking whether, when, and how China would come out of the current global downturn; the broader questions were whether it would come out stronger or weaker, including potential shifts in immediate world rankings. *El Economista* of Mexico reported that China was on its way to becoming the world's second largest economy, likely superseding Japan before the end of 2009 (El Economista 2009). However, medium- to longer-term changes in relative international rankings will determine whether this is fundamental shift in the global economic order.

An important consideration still unacknowledged in the debates is that China appeared to possess latent trade capacity that it did not tap prior to the global crisis. However, as international demand fell in its major export markets, China began to implement a crisis mitigation strategy of shifting downward on the technology ladder, and to unleash latent trade potential with neighbouring Southeast Asian countries.[9] Prior to the crisis, Beijing had strictly regulated manufacturers in a number of export-oriented high technology sectors, such as mobile telephones, in order to push them up the technology ladder and to aim for more advanced foreign markets. However, after the onset of the global downturn, Beijing eased its industrial upgrading demands, and allowed these highly responsive and flexible manufacturers to expand further into less-advanced markets in order to keep assembly lines running and workers employed. Such previously hidden capacity for international diversification is just one dimension of the economic cushion that China possesses to withstand, and adjust to, changes in external demand in ways that may not have been obvious prior to the global crisis.

In terms of geoeconomic and geopolitical contestation, the issue was not whether China would suffer a temporary period of downturn, together with the rest of the world economy. What mattered was whether the country would be on a relative upward growth trajectory over the next few decades. In other words, even if the Chinese economy experiences periodic downturns, and despite the fact that tensions are growing inside certain segments of China's evolving society, is the country on an upward trend over the medium to long term? Is this also the case in relation to rival states? The United States also suffered downturns during the period of its rise from the late 19th century to mid 20th century, during the

---

8   On the challenge of predicting the impact of historical contingency on the international behaviour of Great Powers see Jeffrey Legro (2007).

9   Interview with representative of a mobile telephone manufacturing company in southern China, March 2009.

Great Depression and the inter-war period. Having become the world's major manufacturing centre, America suffered the effects of rising trade protectionism and slowdowns in world demand for its manufactured goods in these periods. However, relative to every other country, including Britain, the U.S. was powerful and still on the rise.

A related question is whether the other BRICs will continue to rise and coalesce. If this happens, there is potential for a more fundamental shift in world order. It is awareness of such a possibility, combined with a crisis of confidence in American leadership among the BRIC countries during the global crisis, that led Brazil's Lula to emphasize that one of the most important effects of the global financial crisis was that it made countries 'more equal' (Zhang Xiang 2009a). During his visit to Kazakhstan—the first visit of a Brazilian president to the area—in June 2009, he said that 'before the crisis, there were many countries that had greater significance than others, and some countries which had no significance at all' (Zhang Xiang 2009a). In essence, the Brazilian president was suggesting that the 'all in the same boat' negative effects of the global crisis had a humbling effect on the traditional powers and highlighted the need for the traditional and the rising powers to be at the same negotiating table in order to address the crisis.

Concluding Observations

A prolonged global downturn and continuing low demand in the developed economies would create difficulty for Russia, and would likely affect the medium-term growth prospects and competitiveness of Brazil and India, and eventually of China as well. In such a scenario, their hard-won gains of the recent past would be difficult to sustain. However, both India and Brazil appear less vulnerable than Russia due to their more diversified economies. Several indicators suggest that the macro fundamentals of Brazil and India are strong and that both these emerging economies have built up a greater degree of resiliency over the past decade than was previously appreciated. China (and, to a lesser extent, India and Brazil) appears to have built up a significant degree of monetary insulation to external shocks and pressure (Chin and Helleiner 2008). The Chinese government has a number of fiscal and monetary tools to sustain the country's upward drive. However, the case of China is not as straightforward as it may seem, based on first impressions. China is still dealing with a number of developmental uncertainties, and has begun to focus on containing a number of vulnerabilities in its current outward-oriented growth scenario, including reducing its reliance on the American and European markets. However, as others have noted, China was well placed to weather the global economic downturn with its high level of reserves, room for policy easing, strong savings rate, and low leverage (Xie Peng and Qiao Jihong 2009). China remained on a priority list to receive asset allocation or portfolio in worldwide markets once liquidity eased.

An important future research question is how and why the BRIC countries came out of the current downturn earlier than the major G7 countries. And whether—over the next three decades—the emerging major economies will be on an overall upward trend, especially relative to the G7 or countries of the Organisation for Economic Co-operation and Development (OECD). At the global level, the crisis revealed serious shortcomings in the international financial and monetary systems. Developing countries will likely continue to be reluctant to borrow from the IMF unless there are changes in its lending operations or those of the World Bank. Given a choice, developing countries may also try to reduce their borrowing from international capital markets and instead look to the BRIC example of building up their own foreign exchange reserves. Or they may press international development banks to provide development financing, on terms that are more favourable to the borrowers. The key research question here is whether some developing countries may indirectly challenge the predominant economic paradigm of the past two decades and choose monetary and fiscal policies that are more economically nationalist, more conservatively financial, and more cautious. Could they take on alternative gradualist and potentially lower but more stable growth models—drawing on lessons learned from the BRIC countries?

While predictions about medium- and longer-term impacts of the global crisis on the BRIC, or the exemplary effects of the BRIC responses remain largely speculative, the sustained rise of the BRIC countries may foreshadow qualitative shifts in world order. This is not to suggest that one should be overly optimistic about the future prospects of the BRIC countries. Each BRIC country has a protean quality—with both resiliency and vulnerability in its makeup. However, their success in mediating the crisis does not simply suggest that the rise of the BRICs merely reinforces another period of more of the same, particularly given that demand from the advanced economies will likely remain lower for some time. It is possible the domestic fiscal needs of those advanced countries are likely to absorb a substantial portion of the world's savings.

Active state intervention from the BRIC countries prior to the global crisis and in the aftermath, have added momentum to the fast growing trade between China (and India, although to a lesser extent) and the other emerging economies. This trade, if not bypassing the West (that is, 'decoupling'), supplements a portion of the trade with the West. From 2003 to 2007, China's trade with the three BRIC partners grew twice as quickly as its trade with the U.S., as China soaked up iron ore from Brazil and oil from Russia and exported consumer goods to India. The new trade flows within the BRIC economies may not replace trade with the West. However, when combined with increasing trade and investment between China and its East Asian neighbours, the new trading patterns appear to be allowing China to ride out the current global downturn and emerge from the crisis more quickly and in a stronger position.

In the current scenario, the major emerging economies will have to take some measures on their own to foster growth, in their own contexts, and across the developing world, including accelerating trade and financial linkages among themselves. Further encouragement of the diversification option would require some degree of internationally coordinated and synchronized action, and shared leadership from the BRIC countries. Some of the major developing countries—especially China—have high levels of savings that could be used for investment in Southern countries with a scarcity of savings and yet significant investment needs. This would be on top of trade adjustments such as increased tariff cuts and preferential trade agreements to further encourage intra-developing country trade. Such an approach to global coordination would lead far beyond 'Chimerica' as problem and solution to the current crisis.

References

Abreu, Marcelo de Paiva, Manmohan Agarwal, Sergey Kadochnikov, et al. (2009). 'The Effect of the World Financial Crisis on Developing Countries:An Initial Assessment.' CIGI Task Force on Developing Countries. <www.cigionline. org/sites/default/files/Task_Force_1.pdf> (August 2010).

Babich, Dmitry (2009). 'Russia Reviews Forecast for its Budget Deficit.' Editorial. *RIA Novosti*, 15 April. <en.rian.ru/analysis/20090415/121134126. html> (August 2010).

BBC (2008). 'Russia Confirms Recession to Come.' 12 December. <news.bbc. co.uk/2/hi/business/7779132.stm> (August 2010).

Chin, Gregory T. (2008). 'China and the End of the G8?' *Far Eastern Economic Review*, December,

Chin, Gregory T. and Eric Helleiner (2008). 'China as Creditor: A Rising Financial Power?' *Journal of International Affairs*, vol. 62, no. 1, pp. 87–102.

Deng Shasha (2009). 'Indian Officials, Scholars Express High Expectations of BRIC Cooperation.' *Xinhua*, 14 June. <english.peopledaily.com. cn/90001/90777/90851/6677880.html> (August 2010).

Economist (2009). 'Getting It Together at Last.' 12 November. <www.economist. com/node/14829845> (March 2011).

El Economista (2009). 'China rumbo a convertirse en la segunda economía del mundo.' [China Due to Be World's Second Largest Economy.], 10 June.

Faulconbridge, Guy (2008). 'Russia's Stocks Shed over $1 Trillion in Crisis.' *Reuters*, 13 November. <www.reuters.com/article/idUSTRE4AC5M020081113> (August 2010).

Faulconbridge, Guy and Michael Stott (2009). 'Crisis Speeds BRIC Rise to Power: Goldman's O'Neill.' *Reuters*, 9 June. <www.reuters.com/article/ idUSTRE5583ZA20090609> (August 2010).

Haas, Richard (2005). *The Opportunity: America's Moment to Alter History's Course* (New York: Public Affairs).

Halpin, Tony (2008). 'Russia Floods Markets with Cash in Shutdown.' *Times*, 18 September. <business.timesonline.co.uk/tol/business/economics/ article4780314.ece> (August 2010).

Hurrell, Andrew (2006). 'Hegemony, Liberalism, and Global Order: What Space for Would-Be Powers?' *International Affairs*, vol. 82, no. 1, pp. 1–19.

Kahn, Annie (2009). 'La demande intérieure des pays émergents reste faible.' [Domestic Demand in the Emerging Economies Remains Weak.] *Le Monde,* 21 April.

Katzenstein, Peter J., ed. (1978). *Between Power and Plenty: Foreign Economic Policies in Adanced Industrial States* (Madison: University of Wisconsin Press).

Kommersant (2008a). 'Gov't Lifts Industrial Equipment Duties.' 5 December. <www.kommersant.com/p1089030/customs_and_duties> (August 2010).

Kommersant (2008b). 'Russia Has Spent $222 Billion on Crisis.' 13 November. <www.kommersant.com/page.asp?id=-13561> (August 2010).

Kuroda, Haruhiko (2009). *Welcoming Remarks.* South Asia Forum on the Impact of Global Economic and Financial Crisis, Manila, 9 March.

Legro, Jeffrey (2007). 'What China Will Want: The Future Intentions of a Rising Power.' *Perspectives on Politics*, vol. 5, no. 3, pp. 1–21.

Maternovsky, Denis (2009). 'Ruble Gain Versus Dollar "Inevitable", Zadornov Says.' *Bloomberg*, 16 December. <www.bloomberg.com/apps/news?pid=new sarchive&sid=aPzxsrEg7GUc> (August 2010).

Mauldin, William (2008). 'Russia Providing $200 Billion for Banks, Builders.' *Bloomberg*, 7 October. <www.bloomberg.com/apps/news?pid=newsarchive& sid=a16BnNfBwIkw> (August 2010).

Ng, Grace (2009). 'BRIC Building Its Own Way Out of Recession: Brazil, Russia, India, and China Are Trading More and Relying Less on West.' *Straits Times,* 15 June <app.mfa.gov.sg/pr/read_content.asp?View,12925> (August 2010).

Niblett, Robin, ed. (2010). *America and a Changed World: A Question of Leadership* (London: Wiley-Blackwell).

Nicholson, Alexander (2009a). 'Medvedev Says Russia Must Modernize "Without Delay".' *Bloomberg,* 18 June. <www.bloomberg.com/apps/news?pid=newsarc hive&sid=aQ4twqk2SDI4> (August 2010).

Nicholson, Alexander (2009b). 'Russian Economy Exited Recession in Third Quarter.' *Bloomberg,* 20 October. <www.bloomberg.com/apps/news?pid=new sarchive&sid=aon.9KAC7AMw> (August 2010).

Nye, Joseph S. (2009). 'American Power in the Twenty-First Century.' 9 September, Project Syndicate. <www.project-syndicate.org/commentary/nye74/English> (August 2010).

PRNewswire (2009). 'Brazil Well Positioned to Weather Global Financial Crisis and Provides Opportunities for Value Investors, According to BNY Mellon ARX.' 6 April. <www.istockanalyst.com/article/viewiStockNews/ articleid/3178866> (August 2010).

Russia Today (2009). 'Industrial Output Down 14.9% January to April.' 19 May. <rt.com/Business/2009-05-19/Industrial_Output_down_14.9__January_to_ April.html> (August 2010).

Shaw, Timothy M., Andrew F. Cooper, and Gregory T. Chin (2009). 'Emerging Powers and Africa: Implications for/from Global Governance.' *Politikon,* vol. 36, no. 1, pp. 27–44.

Stott, Michael (2008). 'Russia Acknowledges Financial Crisis Has Hit Hard.' *Reuters,* 21 November. <www.reuters.com/article/ idUSTRE4AK4L620081121> (August 2010).

Subbarao, Duvvuri (2009). *Impact of the Global Financial Crisis on India: Collateral Damage and Response.* Speech prepared for the Symposium on 'The Global Economic Crisis and Challenges for the Asian Economy in a Changing World', Tokyo, 18 February <www.bis.org/review/r090223b.pdf> (August 2010).

Vasilyeva, Nataliya and Douglas Birch (2008). 'Russia's Effort to Halt Slide of Once-Robust Ruble Has Cost the Kremlin Billions.' *Associated Press,* 20 October.

Wang Yong (2008). 'Domestic Demand and Continued Reform: China's Search for a New Model.' *Global Asia,* vol. 2, no. 4, <globalasia.org/pdf/issue8/v3n4_ Yong.pdf> (August 2010).

Weiss, Linda, ed. (2003). *States in the Global Economy: Bringing Domestic Institutions Back In* (Cambridge: Cambridge University Press).

Wilson, David (2009). '"Bubble of Belief" in China Economy Seen Bursting: Chart of Day.' *Bloomberg,* 17 June. <www.bloomberg.com/apps/news?pid=ne wsarchive&sid=aN5ok_FbkeQw> (August 2010).

Wilson, Dominic and Roopa Purushothaman (2003). 'Dreaming with BRICs: The Path to 2050.' Global Economics Paper No. 99. Goldman Sachs, New York. <www2.goldmansachs.com/ideas/brics/book/99-dreaming.pdf> (September 2008).

Xie Peng and Qiao Jihong (2009). 'China Well Placed to Withstand Global Financial Crisis.' *Xinhua,* 4 January. <news.xinhuanet.com/english/2009-01/04/content_10601248.htm> (August 2010).

Xinhua (2009). 'Brazil Acts Swiftly against Financial Crisis.' 14 June. <news. xinhuanet.com/english/2009-06/14/content_11539953.htm> (August 2010).

Yu Maofeng and Zhao Jialin (2009). 'Russia's Anti-Crisis Measures Take Effect.' *Xinhua,* 20 June. <news.xinhuanet.com/english/2009-06/21/content_ 11575646.htm> (August 2010).

Zhang Xiang (2009a). 'Global Financial Crisis Makes Countries More Equal: Brazilian President.' *Xinhua,* 17 June. <news.xinhuanet.com/english/2009-06/18/ content_11560243.htm> (August 2010).

Zhang Xiang (2009b). 'World Bank Raises China's 2009 Growth Forecast to 7.2%.' *Xinhua,* 18 June. <news.xinhuanet.com/english/2009-06/18/content_11560351. htm> (August 2010).

Chapter 9
Russia: Impact and Response

Victoria Panova

Since the end of the Cold War and Russia's integration into the world economy, the conditions that determine a global crisis affecting the country's economy have changed dramatically. When Russia was enclosed in a rigid and isolated socialist system, it felt few effects from the frequent cyclical turbulence in the capitalist world. Russia's resource wealth added to the short-lived popularity of the Soviet Union and the model of a centrally planned economy, since during the shocks of the mid and late 1970s, neither the Soviet Union nor its allies experienced the problems that hit the liberal capitalist economies of the West. However, that central planning led to long-term disadvantages for the USSR and the whole post-Soviet region. Those countries were not induced by market forces to move away from extensive development. They did not develop energy-efficient and energy-saving technologies, and they were left far behind those countries that were experiencing the vulnerability of those times. The Soviet bloc remained untouched by the economic instability of the period. As a result of short-term thinking and deception, those within the socialist bloc believed that the Soviet-style economy could be more efficient and protective. The USSR also had a huge inflow of petrodollars, which were not used to best economic advantage. When that flow was suddenly interrupted, the economy had no safety cushion and became obsolete. This, along with other factors, led to the collapse of the whole socialist system.

Of course, there had been attempts to introduce new, fairer rules into the world economy and world politics during the Cold War. One such effort came in the form of the Non-Aligned Movement (NAM), a group of countries that did not want to play to the interests of either superpower. There were demands for a 'New International Economic Order', and the Group of 77 (G77)—an institution still in existence with more than 130 members—was formed, although it is not as influential as the smaller Gs.

None of these initiatives managed to push the western powers out of the leadership role. Those efforts had, in fact, a more moderate goal of getting a piece of the economic pie on more favourable terms. Today, Brazil, Russia, India, and China (the BRICs) have similar demands. But the difference is that for the first time the new group on the scene can actually challenge the G7 and the global economic North. That new group is increasingly capable of playing with the developed countries group on equal terms, with concessions not granted but rather negotiated. This shift is due to the significant change of wealth and resulting redistribution of power that has occurred over the past decade.

Within the BRICs grouping there are significant differences of economic, demographic, political, and financial potential. But there is no equality in absolute terms among the post-industrialized countries.

The BRICs do not constitute a political counterweight to the West. Each member continues to pursue its own game plan with the United States, the European Union, Japan, and Canada. Whatever divergences occur on the political front are left for the national polities to decide on their own, without dragging the BRICs as a group into those arguments.

Framing the issue in terms of rivalry and challenge does not bring in the political and military component, regardless of the specificities of each BRIC member in relation to the geopolitical West. This chapter explains the changes in the Russian approach to this grouping as well as to the G8, of which is also a member. These changes are influenced primarily by geopolitical shifts, but are also affected by the global financial and economic crisis.

Pre-crisis Conditions in Russia

When Russia finally opened up, it started to experience both the positive and the negative sides of the market economy and liberal trade agenda. The Asian financial crisis of 1997–99 started with a distant, apparently systemic threat with the devaluation of the Thai currency on 2 July 1997. The crisis quickly spread to the other most dynamically developing Asian economies, causing global gross domestic product (GDP) to lose $2 trillion in value. In the second half of 1998, the crisis went global, starting with Russia, which devaluated its currency and rescheduled its debt, and then spreading further into North and South America.

The crisis hit Russia severely. Among the possible reasons for its default were the huge state debt, plunging world prices for hydrocarbons (on which the Russian economy relied heavily), and the pyramid of short-term bonds that were not paid in time.[1] The ruble plummeted.[2] The country turned out to be less relevant in economic terms as a 'G7+1' partner. It suffered extreme economic, political, and social decline. It later experienced a recovery introduced by import substitution with the assistance of significant sums of underused capital, which allowed for growth without huge investments from outside.

During the following decade, before the U.S.-turned-global crisis erupted in 2007–08, Russia witnessed the strongest growth in history. This growth was in many ways stimulated by the favourable conjuncture of the energy and raw

---

1   When the 2007–08 crisis began, Russia's situation was very different because it had a low level of state debt, especially relative to GDP. As of 1 August 2009, Russia's debt amounted to $39 053.8 million (including the obligations of the Soviet Union that were assumed by the Russian Federation (Russian Federation. Ministry of Finance 2009).

2   Between August 2008 and January 2009 the ruble fell from 6 rubles per $1 to 21 rubles per $1.

materials market. According to the Organisation for Economic Co-operation and Development ([OECD] 2009, 3), 'nominal GDP measured in US dollars rose almost 7-fold during that period, more than in any other major country'. There were large capital inflows, with international reserves reaching nearly $600 billion, surpassing all but the Asian giants of China and Japan. At the time of the 1998 crisis, Russia had a huge public debt, which needed to be rescheduled in order for it to meet its obligations. Later, Russia had 'a string of surpluses and almost extinguished public debt while building up foreign assets amounting to 13% of GDP by the end-2008' (OECD 2009). Its inflation rate remained a concern throughout the decade, although it improved compared the situation of the late 1990s, when the rates reached 85 percent. The notion of inflation as the worst enemy fell off the agendas of the developed countries as the 2007–08 crisis developed, but remained a concern within Russia.

Certain other uncertainties exist despite this robust economic development. With such favourable growth factors as high oil prices and compressed borrowing spreads for emerging markets peaking, and with investment volume remaining low as compared to GDP, Russia's economy began to approach a state of overheating, thanks to increased capacity utilization rates and labour shortages.

Economic, Social, and Political Impacts of the Crisis

For historical as well as geographic reasons, Russia always struggles with a philosophical as well as a political dilemma in defining where it actually belongs: is it a European state or an Asian state, or does it occupy a special position as a bridge between two parts of the world?

Being a superpower during the Cold War frequently made Russia appear to be an imperialistic state, from which the majority of developing countries tried to maintain a distance (hence the creation of the NAM). Today, while sympathetic to the demands of developing countries, Russia does not fully belong among them, nor does it fully share the same needs. China increasingly finds itself in a similar position (and is joined by the other BRIC countries). Many developing countries can no longer identify with the tumultuous growing Asian economic and political giant. Moreover, China is often seen within the Republican part of the American establishment as the most significant potential adversary in the medium term.

With regard to the impact of the crisis on the Russian economy and consequently Russia's role within the BRICs, the G8, the G20, and more widely, experts agree that the country has been badly hurt. Of all the G8 countries, as well as the BRICs, Russia has suffered most.

However, that Russia's economy was hit hardest is a paradox, especially compared to China's economy. After the end of the Cold War, Russia was the first to open itself up to try to join the western family. There were certain drawbacks after it began to reassess its interests and defend its stand as it grew economically stronger, but it nevertheless tried to stay within the global economy. But the paradox comes from the fact that China, being more closed and being ruled by the Communist Party, takes bolder steps commercially. China is a member of the World Trade Organization (WTO), for example, while Russia remains outside. Nevertheless, was it Russia's more intense interrelationship with western economies that brought about its greater vulnerability?

Indeed, there were enormous problems arising for Russia. The economy did suffer and the oil fund reserves were eaten up very fast. Thus, according to the Russian Ministry of Finance, the federal reserve fund dropped by more than two thirds—from its peak of $142.6 billion as of 1 September 2008 to $40.08 billion as of 1 September 2010 (Russian Federation. Ministry of Finance 2010).

One positive tendency was a declining inflation rate, dropping from its previously forecasted 13 percent for 2009. But the budget deficit increased, and budget revenues were expected to be almost half those of the previous year (between 15 percent and 24 percent). Russia would fight its budget deficit and not allow it to reach 13 percent of GDP, as was the case in some other economies hit by the crisis (again not missing the chance to prick the U.S.). Fighting the deficit required reducing budget expenses as well as increasing revenues. Expenditures for 2009 reached 9.7 trillion rubles, compared to 7.6 trillion in 2008.

The constriction of the Russian economy continued, however. According to Russia's Ministry of Economic Development, the turning point had not yet been passed by the summer of 2009.[3] One reason was the record high decrease in investments. During the first six months of 2009 the Russian economy saw an inflow of $32.2 billion in foreign investment, which was 30.9 percent less than during the same period in 2008.[4] Rosstat, Russia's statistical service, reported that real GDP in the first quarter of 2009 fell by 9.8 percent, compared to the same period in the previous year, and by 23.5 percent compared to the last quarter of 2008. The volume of industrial production also fell dramatically. Rosstat reported that in the first quarter of 2009 production fell by 15.4 percent compared to the same period in 2008, with the manufacturing sector suffering even bigger losses (up to 22.4 percent). Between January and June 2009, although the trade balance remained in the positive range, Russia's Federal Customs Service reported that total trade turnover declined by 54.2 percent, compared to the previous year.[5]

The severe drop in Russia's population is one major issue that could lead to long-term problems, regardless of the timing of the emergence of other national economies from the crisis. As for the real expendable income of the population, in July 2009 it fell by 3 percent and by 5.4 percent for the relevant period. Although by the end of 2009 it became clear that situation was better than expected. Previously,

---

3   Between January and May 2009, the Russian economy contracted by 10.2 percent.

4   Federal Statistical Service of Russia <www.gks.ru/bgd/free/b04_03/IssWWW.exe/Stg/d03/159inv20.htm>.

5   The Bank of Russia, however, produced slightly different figures: the total turnover was $208.3 billion, which constituted 55.9 percent of the figure of the first six months of 2009.

the Ministry of Economic Development had forecast an overall decrease by 4.1 percent, but in reality the economy actually grew by 0.7 percent due to higher pensions, social payments, and the sale of foreign currency by the population (Ria Novosti 2009). The real salary fell by as much as 5.8 percent for the same period and continued to fall. Experts forecast that the upward trend would not begin until 2012. The state cash infusions that had been characteristic of the beginning of 2009 ended, with no new expenditures to stimulate demand.

However, one study indicated that expatriates working in Russia felt comfortable and did not want to leave the country. Indeed, in 2009 60 percent of expatriates around the world with biggest incomes (around €250 000 per year) lived in Russia. This provides indirect proof that the Russian economy remained attractive and that foreign capital is at ease.

There was also a big cushion for the country's companies to get out of the crisis: the value of companies (including energy companies) on the stock markets was undervalued. Russia thus had a way to regain its development momentum.

Russia's Response

Russia needs to move into more self-sustaining growth, to rely less on raw materials, and to be more innovative and creative. Thus in 2008, although oil prices were still high, the government adopted its 2020 growth strategy. This strategy came too late, however, for any of the specific policy steps to be implemented before the crisis could devastate its economy.

To make Russia's economy less vulnerable early on in the crisis, action was taken to reduce its dependence on the hydrocarbon sector. The 2008 budget, adopted for three years (which in itself was an innovation), introduced the new concept of a non–oil-and-gas balance. That year was a turning point in the trend of industrial growth being lower than that of GDP. But the steps were not enough, and often remained on paper rather than in practice, probably due to the difficulties of managing a huge country covering 13 percent of the world's territory.

Russia continues to depend heavily on hydrocarbons, which renders its economy fragile even without a global crisis. Yet there are short-term advantages—with oil prices still rising again since the end of 2008. The ways to develop a non-hydrocarbon economy have yet to be discovered, and good alternatives to oil and gas in the fuel and energy balance do not yet exist, notwithstanding certain progress. Also demand will likely continue primarily from the emerging economies, which were hit less hard than were the developed countries.

There is still no consensus on the mid- and long-term impacts of the global crisis on the BRICs. In 2008, forecasts projected that by 2050 the four BRIC members would be among the six largest economies in the world. After the crisis, some experts predicted their collapse. Others believed that the crisis will make that forecast a reality as soon as 10 years. According to interviews with foreign small- and medium-sized enterprises in Russia, many people believe it is a good time to start up businesses there and find a niche in its economy, because even though Russia suffered badly, it is believed to be one of the fastest to rise globally.

Summit Governance

A number of summits and meetings were held in 2009. The most important were the G20 London Summit, the G8 L'Aquila Summit and the Heiligendamm L'Aquila Process within it, the BRIC summit, and the summit of the Shanghai Cooperation Organisation (SCO). All of them, especially the meetings of the emerging economies, consistently supported the idea of reforming the global financial architecture. Although the notion of a supernational currency received little support from those various groups (the biggest proponent being one of the participants in the SCO—Kazakhstan), the fact that this issue exists sends a clear signal. There was more interest in attracting more BRIC resources into special drawing rights (SDRs), which was expressed at all the meetings, including the BRIC encounter in Yekaterinburg.

There was intense speculation that the situation was likely to worsen over the late summer and early autumn of 2009. Finance ministry officials confirmed scenarios that were not very positive. At the G8 L'Aquila Summit in July, Russian officials were among those who remained cautious about prospects for the global economy and about starting to implement exit strategies too soon. Subsequently statistics showed certain positive signs. But the general slowdown was characteristic not only for Russia, but also for the other economies, including the G7 members.

Conclusion

Russia suffered severely from the global financial crisis. It was difficult for it to remain untouched by global turmoil of such size. Nevertheless, the Russian government undertook the appropriate steps to counter the crisis, although some measures, such as the 2020 growth strategy and innovative development, came too late to mitigate the effects of the crisis or to render the economy less vulnerable. There remains the potential within Russia to rise again and resume its development, thus making it to the top of world economic powers in the medium term.

Even once the global recovery was underway by 2010, including in Russia, major questions remain. The recovery is unstable. The flow of cheap money, which now floods developing countries, may well cause a second wave of crisis. Moreover, the main reason for the recovery is the amount of financial stimulus injected by governments world-wide.[6] Governments are wary of stopping such support, for the fear of this new wave, yet such state spending might lead to the other problems, such as inflation and higher interest rates.

Other more global questions arise, with no definite answers as yet. Is the world witnessing a hegemonic transition along the lines of the one in the energy sphere, with the power of rule making shifting to a combination of emerging powers that are both consumers and producers and the national oil corporations? Has the global financial crisis sped up the reorientation of the economy and transfer of power to the BRICs and other emerging economies? Has this realignment brought about an agreement to share power, rather than to replace the dominance of the old powers? Or has the crisis pushed the newcomers back, as was the case with the Asian tigers after the 1997–99 crisis?

It is true that Russia, China, India, and Brazil survived the crisis with little damage, but each still has very different problems that must be solved before their economies can override the old G7 powers and move the centre of financial and economic power firmly away from them. The prospect of this power shift seems unlikely in the medium run. With all the talk and activities directed toward innovation and the modernization of its economy, Russia still depends on the dynamics of world demand for energy resources—and thus remains vulnerable to hydrocarbons exports—as the main driver of its recovery.

References

Gladun, Oleg (2010). 'Академик Гринберг: Спасение нашей экономики в нефтяном наркотике.' [Academician Greenberg: Rescuing the Economy with the Drug of Oil.] *Svobodnaya Pressa,* 18 January. <svpressa.ru/economy/article/19843> (August 2010).

Organisation for Economic Co-operation and Development (2009). *Economic Survey of the Russian Federation, 2009.* Policy Brief, June. Organisation for Economic Co-operation and Development, Paris. <www.oecd.org/dataoecd/50/18/43225190.pdf> (August 2010).

Ria Novosti (2009). 'Реальные доходы населения РФ в 2009 году выросли на 0,7–1,0%—Путин.' [Real Incomes of the Russian Population in 2009 Increased by 0.7–1.0%—Putin.], 30 December. <www.rian.ru/economy/20091230/202411413.html> (August 2010).

Russian Federation. Ministry of Finance (2009). *Структура государственного внешнего долга Российской Федерации по состоянию на 1 августа 2009 года.* [The Structure of Public External Debt of the Russian Federation as

---

6   More than $2 trillion of stimulus has been committed worldwide, meanwhile according to the Ministry of Finance, Russia's crisis management measures in 2009 constituted 3664 trillion rubles (more than $100 billion) or 9.1 percent of Russian GDP (Gladun 2010).

at 1 August 2009.]. Moscow. <www1.minfin.ru/common/img/uploaded/library/2009/08/debt010809.pdf> (August 2010).

Russian Federation. Ministry of Finance (2010). 'Совокупный объем средств фонда.' [Aggregate Reserve Fund.] 1 September. <www1.minfin.ru/ru/reservefund/statistics/volume/index.php?id4=5796> (September 2010).

Chapter 10
Brazil and Latin America: Impact and Response

Raffaele Galano

The 2007–09 financial crisis raises different types of questions about its origins, its characteristics, the factors that strengthened it, and the actions that could be taken to limit its spread and to avoid a repetition of similar crisis. This chapter refers to some aspects common to all financial crises, and then focuses on factors influencing the effects of the crisis on Latin America and on the actions taken there to counteract it. Particular attention is paid to Brazil, not only due to its importance in the Latin American economy, but also because it, along with Russia, India, and China, forms the BRIC group of countries. The chapter ends with reflections on the role that the BRICs could play in promoting a new order that might make it possible to prevent similar situations in the future.

This chapter argues that two elements are common to all financial crises: the existence of an interconnected network through which the problems spread to the different sectors (systemic environment) and the opacity of information, meaning that not all the operators have the same information at their disposal regarding the quality of the assets and the characteristics of the liabilities of the financial intermediaries (Mizen 2008). The network was seen in the AIG bail-out that precluded the bankruptcy of many financial entities whose credit was guaranteed by AIG itself, by means of credit default swaps (CDS), thus avoiding a systemic crisis.[1] Asymmetrical information, in turn, was, at least in the first stage of the crisis, the determining cause of restrictions of bank credit.

The causes of the crisis lie largely in the climate of financial euphoria that developed over recent years in the majority of industrialized countries and in the inability of financial systems to regulate them (Minsky 1982). Even before the Asian, the Russian, and the Latin American crises, many felt that any measures of financial liberalization should be accompanied by better regulation and by efficient and prudential supervision. Nevertheless, the process of deregulation continued, which led to the abolition of the distinction between investment banks and commercial banks in the American financial system and, in 2004, the liberalization of the capital requirements of investment banks, with the consequent doubling of borrowing levels in subsequent years. The absence

---

1 The operation insured amounted to about $450 billion, which included $55 billion in sub-prime mortgages.

of regulations for financial innovation and for proliferating credit derivatives, including CDSs, and the lack of fiscal brakes on multiplying financial assets not included in the financial statements of the financial intermediaries created a favourable environment for sub-prime lending to act as a detonator.

The Impact in Latin America

In the history of Latin America it is difficult to find anything similar, in terms of duration or dimension, to the economic well-being in the period from 2003 to 2007. This was characterized by significant increases in the prices of raw materials, the constant development of international trade, substantial remittances made by emigrants, low interest rates, modest inflation rates, exchange rate stability, low financial volatility, public accounts in balance, and the accumulation of international reserves.

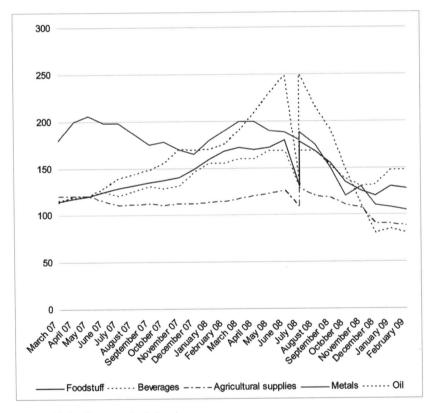

Figure 10.1   Raw material prices

Source: International Monetary Fund (2008).

In a context characterized by a contraction of gross domestic product (GDP) at the global level, starting in September 2008, those same elements that had constituted the push to the development for Latin America became the major external factors that carried the crisis to the region. Of particular importance was the contraction in the volume of international trade, involving essentially countries that export manufactured goods and services. The hardest hit was Mexico, due to its dependence on the United States (Ocampo 2009).

One aspect of particular importance was the marked drop in the prices of primary goods, which began in the second half of 2008 (see Figure 10.1). The fall in price of oil, copper, soy, coffee, sugar, and corn, following the fastest growth ever recorded in Latin America in the past 100 years, had strong repercussions in the countries that are net exporters of raw materials, such as Brazil, Bolivia, Chile, Ecuador, Mexico, and Venezuela, but to differing degrees according to the weight of those products on their export mix. However, in the Central American countries that are net importers of raw materials, the reduction in the price of oil and foodstuffs had favourable repercussions.

One effect produced by the lower prices in raw materials and energy was that projects involving investments in natural resources were put to one side, aggravating the downward trend in the flows of direct investments. Those flows were already compromised by credit restrictions and the scarce liquidity of firms.

In turn, inflation, which during the expansive phase of the economy was fuelled by the increase in prices of raw materials and energy products, reached nearly 9 percent in September 2008. But following the slump in prices and the consequent effects on domestic demand and employment, it decreased considerably. In March 2009 the average inflation rate, on a regional basis, was 6 percent. This left room for the Latin American central banks to implement more flexible monetary policies with the aim of stimulating economic activity.

The sudden reversal of the flows of gross capital, the consequent paralysis of the banking flows, and the usual means of financing, accompanied by escalating costs of banking and non-bank financing, subsequently caused local currencies to depreciate against the U.S. dollar, sometimes used as a refuge currency. The hardest hit countries were Mexico and Brazil, which, between August 2008 and June 2009, witnessed depreciation in the local currency of 50 percent and 42 percent, respectively. These were followed, to a lesser extent, by Argentina, Chile, Colombia, and Peru.[2]

The deterioration of public accounts was another consequence of the crisis. Until 2008, thanks to the increase in commodity prices, the countries of Latin America had recorded an average primary surplus of 1.6 percent of GDP. They had considerably increased their stock of international reserves. The decrease in fiscal revenues, resulting from the slump in economic activities, suggested that in 2009 there would

---

2   For the first time in 10 years, the Bank of Mexico intervened in the exchange market, enabling the Mexican peso to regain ground and to settle, in June 2009, at 13.25 pesos per U.S. dollar. Similar measures adopted by the Central Bank of Brazil brought the real-dollar exchange rate back down to 1.90.

be a deficit in the primary balance of 0.7 percent of GDP, compared to a surplus the year before.

In turn, the external sector, after five consecutive years of constant surplus in the current account balance, recorded a negative balance of 0.6 percent of GDP for the first time in 2008. The only exceptions were Argentina, Bolivia, Ecuador, and Venezuela (see Figure 10.2).

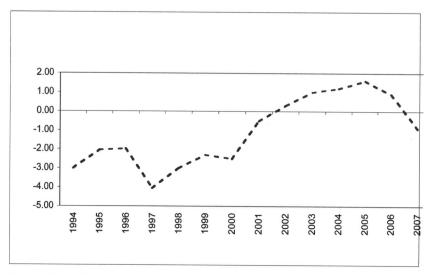

Figure 10.2   Current account balances in Latin America and the Caribbean (percentage of GDP at current prices)

Source: Economic Commission for Latin America and the Caribbean (2008).

Policy Responses

The greater solidity of public finance, the accumulation of international reserves, and the consequent reduction in external dependency enabled the region to implement anti-cyclical policies of both a monetary and fiscal nature, although methods differed from country to country. In monetary policies, the most common interventions were the use of international reserves to stabilize the exchange rates, export credit (Brazil and Argentina), the increase in liquidity by reducing the ratio of the compulsory reserve (Argentina, Brazil, Peru, Colombia, and Venezuela), the reinforcement of the central bank to promote credit (Brazil and Chile), and the reduction of the official discount rate playing on the expectation of a progressive fall in inflation.[3]

---

3   By April 2009 the accumulated reduction of the official discount rate was 650 basis points in Chile, 205 basis points in Brazil, 300 basis points in Colombia, 225 basis points in Mexico, and 150 basis points in Peru.

The Central Bank of Brazil cut the official discount rate five times between December 2008 and July 2009, from 13.7 percent to 9.25 percent. Over the same period behaviour was similar in Colombia, Guatemala, Mexico, and Peru. The Central Bank of Chile made particularly hefty cuts, reducing discount rates from 8.25 percent to 1.25 percent between December 2008 and May 2009.

Despite this expansive monetary policy, there were no substantial benefits to the credit market, which showed very weak signs of recovery. Consumer credit, which reflects economic expectations, contracted further between January and May 2009 in Colombia, Mexico, Peru, and Venezuela, while there was greater dynamism in Brazil and Chile.

The fiscal policy measures adopted vary from country to country according to the different tax structure, as well as the capacity for levying taxes and the sources of financing at their disposal (see Table 10.1). These measures can be divided into two categories: reducing the collectable tax burden directly by lowering the rates or indirectly by widening the margins of deductibility, and increasing public spending through investments in both infrastructure and social housing and programmes to support the productive sector, particularly the small and medium-sized enterprises (SMEs) and agriculture.

In countries with a low level of banking intermediation, monetary policy measures might not generate the expected effects. Furthermore, in situations where there is a high degree of uncertainty, it is possible that the mechanisms for transmitting the expansive measures of monetary policy toward an increase in the credit supply and the effective use of the available financing prove to be ineffective (Bank for International Settlements 2008).

On the other hand, fiscal policies could play a role as protagonist in supporting growth in aggregate demand. However, the effect may be limited in countries where the level of taxation is low and the increases in disposable income do not necessarily translate into greater volumes of demand. Moreover, increasing public spending for investment projects requires time since countries do not usually have projects ready to be implemented. Furthermore, paying subsidies may be effective only when countries have appropriate mechanisms for identifying the possible beneficiaries (Economic Commission for Latin America and the Caribbean [ECLAC] 2009a).

For recovery, much depends on the trend of domestic demand of developed countries and the return to normality on the financial markets. In a context of less uncertainty about the evolution of the international economy, supported by measures of monetary and fiscal policy implemented in various countries, by the second half of 2009 it was possible, on the base of the majority of available indicators, to glimpse signs of not only the end of the decline but also a modest reversal.

Factors that justified such optimism include the attenuation of the risk perceived by the financial market in relation to the interbank loans, the partial recovery of the stock markets in both developed and developing countries, a slowdown in the decrease of house prices in the United States, the increased prices

Table 10.1 Main fiscal measures in Latin America

	Argentina	Bolivia	Brazil	Chile	Colombia	Costa Rica	Ecuador	El Salvador	Guatemala	Honduras	Mexico	Nicaragua	Panama	Paraguay	Peru	Dominican Republic	Uruguay	Venezuela
Taxes																		
Corporate tax reduction/depreciation	X			T	X	T	X		X	X	T				X		T	
Personal income tax reduction	X		T	T	X				X	X	T							
Taxes on foreign trade reduction				X	X		X				X	X	X					
Other	T		X	X	X		T					T			T		X	
Public spending																		
Investments in infrastructure	X	X	X	X	X	X	X	X	X	X	X	X		X	X	X	X	
Construction		X		T	X	X			X	X	X	X		X	X	X	X	
Support to SMEs and farmers			X	X	X	X		X	X	X	X		X	X	X	X	X	X
Support for strategic sectors		X	X	X					X		X				X			
Other	T							X		X	X	X						

Notes: SME = small and medium-sized enterprise; T = temporary measures.

Source: Economic Commission for Latin America and the Caribbean (2009c).

of raw materials, and the improvement of access to credit. Further confirmation was found in the improvement in the consumer confidence index.

From the data available in June 2009 related to Latin America and the Caribbean, it seemed that international trade had stopped contracting, the prices of primary goods were recovering, and the conditions to credit access were improving. This combination of factors suggested that in the second half of 2009 there would be a recovery in the level of activity in the region, even if a modest one.

The expectations of the leading international organizations (International Monetary Fund [IMF], ECLAC) and of the multilateral banks (Inter-American Development Bank, Corporación Andina de Fomento), indicated a negative rate of growth for GDP in 2009, inasmuch as it was penalized by the marked repercussions of the Mexico crisis. In 2010 positive growth in GDP would be recorded by all Latin American countries (see Figure 10.3).

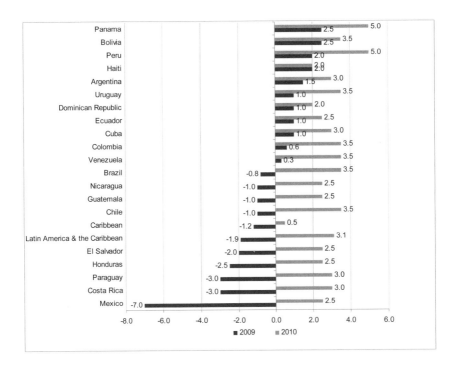

Figure 10.3   Growth estimates for Latin America and the Caribbean, 2009–10 (percentage)

Source: Based on data from the Economic Commission for Latin America and the Caribbean (2009b).

Brazil

Brazil is worth considering on its own, both because it is one of the major economies of Latin America, vying with Mexico for leadership, and because it is one of the BRICs, which are discussed below.

In 2003 Brazil's GDP began growing constantly, at an average of 5 percent annually, fuelled by the increase in domestic demand. This increase was in turn sustained by the rise in direct investments and in consumption, the latter being encouraged by the increase in real salaries and the expansion of credit. Further support for aggregate demand came from rising public spending, where the GDP ratio had increased from 1.6 percent in 2006 to 1.8 percent in 2008 without any particular pressure on the public accounts, thanks to high fiscal revenues.

The first signs of the crisis arose in the fourth quarter of 2008 after the sharp drop in domestic demand, whose contribution to GDP growth fell from 9.8 percent to 3.2 percent between the third and fourth quarters that year. It was driven by the collapse in investment and the contraction in domestic consumption. In the first quarter of 2009 the main macroeconomic indicators showed a further weakening of the economy, characterized by rising unemployment rates, high warehouse stocks (largely due to lower external demand), lack of liquidity, difficulty in accessing credit, and high financing costs.

Brazil faced the world with more optimism than in the past, despite decreased industrial production, affected by the performance of the Chinese economy, the rise of unemployment, and the mass cancellation of purchasing orders from developed countries. This was thanks to broader margins available to the government and central bank to implement expansive monetary and fiscal policies.

Prior to the crisis, one of the main criticisms of the Brazilian economy was the considerable influence the state had over the financial system. Banco do Brasil and the Banco Caixa Econômica Federal (retail sector) are both owned by the state. This anomaly makes Brazil and China very similar. In both countries there is a massive state presence in the financial system, which made it possible not only to mitigate the effects of the crisis on the credit market but also to draw up sectoral development plans, orienting credit toward those sectors considered to be of greater interest.

To stimulate domestic demand and activate the economy, Brazilian authorities adopted several measures: the reduction of the official discount rate, tax reduction, injections of liquidity, and public spending. The government injected $100 billion into the banking system, reduced some taxes, and offered special lines of financing through state banks to the agricultural and industrial sectors.

Between December 2008 and June 2009, Brazil's official discount rate was lowered five times, from 13.75 percent to 9.25 percent. However, the benefits for firms and consumers were scarce. The spread remained very high due to the particular cost structure of Brazilian banks, conditioned by the distortional effect of the massive presence of the public bank, the compulsory reserve of 50 percent, the taxes on banking operations, and the slowness of the legal system that forced banks to pay a higher risk premium. Furthermore, commercial banks were obliged to grant credit to farmers at preferential rates, so the banks had to ask for higher interest rates in other areas to compensate for the losses.

The most important public investments were those in infrastructure that involve the energy sector, the extraction of gas and oil, transport (with particular reference to the construction of a high-speed rail network between Rio de Janeiro and São Paulo), and investments in ports and airports.

The first results were soon seen. The main macroeconomic indicators surveyed in the first half of 2009, from both the IMF (2009) and ECLAC (2009a), suggested a recovery starting in the second half of 2009, indicating an annual GDP change of –0.8 percent, considerably lower than that predicted in March by the same sources (–2 percent). The forecasts for 2010 predicted growth in GDP of 3.5 percent, which, even though still far below the pre-crisis levels, would indicate a clear trend to restoring normality.

There were some unknown factors. One was fear of public accounts worsening, following the increase in public spending to prevent lower fiscal revenue resulting from decreased economic activity. This was partly compensated for by issuing state bonds, which produced an extremely positive market response in May 2009.

Greater perplexities derived from the increase of unemployment, which stood at 9 percent in March 2009, showing an upsurge compared to December 2008 (6.8 percent), and from the repercussions this might have on the presidential elections of 2010, jeopardizing the expectations of President Luiz Inácio Lula da Silva. Although he could not be re-elected due to constitutional constraints, Lula had high hopes that the Partito de Trabajadores ([PT], Workers' Party) would win, and that his right-hand, Dilma Roussef, would be elected (as she was in October 2010).

The chance of a new victory for the PT depended to a large degree on the success of the Programma de Aceleracion de Crecimiento (PAC), coordinated by Roussef, pointing to investments in logistics, energy, and urban infrastructure. With a total value of $260 billion, one of the main aims of the programme was to promote employment.

Brazil strove to carve for itself an international role as one of the BRICs. The confirmation of this role, however, required that structural choices be made to reduce the excessive dependency of the international trade on exports of raw materials, which in 2009 accounted for 46 percent of total exports, compared to the 12 percent for technology exports. The ball and chain was the predominant weight of agriculture in international trade, which was concentrated in a few hands. Brazil here is similar to India, with which it shares a highly insidious colonial history. It is very different from China.

The international position of Brazil was strengthened by its presidency of the G20 in 2008. At the November 2008 meeting of the finance ministers and cenral bank governors, Brazil defended the idea of laying the basis for a new world order in the financial market, stressing the need for greater participation of emerging countries in decision-making mechanisms.

The BRICs

The term BRIC, coined by British economist Jim O'Neill, was used in 2001 to refer to four emerging economies with high growth potential—Brazil, Russia, India, and China. These countries account for 25 percent of the world's land mass, 40 percent of the world's population, and 35 percent of foreign exchange reserves. Between 2002 and 2007 annual GDP growth averaged 3.7 percent in Brazil, 6.9 percent in Russia, 7.9 percent in India, and 10.4 percent in China (Fitzgerald 2007).

Within the BRICs, the true catalyst for growth is China. Its GDP increased by 9.9 percent between 1980 and 2008, compared to an average rate of 2.8 percent in Latin America. China has the largest GDP after the United States (at purchasing power parity) and is third after Japan if measured in current U.S. dollars.

All international indicators show the increasing presence of China in the global aggregates. This has given rise to a new scenario where the Asia-Pacific area adjusts its productive chains around China, which in turn actively develops its trade with Africa and Latin America.

Asian economies hold more than 60 percent of the world's international reserves and 53 percent of U.S. treasury bonds, contributing to the stability of the world economies with their large surplus of the current balance of payments. Brazil finds itself at the centre of the prosperous South-South trade, which accounts for 41 percent of the world trade of all developing countries (ECLAC 2008).

In light of the changes in the world ranking of exporting countries, China rose from 11th position in 1995 to first in 2008—an impressive competitive jump. China's role as a global player is further strengthened thanks to its capacity to establish alliances with the other emerging economies, in the fields of commerce and finance.

According to a projection by Goldman Sachs, in 2043 Chinese GDP should overtake that of the United States (Goldman Sachs Economic Group 2003). In 2040 the countries of the European Union will no longer be part of the G8 leading industrialized economies, having been replaced by China, India, and Brazil (see Table 10.2).

According to some, the contraction in world economic growth in 2008–09 would have been far more severe, at least until September 2008, if not for the

Table 10.2   Classification of the major economies in the world, 2000–2040, ranked according to GDP

	1	2	3	4	5	6
2000	United States	Japan	Germany	United Kingdom	France	Italy
2020	United States	China	Japan	Germany	United Kingdom	India
2030	United States	China	Japan	India	Russia	Germany
2040	United States	China	India	Japan	Russia	Brazil

Source: Based on information contained in Goldman Sachs Economic Group (2003).

large emerging markets, such as the BRICs. In fact, more than 40 percent of the expansion in the world economy between 2003 and 2007 was due to the growth of the BRICs. They jointly recorded a significant development of international trade at a growth rate of investments never seen before. In five years China made more investments, in real terms, than throughout the 20th century (Economist 2008).

In 2007 the BRICs accumulated more than 40 percent of total international reserves. About 42 percent of global savings, nearly half of which was used to finance U.S. development, came from China, Russia, Saudi Arabia, Kuwait, the United Arab Emirates, and Singapore.

Global Governance and the BRICs

These figures clearly indicate that it was not conceivable to solve the crisis, let alone reform the financial international system, without giving emerging countries and BRIC greater voice in global financial governance.

One of the most significant aspects of the G20's London Summit in April 2009 was the acknowledgement of the specific role of emerging countries in the decision-making process of the leading international institutions. This is a first step that was inconceivable four years earlier during the G8's Gleneagles Summit in 2005, not only because the G8 does not hold any legal status but also because it does not have an acknowledged representation. While almost all developed countries are directly or indirectly present in the G20, the presence of emerging countries is limited to the most prosperous ones, which are also BRIC.

The need for a more democratic and transparent mechanism in the decision-making processes of international organizations, based on a larger presence and stronger decision powers of emerging countries, was reaffirmed during the first meeting of BRICs. That meeting was held in Russia on 16 June 2009 at Yekaterinburg.

The arguments supported by Brazil and Russia, about the need for a lesser role for the U.S. dollar in international business and its replacement with a super national currency, were not mentioned in the BRICs communiqué, as a result of China's opposition (China holds U.S. treasury bonds equalling near $2 billion). This further supports the position of those who maintain that the BRICs are identified only by their strong economic growth during past years, while their political interests and global priorities are largely different. This thwarts the creation of strong and common positions.

Apart from these considerations, relevant in terms of the capacity to affect global governance, the astonishing development achieved during the last years by some emerging countries, with the BRICs among them, indicates an intense process of transition resulting from increasing globalization, the intensity of technological changes, and the coming of new competitors.

The global economy, according the structuralist paradigm of Raúl Prébisch (the first director of ECLAC), would include two important poles that interact with each other, centre and periphery, with profoundly different productive structures (Rodríguez 1980). Here central countries are characterized by homogeneous and diversified economies, and the peripheral ones by heterogeneous and scarcely diversified economic structures. The essence of commercial trade and the transfer of technology in the world economy depend on these differences.

In the long run the traditional international division of labour that would have generated an asymmetric international system would also bring about an increasing distance between peripheral and central countries, causing a productive and technological slowdown in peripheral countries and a deterioration of trading terms

The explanation could be found in the fact that the productive sector of the capital goods manufacturing sector in central economies allows them to access technological progress. However, in the peripheral countries, the new technologies are essentially imported, as a result of the absence (or the marginal presence) of production of capital assets that in turn are limited to the export sector of primary goods. The experience of China, on the contrary, as other countries of the BRICs, as well as other Asian economies, demonstrates that convergence with the level of income of central economies, however slow, is possible (Rosales and Kuwayama 2007).

Conclusion

The international financial system does not reflect the current equilibrium of the world economy and specially the weight of emerging economies. The IMF's quota distribution enables a small group of developed economies to block a number of initiatives, including those that could improve the current equilibrium of power of the executive director.

To achieve a large and solid legitimacy, the new financial architecture will have to take into account the needs of each country and grant the developing countries voice and vote in the decision processes of both the IMF and the Bank for International Settlements. The latter has increased the number of permanent member countries in the Basel Committee on Banking Supervision, incorporating some emerging countries, as well as the BRICs.

The crisis demonstrated that the G groups (G7, G8, G20, G24) can play an important role. However, the support of the international community was required to coordinate actions directed to combating the crisis and to adopt the necessary reforms of the financial architecture to reduce systemic risk and minimize the contagious effect.

The current prudential regulation is procyclical, including the rating system contemplated in Basel II. The discussions related to the applications of Basel II in Latin America concentrated on two aspects. The first was the potential uneven competition between internationally active banks and domestic banks in relation to the different capacity to adopt advanced models of economic capital determination.

The second aspect was the implications of the parametrization models of Basel II to capital needs in countries with greater volatility of macroeconomic variables. In such a context the presence of more marked economic cycles can exacerbate the procyclical aspect of Basel II.

The need for a more active role for the international financial organizations would be even greater if the recovery of the international financial system were delayed and difficult conditions of access to external financing persisted.

It is likewise important to adjust the duration and costs of financing to the needs of emerging countries. It would also be useful if all those diverse international organizations acted in a coordinated manner with the aim of strengthening the effects.

This is the appropriate time to question the possible changes in the global economy and the effects on Latin American and Caribbean countries.

It is probable that developed countries will grow at a low rate and that consequently the importance of emerging countries in supporting global demand will increase. The BRIC countries have demonstrated it. As a result new challenges arise in terms of competitiveness as does the strong need to diversify export by products and by market.

It is possible that the international financial systems will be subjected to more strict regulation and supervision. In such a case the dynamism of the credit market would be reduced and interest rate increased. Such a scenario would make it necessary to maintain adequate levels of domestic savings in order to finance economic activity. In the short term it would be necessary to put in place public policies that contribute and assure an adequate level of competition to guarantee social cohesion.

References

Bank for International Settlements (2008). *Monetary and Financial Stability Implications of Capital Flows in Latin America and the Caribbean.* BIS Paper No. 32. Bank for International Settlements, Basel. <www.bis.org/publ/bppdf/bispap43.htm> (August 2010).

Economic Commission for Latin America and the Caribbean (2008). *Preliminary Overview of the Economies of Latin America and the Caribbean, 2008.* Santiago, Chile.

Economic Commission for Latin America and the Caribbean (2009a). *Countercyclical Policies to Buffer the Impact of Economic Crisis Predominate in Latin America.* Press release, 10 February. Santiago, Chile.

Economic Commission for Latin America and the Caribbean (2009b). *Economic Survey of Latin America and the Caribbean, 2008–2009.* Santiago, Chile.

Economic Commission for Latin America and the Caribbean (2009c). *The Reactions of Latin America and the Caribbean Governments to the International Crisis: An Overview of Policy Measures up to 20 February*

2009. Santiago, Chile. <www.eclac.org/publicaciones/xml/2/35362/2009-122-Rev.2-Thecurrentinternationalcrisis-february2009.pdf> (August 2010).

Economist (2008). 'Building BRICs of Growth.' 5 June. <www.economist.com/node/11488749> (August 2010).

Fitzgerald, Valpy (2007). *Los nuevos colosos emergentes y su efecto sobre la economía internacional.* [*The New Emerging Giants and Their Impact on the Global Economy*]. Instituto Español de Comercio Exterio, Madrid.

Goldman Sachs Economic Group (2003). 'Dreaming with the BRICs: The Path to 2050.'

International Monetary Fund (2008). *World Economic Outlook Database.* October. <www.imf.org/external/pubs/ft/weo/2008/02/weodata/index.aspx> (August 2010).

International Monetary Fund (2009). *World Economic Outlook Update: Global Economic Slump Challenges Policies.* January. <www.imf.org/external/pubs/ft/weo/2009/update/01/> (August 2010).

Minsky, Hyman (1982). 'The Financial Instability Hypothesis: A Restatement.' In *Can "It" Happen Again? Essays on Instability and Finance* (Armonk NY: M.E. Sharpe).

Mizen, Paul (2008). 'The Credit Crunch of 2007–2008: A Discussion of the Background, Market Reactions, and Policy Responses.' *Federal Reserve Bank of St. Louis Review*, September/October <research.stlouisfed.org/publications/review/08/09/Mizen.pdf> (August 2010).

Ocampo, José Antonio (2009). 'Impactos de la crisis financiera mundial sobre América Latina.' *Revista CEPAL,* no. 97, April, pp. 9–32.

Rodríguez, Octavio (1980). *La teoría del subdesarrollo de la CEPAL* [*ECLAC's Theory of Underdevelopment*]. (Mexico City: Siglo Veintiuno Editores).

Rosales, Osvaldo and Mikio Kuwayama (2007). 'Latin America Meets China and India: Prospects and Challenges for Trade and Investment.' *Revista CEPAL,* no. 93, December, pp. 81–103.

PART V
Impacts and Responses in Developing Countries

Chapter 11

Sub-Saharan Africa: Impact and Response

Diéry Seck

The countries of sub-Saharan Africa experienced a wave of accession to political independence between the mid 1950s and the mid 1960s, with the exception of the Portuguese-speaking countries whose liberation from Portugal occurred in the 1970s. The 50 years of sub-Saharan history since 1960 have been marked by dramatic events in the political and human spheres, while decades of economic strategies have sought to uplift the region. The main doctrines attempted for the region's economic development included state-controlled economies with the underlying theories of accelerated industrialization and import-substitution strategies of the 1960s and '70s, structural adjustment programmes (SAPs) supported by market liberalization and government disengagement from the economy during the 1980s and '90s, and poverty reduction strategies brought about in the 2000s. In parallel, the years since 1985 have witnessed sub-Saharan Africa's efforts to deal with its crippling external debt with the help of the international community through various debt relief packages, the most notable being the 1985 Baker Plan, the 1989 Brady Plan, and the 1997 Heavily Indebted Poor Countries (HIPC) Initiative.

In spite of these efforts, sub-Saharan Africa's situation, which varies across countries, remains mostly unfavourable. The region has the highest number of countries in the bottom quarter of the rankings of the Human Development Index of the United Nations Development Programme (UNDP). It is plagued with pandemics such as HIV/AIDS and malaria, crop-ravaging natural disasters, famine, civil wars, and chronic constitutional crises that often lead to civil unrest. Although there was an upturn after 2000 for some of its countries, due mostly to increases in the prices of export commodities and short-term gains from sound macroeconomic management, sub-Saharan Africa has proven to be vulnerable to global economic crises with little capacity to tackle them. Moreover, the region faces increasing marginalization from global trade and investment, as well as a digital divide that may preclude large sections of its population from joining the information society.

The challenge, then, is not to seek to achieve a level of economic growth that would bring sub-Saharan Africa closer to the leading economies of the world, with the attendant improvement in the living conditions of its residents. Rather, it is to ensure that, given the absence of appropriate policies to turn things around, some parts of the region will not slip further into economic and social regression. This rather sobering concern dictates that the goals of policy making for sub-Saharan

Africa be aimed at making it behave more like any other developing region with the expectation that similar economic growth will ensue.

In the context of the recent financial crisis, these long-term considerations have been compounded by the fear that sub-Saharan countries have been negatively affected beyond their capacity to cope given their vulnerability to external shocks. In other words, the issue is whether the chronic dire financial situation of these countries has worsened as a result of the crisis, and if they were more or less affected than advanced and emerging countries by the fallout of the global financial crisis of 2007–08. The debate on this topic presents two opposing points of view. On the one hand, it is argued that African countries' economies are not sufficiently integrated into the world economy and, as a result, their relative isolation spared them the adverse impacts of the crisis. On the other hand, it is argued that these countries have small open economies and may have been affected at least through financial flows with the rest of the world because global credit dried up and limited their capacity to borrow, while the contracting world economy reduced their capacity to export. In this chapter, the issue of the short-term impact of the global financial crisis will be investigated first. The longer term developmental and financial challenges of sub-Saharan countries will then be addressed.

In particular, this chapter investigates the impact of the recent global financial crisis on sub-Saharan countries relative to other groups of countries. It also addresses the adequacy of current development strategies, especially in the area of finance, that are applied to sub-Saharan Africa and proposes measures to help make them more relevant and effective.

The Impact of the Financial Crisis on Sub-Saharan Countries

The impact of the global financial crisis on sub-Saharan African countries is assessed on the basis of three financial flow-related criteria, namely the stock market performance, changes in the nominal exchange rate, and variations in the level of total reserves (not including gold). A fourth variable, changes in the level of export revenues (see Table 11.1), will serve to measure the impact on real economic activity, in the absence of data on the gross domestic product (GDP) of some countries. Table 11.2 displays the annual rates of return on the national stock market indices of a number of sub-Saharan countries, a group of emerging countries (Brazil, China, India, and South Africa), and three advanced economies (France, the United Kingdom, and the United States). The last column of Table 11.2 lists the value at the end of 2009 of $100 invested in the national stock exchange index at the end of 2007. The evidence suggests that sub-Saharan African countries were as heavily affected by the global financial crisis through their stock markets as were advanced economies and indeed fared far worse than emerging countries.

Table 11.1   Trade statistics of selected countries

	Annual Change in Export Revenues, in %			Statistics on Annual Change in Exports, 1980–2009		
	2007	2008	2009	Average	Standard deviation	Coefficient of variation
Cameroon	4.9	16.0	−28.7	1.7	16.1	9.5
Côte d'Ivoire	−1.2	22.1	−5.4	2.5	14.7	5.9
Ghana	15.6	30.8	−2.1	10.4	44.8	4.3
Kenya	18.7	21.9	−10.2	3.0	12.8	4.3
Nigeria	13.4	23.8	−34.9	4.4	30.0	6.8
Uganda	60.3	40.2	63.3	11.1	36.6	3.3
Zambia	29.3	4.4	−16.8	5.5	30.0	5.5
Average	20.2	22.7	−5.0	5.5	26.4	5.6
Brazil	16.6	23.2	−22.7	5.4	10.7	2.0
China	25.6	17.3	−15.9	13.4	10.0	0.7
India	23.1	29.7	−16.4	8.6	9.1	1.1
South Africa	20.0	21.3	−26.0	1.4	10.6	7.6
Average	21.3	22.9	−20.3	7.2	10.1	2.8
France	12.4	10.1	−19.9	3.1	9.8	3.2
United Kingdom	1.7	5.8	−22.6	2.1	8.4	4.0
United States	12.0	11.9	−18.8	3.3	7.0	2.1
Average	8.7	9.3	−20.4	2.8	8.4	3.1

Source: International Monetary Fund; IFS, Online, July 2010, Author's calculations.

Table 11.2   Annual performance of national stock market indices

	2007	2008	2009	Value of $100, 2007–09
Côte d'Ivoire	77.0	−10.7	−25.9	$66.22
Ghana	5.4	31.8	−15.6	$111.31
Kenya	−3.6	−35.3	−7.8	$59.64
Nigeria	74.7	−45.8	−33.8	$35.92
Zambia	88.2	31.6	−31.3	$90.35
Average	48.4	−5.7	−22.9	$72.76
Brazil	43.7	−41.2	82.7	$107.36
China	161.1	−28.1	−10.0	$64.66
India	49.5	−50.4	72.9	$85.71
South Africa	32.8	−7.1	−45.8	$50.34
Average	71.8	−31.7	24.9	$85.29
France	1.3	−42.7	22.3	$70.12
United Kingdom	9.4	−17.5	−14.7	$70.37
United States	15.4	−14.6	−21.1	$67.40
Average	8.7	−24.9	−4.5	$71.71

Sources: International Monetary Fund; IFS, Online, July 2010; Nigeria: Central Bank of Nigeria; Ghana: Bloomberg.com; Côte d'Ivoire: CGF Bourse, Sénégal, Lettre Mensuelle.

The effect on sub-Saharan African countries was also delayed. The biggest drop in their stock markets occurred in 2009, while for emerging and advanced countries the bottom was reached in 2008 and the rebound commenced in 2009.

The compound stock market effect is illustrated the amount listed in the last column of Table 11.2. During the specified two-year period, the sub-Saharan African countries experienced an average reduction in the values of their respective portfolios from $100 to $72.76. This amount is similar to $71.71, the end value of advanced countries' portfolios. But it is significantly smaller than that of emerging countries, which was $85.29. Three sub-Saharan African countries—Nigeria, Kenya, and Côte d'Ivoire—were among the worst affected countries. Only Ghana and Brazil scored positive compound returns during that period.

Table 11.3 reports the annual rates of change in the nominal official exchange rates (the number of U.S. dollars per unit of local currency) and the annual rates of change of total reserves (excluding gold) of the selected countries from 2006 to 2009. For all groups of countries, the impact of the crisis on the nominal exchange rate was very similar. Local currencies rose against the dollar in 2007, declined significantly in 2008, and suffered a sharp drop in 2009. The speed of the transmission of the crisis was about the same for all groups, emerging economies being the least affected and sub-Saharan African countries experiencing the largest decline during the crisis years of 2008 and 2009. A slightly softer image is reflected in the annual change in total reserves, for which the negative impact of the crisis was simultaneous and of comparable magnitude for all groups. In summary, sub-Saharan African countries were adversely affected by the global financial crisis through their reserves at the same time as were emerging and advanced countries, and through their nominal exchange rates with a delayed effect, both responses being of a magnitude that is approximately similar for the three groups of countries.

Table 11.1 also illustrates that the export revenues of African countries were not as affected as they were for advanced and emerging countries when, in 2009, the impact of the crisis was first felt on trade. This effect was delayed for all groups of countries but was more pronounced for Africa. Data for 2010 and subsequent years should establish the real pattern of the impact on Africa. The table also points to a significantly higher variability of export revenues for sub-Saharan Africa than for emerging or advanced countries. Indeed, sub-Saharan Africa has a coefficient of variability of the annual changes of its export revenues that was about twice as high as for the other groups of countries. This factor has important implications for the predictability of future financial resources of African countries and their capacity to honour external obligations related to imports and foreign debt.

The evidence presented in Tables 11.1, 11.2, and 11.3 shows that sub-Saharan African countries were not spared from the negative impact of the financial crisis. They were as affected as advanced countries were and significantly more affected than emerging countries were. They experienced a delayed impact with respect to stock market performance and export revenues, but the duration of the impact was similar for all groups of countries. Given that, unlike advanced countries, sub-

Table 11.3 Annual rates of change of nominal exchange rate and of total reserves for selected countries

	Nominal official exchange rate			Total reserves		
	2007	2008	2009	2007	2008	2009
Cameroon	9.1	7.0	−5.2	69.4	6.2	19.1
Côte d'Ivoire	9.1	7.0	−5.2	40.1	−10.6	45.0
Ghana	−2.0	−11.6	−24.9	N.A.	N.A.	N.A.
Kenya	7.1	−2.7	−10.6	38.9	−14.2	33.7
Nigeria	2.3	6.1	−20.4	21.4	3.2	−15.5
Uganda	6.3	0.2	−15.3	41.4	−10.1	30.2
Zambia	−10.0	6.9	−25.8	51.4	0.5	72.7
Average	3.1	1.8	−15.3	43.8	−4.2	30.9
Brazil	11.7	6.2	−8.3	110.7	7.5	23.1
China	4.8	9.5	1.7	43.2	27.4	23.9
India	9.6	−5.0	−10.1	56.4	−7.3	7.2
South Africa	−3.9	−14.7	−2.5	28.3	3.4	15.2
Average	5.6	−1.0	−4.8	59.7	7.7	17.4
France	9.1	7.0	−5.2	7.2	−26.5	38.7
United Kingdom	8.6	−7.4	−15.6	20.3	−9.4	25.6
United States	–	–	–	8.5	11.9	79.7
Average	8.9	−0.2	−10.4	12.0	−8.0	48.0

Source: International Monetary Fund; IFS, Online, July 2010.

Saharan African countries were unable to implement massive remedial policies in support of their economies and in response to the crisis, the negative impact on their economies might be expected to last a little longer but to subside eventually thanks to improving conditions at the global level. The analysis will now focus on the long-term development challenges of sub-Saharan Africa.

Sub-Saharan Africa's Unfavourable Initial Conditions for the Long Term

Two basic observations motivate the analysis and recommendations. The first is that sub-Saharan Africa has been economically and socially underdeveloped over the last century, and most of its sub-regions are likely to remain underdeveloped in the foreseeable future if drastic measures are not taken to change its course. The second is that, from a situation of relative parity about 50 years ago, sub-Saharan Africa has increasingly been losing ground to other developing regions and experiencing economic divergence, a process that seems unstoppable with the policy packages that are applied today. Therefore, if sub-Saharan Africa is not able to achieve its absolute development goals as set by the United Nations Millennium Development Goals (MDGs) despite decades of efforts on its part with the assistance of the international community, it would be more realistic and equally instructive to aim for the objective of converging toward other developing regions of the world. This implies that something different must be done almost exclusively for sub-Saharan Africa.

Three Unfavourable Characteristics

The comparison between sub-Saharan Africa and other developing regions assumes a certain degree of homogeneity within regions. This is not the case, but it serves to underscore the vast disparities that exist and justify remedial action more on behalf of sub-Saharan Africa than other regions. To be justified, such differentiated treatment must be based on characteristics that set sub-Saharan Africa apart and unquestionably hamper its development, even in comparison to other developing areas. Three characteristics emerge. The first one is related to the magnitude and degree of satisfaction of social demand; the second one highlights impediments to trade through the high incidence of landlocked countries; and the third one captures the uncertainty surrounding future economic prospects as measured by the variability of export earnings over time.

As Table 11.4 shows, sub-Saharan Africa has a low per capita gross national income (GNI), and the lowest life expectancy at birth at only 51 years. South Asia has an average production lifetime that is longer than that of sub-Saharan Africa by 14 years. For other developing regions the difference ranges between 19 and 22 years. Sub-Saharan Africa's considerably larger rate of population growth underscores the growing social dimensions of its underdevelopment, which its workforce may not be able to remedy considering its low life expectancy. This

Table 11.4   Key statistics and indicators of selected developing regions, 2007

Region	Per capita GNI in $, Atlas method	Life expectancy at birth in years	Rate of population growth, %	Primary school enrolment, %	Number of landlocked countries
Sub-Saharan Africa	951	51	2.4	69.5	15
Latin America and Caribbean	5801	73	1.2	93.9	2
South Asia	880	64	1.5	85.2	3
East Asia and Pacific	2182	72	0.8	93.0	2
Middle East and North Africa	2820	70	1.7	90.1	0

Note: GNI = gross national product.

Sources: World Bank Key Development Data and Statistics, World Bank.

challenge is compounded by the region's low net rate of primary school enrolment, which assigns the lowest per capita productivity to sub-Saharan Africa. Compared to other developing regions, sub-Saharan Africa is thus likely to have larger social needs that it may have difficulty satisfying because the proportion of unproductive young people is higher and grows faster, and its workforce dies younger and has lower productivity than anywhere else in the world.

The last column of Table 11.4 indicates the number of landlocked countries in each developing region. Of the 15 landlocked sub-Saharan Africa countries, 12 are among the 26 countries that have the lowest rankings according to the UNDP's 2006 Human Development Index. Landlocked countries in other developing regions also tend to rank low in their respective regions. This strong correlation between lack of access to the coastline and lack of human development afflicts sub-Saharan Africa more than any other region. As has been often pointed out, being landlocked can hinder development (MacKellar et al. 2000; Limão and Venables 1999; Faye et al. 2004).

Recent instances of strong and sustained economic growth in the developing world have been led by exports. This is the case for China and India now, and for Singapore, Taiwan, Korea, and Malaysia two decades ago. Therefore, the economic growth of developing countries can be significantly affected by the rate of growth and variability of their export earnings. More specifically, fast expansion of exports fuels economic growth, while highly variable exports may affect growth negatively. Table 11.5 provides a comparison among regions. The annual rate of growth of nominal exports of goods and services freight on board (in U.S. dollars and deflated with the U.S. producer price index) is calculated for each sampled country for the period of 1970 to 2008. Then the average, standard

Table 11.5   Statistics of real freight-on-board export growth by selected developing regions, 1970–2007

Region	Mean Average Rate of Export Growth, in %	Mean Standard Deviation of Rate of Export Growth, in %	Mean Coefficient of Variation
Sub-Sahara Africa	8.3	33.4	5.1
Latin America and Caribbean	6.4	19.4	3.4
South Asia	7.7	15.3	2.1
East Asia and Pacific	9.4	26.0	3.9
Middle East and North Africa	9.4	24.9	3.1

Source: International Monetary Fund, International Financial Statistics Online; computations by the author.

deviation, and coefficient of variation are computed for each country over the same period. The means of these statistics are calculated across countries in each developing region. The list of sampled countries appears in Appendix 11.1.

Column 1 in Table 11.5 shows that, over the 38-year sample period, sub-Saharan Africa has recorded an average export growth performance of 8.3 percent. This ranks it in the middle of developing areas. It has done better than South Asia and Latin America and the Caribbean, but not as well as East Asia and the Pacific or the Middle East and North Africa. However, the variability of export growth in sub-Saharan Africa is markedly higher than in other regions. At 5.1 its coefficient of variation of export growth is 31.8 percent higher than that of the region with the next highest coefficient of variation (East Asia and Pacific) and almost two and a half times that of South Asia. Thus, the third characteristic that adversely affects sub-Saharan Africa's economic growth prospects is that its export earnings are highly volatile, even when compared to those of other developing regions and export diversification may not be readily available to most sub-Saharan Africa countries given their lack of competitiveness outside their traditional export sectors.

The Impact of Adverse Initial Conditions

The extent to which these disparities harm sub-Saharan Africa's economic development prospects requires further scrutiny. With respect to its capacity to generate enough wealth to meet its social needs, sub-Saharan Africa is at a major disadvantage. The average lifetime per capita production (the product of the number of productive years and the average annual productivity) is lower than in other regions because both elements are lower for sub-Saharan Africa than for other developing regions. Furthermore, the level of social demand is higher and will be increasingly higher for sub-Saharan Africa than for other developing areas. Indeed, the region's rate of population growth is higher, while its larger proportion of poor arising from lower primary school enrolment will reduce, through social spending, the level of resources otherwise invested in other aspects of economic development.

A vast empirical literature has uncovered the negative impact of a country's distance from the coastline on its economic growth. This relationship points to the cost of transportation as a key determinant of a country's ability to open up and integrate into the world economy. In the absence of a competitive advantage that fuels international trade, a country is isolated and lags behind in the acquisition of trade-induced technological advances, whether through invention or transfer. This lag further compounds the adverse effects of its landlocked status. Because technology embodies technical knowledge, a landlocked country tends to fall behind in developing human capital. Moreover, most landlocked sub-Saharan Africa countries have neighbours that are hardly more developed than they are,

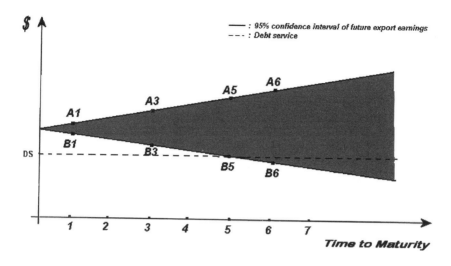

Figure 11.1   Static forecast of future debt service difficulties

which limits the potential trade-induced developmental gains that arise through land-based cross-border transactions.

Figure 11.1 illustrates the adverse impacts of the high variability of a country's export proceeds on its future economic prospects. In this example, an African country borrows externally and commits to make annual payments equal to debt service until the maturity of the loan. The equal payments of debt service are represented by the horizontal dotted line. The horizontal axis depicts years to maturity while the vertical line indicates dollar amounts. Export earnings of African countries follow a random pattern, which means that the variance of their underlying probabilistic distribution increases proportionally as the time horizon over which it is calculated increases (Seck 2006). Therefore, the confidence interval within which export earnings are expected to fall with a given confidence level will also increase over time and has a conical graphic shape. For instance, in Figure 11.1, at a 95 percent confidence level, the country's export earnings one year from now will fall between A1 and B1. If the forecast is extended to three years the corresponding 95 percent boundaries are A3 and B3 (see Seck 2008).

If external debt is serviced solely with a country's export proceeds, a country is almost sure to repay its annual debt instalment equal to debt service, although a residual risk of non-payment remains, as long as the dotted line is below the grey area. However, as the maturity of the loan increases, the dotted debt service line eventually intersects with the lower boundary of the confidence interval of the export earnings distribution and there is stronger likelihood that the country will face debt-servicing difficulties after that date. This eventuality is higher the higher the variability of a country's export earnings, which is the case of African countries compared to countries in other developing regions.

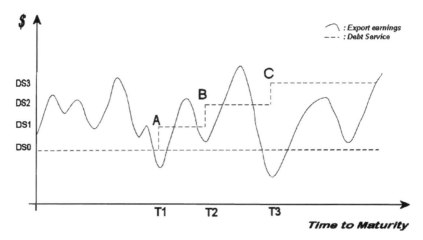

Figure 11.2   Dynamic forecast of future debt service difficulties

Note: DS = debt service.

In Figure 11.1, the analysis is static because it is entirely conducted at the time of the loan contract. Figure 11.2 depicts a dynamic forecast of the country's future external debt difficulties because it includes events that emerge after the loan contract has been signed. The actual value of exports earnings is represented by the continuous line, and replaces the confidence interval represented by the grey area in Figure 11.1. The initially contracted debt service amount that was denoted by debt service in Figure 11.1 is denoted by DS0 in Figure 11.2. If a borrower country with export proceeds higher than its contractual debt service up to the year T1, its export earnings fall below DS0 and it cannot service its external debt.

As a result, the accrued interest on its debt service payment is capitalized and its new annual debt service payment is increased to DS1, as indicated by the stepped-up dotted line starting at point A. Therefore, the country's debt service is higher than its initial value, and the probability that its future export earnings will cover it decreases. With future debt service difficulties, the country experiences new capitalizations of accrued interest on its unpaid debt service obligations. Consequently, increasing higher debt service amounts, denoted by points B and C, burden the country's development efforts and debt crises become more frequent. This process of ballooning external debt obligations is more likely to happen the longer the initial maturity of the debt contract. In summary, the long-held view that developing countries must borrow long term to finance their long-term development must be challenged because with extended maturities there is an increasingly higher probability of debt service difficulties, given the characteristics of the probabilistic distribution underlying their export earnings.

This analysis provides evidence that sub-Saharan Africa suffers from initial conditions that put it at a disadvantage compared to other developing regions. Some of these conditions stem from the region's demographic and geographic characteristics, while the high variability of its export earnings makes it difficult to undertake long-term development planning or make effective use of external sovereign borrowing without facing a high probability of future debt service crises. Consequently, any attempt to improve the development prospects of sub-Saharan Africa, even to meet the level of other developing regions, must seek to level the playing field by implementing remedial measures that will be organized around a new development finance architecture, supported by consistently sound macroeconomic policies that help prevent major domestic imbalances.

A New Development Finance Architecture for Sub-Saharan Africa

In light of the adverse characteristics that beset sub-Saharan Africa's growth potential and make it diverge economically from other developing regions, what appropriate policy reforms are needed to remedy the current situation? Based on the evidence, the policy package needs to include identification of sectoral priorities to address the demographic and geographic challenges of the sub-region as well as financial arrangements, not just financial flows that ensure long-term sustainability of economic development.

Sub-Saharan Africa's Sectoral Priorities

Table 11.4 illustrates the demographic challenges faced by sub-Saharan Africa with respect to its lowest life expectancy, highest population growth, and lowest primary school enrolment among developing regions. This combination of factors is incompatible with autonomous sustainable development because the region cannot finance its spiralling social needs. In order to break the vicious circle of current needs exceeding available resources, priority must be given to significantly larger expenditures in the human development sector, particularly in health and education. Such a policy will raise the life expectancy and, consequently, the per capita lifetime production, and will enhance the average productivity of sub-Saharan Africa. As household incomes increase, the rate of population growth will decrease, a demographic process that has been observed in other developing regions. This will, in turn, reduce the extent of sub-Saharan Africa's social needs and release additional resources that can be devoted to other requirements for development.

The second sectoral priority arises from the high incidence of landlocked countries in sub-Saharan Africa compared to other developing regions, as also indicated in Table 11.4. While geographic location is exogenous, it is one element in a country's transport cost function. Other arguments in the same function can play a countervailing role and help reduce the negative impact of distance from the coastline. Trade-facilitating infrastructure can be considered a prime candidate to offset landlocked status. Even within the borders of large countries, rail and road transport have historically brought secluded regions closer to markets and ensured their economic development. Air transport also plays an increasingly important role. Landlocked sub-Saharan Africa countries have very poor infrastructure in general and trade-related infrastructure in particular. They must therefore make efforts to increase their level of trade-facilitating infrastructure to lessen the adverse impact of their geographic location and further integrate into the world economy.

Thus investment in social development and trade-related infrastructure can be considered imperative requirements that will help sub-Saharan Africa catch up with other developing regions. To be successful, a financial architecture aimed at supporting the region's development efforts needs to take these two sectoral priorities into account. The main characteristics of the development finance architecture proposed for sub-Saharan Africa are discussed below.

The Architecture for Sub-Saharan Africa's Development Finance

The current architecture of sub-Saharan Africa's development finance has the following main components. Domestic financial sources include a government's fiscal revenue, domestic borrowing, and private sector finance (which comprises bank lending and equity including household self-financing). International sources of funding refer to grants, sovereign and private sector borrowing, private inflows composed of foreign direct investment, portfolio investment, and foreign remittances. To remain practical, the discussion on the new architecture will focus here on sources of funding over which the international development community has some control. This excludes all domestic sources and private international inflows. In other words, attention will be paid to foreign grants and sovereign and private sector international borrowing from public lenders. These channels are more amenable to public policy reform at the regional level. The other sources of funding are within the scope of private sector or sovereign national decision making.

Have foreign grants and international loans prevented sub-Saharan Africa from falling increasingly behind? If not, what remedial measures can be taken? With respect to grant making, the consensus on its historical performance and shortcomings is captured by the Paris Declaration and the ongoing debate on aid (see Organisation for Economic Co-operation and Development [OECD] 2005). The list below enumerates the main critiques levelled at official development assistance (ODA) (see Appendix 11.2).

- Recipient countries do not have a strong sense of ownership of aid packages.
- There is poor alignment of donor practices with recipient countries' procurement and accounting policies.
- Donors display limited willingness to harmonize their practices and to work in unison.

Table 11.6   Aid to all recipients by major purposes in 2007, in percentage

	Total Development Assistance Committee	European Commission	World Bank	Regional development banks
Social and administrative infrastructure	40.5	39.2	31.8	25.2
Education[a]	9.1	5.7	7.7	3.4
of which: Basic education	2.5	0.8	1.6	2.0
Health	4.7	3.0	1.6	1.2
of which: Basic health	3.3	2.1	0.6	0.3
Population[b]	6.1	0.7	2.0	–
Water supply and sanitation	4.7	3.7	10.5	7.7
Government and civil society	12.5	17.8	5.3	12.0
Other social infrastructure/service	3.5	8.4	4.8	0.8
Economic infrastructure	12.7	15.1	31.8	46.7
Transport and communications	4.4	7.7	17.0	30.2
Energy	4.1	4.7	11.2	11.4
Other	4.1	2.7	3.7	5.1
Production	6.1	9.6	9.1	14.2
Agriculture	4.6	3.4	8.1	5.6
Industry, mining and construction	0.9	3.8	0.7	8.1
Trade and tourism	0.6	2.3	0.3	0.5
Multisector	7.1	10.2	1.4	12.3
Program assistance	4.5	9.2	25.8	0.8
Action relating to debt[c]	10.5	0.2	–	–
Humanitarian aid	7.5	10.7	0.0	–
Administrative expenses	5.3	5.1	–	–
Other and unspecified	5.8	0.9	–	0.8
Total	00.0	100.0	100.0	100.0
Memo item:				
Food aid, total	2.9	4.5	–	–

Notes:
[a] Including students and trainees.
[b] Population and reproductive health.
[c] Including forgiveness of non-official development assistance debt.
Source: Organisation for Economic Co-operation and Development, Development Assistance Committee Statistics Online, Table 19.

- ODA needs to move away from process-based mechanisms in favour of a results-based framework.
- Recipient countries suffer from asymmetric accountability in favour of donors.
- The technical assistance component of ODA is costly, is inadequate, is often imposed through tied aid, and does not empower local staff.
- Donors impose excessive conditionality.
- Politically motivated allocation of aid distorts priorities and does not reflect recipients' actual needs.
- The unpredictability of the level and composition of aid flows makes recipient countries' long-term planning difficult.
- Aid flows to sub-Saharan Africa have historically been deemed insufficient.

In view of all these critiques and the results ODA has yielded, one may wonder why the current ODA system has managed to remain in place for so long, and is consistently utilized by so many in the donor community. The Paris Declaration recognizes many of the pitfalls listed above but has not been very successful at removing them. Consequently, the search for new aid mechanisms is still warranted, especially in light of the increasing role of new donors such as China that espouses an approach to aid that is different from the current practice of traditional donors to the Development Assistance Committee (DAC) of the Organisation for Economic Co-operation and Development (OECD). Table 11.6 reports the major uses of aid in 2007 and illustrates the lack of adequacy of DAC aid relative to the development needs of developing countries in the areas of social development and infrastructure. The World Bank and the regional development banks seem to do better in economic infrastructure but not in social development.

Table 11.7 summarizes for each developing region the evolution of external debt of various sources and maturities over a 15-year period. Four observations are relevant. First, sub-Saharan Africa carries too much external debt compared to other developing regions, not in absolute amount, but in view of the high variability of its export earnings. Indeed, the higher its total indebtedness, the higher its expected debt service obligations and the higher the probability of occurrence of future debt service difficulties. In other words, sub-Saharan Africa should borrow significantly less than other developing regions, which was not the case in 1990 or in 2005. Second, sub-Saharan Africa has too much long-term debt considering that its highly volatile export earnings may be insufficient to service debt obligations that are very distant in the future.

The third observation relates to the inadequacy of the level of private non-guaranteed external debt compared to the other regions and to the need to develop the private sector in sub-Saharan Africa. The long-held view that the private sector is the engine of economic growth in the developing world seems to have been backed up by external debt finance in every developing region except in sub-Saharan Africa where, arguably, it was most needed given previous decades

Table 11.7 External debt statistics of selected developing regions, in $ billions

	Total external debt		Long-term debt		Public and publicly guaranteed debt		Private nonguaranteed external debt		EBRD loans and IDA credit		Use of IMF credit	
	1990	**2005**	**1990**	**2005**	**1990**	**2005**	**1990**	**2005**	**1990**	**2005**	**1990**	**2005**
Sub-Saharan Africa	176.6	214.8	149.4	176.7	144.1	163.8	5.3	13.0	24.9	50.5	6.6	5.9
Latin America and Caribbean	444.6	727.6	352.7	621.9	327.7	419.6	25.0	202.3	35.9	40.4	18.3	13.1
South Asia	124.4	191.5	107.5	177.4	105.8	141.7	1.7	35.8	30.7	50.3	4.5	2.2
East Asia and Pacific	234.1	621.2	194.6	400.2	173.0	256.3	21.6	143.9	25.3	39.9	2.1	8.5
Middle East and North Africa	139.5	152.7	118.0	124.3	116.6	113.3	1.4	11.0	10.1	10.1	1.8	0.5
Total	1119.2	1907.8	922.2	1500.5	867.2	1094.7	55.0	406.0	126.9	521.2	33.3	30.2

Notes: EBRD = European Bank for Reconstruction and Development; IDA = International Development Association; IMF = International Monetary Fund.

Source: World Bank, World Bank Indicators 2007, Online, Table 4.16.

of government-controlled economic activity. Indeed, between 1990 and 2005, sub-Saharan Africa's private sector borrowing from external sources increased by only $7.7 billion. Finally, while separate statistics are not available in Table 11.7 for credit granted by the International Development Association (IDA), the possible inadequacy of this facility must not be overlooked. Although its loans are extended on concessionary terms, they carry fixed debt obligations over very long maturities for debtor countries deemed poor but also saddled with highly volatile export earnings. In this regard, it is legitimate to examine whether this soft loan window should be replaced by a pure grant facility. The same can be said of the African Development Fund of the African Development Bank (AfDB).

Proposals for a New Development Finance Architecture

The foregoing analysis has uncovered three characteristics that are thought to be related to sub-Saharan Africa's lack of economic convergence with other developing regions. It is proposed that sectoral priorities that include social development and infrastructure be the focus of future policies to remedy the current situation. This section makes recommendations on financing packages aimed at achieving this goal. The discussion will first address the financing facilities that are deemed adequate for the programme. The key institutional actors that could help in its success will be identified afterward.

Financing Facilities for Sub-Saharan Africa

The financing facilities that could help enhance sub-Saharan Africa's economic prospects relate to the design and management of sub-Saharan Africa's external borrowing and to grant-making policies. Two new approaches are proposed with respect to external debt facilities. The first one seeks to substitute sub-Saharan Africa's sovereign credit risk with liquidity risk. The rationale is that after 25 years of external debt crises with a long string of *ex post* debt relief plans, sub-Saharan Africa needs to be shielded from the uncertainty of future debt service difficulties and plan for its long-term economic growth. Given that historically debt relief packages mostly addressed the consequences of debt crises rather than their causes, the purpose of the three facilities proposed below is to prevent these crises in the future.

The first facility is to reduce the stock of sovereign external debt in order to lower future debt service obligations. Here, initiatives such as the HIPC Initiative and other debt forgiveness and debt exchange mechanisms can play a significant role. The goal of the second facility is to make service on external sovereign debt contingent on the export earnings performance of the debtor country. If the contractual periodic debt service payment is manageably low as prescribed in the first facility, a country can be considered fundamentally solvent and shortfalls in its export revenues will be expected to be minor and of limited duration. In such instances, the debtor country could be authorized to postpone all or part of its contractual debt service payment, with or without recapitalization of interest, and resume its scheduled payments when its export performance improves. Through this facility the credit risk that has plagued sub-Saharan Africa countries for many years is transformed into a mere liquidity risk. Lenders that are unwilling to carry the liquidity risk could sell it to other market participants more adept at pooling it and therefore diversifying across borrowers. By the same token, private foreign lenders could also be given protection by their governments through insurance schemes comparable to those offered to exporters.

The goal of the third facility is to replace concessionary lending instruments such as the IDA with pure grant windows to maintain sub-Saharan Africa countries' access to external sovereign financing without the pitfalls of fixed long-term debt service obligations described above. Its implementation would constitute a suitable substitute for the current practice toward sub-Saharan Africa countries. Indeed, the combination of the *ex ante* grant element in concessionary loans and increasingly generalized loan forgiveness, especially under the HIPC Initiative, yields a present value of debt service inflows going to lenders that is close to zero. The pure grant facility has the dual advantage of removing the burden of future debt service payments for cash-strapped sub-Saharan Africa governments and significantly reducing the financial uncertainty surrounding future development planning. Arguably, a pure grant facility is more likely to yield satisfactory results if recipients are held to high standards of external accountability and domestic governance that satisfy the requirements of fiduciary responsibility of donors. Such standards should be an integral part of the proposed financial architecture.

The second approach is to strengthen its process of international crowding in. Table 11.7 documents the low recourse of sub-Saharan Africa's private sector to external borrowing, unlike other developing regions, which is detrimental to the unleashing of its growth potential. Countries that have recently experienced episodes of high economic growth have also promoted their private sector, notably in the cases of export-induced growth. Given the region's scarcity of domestic capital and low savings rate, sub-Saharan Africa needs to fund its private sector through international borrowing.

Although most of the critiques levelled at ODA are known and discussed in the Paris Declaration and elsewhere, the record for sub-Saharan Africa does not provide evidence of improvement likely to enhance the region's prospects for economic development. Therefore, a new initiative could complement the current architecture in the pursuit of sub-Saharan Africa's grant-aided development efforts. The proposal seeks to establish two grant-making pools to provide exclusive support for sub-Saharan Africa: the development pool and the common pool. The development pool will help finance individual countries' development programmes in priority sectors such as social development and infrastructure, while the common pool will fund all other eligible programmes and projects that are submitted by countries, the African Union (AU), and regional economic communities of the region. All sub-Saharan Africa countries

Table 11.8   Proposed design for Aid Council for Africa

	Development Pool	Common Pool
Panel A: Financing		
Initial contribution	To be determined	To be determined
Annual contribution	To be determined	To be determined
Funding sources Foreign contributions	• Bilateral: ODA expenditure; International Finance Facility • Multilateral: reserve draw-down; special drawing rights (International Monetary Fund) • International levies: airline ticket tax	• Bilateral: ODA expenditure; International Finance Facility
Africa's contributions	• Governments: tax revenues • International levies: Penny-a-Pack cigarette tax; Dime-a-Bottle alcohol tax; Dollar-a-Transfer tax on international personal bank transfers	• Governments: tax revenues
Private sector contributions	• Donations • Import price reductions	• Private investment flows
Civil society contributions	• Charitable donations • Volunteer work	• Purchase of development shares
Terms of funding for recipients	• Pure grants for all sources	• Pure grants for foreign, African and civil society contributions • Market profitability for private sector investments
Timetable of funding delegation	• DAC countries to transfer to pool 0.1% of GNI at start and 0.5% of GNI by year five.	• No mandatory transfer required
Duration of pool	Pool expires in 2025	Pool expires in 2025
Panel B: Eligibility		
Type of support	Budget support	Economic growth projects
Recipients	• Sub-Saharan African countries	• All African countries • African Union • RECs
Eligibility threshold	Per capita GNI less than $1000	None
Submission document	• Poverty reduction strategy paper or accelerated growth strategy	• Country sector-wide Investment projects • NEPAD implementation documents • RECs implementation documents
Institutional external vetting	Non-objection by World Bank, International Monetary Fund, African Development Bank	Non-objection by World Bank, International Monetary Fund, African Development Bank

Main conditionality	• Observance of governance requirements and expenditure standards	• Observance of governance requirements and expenditure standards • Evidence of economic impact
Panel C: Governance, Monitoring and Reporting		
Governance body	Aid Council for Africa	Aid Council for Africa
Composition of Council	• Donors • African countries • Appointed by United Nations secretary general	• Donors • African countries • Appointed by United Nations secretary general
Observers	World Bank, International Monetary Fund, African Development Bank, African Union, Organisation for Economic Co-operation and Development	World Bank, International Monetary Fund, African Development Bank, African Union, Organisation for Economic Co-operation and Development
Administration of funds	World Bank and African Development Bank	World Bank and African Development Bank

Notes: DAC = Development Assistance Committee; GNI = gross national income; IDA = International Development Association; IMF = International Monetary Fund; NEPAD = New Partnership for Africa's Development; ODA = official development assistance; REC = regional economic community.

Source: Seck (2006).

with a per capita GNI not exceeding $1000 will be eligible for the development pool while the common pool will be open to all African countries, the AU, and the regional economic communities.

The private sector will be encouraged to participate in the development pool with grants and in the common pool possibly with profit-seeking joint venture investments. Civil society's contribution will be in the form of charitable donations and purchase of non-refundable, non-income bearing development shares. The donor community will provide funding through ODA, the International Finance Facility, other development facilities, international levies such as the airline tax, and special drawing rights (SDRs) to be issued by the International Monetary Fund (IMF). The domestic funding counterpart of African countries will include tax revenues and a number of new levies. The levies include a penny of additional excise tax for each pack of cigarettes sold (Penny-a-Pack or PAP tax), a dime for each bottle of alcoholic beverage sold (Dime-a-Bottle or DAB tax) and one U.S. dollar for each international personal money transfer originating in an OECD country and destined to sub-Saharan Africa (Dollar-a-Transfer or DAT tax). DAC members will be urged to channel the equivalent of 0.1 percent of their GNI to the development pool at its inception and 0.5 percent of their GNI after five years. Their contributions to the common pool will be voluntary and the amounts discretionary.

To be eligible for development pool assistance, countries will be requested to submit a poverty reduction strategy paper (PRSP), a strategy for accelerated growth, or a comparable document. Standard economic documents such as sector-wide investment programmes or implementation strategy briefs by the New Partnership for Africa's Development (NEPAD) will be adequate for requests submitted to the common pool. For each proposal the World Bank, the IMF, and the AfDB will, in their capacity as knowledge institutions, be requested to provide written non-binding observations on technical assistance to the selection process. To lessen the incidence of tied aid, donor-specific conditionality, political targeting of recipients and the practice of trust funds will be kept to a minimum. To mitigate the incidence of information asymmetry and reduce the incentive for moral hazard, accountability and governance standards coupled with verifiable monitoring benchmarks will be put in place to govern eligibility criteria and compliance rules. The two pools will be administered by the Aid Council for Africa (ACA), which would report to the secretary general of the United Nations. The composition of the ACA will comprise representatives of sub-Saharan Africa countries, of participating donors as well as institutions and individuals appointed by the UN secretary general. The AU, the World Bank, the IMF, and the AfDB will serve as observers. Table 11.8 summarizes the main features of the two pools.

Roles of Institutional Actors

The changes and innovations proposed would have direct implications for the roles and operations of the financial institutions that serve Africa. The role and mode of operation of the ACA are described above. Current financial and development institutions could be reviewed and mandated as follows.

- The World Bank and the AfDB
  - Reduce the total stock of outstanding external sovereign debt of sub-Saharan Africa, refrain from further sovereign lending, and terminate concessionary loans, usually extended through IDA and the African Development Fund.
  - Transform these windows into pure grant facilities.
  - Increase significantly loans to sub-Saharan Africa's private sector.
  - Provide technical assistance to recipient countries and the ACA.
- Bilateral and other multilateral donors
  - Reduce the stock of outstanding external sovereign debt of sub-Saharan Africa and refrain from further lending to sub-Saharan Africa sovereign borrowers.
  - Replace loans with sovereign grants.
  - Support private sector funding schemes.

- The IMF
  - Increase resources available for balance-of-payments relief interventions on behalf of sub-Saharan Africa countries.
  - Provide exceptional SDRs to sub-Saharan Africa countries to support their development efforts.
  - Provide technical support to recipient countries and the ACA.

It is noteworthy that the AU is in the process of establishing a number of continent-wide financial institutions. Their roles and collaboration with existing institutions could be the focus of future discussion when they become fully operational.

Conclusion

This chapter investigates two key issues related to sub-Saharan Africa's development prospects. The first one focused on the adverse short-term impact of the recent financial crisis on African economies and the magnitude of that impact compared to advanced and emerging economies. Based on the data available so far, there is empirical evidence that financial flow-related variables such as stock market performance, changes in the nominal exchange rate, and changes in the level of total reserves point to a negative effect of the financial crisis that is of the same magnitude for African countries and advanced economies but not as severe for emerging countries. The impact of the crisis on export revenues has been slow for all groups of countries and seems more delayed for African countries than for their emerging and advanced counterparts. Data on subsequent years will be needed to establish the pattern of the trade-related impact of the crisis. One striking feature of sub-Saharan African countries is the significantly higher volatility of their export revenues than those for other groups of countries. These short-term adverse shocks have unavoidably hampered African countries' current development efforts and may also have created longer term hurdles for their economies.

The second issue that was investigated was whether there are factors that may cause long-term impediments to sub-Saharan Africa's development prospects in addition to the typical features that characterize developing countries around the world. If such is the case, a new development architecture could be designed to alleviate these long-term constraints. Sub-Saharan Africa has been afflicted by more than a century of economic underdevelopment and is increasingly losing ground to other developing regions. Characteristics that set it apart and could contribute to its unfavourable situation include demographic challenges such as lower life expectancy, higher population growth, and lower primary school enrolment. These factors limit sub-Saharan Africa's ability to address its social needs, a situation that will be exacerbated if nothing is done to remedy it. Furthermore, sub-Saharan Africa is the developing region with the highest number of landlocked countries, which constitutes a major impediment to trade and integration into the world economy. Moreover, export proceeds of sub-Saharan Africa countries are significantly more variable than in other developing countries, a factor that undermines their capacity to fulfil external debt obligations with certainty and consequently to plan for sustainable long-term development.

In order to achieve the more modest objective of securing economic convergence between sub-Saharan Africa and other developing regions the adverse impact of the characteristics identified above must be mitigated. Sub-Saharan Africa's sectoral priorities should thus include significantly larger expenditures in social development and trade-facilitating infrastructure. New facilities should be integrated into a development finance architecture designed to address the region's needs. With respect to external borrowing, the stock of sub-Saharan Africa's sovereign debt, including that on concessionary terms, should be reduced drastically and replaced with pure grants to sovereign recipients. Debt service payments on outstanding external sovereign debt should be made contingent on a debtor country's export earnings. Given the strong growth potential usually ascribed to the private sector of export-led fast-growing economies, sub-Saharan Africa's private sector should have expanded access to international lending markets.

Aid-assisted development of sub-Saharan Africa could be better achieved through establishment of a development pool and a common pool under the auspices of the United Nations with financial contribution from bilateral and multilateral donors, the private sector, and civil society. The development pool will support sub-Saharan Africa countries' investment in priority sectors such as social development and infrastructure, while the common pool will be open to projects and programmes of countries, regional economic communities, and the AU. A number of levies could provide additional funding to the ACA in charge of administration of the two pools as well as to African countries' revenue base. The proposed innovations would entail changes in the mandate and operations of the key financial development institutions to facilitate the enhanced economic growth of sub-Saharan Africa.

References

Faye, Michael, John McArthur, Jeffrey Sachs, et al. (2004). 'The Challenges Facing Landlocked Developing Countries.' *Journal of Human Development and Capabilities*, vol. 5, no. 1, pp. 31–68.

Limão, Nuno and Anthony Venables (1999). *Infrastructure, Geographical Disadvantage, and Transport Costs*. World Bank Policy Research Working Paper No. 2257. World Bank, Washington DC.

MacKellar, Landis, Andreas Woergoetter, and Julia Woerz (2000). *Economic Development Problems of Landlocked Countries*. Transition Economic Series No. 14, January. Institute for Advanced Studies. <ideas.repec.org/p/ihs/ihstep/14.html> (August 2010).

Organisation for Economic Co-operation and Development (2005). *The Paris Declaration on Aid Effectiveness: Ownership, Harmonisation, Alignment, Results, and Mutual Accountability.* Paris. <www.oecd.org/dataoecd/11/41/34428351. pdf> (August 2010).

Seck, Diery (2006). 'A New Architecture for the Financing of Africa's Development'. United Nations African Institute for Economic Development and Planning, Unpublished.

Seck, Diery (2008). 'On the Design of a New Mechanism for Africa's External Debt.' In S. Boko and D. Seck, eds., *NEPAD and the Future of Economic Policy in Africa* (Trenton, NJ: Africa World Press).

Appendix 11.1   List of countries sampled for the computation of statistics of real growth of export earnings, 1970–2007

Sub-Saharan Africa	Latin America and Caribbean	East Asia and Pacific
Benin	**Caribbean**	**China**
Burkina Faso	Argentina	Indonesia
Burundi	Bahamas	Laos
Cameroon	Barbados	Malaysia
Republic of Congo	Belize	Myanmar
Cote d'Ivoire	Bolivia	Papua New Guinea
Equatorial Guinea	Brazil	Philippines
Ethiopia	Chile	Thailand
Gabon	Colombia	Tonga
The Gambia	Costa Rica	Vanuatu
Ghana	Dominican Republic	
Guinea	Ecuador	**Middle East and North Africa**
Kenya	Guatemala	**Bahrain**
Lesotho	Haiti	Egypt
Madagascar	Honduras	Iran
Malawi	Jamaica	Jordan
Mali	Mexico	Kuwait
Mozambique	Paraguay	Lebanon
Nigeria	Peru	Libya
Senegal	Trinidad and Tobago	Morocco
South Africa	Uruguay	Oman
Swaziland	Venezuela	Saudi Arabia
Tanzania		Sudan
Togo	**South Asia**	Syrian Arab Republic
Uganda	Bangladesh	Tunisia
Zambia	Bhutan	
Zimbabwe	India	
	Maldives	
	Nepal	
	Pakistan	
	Sri Lanka	

Note: The sample period is shorter for some countries.

Appendix 11.2   Net disbursements of official development assistance to sub-Saharan Africa by recipient

(US$ million at 2006 prices and exchange rates)

	1991–92 average	1996–97 average	2004	2005	2006	2007
Angola	400	517	1217	449	171	225
Benin	356	298	410	356	375	429
Botswana	167	120	50	50	66	97
Burkina Faso	557	477	675	714	870	848
Burundi	365	103	380	375	415	425
Cameroon	800	553	819	429	1,689	1,746
Cape Verde	142	140	152	168	138	148
Central African Republic	223	147	115	95	133	161
Chad	324	312	346	395	284	324
Comoros	72	40	27	26	30	40
Congo, Democratic Republic of	482	198	1920	1847	2049	1112
Congo	159	435	121	1,493	259	116
Côte d'Ivoire	894	829	170	115	251	152
Djibouti	139	106	66	78	117	103
Equatorial Guinea	81	36	31	40	26	28
Eritrea	–	175	281	365	129	142
Ethiopia	1463	846	1914	1973	1948	2227
Gabon	139	98	42	54	31	44
Gambia	136	46	58	63	74	67
Ghana	958	673	1469	1179	1176	1055
Guinea	526	412	286	206	161	207
Guinea-Bissau	142	187	80	81	82	112
Kenya	1126	616	682	786	943	1184
Lesotho	175	120	101	71	72	120
Liberia	180	147	227	240	268	645
Madagascar	521	734	1313	942	750	828
Malawi	732	505	534	599	684	676
Mali	577	552	617	731	825	926
Mauritania	269	300	197	205	190	333
Mauritius	73	40	34	34	19	67
Mayotte	96	141	219	208	338	365
Mozambique	1659	1154	1319	1332	1605	1619
Namibia	212	217	183	117	145	190
Niger	468	355	575	534	514	498
Nigeria	338	236	610	6603	11 432	1867
Rwanda	459	434	516	595	586	655
Sáo Tomé and Principe	72	51	35	33	22	33

Senegal	823	594	1104	707	826	771
Seychelles	27	22	11	15	14	3
Sierra Leone	152	186	396	361	344	489
Somalia	549	106	215	248	392	351
South Africa	-	540	662	701	720	733
St. Helena	23	22	28	23	28	39
Sudan	917	220	1061	1892	2052	1951
Swaziland	72	34	23	46	35	58
Tanzania	1562	1118	1860	1534	1825	2643
Togo	269	159	68	86	79	110
Uganda	900	929	1288	1229	1549	1592
Zambia	1218	756	1194	1191	1426	967
Zimbabwe	762	428	199	386	279	430
South of Sahara region	909	1007	1513	1153	1590	1577
Total	23 668	18 472	27 412	33 154	40 025	31 521

Source: Organisation for Economic Co-operation and Development, Development Assistance Committee, Statistics Online, Table 30.

Appendix 11.3 Total net flows from development assistance committee members by type of flow (in million U.S.\$)

	1991–92 average	1996–97 average	2003	2004	2005	2006	2007
Official development assistance	58 453	52 028	69 065	79 432	107 078	104 370	103 491
1. Bilateral grants and grant-like flows	35 678	33 925	50 888	57 246	83 432	79 440	75 326
of which: technical cooperation	13 143	13 515	18 352	18 672	20 732	22 242	14 779
Developmental food aid	1707	951	1196	1169	887	956	1051
Humanitarian aid	2003	1783	4360	5193	7121	6751	6278
Debt forgiveness	4508	3260	8317	7134	24 999	18 600	9624
Administrative costs	2314	2788	3545	4032	4115	4250	4618
2. Bilateral loans	7139	1818	-1153	-2942	-1008	-2531	-2433
3. Contributions to multilateral institutions	17 513	16 286	19 330	25 127	24 653	27 461	30 598
of which: United Nations	4694	4209	4828	5129	5469	5239	5801
European Commission	4350	4794	6946	8906	9258	9931	11 714
International Development Association	5505	4027	3120	5690	4827	6787	5609
Regional development banks	1503	1564	1734	2274	2096	2466	2361
Other official flows	8097	5926	-350	-5601	1430	-10 728	-6438
1. Bilateral	7474	6164	-820	-5349	2262	-10 551	-6962
2. Multilateral	622	-238	470	-252	-832	-177	524
Private flows at market terms	29 996	126 216	46 573	75 262	179 559	194 761	325 350
1. Direct investment	25 495	68 008	49 340	76 901	100 622	127 925	188 696
2. Bilateral portfolio investment	6324	59 222	-6164	-3544	73 335	60 910	133 199
3. Multilateral portfolio investment	-1075	-3537	1083	-4657	40	2789	-9727
4. Export credits	-748	2523	2313	6561	5563	3137	13 182
Net grants by non-governmental organizations	5704	5480	10 239	11 320	14 712	14 648	18 508
Total	102 249	189 649	125 527	160 412	302 779	303 051	440 912

Sources: Organisation for Economic Co-operation and Development, Development Assistance Committee, Online Statistics.

Chapter 12

Africa in the Face of the Crisis

George M. von Furstenberg

For more than 25 years prior to 2000, sub-Saharan Africa, excluding the Republic of South Africa, has been growing more slowly than other developing regions. On a per capita purchasing power basis, sub-Saharan Africa often did not grow at all or even declined. After a decade during which the average annual rate of growth of real per capita income had been –0.7 percent, that rate averaged 2 percent between 2000 and 2006. By 2009, that rate had again turned negative, and might be close to –1 percent according to one forecast (World Bank 2009, 30). Because of its abysmal record, Africa has become home to an undue share of 'the bottom billion', 70 percent of whom are in the continent of Africa, many in sub-Saharan Africa (Collier 2007, 7).

This chapter gives reason to doubt that tinkering with existing aid mechanisms can change this dismal situation as long as those in power in sub-Saharan Africa, along with their western partners, serve themselves first. This is what many of them still do with remarkable regularity and brutality, and no durable change is in sight. There is also no blanket justification for using the 2007–09 financial crisis and its aftermath as an emergency fundraising tool for sub-Saharan Africa. Aid is wasted at best and poisonous at worst as long as considerable parts of this region, including some of its largest states, are governed to heap abundance on their rulers and their retinue and on foreign and domestic cronies and affiliates, while also oiling the machinery for repressing popular discontent.

This judgement may be viewed as harsh and presumptuous coming from a 'westerner', and its morality is in need of immediate defence, for what African potentates, from petty to supreme, hate most is for the postcolonial West, which immiserized and brutalized the African people long before they did, to take them to task for being corrupt. Jean Ziegler (2008, ch. 4) argues for those potentates that corruption may be useful for the West because, by discrediting local governments, it makes them willing accomplices of transcontinental exploitation schemes and enterprises, eager to share in the spoils and repressive methods of neo-colonization. In recent decades, new foreign partners and promoters of local corruption have come to offer their services, such as discreet entities sponsored by the Chinese government, although 'perhaps the material distinction is not between Chinese capital and Western, but rather between the merely rapacious, and the more sophisticated' (Marks 2007, 3).

Still, if the West is to blame for so much evil, past, and present, in sub-Saharan Africa and elsewhere in the 'South' and justly hated as Ziegler claims, it should perhaps just pull itself together and engage in moral and financial acts of contrition, no longer daring to wag its forked tongue at its former colonies from pedestals above. What right have those who are condemned by their own professions of ethics and humanity to make restitution, to ask whether their reparation payments are going to be well spent? The answer is that they have no such right, but a compelling moral duty and practical obligation to insist on aid effectiveness nonetheless. Absent such a caveat, any attempted atonement or expiation would end up in the wrong coffers and, by encouraging defrauding and abuse of power, become its own mockery.

An Untrustworthy New Aid Mechanism to the Rescue?

The reason for sub-Saharan Africa's extraordinary plight cannot be that it has been disproportionately neglected or mismanaged by donors in the official development assistance (ODA) process. By relying more on home-grown development strategies rather than on outside aid and intervention, a number of developing countries have succeeded while getting far less per head, and on less concessionary terms, through the same channels (see Easterly 2008). Proposals like that advocated by Diéry Seck in Chapter 11 are not a hopeful new beginning but amount to more, indeed much more, of the same, although there may be some incidental turnover in the privileged cast of principal beneficiaries and beneficiary institutions. The proposal is henceforth to shun sovereign debt and to establish pools of grant funds to be fed from various sources, including ODA, which are to be administered by recipient committees such as the, as-yet non-existent, Aid Council for Africa (ACA) that would 'report to the secretary general of the United Nations'. Bad debts create a stench as they rot and thus send a warning. But wasted or misappropriated and mismanaged grants, whether for social development, infrastructure, or various negotiation-intensive construction projects that are corruption's delight are a feast for aid administrators: Grants *à fonds perdu* do not talk, and the donors are not very welcome, able, or motivated to monitor what became of them. As Chinese representatives and their government-sponsored enterprises have been quick to learn from the old postcolonial masters, opaque transfers in aid into government pockets may be lost to the receiving country but not to them. Rather, they are investments that may be expected to be richly repaid by the future spoils from preferential contract awards whose terms and accounts remain well hidden.

The ACA, as already described years ago in an unsigned paper put out by the United Nations Economic Commission for Africa (UNECA), 'would include representatives of donor countries ..., of African countries, and of the private sector and civil society' (UNECA 2006, 29). Seck wants this checkered assembly to administer two pools mostly of grant funds, a development pool and a common pool, whose current description is the same as in the UNECA paper. The common pool established 'under the auspices of the United Nations', would be available for 'projects and programmes of [sub-Saharan African] countries, regional economic communities and the AU [African Union]'. Its funding base is to be diverse. Members of the Development Assistance Committee (DAC) of the Organisation for Economic Co-operation and Development (OECD) are urged to channel increasing amounts principally to the development pool for social development and infrastructure. Their contributions are to top out within five years at 0.5 percent of their gross national income (GNI). Since the GNI of high-income OECD countries in 2007 was $35 642 billion in purchasing power parity (PPP) international dollars, this cash-equivalent aid contribution would have been $178 billion if applicable at that time.

The proposed half-percent target, unchanged from 2006, would involve severe aid overload. The World Bank's World Development Indicators database shows that in 2007, the last year for which such data were as yet available, the GNI of high-income OECD members that essentially constitute the membership of the DAC is 24 times greater than that of sub-Saharan Africa as a whole and 46 times greater than sub-Saharan Africa minus Nigeria and South Africa. Hence if the DAC members were to give 0.5 percent of their GNI to sub-Saharan Africa each year, the region would receive an amount equal to 12 percent of its GNI from that source and equal to 23 percent if the aid is focused on sub-Saharan Africa net of South Africa and Nigeria. These two largest countries in sub-Saharan Africa may not qualify for parts of the development pool funding because they exceed the per capita income limit to be set on eligibility. Since there would still be a number of other sources of grants-in-aid for sub-Saharan Africa, the resulting aid shock could very well overwhelm any prospect of prudent use and accountability.

Neither the UNECA document nor the present proposal makes any attempt to explain where the target aid percentage for the benefit of sub-Saharan Africa comes from. In 2008, total net ODA from DAC countries represented 0.3 percent of members' combined GNI (OECD 2009, 30). Hence asking 0.5 percent for sub-Saharan Africa alone from 2013 on is politically unattainable as long as the economic and social returns to ODA flows remain low. It is also unneeded if prospective returns, while high on average, threaten to become low or even negative at the margin on account of debt overload.

Donors Undermine Aid Effectiveness But Should Give More Anyway?

Buttressed only by repeated references to the Paris Declaration, the proposal rarely misses an opportunity to pillory the bad aid practices of donors while never blaming the recipients. The proposal states that 'although most of the critiques levelled at ODA are known and discussed in the Paris Declaration and elsewhere, the record for sub-Saharan Africa does not provide evidence of improvement likely to enhance the region's prospects for economic development'. In fact the Paris Declaration on Aid Effectiveness can be read rather differently (see OECD 2005). It can be seen to emphasize the mutuality of obligations between donors and recipients, and to recognize difficult facts of life in Africa. Thus, among the remaining five challenges to address it includes

> corruption and lack of transparency, which erode public support, impede effective resource mobilisation and allocation and divert resources away from activities that are vital for poverty reduction and sustainable economic development. Where corruption exists, it inhibits donors from relying on partner country systems (OECD 2005, 1).

Perhaps there is a problem not so much with the bad practices of the donors as with the governance failures of the recipients. Requiring donors to place their trust in local systems with processes that are intentionally obscure and prone to corruption is an affront to donors' fiduciary responsibilities toward their own taxpayers. While the proposal may seek to find fault with the donors' *modus operandi* at every turn, there is a refreshing candor in other parts of it, as when it concedes that soft loan flows from official sources have not strangled development in sub-Saharan Africa, and that debt forgiveness has become routine. The proposal therefore wants to do away with (all but perhaps some temporary countercyclical) sovereign borrowing that does not mean what it says in favour of grants front-up. It does not explain how the temptation to go for sovereign borrowing that is so forgiving and attractive can in fact be resisted by developing countries at any time, good or bad, or how debt forgiveness can be prevented from opening the door to a new round of heavy borrowing. Worrying about the details of implementation of its proposed directives is not the proposal's business.

Carmen Reinhart, Kenneth Rogoff, and Miguel Savastano have documented serial default and debt intolerance for a number of countries (Reinhart and Rogoff 2009, ch. 2; Reinhart et al. 2003; Reinhart and Rogoff 2004). Many of those countries are developing, and many of those are now past the completion point for debt forgiveness under the Heavily Indebted Poor Countries (HIPC) Initiative. The reasons for their recurring debt crises usually are found in lack of fiscal control and other agency and coordination problems—including time inconsistency—characteristic of misrule in states whose elites are good at living off their own people in cahoots with the rest of the world. Even not so poor countries in this political condition will seek to borrow over and over again as much and as quickly as they can, as Argentina has demonstrated unfailingly for many decades. The international lending process with developing countries, like sub-prime lending and securitization in advanced countries, is so riddled with agency problems that it is hard to keep overlending from accommodating the appetite for overborrowing, thereby sustaining the pattern of serial default.

There is a need to consider continued reforms of governance and legal systems, including land law, in more sub-Saharan Africa countries, because from 1998 to 2007 their record on those crucial issues has been decidedly mixed. As Daniel Kaufmann, Aart Kraay, and Massimo Mastruzzi (2008) have documented with their World Bank Institute World Governance Indicators, changes in the categories 'voice and accountability', 'political stability and absence of violence', 'government effectiveness', 'regulatory quality', 'rule of law', and 'control of corruption' have been significantly positive in some cases and negative in other sub-Saharan African countries, and horror cases remain. Avinash Dixit (2009) has dealt sensitively with the subject of governance institution building and economic activity and with incorporating polycentric planning in poverty reduction strategies.

As Seck finds no fault, and hence no needed reforms, within sub-Saharan African countries or their government institutions, the focus is put on external afflictions that have made the region fall ever farther behind at least until the turn of the last century. Sub-Saharan Africa contains many land-locked countries, and short of political realignment, that adverse circumstance is truly exogenous. UNECA (2009) has written, however, that 'it is not just high transport costs that impede intraregional and external trade in the African sub-region; bribery and long delays on the trade corridors are also hampering factors, according to the conclusions of a trade facilitation workshop on the promotion of intra-African trade'. When it comes to the prevalence of scourges such as malaria, HIV/AIDS, and high fertility and infant mortality rates, the causes and effects of poverty easily get muddled. Indeed, all the proposal has to say about Africa's fertility rates is that with higher income per capita they may well fall.

Has Sub-Sahara Africa Suffered Disproportionately from the Crisis?

Another external susceptibility that apparently cannot be changed according to Seck's proposal is that sub-Saharan Africa has 'proven to be vulnerable to global economic crises with little capacity to tackle them'. This kind of victim's lament has gained credibility through frequent repetition in policy circles (see, for instance, Kirton 2009; Lombardi 2009). Yet its factual predication does not hold, at least not in the latest global financial crisis that affected advanced economies first and foremost. The *World Economic Outlook* (WEO) published by the International Monetary Fund ([IMF] 2009b, 69) in October 2009, for instance, has real growth in gross domestic product (GDP) in advanced economies fall from 2.7 percent in 2007 to 0.6 percent in 2008 and –3.4 percent in 2009, before staging a tepid recovery to 1.3 percent in 2010. Growth in sub-Saharan Africa (excluding South Africa and Nigeria), by contrast, is expected to decline from a much higher level in 2007 and then to recover quickly and impressively by 2010. The GDP growth numbers for sub-Saharan Africa just characterized fall from 8.1 percent per annum in 2007 to 6.6 percent in 2008 and to 2.6 percent in 2009 before rebounding to 5.1 percent in 2010 (IMF 2009c). Thus the reflection of the 2007–09 global financial and economic crisis in sub-Saharan Africa looks like a small 'v' centred on 2009, while it appears like a large 'U' in advanced economies with its sides distended from 2007 to 2010. Claims that the crisis would hit sub-Saharan African countries harder than advanced economies in the IMF classification, and most likely with a lag, have both been refuted by the available evidence and by WEO forecasts.

Instead, the sub-Saharan African countries were last in and first out of the crisis. With regard to major sub-Saharan African regions, annual growth expected for 2009 (compared with 2008, in parentheses) is 5.4 percent (8.7 percent) in the Horn of Africa, 4.3 percent (5.8 percent) in the Great Lakes Region, and 2.6 percent (5.3 percent) in West and Central Africa, including Ghana and Nigeria (IMF 2009b). All advanced countries, including newly industrialized Asian economies (Korea, Taiwan, Hong Kong, and Singapore), can only wish they would have been so lucky with respect to their recent growth.

The picture is less favourable to sub-Saharan Africa on a per capita basis on account of its high annual population growth of 2 percent. But even on that basis, the high-income countries do much worse in the forecast. Obviously, since the objective must be to compare not just dollar magnitudes of damage but also their welfare equivalents to judge which group has been hit hardest, it is necessary to specify a social welfare or utility function and an aggregation routine to explain what is meant by such comparative judgements. For instance, subsuming a logarithmic utility function for the representative person in every $i=1,\ldots s$ region distinguished in a world of s regions, as was implicitly done in the comments above, implies the following judgement: Comparing two regions with the same population but a 46-fold difference in per capita income to start with, an absolute decline in per capita income that is 46 times as large in the rich than the poor region would imply an equal percentage decline and hence welfare loss in each region and in world welfare. Hence only if the GNI per capita of the poor region would shrink by more than $\frac{1}{46}$th of the absolute decline experienced in the rich region's per capita income would the poor region do worse by the log-utility standard for welfare comparisons with these data.

The reason for the relatively benign outcome for sub-Saharan Africa by this standard is that although steeply falling demand in advanced countries, lower commodity prices and remittances, and greater risk aversion in foreign lending and foreign direct investment have had an adverse effect, the importance of oil exports and exports of other commodities differs greatly among sub-Saharan Africa countries, and their financial systems are relatively insulated. As the IMF's *Regional Economic Outlook* pointed out in 2009, 'sub-Saharan African economies [were] somewhat more resilient in 2008 than those in other regions, mainly due to lags in the transmission of real sector shocks but partly because sub-Saharan African financial systems are less integrated with global financial markets' (IMF 2009a, 5). Furthermore, a study by Laura Beny and Lisa Cook (2009) with data for 1960–2005 concluded that while both policy reforms and the commodity boom contributed to Africa's high-growth experience in 2000–05, the fact that the former has not been found less important than the latter factor suggests that continued policy reform, now sadly stalled in most sub-Saharan African countries, could have compensated for the subsequent commodity bust.

Variability of Export Proceeds and Debt Capacity

One of the distinguishing characteristics of sub-Saharan Africa, according to the proposal, is the high variability of its export revenue. The subject needs to be examined, as follows. The time (t) rate of change in the export proceeds, P_xX, of a sub-Saharan African country, in U.S. dollars deflated by the U.S. producer price index, PPI_{US}, is:

$$(d/dt)\ln[(P_x/PPI_{US})X] = (p_x-ppi_{us}) + rxq = rtt + rx \qquad (1)$$

where lower-case letters indicate rates of change, rtt is the rate of change (r) in the terms of trade (tt) which is a relative price index of exports over imports, and rxq is the rate of change in the quantity of exports, xq. Thus the variance (var) of the rate of growth of export proceeds deflated by the U.S. PPI can be decomposed into:

$$E[rtt + rxq-E(rtt+rxq)]^2 = var(rtt)+var(rxq)+2covar(rtt, rxq) \qquad (2)$$

where E is the expectations operator.

Compared with most of the developing countries elsewhere, in particular China and India, sub-Saharan Africa experiences greater variance in its terms of trade and a smaller variance in quantity to the extent there is short-run inelasticity of supply and demand in the agricultural, metal, and mineral segments of its exports. Then large price fluctuations caused by shifts in world demand meet with little quantity response. However, the covariance (covar) between the rates of change in the terms of trade and in export volume is positive. In countries such as China and India, on the other hand, the price elasticities of supply and demand for their exports are high and the variance of the terms of trade is low, while the variance of the quantity response is large. Rapid productivity growth in manufacturing and service sectors makes supply the active element, rather than global demand, that most affects these countries. As a result, the more the terms of trade with the United States decline, the more disproportionate are the growth in productivity and international competitiveness in these countries and hence in their export volume. In short, the covariance between rates of change in the terms of trade and in export quantity in much of South-East Asia is likely to be negative.

Hence the principal reason for the volatility of export proceeds being higher in sub-Saharan Africa than in other developing countries according to this conjecture is that the last term in equation (2), the covariance between price and quantity change, is positive for sub-Saharan Africa—as it is for undiversified exporters of highly storable, internationally traded raw and processed materials and of natural resources anywhere—but negative for most other developing countries, particularly in South-East Asia. Being indicative of, but not a cause of, a low level of development, the sub-Saharan African positive price and quantity covariance condition may well have applied in other countries at past stages of development, including Bolivia, Chile, and Venezuela. That condition adds urgency to sub-

Saharan Africa saving more in good times to be better prepared for the bad times, and diversifying and expanding its sources of wealth further beyond natural resources.

Economists usually see at least two opportunities that come from operating in an open economy rather than closed one. Access to international capital markets may be beneficial if it is used to draw more resources into the country that are applied to productive capital formation and technology transfer, and if international borrowing and lending are used for greater smoothing of domestic consumption. If all is well managed and on market terms, high variability of trend-stationary export proceeds reduces countries' debt capacity to a level sufficiently low to allow them to be net international borrowers when export proceeds temporarily fall short. Instead of treating high variability of export proceeds as something to be managed and reduced through diversification, Seck's proposal fatalistically treats it as driven by chance, indeed as a one-dimensional unit-root process. It does not say whether trend-adjusted mean reversion could credibly be rejected in long time series or whether there is co-integration with other variables that could be subject to a degree of policy control. It pictures the confidence interval for a country's total export revenues expanding like a cone linearly with the length T of the forward time horizon. It does not explain why it specifies export proceeds as a random walk in the first place where things could go from bad to worse all the way to hell purely by chance and not by human agency, and why then the confidence interval would grow at the rate T in Figure 11.1, rather than at the rate $\sqrt{T}$ which would be the correct answer for a random-walk process.

Technical grumbles aside, many entrepreneurial development projects in the real world benefit from seasoning so that the risk of failing falls as they succeed in becoming firmly established. Similarly, entering into new foreign markets with fresh borrowing is riskier than defending a well-established turf built long ago with debt. Debt tends to be seasoned and amortized as it ages. It may be collateralized and have seniority over later debts. Lengthening the average maturity of debt is exactly what the doctor ordered for countries with volatile prospects that do not want to depend entirely on the fickle mercies of the short-term international debt market. Indeed, the entire notion that debt becomes more vulnerable to balance-of-payments crises as it ages takes a very disjointed view of the process since such a crisis may throw the timely servicing of any kind of foreign-currency debt, long or short, into doubt. Cross-default clauses help make this so. Addressing none of these points, the proposal's diffusion process on export revenue and its improper coupling of gross current-account proceeds to net repayment of a particular debt, mechanically make repayment of debt less certain the longer the pay-back period. It concludes that there should be less of such debt, even debt extended on highly concessionary terms by official development agencies, in the first place.

Internal consistency is not always strictly observed in Seck's proposal. After first characterizing export proceeds as a random walk, he argues for making servicing external debt legally contingent on the export-earnings performance of the debtor country because 'shortfalls in its export revenues will be expected to be minor and of limited duration'. Debt contracts with interest rates that vary inversely with the price indexes of certain export commodities have existed in the market, and other insurance arrangements, such as catastrophe bonds based on weather and rainfall, have developed. All such instruments are based on triggers entirely beyond the control of the insured. For lack of this qualification, indexing debt contracts to officially registered export proceeds is a bad idea. Take a country that has insisted on letting its official exchange rate appreciate excessively in real terms while smuggling and a grey market conducted at a realistic exchange rate flourish. Should such a country get automatic debt relief because its officially recorded exports have plummeted?

Until about two decades ago, the IMF ran a compensatory financing facility based on entitlement to drawings by a formula that was much abused by sub-Saharan Africa countries. These automatic drawings were ostensibly designed to compensate those countries for unexpectedly large declines in their proceeds from resource exports that were beyond their control (but not their statistical manipulations). In sub-Saharan Africa as elsewhere in aid-gathering communities, bad ideas for automating aid flows may change their pitch but never die.

What's the Use: *Cui Bono*?

Cronyism and log rolling among fellow recipient countries are built into the aid seeking of official regional bodies. Seck's proposal is silent on these internal obstacles to aid effectiveness while reflecting adversely on donor-specific conditionality or political targeting of recipients by donors. It makes only a single grudging reference to accepting credible external accountability, not further specified, for the torrent of grants it proposes, and any mechanism for accountability to a country's own citizens for the grants' best use appears absent entirely. Zimbabwe's Robert Mugabe and his Chinese supporters and other 'aid' givers and receivers operating in the dark would rejoice. As William Easterly has noted about the objectives of aid recipients,

> many developing countries are characterized by 'clientelism'—the giving and granting of favours and patronage; the distribution of economic rents in order to ensure political stability ... The funnelling of aid away from the intended recipients and into the hands of the state elite is an unsurprising result of pervasive clientelism ... Bad governance may not only lead to misappropriation of aid, but aid flows may actually have worsened governance in Africa (Easterly 2007, 672).

Easterly and Tobias Pfutze (2008, 48) also find 'the UN agencies typically having the highest ratios of operating costs to aid by a large margin. The UN Development Programme is the worst, spending much more on its administrative budget than it gives in aid'. Obviously in order to continue their wasteful ways in league with their development partners in official positions, these supposedly legitimating agencies like more grant money to administer with little accountability and oversight.

As others have also found, because of political obstacles to good use, the case for foreign aid to Africa is weak (see, for example, Cancutt and Kumar 2008). Yet realism requires a closing comment. Evidence-based examinations, no matter how disillusioning their findings, will not stop aid from continuing to be given without public accountability in either donor or recipient countries. The reason is that such aid has much more potent and interconnected advocates than aid effectiveness. The notional advocates of the latter mostly are the wretchedly poor, who politically count for little beyond being used in the rigged, confusing, and sometimes bloody elections and election riots in sub-Saharan African countries. The beneficiaries of aid, by contrast, are all those who can render such aid ineffective for their own account. So they push for more aid to let negligent taxpayers in donor countries, who do not know how or why they pay for what abroad, better grease the skids. Perverse as it seems, aid ineffectiveness thus drives the aid business: if aid were highly effective, it would have far fewer powerful advocates and friends. Conversely, those exceptional countries that have made a success of home-grown development already may also be in good shape to absorb foreign aid and coordinated foreign technical assistance without serious adverse economic and political side effects (Annen and Kosempel 2009).

References

Annen, Kurt and Stephen Kosempel (2009). 'Foreign Aid, Donor Fragmentation, and Economic Growth.' *B.E. Journal of Macroeconomics*, vol. 9, no. 1 (Contributions), art. 33.

Beny, Laura N. and Lisa D. Cook (2009). 'Metals or Management? Explaining Africa's Recent Economic Growth Performance.' *American Economic Review*, vol. 99, no. 2, pp. 268–275.

Cancutt, Elizabeth M. and Krishna B. Kumar (2008). 'Africa: Is Aid an Answer?' *B.E. Journal of Macroeconomics*, vol. 8, no. 1 (Advances), art. 32.

Collier, Paul (2007). *The Bottom Billion: Why the Poorest Countries Are Failing and What Can Be Done About It* (Oxford: Oxford University Press).

Dixit, Avinash K. (2009). 'Government Institutions and Economic Activity.' *American Economic Review*, vol. 99, no. 1, pp. 5–24.

Easterly, William (2007). 'Are Aid Agencies Improving?' *Economic Policy*, vol. 22, no. 52, pp. 633–678.

Easterly, William (2008). 'Can the West Save Africa?' *Journal of Economic Literature*, vol. 47, no. 2, pp. 373–447.

Easterly, William and Tobias Pfutze (2008). 'Where Does the Money Go? Best and Worst Practices in Foreign Aid.' *Journal of Economic Perspectives*, vol. 22, no. 2, pp. 29–52.

International Monetary Fund (2009a). *Regional Economic Outlook: Sub-Saharan Africa.* World Economic and Financial Surveys, April. International Monetary Fund, Washington DC. <www.imf.org/external/pubs/ft/reo/2009/afr/eng/sreo0409.htm> (August 2010).

International Monetary Fund (2009b). *World Economic Outlook: Sustaining the Recovery.* October. International Monetary Fund, Washington DC. <www.imf.org/external/pubs/ft/weo/2009/02> (August 2010).

International Monetary Fund (2009c). *World Economic Outlook: Sustaining the Recovery – List of Tables, Part B.* Statistical Index. International Monetary Fund, Washington DC. <www.imf.org/external/pubs/ft/weo/2009/02/pdf/tblpartb.pdf> (August 2010).

Kaufman, Daniel, Aart Kraay, and Massimo Mastruzzi (2008). *Governance Matters VII: Aggregate and Individual Governance Indicators, 1996–2007.* World Bank Policy Research Working Paper No. 4654. World Bank. <ssrn.com/abstract=1148386> (August 2010).

Kirton, John J. (2009). 'Prospects for the 2009 L'Aquila G8 Summit.' In J.J. Kirton and M. Koch, eds., *The G8 2009: From La Maddalena to L'Aquila* (London: Newsdesk Publications).

Lombardi, Domenico (2009). 'Under Pressure.' In J.J. Kirton and M. Koch, eds., *The G8 2009: From La Maddalena to L'Aquila* (London: Newsdesk Publications).

Marks, Stephen (2007). 'Introduction.' In F. Manji and S. Marks, eds., *African Perspectives on China in Africa* (Cape Town: Fahamu Books).

Organisation for Economic Co-operation and Development (2005). *The Paris Declaration on Aid Effectiveness: Ownership, Harmonisation, Alignment, Results, and Mutual Accountability.* Paris. <www.oecd.org/dataoecd/11/41/34428351.pdf> (August 2010).

Organisation for Economic Co-operation and Development (2009). 'Development Aid: The Funding Challenge.' *OECD Observer*, April, pp. 30–31. <www.oecdobserver.org/news/fullstory.php/aid/2866/Development_aid:_The_funding_challenge.html> (August 2010).

Reinhart, Carmen M. and Kenneth Rogoff (2004). *Serial Default and the 'Paradox' of Rich to Poor Capital Flows.* NBER Working Paper No. 10296. National Bureau of Economic Research. <www.nber.org/papers/w10296> (April 2007).

Reinhart, Carmen M. and Kenneth Rogoff (2009). *This Time Is Different: Eight Centuries of Financial Folly* (Princeton: Princeton University Press).

Reinhart, Carmen M., Kenneth Rogoff, and Miguel A. Savastano (2003). 'Debt Intolerance.' *Brookings Papers on Economic Activity*, vol. 2003, no. 1, pp. 1–74.

United Nations Economic Commission for Africa (2006). 'Emerging Aid Architecture'. Paper presented to the Conference of African Ministers of Finance, Financing for Development: From Commitment to Action in Africa,

Abuja, Nigeria, 21–22 May. <www.uneca.org/f4d/docs/past-f4d/Technical papers/F4D_Emerging Aid Architecture.pdf> (August 2010).

United Nations Economic Commission for Africa (2009). *High Transport Costs, Bribery, Long Delays Impede Intra-African Trade.* <www.uneca.org/eca_ programmes/nrid/default.htm> (August 2010).

World Bank (2009). *Global Development Finance: Charting a Global Recovery.* World Bank, Washington DC. <siteresources.worldbank.org/INTGDF2009/ Resources/gdf_combined_web.pdf> (August 2010).

Zeigler, Jean (2008). *La haine de l'Occident* (Paris: Michel Albin).

Chapter 13
The Broader Impacts
on the Developing World

Sara Savastano

From 2007 to 2009, the global financial system and economy entered an unprecedented severe crisis and the deepest recession since World War II. If losses by financial intermediaries in the 1929 and 1933 crises were estimated to account for 4 percent of the United States gross domestic product (GDP), the overall cost of the 2007–09 crisis far exceeded the previous one, with the banking sector losing $1.7 trillion, equivalent to 11.8 percent of U.S. GDP (White 2008).

Throughout 2009, there was great debate over the origin and development of the crisis. Even though most of the fundamental causes have been widely treated, there is concern about its consequences and the global economic recession that it brought. While developed economies struggled to find more suitable economic policies to cope with this exceptional recession, growth estimates for 2008 and 2009 in developing countries, such as those in Africa, were continuously revised. A key question is, therefore, to what extent the global crisis affected the developing world as the full spread of the global economic crisis.

This chapter reviews the main causes of the crisis in more advanced countries and then analyses the situation of the developing countries, to investigate the extent to which the crisis affected their macroeconomic conditions. It ends with a review of the policy response and the role of the leading economies and the international institutions, in this period of liquidity constraint, to identify economic priorities to help those countries recovering from the crisis and increasing their well-being.

The Global Crisis: Macro and Micro 'Culprits'

There is considerable uncertainty about the resolution of the crisis and its future global repercussions. In January 2009, the *World Economic Outlook* published by the International Monetary Fund (IMF) projected that global growth in real GDP in 2009 would fall by 0.5 percent, its lowest rate since World War II, a downward revision of 1.75 percent from its November projection (IMF 2009a, 2009b). However, in early July, a new update of the projections was released with growth during 2009–10 being a 0.5 percentage point higher than projected in April 2009.

As of January 2010, IMF estimate have been revised. The overall loss in the world GDP output, throughout 2009, has been –0.8 percent. Although growth figures are constantly updated and adjusted, there are some stylized facts about the recent 2007–09 crisis, its origins, and causes. The answers are still very complex, but a consensus is now taking shape. Two sets of factors can be distinguished: macroeconomic and microeconomic conditions (Baily et al. 2008; van den Noord 2009).

Global imbalances, excess liquidity creation, global savings surplus, and excessive investment in housing, notably in the United States, are the most recurrent macroeconomic causes. Global monetary expansion was further amplified by emerging countries that used their savings to finance U.S. current account deficits, imported U.S. monetary policy, and accumulated large reserves (Masera 2009). The crisis became apparent in September-October 2008, when the major investment banks and mortgage loan institutions collapsed. This was followed by credit compression, and the London interbank offered rate (LIBOR) reached an unprecedented 6 percent in September. The result was general panic, together with the collapse of confidence. Credit conditions froze almost everywhere.

Those macroeconomic factors were accompanied by microeconomic dynamics such as poor management risk, and lack of monitoring and supervision from national and international institutions. In addition the downward spiral of the bank's assets due the mark-to-market valuation of 'sub-prime securities' created a distortion between financial and real economy (van den Noord 2009).

To summarize the existing literature, the causes can be summarized as easy credit, bad loans, weak regulation and supervision of complex financial instruments, debt default, insolvency of key financial institutions, a loss of credibility and trust, and financial panic and mass selling-off of stocks and a hoarding of cash by banks and individuals (Barth 2008; Bicksler; Taylor 2009; Naudé 2009). These factors contributed to a widespread credit crunch and a subsequent decrease in most of the macroeconomic variable such as consumption, investment, and trade. Policy makers responded to mitigate the difficulties in the financial system by cuts in interest rates and liquidity expansion and to support spending by a fiscal package.

From a mere micro perspective, looking at the impact of the crisis on household and global poverty, two distinct approaches should be considered. On the one hand, Shaohua Chen and Martin Ravallion (2009) analyse the impact of the crisis on household income and consumption and use those variables to estimate the overall impact on poverty. On the other hand, Maros Ivanic and Will Martin (2009) predict changes in prices and income flows to analyse the impact of the crisis on household, and therefore on poverty estimates of group of households. Using the first approach, Chen and Ravallion find that the impact of the crisis on poverty would add 64 million people to the total living on less than $2 a day. Compared to the pre-crisis projections, this is equivalent to increase poverty of an additional 1 percent. The pre-crisis poverty estimates pointed toward a poverty reduction from 42 percent to 38 percent. The crisis added an additional 1 percent, namely the poverty reduction would fall from 42 percent to 39 percent, reducing the global poverty rate from 42 percent to 39 percent, just a percentage point higher than the level estimated prior the crisis. Ivanic and Martin use the results of a modelling study by Warren McKibbin and Andrew Stoeckel (2009) to assess the impacts on rural and urban poverty rates in 10 developing countries. The authors found that the declines in consumer prices seem to have a positive impact on poverty, but this trend could be reversed by declines in wages and employment and by reductions in transfers and remittances.

There were positive signs of a rapid economic upturn, thanks to the macroeconomic and financial policy support implemented by leading economies. However, recovery has been difficult to achieve, at least in the short run. According to the IMF in mid 2009, world economic growth during 2009–10 was expected to be about 0.5 percentage points higher than projected in April 2009, reaching 2.5 percent in 2010 (IMF 2009a, 2009b). The success and the speed of the recovery depend on which of the signals would prevail. Financial shock and decreased global trade must be balanced with decreasing uncertainty and global confidence upsurge.

The Impact of the Crisis on Developing Countries, Including Sub-Saharan Africa

Because most African economies do not have highly developed financial systems and are less integrated into the global financial market, the impact of the crisis was expected to be less drastic on the continent. In addition, even though African countries are far from reaching the Millennium Development Goals (MDGs), their growth rate and sound macroeconomic policies had helped some countries reach higher rates of growth. This achievement was fuelled by a favourable external environment, especially rising commodity prices, debt relief, and aid from the international community (IMF 2009a). After experiencing an average growth rate of 7.8 percent in 2006–07, a drop of several percentage points was projected for 2009.

According to the estimates of the IMF in July 2009, only emerging Asia was expected to reverse its downward trend in the second half of 2009 (IMF 2009a). Growth projections were estimated up to 7 percent in 2010. The improvement was driven by macroeconomic stimulus in China and India, and a faster increase in capital flows, as long as gradual recovery would be confirmed in advanced economies. Latin America was suffering a production shortfall because of slowed down global trade. This contraction would be compensated, however, by rising commodity prices that contributed to growth of about 0.7 percentage points in 2010. Estimates for Central and Eastern European countries were revised downward by 0.7 percentage points for late 2009, but upward by 0.8 percentage points for 2010. Growth projections for emerging Africa and the Middle East were revised downward by 0.3 percentage points and 0.5 percentage points in 2009, respectively, while those for 2010 remained broadly unchanged. Both regions were more negatively affected by the drop in global trade than previously expected.

While the channels of transmission might differ, many developing countries, be they emerging market countries or poor countries in Africa, escaped the impact of the widening crisis. The main channels through which the crisis affected those countries were trade and financial markets.

Although the global crisis started in 2007, the main impact on developing countries started to emerge only in late 2008. The interest rate spread on sovereign lending of developing countries started to increase to a peak in the last quarter of 2008 (Ivanic and Martin 2009). Higher interest rates, together with credit shortages, caused a decline in investment of both developing and more advanced countries.

While countries' exposure to sophisticated securitized instruments of developed country markets was limited, the impact of the crisis on developing countries was been smoother (Lin 2008). In countries such as China, where the banking system is still mostly under public control, the contagion of the sub-prime crisis was been contained. The relationships with international financial institutions are also restricted in countries such as Latin America and, to some extent, Africa. However, most of the Eastern and Central European countries, such as Estonia, Latvia, Lithuania, Belarus, Russia, Ukraine, and Bulgaria, chose fixed exchange rate policies that resulted in large private international inflows of short-term lending, at the cost of a high inflation rate. Even India, where the banking sector was not excessively exposed to the sub-prime crisis, credit flows suddenly contracted; after the collapse of Lehman Brothers in September 2008, money market interest rates spiked higher than 20 percent and remained high for the next month. Foreign direct investment (FDI), one of the main assets of Indian economy, also declined rapidly for the whole period of the crisis.

However, even with limited direct effect given due consideration, the indirect implications of the crisis for developing countries were still profound. Two of the most important impacts were reductions in export earnings and reductions in financial flows to developing countries.

Impact on Export Earnings

Although low-income countries were less affected by financial contagion, declining exports and deteriorating terms of trade for commodity exporters undermined growth prospects in 2009.

For Southern African countries, trade flows have always been dominated by developed countries, reflecting trading patterns established during colonial times. Recently, the traditional trade corridor with these countries has shifted toward emerging economies (Adjepong-Boateng 2009). It has been reinforced with other developing partners.

Consequently, exports have been the major driver of African growth, and the contraction of global demand affects those countries. For 2009 world trade was expected to shrink (a −12 percent change since 2008) for the first time since 1982, due to recessions in high-income countries, the credit crisis, poor private investment, and exchange rate volatility. The largest share of trade of African countries was with Europe and United States. The continuous slowdown of global demand profoundly affected those countries.

In emerging markets such as India, the global downturn has been evident in the steep decline in demand for the countries' exports in major markets, especially in the sectors where the multiplier effect for economic activity is large compared to relative import content, as with garments and textiles, leather, handicrafts, and auto components (Kumar et al. 2009).

The crisis erupted in the wake of sharp increases in the international price of food and fuel, when the continent was trying to recover from negative effects, such as the decline of more than 50 percent, and 20 percent for crude oil, and copper, coffee, and sugar prices respectively between February 2008 and 2009. Those price reductions lowered export revenues and earnings of net-exporter countries. In Burundi, coffee earnings fell by 36 percent between October and November 2008, while in Angola, Cape Verde, and Côte d'Ivoire, agricultural export earnings were expected to decline in 2009 when compared to 2008 (United Nations Economic Commission for Africa [UNECA] 2009).

For commodity import countries the reduction in export earnings came at a time when their balance of payments was already under pressure due to rising food and fuel prices in 2007 and 2008. After the initial slump of the first half of 2008, the crisis was transmitted through capital outflows and primarily through a fall in the price of export commodities such as oil and declines in the volume of commodity exports. A difference emerged between oil-exporting and oil-importing countries. The former were able to cushion the crisis thanks to a prudent financial and economic management, but also because they could rely on large reserves. The impact of the global slowdown was less pronounced in their economies and the economies of their neighbouring countries with which they had growing economic links.

The Impact on Financial Flows

The impact of reduced financial flows was different. Developing countries rely on financial inflows from the rest of the world to facilitate and accelerate economic growth, trade and development. These flows include official development assistance (ODA), investment flows, portfolio flows, flows of remittances, and FDI.

Portfolio flows are, in general, more volatile than those of FDI, especially during a crisis (World Bank 2004). Developing countries that financed growth through lending from foreign banks are expected to experience larger losses. This was the case for most of the developing countries in Central Asia and in Central and Eastern Europe, compared to those in Southern Africa. However, after an earlier tremendous increase, FDI flows to developing countries were expected to decline. According to estimates from the United Nations Conference on Trade and Development ([UNCTAD] 2009), FDI decreased by more than 20 percent in 2008 due to the global financial crisis. Because the crisis originated in developed countries, this decline primarily hit those countries. For the developed world at large, the drop was about 33 percent from the 2007 level. In developing and transition economies, FDI remained more resilient. While in 2007 it exceeded 20 percent, it was estimated to be 4 percent in 2008, before the worst impact of the global financial crisis on FDI inflows was transmitted in 2009. The fall in global FDI in 2008–09 was the result of international investment and two major factors affecting domestic. First, the capability of firms to invest was reduced by decreased access to financial resources, both internally—due to a decline in corporate profits— and externally—due to lower availability and higher costs of finance. Second, the propensity to invest was diminished by negative economic prospects, especially in developed countries hit by the most severe recession of the post-war era.

In economies with very low domestic savings and poor access to capital, migrant workers' remittances can play a vital role in development finance. During economic downturns, migrant workers are often the first to lose their jobs while some may choose to return home. Remittances tend to be more stable than other private capital flows. However, during a deep recession, migrants in developed countries are likely to slow down the remittance flows to their home country. After several years of strong growth, remittance flows to developing countries began to decelerate in the second half of 2008 in response to the global financial crisis (Ratha and Mohapatra 2009). The slowdown of remittances to developing countries was expected to deepen in by 7.3 percent in 2009, although remittances were expected to be more resilient than private capital flows. This extent of the slowdown was hard to predict given uncertainties regarding global growth, commodity prices, and exchange rates. The relationship between global growth and remittances flow is even more complicated because official estimates record only the amount of formal remittances. World Bank remittances data are based on officially recorded remittances. The data do not include estimates of informal remittances. Sub-Sahara Africa only comprises 6.6 percent of global remittances to developing countries. Western Europe and United States are the major sources of sub-Sahara Africa's remittance receipts at 44 percent and 31 percent respectively. Although sub-Saharan Africa's remittances increased by 6.3 percent from 2007 to 2009, they were estimated to fall by just 4.4 percent in 2009, declining from 2.2 percent to 1.9 percent as a share of GDP (Organisation for Economic Co-operation and Development [OECD] and African Development Bank 2009).

Another source of fear for African countries during this period of crisis was represented by the uncertainty about the future flows of ODA, which is among the most important source of funding for financing development. Starting from the Monterrey consensus in 2002, ODA flows to Africa increased from $21 billion to some $40 billion in 2007, and accounted for more than 10 percent of the region's gross national income over the same period (UNECA 2009). Aid volatility can seriously affect some African countries. As a percentage of GDP, ODA plays a procyclical role in less advanced economies, being higher in periods of growth and lower during bad times. ODA fluctuations tend to amplify real business cycles in recipient countries. During a severe crisis, development aid must be transformed into a countercyclical policy (Page 2009). This trend needed to change, to make development act as countercyclically. The G8's 2009 L'Aquila Summit seemed to go in that direction.

Policy Responses

What policy responses were implemented by most African countries and by the international community to help mitigate the impact of the crisis?

The actions undertaken by African countries varied among countries and across regions, subject to their exposure to the crisis and the availability of fiscal stimulus. Such actions included an array of interest rate reductions, the recapitalization of financial institutions, increased liquidity to banks and firms, fiscal stimulus packages, trade policy changes, and regulatory reforms (UNECA 2009). Oil-exporting countries that accumulated foreign reserves after the rise in oil prices in 2008 were able to implement more stringent fiscal policies. Botswana, Egypt, Nigeria, Kenya, Mauritius, and most of the Central African states reduced their interest rates of on average 1 percentage point during the first half of 2009. Contrary to this generalized behaviour, the Democratic Republic of Congo increased its interest rate a few times after December 2008 to overcome high inflation rates.

Some countries also supported their central bank to strengthen their financial system. The actions were diverse such as increasing the minimal capital requirements (Kenya and Algeria), facilitating the financing of small and medium-sized enterprises, and enhancing domestic investment.

Even as countries were in the process of formulating their strategies to face the crisis, there was a general consensus in implementing common policy action.

In emerging countries, and in particular in India, the government launched several economic stimulus packages to face the impact of the crisis. By the end of March 2010, India was able to reach considerable economic recovery, by boosting consumer and public demand. Fiscal stimulus was accompanied by expansionary monetary policy. The Reserve Bank of India drastically cut the interest rate from 9 percent to 4.75 percent, the lowest level since 2004.

The main policy response to the crisis, in developing and emerging economies, was vigorous fiscal stimulus together with an aggressive easing of monetary policy (Lin and Martin 2009). The latter should, in any case, remain supportive, while growth and deflationary risk remained alive (IMF 2009b).

Although some developing countries benefited from the oil shock, thereby accumulating large foreign reserves, countercyclical fiscal policies were needed. In this respect the international community should increase is financial flows. Fiscal policy can help mitigate the spillover effect of lower external demand. External aid should concentrate on the creation of ad hoc social safety nets to protect the poor and vulnerable households from the negative effects of the economic crisis.

In terms of trade policy, measures to support open markets are extremely important for restoring confidence, avoiding protectionist responses, and delivering real opportunities for recovering economic growth in the medium term (OECD 2009). In the 1929 crisis, the U.S. increased import taxes, thereby the prolonging depression, but in the recent crisis countries such as China and India, which opened up their economies, were able to experience rapid economic growth.

Recovery from the Crisis

By the end of 2010, the European Central Bank and the IMF were noticing signs of recovery. According to the January 2010 update of the IMF *World Economic Outlook*, the world economy was slowly recovering after two years of severe crisis (IMF 2010). Policy actions and decisions implemented by most of the developed and developing world were being transformed into positive forecasts on overall economic condition: +3.9 percent in 2010 and +4.3 percent in 2011 of projection on global GDP growth. The recovery was predicted to be driven mostly by newly industrialized Asian economies as well as emerging market and developing economies. GDP growth projections for 2010 were estimated to be about 4.8 percent for newly industrialized Asian economies and 6 percent for emerging market and developing economies. Those numbers confirm the extraordinary circumstances of the recent 2007–09 financial crisis: it originated in what was the largest economy of the world and spread out across the developed world at various speeds and with different magnitudes. The recovery was thus being led by emerging markets, with advanced economies still relying on government stimulus measures. However, the negative side effects of the crisis are not over yet. The financial sector still requires restructuring to reduce the risk of instability and to develop the means to face future and unexpected economic downturns, and the effectiveness and resilience need to be bolstered.

Conclusion

The economic and financial crisis clearly reinforced the need for enhanced international and multilateral cooperation

At the G8 L'Aquila Summit in July 2009, the initial concerns about the support of the international community to help developing countries recovering from the crisis were resolved. In particular, the governments present at L'Aquila recognized the close links among food security, economic growth, social progress, and political stability and peace. Their action plan encompassed general support to less advanced economies and a commitment to substantially increase aid to agriculture and food security. They pledged to mobilize $20 billion over three years (G8 2008).

Each crisis has its own character, and it is difficult to estimate the impact of the crisis on developing and developed economies. The crisis continued, although, by the summer of 2009, the media tried to highlight a slow but perceptible economic recovery. Whether this was a natural policy strategy to boost consumer confidence and relaunch aggregate demand, or whether this upward trend would be confirmed in the long run remained to be seen. However, the continuing effect of the economic downturn remain clearly identifiable.

Each economic or financial crisis exhibits similar characteristics and passes through similar phases. However the 2007–09 crisis has been peculiar in many respects. Most of the crises over the past few decades have had their roots in developing and emerging countries, often resulting from abrupt reversals in capital flows, and from loose domestic monetary and fiscal policies. In contrast, the crisis had had its roots in the U.S. and extended to the rest of the world. In addition, policy makers did not immediately realize that they faced two different crises at the same time: one in the financial system and the other in the real economy.

The governments and international and regional organizations that met at L'Aquila agreed on a strong procyclical political support for food security and agriculture. Additional political support should be addressed as a priority for investments in education, health, and infrastructure as well as protecting government spending on programmes that target the poor.

While there is no guarantee that the success of these international commitments can be ensured, previous experience provides a strong case on the need for a deep analytical *ex ante* and *ex post* evaluation of government development programmes and projects. Governments and international organizations should thus commit themselves to develop further more monitoring and impact evaluation activities.

References

Adjepong-Boateng, Kofi (2009). 'What Are Bankers For...?' Keynote speech presented at the CSAE Annual Conference on 'Africa and the Banking Crisis,' St. Catherine's College, Oxford, 29 March. <www.csae.ox.ac.uk/output/presentations/csaeconference/2009/Keynote-text-2009.pdf> (August 2010).

Baily, Martin N., Robert E. Litan, and Matthew S. Johnson (2008). *The Origins of the Financial Crisis*. Fixing Finance Series, No. 3. Brookings Institution. <www.brookings.edu/papers/2008/11_origins_crisis_baily_litan.aspx> (August 2010).

Barth, James R. (2008). 'U.S. Subprime Mortgage Meltdown.' Paper presented at the 14th Dubrovnik Economic Conference, Dubrovnik, 25 June.

Bicksler, James L. 'Subprime Mortgage Debacle and Its Linkages to Corporate Governance.' *International Journal of Disclosure and Governance*, vol. 5 (November), pp. 295–300.

Chen, Shaohua and Martin Ravallion (2009). 'The Impact of the Global Financial Crisis on the World's Poorest.' 30 April, VoxEU <www.voxeu.org/index.php?q=node/3520> (August 2010).

G8 (2008). 'L'Aquila Joint Statement on Global Food Security: L'Aquila Food Security Initiative.' 9 July, L'Aquila, Italy. <www.g8.utoronto.ca/summit/2009laquila/2009-food.html> (August 2010).

International Monetary Fund (2009a). *World Economic Outlook Update: Contractionary Forces Receding But Weak Recovery Ahead.* July. International Monetary Fund, Washington DC. <www.imf.org/external/pubs/ft/weo/2009/update/02> (August 2010).

International Monetary Fund (2009b). *World Economic Outlook: Crisis and Recovery.* April. International Monetary Fund, Washington DC <www.imf.org/external/pubs/ft/weo/2009/01> (August 2010).

International Monetary Fund (2010). *World Economic Outlook Update: A Policy-Driven, Multispeed Recovery.* January. International Monetary Fund, Washington DC. <www.imf.org/external/pubs/ft/weo/2010/update/01> (August 2010).

Ivanic, Maros and Will Martin (2009). *The Financial Crisis and Vulnerability in Developing Countries.* Paper presented at the conference of the International Association of Agricultural Economists, Beijing, 16–22 August.

Kumar, Rajiv, Bibek Debroy, Jayati Ghosh, et al. (2009). *Global Financial Crisis: Impact on India's Poor—Some Initial Perspectives.* United Nations Development Programme, India, Delhi. <data.undp.org.in/FinancialCrisis/FinalFCP.pdf> (August 2010).

Lin, Justin Yifu (2008). *The Impact of the Financial Crisis on Developing Countries.* Paper presented at the Korea Development Institute, Seoul, 31 October.

Lin, Justin Yifu and Will Martin (2009). 'The Financial Crisis and Its Impact on the Global Agricultural Landscape.' International Association of Agricultural Economists 2009 conference, Beijing, 16–22 August. <purl.umn.edu/53208> (August 2010).

Masera, Rainer (2009). *Credito e Finanza Oltre la Crisi: come ricostruire un 'buon mercato'.* Università Cattolica del Sacro Cuore, Milan, 8 May.

McKibbon, Warwick J. and Andrew Stoeckel (2009). *The Potential Effects of the Global Financial Crisis on World Trade.* World Bank Policy Research Working Paper No. 5134. World Bank, Washington DC. <go.worldbank.org/A8ZSXCOL60> (August 2010).

Naudé, Wim (2009). *The Financial Crisis of 2008 and the Developing Countries.* WIDER Discussion Paper No. 2009/01. United Nations University, Tokyo. <www.wider.unu.edu/publications/working-papers/discussion-papers/2009/en_GB/dp2009-01> (August 2010).

Organisation for Economic Co-operation and Development (2009). *The Road to Recovery: Update on the OECD's Strategic Response to the Financial and Economic Crisis.* 27 March. <www.oecd.org/dataoecd/40/14/42528786.pdf> (August 2010).

Organisation for Economic Co-operation and Development and African Development Bank (2009). *African Economic Outlook 2009*. Organisation for Economic Co-operation and Development, Paris.

Page, John (2009). *Africa and the Global Crisis: Three Reasons to Be Really Worried.* 8 June. International Growth Centre, London.

Ratha, Dilip and Sanket Mohapatra (2009). *Revised Outlook for Remittance Flows 2009–2011: Remittances Expected to Fall by 5 to 8 Percent in 2009.* 23 March. World Bank, Washington DC.

Taylor, John B. (2009). *The Financial Crisis and the Policy Responses: An Empirical Analysis of What Went Wrong*. NBER Working Paper No. 14631. National Bureau of Economic Research, Washington DC.

United Nations Conference on Trade and Development (2009). *Global FDI in Decline Due to the Financial Crisis, and a Further Drop Expected*. UNCTAD Investment Brief, No. 1. <www.unctad.org/en/docs/webdiaeia20095_en.pdf> (August 2010).

United Nations Economic Commission for Africa and African Union Commission (2009). *The Global Financial Crisis: Impact, Responses, and Way Forward.* E/ECA/COE/28/6 AU/CAMEF/EXP/6(IV). Meeting of the Committee of Experts of the 2nd Joint Annual Meetings of the AU Conference of Ministers of Economy and Finance and ECA Conference of Ministers of Finance, Planning and Economic Development, Cairo, 13 May.

van den Noord, Paul (2009). *From Global Imbalances to Excess Liquidity: A Political Economy View*. Paper presented at the 6th Euroframe Conference on Economic Policy Issues in the European Union, London, and at the Journées d'Économie Publique Louis-André Gérard-Varet, Marseille, 12 June and 15–16 June.

White, Eugene N. (2008). 'Lessons from the History of Bank Examination and Supervision in the United States, 1863–2008.' In A. Gigliobianco and G. Toniolo, eds., *Financial Market Regulation in the Wake of Financial Crises: The Historical Experience* (Rome: Banca d'Italia) <www.bancaditalia.it/pubblicazioni/seminari_convegni/Financial_Market_Regulation/1_volume_regolazione.pdf> (August 2010).

World Bank (2004). 'Patterns of Africa-Asia Trade and Investment: Potential for Ownership and Partnership.' Asia-Africa Trade and Investment Conference, Tokyo, 1–2 November. <www.ticad.net/Publications/pattern-full.pdf> (August 2010).

PART VI
Innovation in Global Economic Governance

Chapter 14

From the Dollar Standard
to a Supernational Money

Pietro Alessandrini and Michele Fratianni

The 2007–09 financial crisis underscored the inherent fragility of the international financial system and its regulatory structure. Having originated in the United States—the country that enjoys the most advanced financial markets, and is also at the centre of the international monetary system—the crisis was preceded by a bubble in the housing and share markets, fuelled by an expansive monetary policy (Fratianni 2008). In its wake a consensus developed that the financial regulatory structure needed a significant overhaul. Much less attention was given to the instability of the dollar-based international monetary system and its potential to spark another severe crisis. The fact that the financial tsunami did not instigate a confidence crisis in the U.S. dollar fed optimism that the financial crisis might be resolved without substantive changes in the existing international monetary regime. Ben Bernanke (2007) reaffirmed the thesis of a global saving glut. This thesis has two important implications: the first is that the large U.S. external imbalances were largely a temporary phenomenon, rather than structural, and thus would find a natural solution in time; the second is that the onus of the adjustment problem fell on the periphery rather than on the centre country of the dollar-based international monetary system.

The global saving glut hypothesis diverts attention from the long-term deterioration of the dollar standard. The external deficits of the U.S., with the attendant dramatic rise in its net foreign indebtedness, are long dated and result from a fundamental weakness of an international monetary system in which a single national money functions also as an international money.

With this premise, this chapter argues that the current international monetary system is fragile because the dollar standard is deteriorating. The dollar remains at the top of the money pyramid because none of the competing international monies, and especially the euro, is ready to fully replace the dollar. However, fundamental changes are required. Money and finance are closely intertwined; it is wishful to think that robustness in the international monetary system will come by concentrating exclusively on fixing the financial system. The system itself needs to be fixed. The best time for doing it is now for the simple reason that radical changes in the rules of the game are affected in times of crises.

The ideal solution would be the creation of a supernational bank money that would coexist alongside international monies. Inspiration can be drawn from the principles underlying Keynes's plan for bancor and an international clearing union (Alessandrini and Fratianni 2009b). These principles tend to resurface in times of stress. In 2009, Zhou Xiaochuan, the governor of the People's Bank of China, made the case for restructuring the international monetary system based on a supranational money, but for practical reasons then opted for the revitalization of the special drawing rights (SDRs). This found a policy echo in the recommendation of the G20 leaders, at their April 2009 meeting in London, to produce a new allocation of 250 billion in SDRs. Dropping more SDRs from a helicopter, without changing the essential characteristics of a special drawing right, is not a long-term solution. Significant structural changes must be introduced to make them work.

The chapter first deals with the fundamental weakness of an international money that is also a national money; in particular, it discusses the long-term deterioration of the dollar standard and raises the issue of how long the U.S. can continue to borrow foreign capital without paying a sovereign risk premium. It then details the limitations of the SDR scheme, followed by a synthesis of a proposal of supranational bank money. Conclusions are drawn in final section.

The Dollar Standard

Historical evidence indicates that one currency tends to dominate others both as an international medium of exchange and as a store of value. In the 19th century, Britain was the leading industrial economy in the world and its currency, the British pound, was the leading but not the exclusive international money in the world. Britain was at the top the pyramid in the international gold standard.[1] World War I marked the end of Britain's economic and financial leadership; yet the key status of the pound lasted for more than four more decades. The interwar period left a vacuum in both currency and trade (Kindleberger 1973). The Bretton Woods Agreement of 1944 had sanctified the pre-eminence of the U.S. dollar. The agreement broke down in 1973 because the U.S. 'abused' the privileges emanating from its national currency functioning also as the key international currency.

The creation of the European Monetary Union (EMU) in 1999 consolidated 11 separate currencies of industrialized countries into a brand new currency, the euro.[2] Today the euro is an established international money, second only

---

1   The standard reference on the pyramidical structure of the gold standard is Peter Lindert (1969); see also Barry Eichengreen (1985); Marc Flandreau, Jacques Le Cacheux, and Frédéric Zumer (1998); and Michele Fratianni, Andreas Hauskrecht, and Aurelio Maccario (1998).

2   The event was enthusiastically received by authors such as C. Fred Bergsten (1997), George Alogoskoufis and Richard Portes (1997), and Richard Portes and Hélène Rey (1997), while Martin Feldstein (1997) made the strongest argument against the euro (see Fratianni et al. 1998).

to the dollar.[3] Following the depreciation of the dollar relative to the euro starting in 2002, increasing attention has been given to the prospect that central banks, especially those in Asia, may want to diversify their holdings out of dollars and into euros and, in the process, bring an end to the dominance of the dollar in official portfolios. There is a growing sense that the status of today's international monies is rapidly evolving with no clear direction, because the end point will be determined by future and thus uncertain policy actions. Other things being equal, there is a positive correlation between the relative economic size of the country and its international-currency status (Kindleberger 1967; Flandreau and Jobst 2009). Relative economic size may be a proxy for the relative transaction domain of the currency; as this shrinks so does the network value of that currency. On this score, the formation of EMU gave the euro a big push in competing against the dollar for the position of dominant currency. On the other hand, the euro has to overcome the serious handicap caused by political unification not being on the horizon in the European system. Without political unification, the euro project will remain incomplete and so will the euro's challenge to the dollar's pre-eminence. In sum, the dollar remains the leading international currency, but with the ascent of the euro the system is becoming increasingly bipolar.

The Deteriorating Dollar Standard

The inherent flaw in using an international money that is also a national money is that the issuing country faces a conflict between pursuing domestic objectives of employment and inflation and maintaining the international public good of a stable money. There are circumstances in which the twin objectives cannot be reconciled simultaneously, and a choice must be made as to which objective dominates. Since World War II—with complete suffrage and a political system more reactive to pressure groups—conflicts between domestic and external objectives tend to be resolved in favour of the former, except when the external constraint is really binding. This has been particularly true for the United States, which has enjoyed a soft external constraint. The costs of being a reserve currency country were perceived to be too large relative to the benefits; the U.S. generated an inflation rate that was consistent neither with the fixed dollar-gold conversion price nor with the preferences of major players such as Germany.

The dollar standard has been deteriorating over the last three decades as a result of the U.S. economy systematically spending beyond its domestic output and becoming, in the process, the largest net debtor in the world. Table 14.1 presents data on the U.S. current account balance—which captures the difference of the excess of domestic absorption over domestic output—from 1973 to 2007, both in billions of dollars and as a percent of U.S. gross domestic product (GDP).

---

3   Elias Papaioannou and Richard Portes (2008) discuss the costs and benefits of the euro as an international currency.

To emphasize trends, this chapter considers periods of at least five years. From the end of Bretton Woods to 2007, the U.S. has accumulated deficits of $6665 billion at an average yearly rate of 2.1 percent of U.S. GDP. More importantly, external deficits have been rising over time: from virtual balance in the 1970s to yearly deficits averaging 1.8 of GDP in the 1980s, 1.9 percent of GDP in the 1990s, and 5.1 percent of GDP in the most recent period of 2001–07.

Table 14.1   U.S. current account balances, 1973–2007

Period	Cumulative surplus (+) or deficits (–), billions of dollars	As a percent of U.S. gross domestic product, annual average
1973–1980	+4.1	+0.1
1981–1985	–251.7	–1.3
1986–1990	–607.4	–2.4
1991–1995	–367.2	–1.1
1996–2000	–1199.6	–2.7
2001–2007	–4242.7	–5.1
1973–2007	–6664.5	–2.1

Source: Data for the U.S. current account balance drawn from *Economic Report of the President: 2009 Report Spreadsheet Tables* (see <www.gpoaccess.gov/eop>); data for U.S. gross domestic product drawn from Federal Reserve Economic Data data base, Federal Reserve Bank of St. Louis (see <research.stlouisfed.org/fred2>).

U.S. net foreign debt at the end of 2007 was $2442 billion. In the 21st century this debt has increased by $1111 billion, far less than the cumulative current account deficits of $4243 billion. The reason for this remarkable discrepancy between the sum of deficit flows and changes in net foreign debt was due to the international role of the dollar, which permitted the U.S. not only to earn foreign seigniorage, but also to act as the 'banker of the world' (Despres et al. 1966). That is, the U.S. borrows short at relatively low rates of interest and lends long at high rates of return. The banker-to-the-world analogy can be extended into a modern leveraged-financial-intermediary view (Gourinchas and Rey 2005). Under this scenario, the U.S. is issuing short-term liabilities as well as fixed income liabilities that are leveraged to make investments abroad in the form of illiquid foreign direct investments and equities that have a high potential for capital gains. The excess rates of return on U.S. assets over U.S. liabilities captures the 'exorbitant privilege' the U.S. earns because of its special role in the international monetary system.[4]

---

4   Between 2001 and 2007, the United States enjoyed an excess of foreign price appreciation on its foreign assets over price appreciation on foreign holdings of U.S. assets valued at $1,263 billion, an exchange rate adjustment worth $950 billion (due to the depreciation of the dollar relative to the foreign currencies that denominate U.S. foreign

Exorbitant Privilege and Benign Neglect

The exorbitant privilege extracted by the U.S. because the special role of the dollar translates into a soft external constraint. Unlike any other country in the world, the U.S. can finance a significant amount of its imports of goods and services plus income payments through increases of liquid liabilities at low interest rates (primarily short-term U.S. government securities and deposits with U.S. banks) held by foreign monetary authorities. For almost half a century, foreign central bank financing has accounted, on average, for approximately 6.5 percent of total U.S. imports, but has been higher when the dollar has been weak against major currencies and lower when the dollar has been strong (Alessandrini and Fratianni 2009b, fig. 1). Central bank financing ratios rose to 40 percent in the first half of the 1970s, in conjunction with the end of Bretton Woods and the first oil shock; they declined to below 1 percent as the dollar experienced a sizeable appreciation in the first half of the 1980s and rose again with the depreciation of the dollar after 1985 before settling at an average of 4 percent in the 1990s. Between 2001 and 2008, financing ratios rose again to an average in excess of 12 percent of total imports, peaking at 19 percent in 2004 (see Figure 14.1). In absolute numbers,

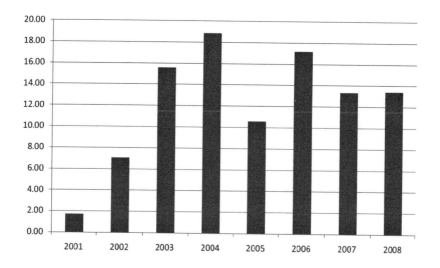

Figure 14.1   Central Bank financing of U.S. total imports, percent, 2001–08

assets), and higher valuation valued at $956 billion (due to changes in coverage and capital gains on direct investment affiliates). The end result was that the increase in net foreign debt between 2001 and 2007 was approximately one fourth of the cumulative current account deficits.

over that eight-year span, the stock of central bank financing rose by $2399 billion, according to U.S. balance of payments statistics.

These trends reflect the propensity of many emerging economies, especially in Asia, and of oil-producing countries to set undervalued exchange rates with respect to the dollar and to accumulate foreign reserves (Dooley et al. 2003; Alessandrini and Fratianni 2009b). This propensity has risen since the start of the new millennium and has financed a growing share of U.S. current account deficits. International reserves have been growing at an average annual rate of 11 percent between 1995 and mid 2007, with a sharp acceleration taking place after 2003, when China began sharply increasing its stock of international reserves.[5] China alone holds 15 percent of U.S. treasuries and is concerned about its undiversified position. Russia, with the third largest stock of international reserves, instead diversified significantly away from the dollar.[6] However, the U.S. government increasingly relies on foreign official agencies to fund its current and prospective budget requirements.[7]

In sum, foreign ownership of U.S. government debt, especially in the hands of a few central banks, raises the risk of a precipitous fall in the value of the dollar, following a readjustment in the currency composition of international reserves. The critical question asked in the market is how long the U.S. can continue to borrow foreign capital at existing rates without incurring a sovereign risk crisis.

The relative indifference of U.S. policy makers toward balance-of-payments deficits and, later, the value of the dollar in relation to other important currencies became known as 'benign neglect'. A resurgence of this policy occurred in 2005 and is known as the saving glut hypothesis (Bernanke 2005, 2007). According to this view, an exogenous upward shift of the saving functions in fast-growing Asian and oil-producing economies, unmatched by a comparable shift in their investment functions, was the cause of the large U.S. capital inflows since the mid 1990s. The resulting *ex ante* gap between saving and investment was responsible for current account surpluses in the emerging countries and falling real rates of interest in the world. According to the saving glut hypothesis, the industrialized world, but primarily the U.S., had to absorb the capital inflows generated by Asian and oil-producing countries. Once the shock petered out, current account

---

5   At the end of 2002, China's reserves were $286 billion; two years later they more than doubled to $610 billion; two years later they almost doubled again to $1066 billion; in 2009 they exceeded $2000 billion, 75 percent of which are dollar denominated (see Center for Geoeconomic Studies 2009).

6   At the end of 2008, the euro share of Russia's foreign reserves was 47.5 percent against the 41.5 percent share of the dollar (Fabrichnaya 2009).

7   In the 2001–07 period, foreign official holdings of U.S. government securities rose by $1746 billion, an amount that is about 50 percent higher than the increase in net foreign debt. In 2008, central banks and sovereign funds purchased close to $600 billion of treasuries (Setser 2009). The 2009 fiscal stimulus of about $800 billion added further pressure on the U.S. government borrowing requirements and likewise on efforts to diversify out of dollars.

imbalances would be reduced. The implication of the Bernanke thesis is that the onus of the adjustment problem falls on the periphery rather than on the centre country of the dollar-based international monetary system; in others words, the appropriate U.S. policy is benign neglect.

In sum, a national money that becomes an international money cannot serve two masters equally well. In the tug of war between domestic and international objectives, political economy considerations dictate that domestic goals of employment and inflation tend to win at the expense of the maintenance of the international public good. It follows that an effective reform of the international monetary system must resolve the dual role of domestic and international money. At the moment, policy makers are betting on resuscitating the SDRs.

Special Drawing Rights

The G20 recommendation of a new SDR allocation worth $250 billion at the April 2009 London Summit brought the SDR back to centre stage as an international reserve asset. As it is the only official proposal to strengthen the international monetary system, it deserves careful examination, not only on its own merit, but also for the prospect of a positive evolution of the monetary system. Policy makers have underscored that the new allocation can be effected rapidly because it is part of an existing institution codified by the Articles of Agreement of the International Monetary Fund (IMF). They also claim that the decision would create sufficient new international liquidity to finance external imbalances and put the IMF back at the centre of the international monetary system. In fact, the London recommendation builds on a weak scheme that has produced few results in the past.[8] Furthermore, the size of the new allocation is small relative to the size of external imbalances, especially those of the United States. Finally, the very structure of the SDRs

---

8   Michele Fratianni and Paolo Savona (1974) formally demonstrated the intrinsic weakness of the SDR scheme, defined as 'a classic jump in the dark' (see also Fratianni 1974). SDRs were created by the IMF in 1969 to supplement the stock of official reserves. The original intent of the programme was to revitalize the dying Bretton Woods system by altering the composition of international reserves between the scarce quantity of monetary gold and the abundant stock of dollar liabilities. The initial allocation of SDR 9.3 billion, over the 1970–72 period, failed to achieve this objective. Not surprisingly, in 1971 the gold convertibility of the dollar was suspended. A second allocation of SDR 12.1 billion took place between 1979 and 1981 in the wake of the second oil shock. Also this allocation failed to achieve the intended results of stabilizing the dollar-based international monetary system. Since then, SDRs have played a marginal role as international reserve, in parallel with the declining importance of the IMF. The SDR has remained mainly a unit of account, defined in terms of fixed quantities of a few important national monies that are adjustable every five years. At the moment, the basket includes the dollar, the euro, the yen and pound sterling.

assigns to the international monetary system a largely passive role (Alessandrini and Fratianni 2009a).

The discrepancy between policy makers' expectations and likely outcomes is pointed out by the IMF (2010) itself: 'The SDR is neither a currency, nor a claim on the IMF. Rather, it is a potential claim on the freely usable currencies of IMF members'. Once a decision has been made by an allocation of SDRs, the IMF has no discretionary power over its use. Under the current system, exchanges of SDRs for national currencies occur either through voluntary bilateral transactions or through the IMF, which may designate member countries with external surpluses to accept SDRs in exchange for their currencies. Thus, the IMF acts as a broker, matching deficit to surplus countries to exchange SDRs for international monies. The transactions remain bilateral.

Each member country receives an amount of SDRs that is proportional to its quota in the IMF, without any necessary *ex ante* consideration about the external liquidity of the country. After the allocation, a deficit country can swap SDRs for an equivalent amount of international money, for example dollars, with a surplus country. The SDR scheme is designed to activate hoarded international money, redistributing it from a surplus country to a deficit country. But there is very little that SDRs can do to improve the position of the largest deficit and net external debtor country in the world. The U.S. share of the new SDR 250 billion is paltry relative to the size of the U.S. external imbalance. To make a dent on the problem would require a large allocation only for the United States. Under such circumstances, the U.S. Federal Reserve could exchange SDRs for dollar assets at surplus countries, starting from the dollar-rich People's Bank of China, and reduce the high weight of dollars in official reserves.[9] But apart from the large size of SDRs involved, the bilateral SDR-dollar swap would be incapable of making the necessary adjustment required to mop up the 'excess' supply of dollars. The swap, in fact, leaves the size of the U.S. monetary base unchanged (only the composition changes in favour of domestic assets). To effect a reduction of the U.S. monetary base, the Federal Reserve would have to sell in the market place the treasury bills received from surplus countries in exchange of SDRs. The Federal Reserve and the U.S. government would have to explicitly agree to such a policy.

Supernational Money

The importance of reforming the existing SDR mechanism in a supernational direction has been raised by Zhou Xiaochuan (2009), the governor of the People's Bank of China. China, more than any other country, is exposed to the risk of an implosion of the dollar standard and urgently feels the need to diversify out of dollar assets. Given that the renmimbi is not an international money, there is

---

9 In the balance sheet of the U.S. Federal Reserve, the exchange would imply a reduction of SDRs and an equivalent increase of dollar assets (treasury bills).

obvious Chinese interest in seeing the transformation of the dollar standard into a supernational money standard. Zhou has chosen to endorse the SDRs and suggests at the same time a series of recommendations that would make them converge progressively to a supernational money. Among the recommendations, it is worth highlighting the following three: transforming the SDR from an artificial basket currency into one backed by assets; establishing a settlement system between the SDR and national currencies so as to make the SDR a fully fledged money; and linking the SDRs to a specific institution that would be responsible for their management and their value, in other words they have to be someone's liability (Alessandrini and Fratianni 2009a).

The 2007–09 financial crisis created an almost unique opportunity for a gradual introduction of a supernational money aimed at reducing the asymmetries of the key currency system. The natural reference for this gradual approach is European monetary unification. Before unification, the European currency unit (ECU) was as much an artificial currency as the SDR is today. Actual transactions and assets denominated in ECUs represented a small share of the market. The ECU was no one's liability. The big change occurred when the ECU became the euro issued by a supernational central bank with a clear mandate for price stability. Something similar must occur at the world level before the SDR can become a true supernational money. But the experience of European monetary unification indicates that the objective of economic convergence among member countries is a precondition that at the world level appears economically and politically insurmountable.

The alternative to a politically unfeasible autonomous world central bank is to create a cooperative agreement among a restricted group of key countries that find it in their interest to share responsibility to stabilize the international monetary system. Theory and practice suggest that cooperation is more likely the smaller the number of participating countries and the more homogenous they are.

The proposal to reform the international monetary system contained in this chapter is based on a cooperative agreement among a restricted group of key countries that find it in their interest to stabilize the system (Alessandrini and Fratianni 2009b). The U.S. Federal Reserve and the European Central Bank (ECB), the two most important central banks with an anti-inflation reputation, could take the initiative by establishing at the IMF a multilateral clearing system of debit and credit entries restricted to central banks. The first step would involve the Federal Reserve and the ECB transferring to the clearing institution earning assets denominated in dollars and euros, respectively, against an equivalent amount of supernational bank money. Supernational bank money would have the property of a basket currency with the attendant risk-diversifying characteristics. The mechanics would be similar to the SDR with a very critical difference: supernational bank money, unlike SDRs, would be a liability of a supernational institution. Unlike SDRs, it would become supernational money for central banks.

The clearing system would be a big step forward from the SDR system in two fundamental ways. The first is that supernational bank money would be created endogenously as a result of actions taken by participating countries, whereas SDRs are created exogenously as a sort of international helicopter money. The second is that the clearing system operates on a banking principle. The settlement of credit and debit between central banks would occur through their supranational bank money accounts: central banks in deficit countries would reduce their stock of supranational bank money, while central banks in surplus countries would increase their stock. In addition to redistributing supranational bank money, the clearing institution could create it through an overdraft facility, the size of which would have to be agreed *ex ante* by the participating countries. Deficit countries could activate their overdraft facility on their supranational bank money accounts and become net debtors with regard to the clearing institution. Unlike the SDR scheme, each country would have a credit or debit position *vis-à-vis* the clearing institution; that is, the payment structure would be multilateral rather than bilateral.

The clearing proposal draws from five principles used by Keynes in his plan to reform the international monetary system at the end of World War II (Alessandrini and Fratianni 2009b).[10] The clearing system would solve the impasse that impeded the adoption of the substitution account in the 1970s.[11] In the clearing system, the IMF would bear no exchange rate risk because it would not hold open positions in assets denominated in national currencies. A central bank in a surplus country would exchange supranational bank money for dollar reserves first by selling dollar assets in the open market and then by converting dollar deposits at the U.S. Federal Reserve in deposits of supranational bank money at the clearing institution. The monetary base of the Federal Reserve would fully reflect the conversion of supranational bank money for dollar assets. The automatic sterilization permitting the United States to insulate its monetary base from the effects of external deficits would disappear. By having to align the monetary base to net foreign payments, the exorbitant privilege of the United States as a key currency country would cease. Clearly, the Federal Reserve would have to accept such a mechanism.

The clearing system could not work without explicit rules of the game, such as the size of the overdraft facility, the terms of repayment of the overdraft, and the

---

10   For the International Clearing Union, see John Maynard Keynes ([1943] 1969). Keynes ([1930] 1971, 358) used the denomination of supranational bank money in 'The Treatise on Money': 'Its assets should consist of gold, securities and advances to central banks, and its liabilities of deposits by central banks. Such deposits we will call supranational bank money.' This chapter takes the same approach but excludes gold.

11   In the 1970s the Committee of Twenty produced a proposal, known as the substitution account, which was later evaluated by the Interim Committee of the IMF in 1978–79 (Kenen 1981; Micossi and Saccomanni 1981). Central banks would be able to open an account denominated in SDRs by depositing dollar assets at the IMF. SDRs would thus be created endogenously by the actions of those central banks that deemed to have too many dollar assets in their official reserves. The substitution account never came to light because neither the IMF nor the U.S. was willing to bear the exchange rate risk arising from an unhedged position of the IMF having dollar assets and SDR liabilities (Boughton 2001, ch. 18).

identification of who bears the burden of external adjustment. In an inflationary environment, it would be up to deficit countries to contract domestic spending; consequently, overdraft facilities would have to be contained. In a recessionary environment, it would be up to surplus countries to raise domestic spending; consequently, overdraft facilities would have to be more expansive than in an inflationary environment.

Conclusion

The dollar-based international monetary system is fragile. This fragility manifests itself in large and long-lived external deficits of the dominant key currency country. The end result is that the net foreign debt of the United States is growing; with that increase grows the risk of an implosion of the international monetary system. The inherent weakness of the current system is that it relies on an international money that is also a national money. This conflict is typically resolved in favour of domestic objectives.

Radical changes are best made in times of crises. China, the largest creditor country and the most exposed to a possible implosion of the dollar-based international monetary system, has expressed—through its central bank governor, Zhou Xiaochuan—the merits of restructuring the international monetary system based on a supernational money. However, for practical reasons, China has advocated the revitalization of SDRs. The G20 leaders obliged in 2009. But the SDR scheme is weak. As a supplement to international reserves, the SDR has failed in the past.

The preferred solution would be the creation of a supernational bank money within the institutional setting of a clearing union. This union goes beyond the simple accounting of recording credit and debit entries. It is the result of a full-fledged agreement by participating central banks on specific rules of the game, such as size and duration of overdrafts, designation of countries that would bear the burden of external adjustment, and coordination of monetary policies. The IMF is the international organization best positioned to monitor and enforce these rules—not an easy task, yet nonetheless feasible. Cooperation, even when it is compatible with incentives, requires the institutionalization of objectives, ways, and means. The interest of the U.S. in cooperating would be linked to maintaining and improving the international brand name of the dollar, which would continue to be used as a means of payment and store of value. A supernational bank money would only substitute (and not completely replace) the dollar in official reserves. The interest of China in cooperating would come first from the benefits of diversification away from dollar assets and, second, from the larger role the country would play in the international monetary system.

References

Alessandrini, Pietro and Michele Fratianni (2009a). 'Dominant Currencies, Special Drawing Rights, and Supernational Bank Money.' *World Economics*, vol. 10, no. 4, 45–67.

Alessandrini, Pietro and Michele Fratianni (2009b). 'Resurrecting Keynes to Stabilize the International Monetary System.' *Open Economies Review*, vol. 20, no. 3, pp. 339–358. <www.springerlink.com/content/dn56083066l27818> (August 2010).

Alogoskoufis, George and Richard Portes (1997). 'The Euro, the Dollar, and the International Monetary System.' In P.R. Masson, T.H. Krueger, and B. Turtelboom, eds., *EMU and the International Monetary System* (Washington DC: International Monetary Fund).

Bergsten, C. Fred (1997). 'The Impact of the Euro on Exchange Rates and International Policy Coordination.' In P.R. Masson, T.H. Krueger, and B. Turtelboom, eds., *EMU and the International Monetary System* (Washington DC: International Monetary Fund).

Bernanke, Ben S. (2005). 'The Global Saving Glut and the U.S. Current Account Deficit.' 10 March, Sandrine Lecture, Virginia Association of Economics. <www.federalreserve.gov/boarddocs/speeches/2005/200503102/default.htm> (August 2010).

Bernanke, Ben S. (2007). 'Global Imbalances: Recent Developments and Prospects.' 11 September, Bundesbank Lecture, Berlin. <www.federalreserve.gov/newsevents/speech/bernanke20070911a.htm> (August 2010).

Boughton, James (2001). *Silent Revolution: The International Monetary Fund, 1979–1989* (Washington DC: International Monetary Fund).

Center for Geoeconomic Studies (2009). 'China's Foreign Assets.' *Geo-Graphics* (blog), Council for Foreign Relations, 15 May. <blogs.cfr.org/geographics/2009/05/15/china%E2%80%99s-foreign-assets> (August 2010).

Despres, Emile, Charles P. Kindleberger, and Walter Salant (1966). 'The Dollar and World Liquidity: A Minority View.' *Economist*, 5 February, pp. 526–529.

Dooley, Michael P., David Folkerts-Landau, and Peter Garber (2003). *An Essay on the Revived Bretton Woods System*. National Bureau of Economic Research, Cambridge, MA. <www.nber.org/papers/w9971> (August 2010).

Eichengreen, Barry J. (1985). 'Editor's Introduction.' In B.J. Eichengreen, ed., *The Gold Standard in Theory and History* (New York: Methuen).

Fabrichnaya, Yelena (2009). 'Euros Overtake Dollars in Russia's Reserves.' *Reuters*, 18 May.

Feldstein, Martin (1997). 'The Political Economy of the European Economic and Monetary Union: Political Sources of an Economic Liability.' *Journal of Economic Perspectives*, vol. 11, no. 4, pp. 23–42.

Flandreau, Marc and Clemens Jobst (2009). 'The Empirics of International Currencies: Network Externalities, History, and Persistence.' *Economic Journal*, vol. 119, no. 537, pp. 653–664.

Flandreau, Marc, Jacques Le Cacheux, and Frédéric Zumer (1998). *Stability Without a Pact? Lessons from the European Gold Standard 1880–1914.* <www.ofce.sciences-po.fr/pdf/dtravail/wp98-01.pdf> (August 2010).

Fratianni, Michele (1974). 'The Problem of Coexistence of SDRs and a Reserve Currency: A Comment.' *Journal of Money, Credit, and Banking*, vol. 6, no. 1, pp. 115–118.

Fratianni, Michele (2008). 'Financial Crises, Safety Nets, and Regulation.' *Rivista Italiana degli Economisti*, vol. 13, no. 2.

Fratianni, Michele, Andreas Hauskrecht, and Aurelio Maccario (1998). 'Dominant Currencies and the Future of the Euro.' *Open Economies Review*, vol. 9, Supp. 1, pp. 467–492. <www.springerlink.com/content/w3v604631nl352mq> (August 2010).

Fratianni, Michele and Paolo Savona (1974). 'Un modello esplicativo della tesaurizzazione e degli usi dei diritti speciali di prelievo.' *Economia Internazionale*, no. 1, February.

Gourinchas, Pierre-Olivier and Hélène Rey (2005). *From World Banker to World Venture Capitalist: U.S. External Adjustment and the Exorbitant Privilege.* National Bureau of Economic Research Working Paper No. 11563. <www. nber.org/papers/w11563> (August 2010).

International Monetary Fund (2010). 'Special Drawing Rights (SDRS).' 29 September. <www.imf.org/external/np/exr/facts/sdr.htm> (September 2010).

Kenen, Peter B. (1981). 'The Analytics of a Substitution Account.' *Banca Nazionale del Lavoro Quarterly Review*, no. 139, December.

Keynes, John Maynard ([1930] 1971). 'A Treatise on Money.' In, *The Collected Writings of John Maynard Keynes*, Vol. VI. (London: Macmillan).

Keynes, John Maynard ([1943] 1969). 'Proposals for an International Clearing Union.' In J.K. Horsefield, ed., *The International Monetary Fund 1945–1965,* Vol. III: Documents (Washington DC: International Monetary Fund).

Kindleberger, Charles P. (1967). 'The Politics of International Money and World Language.' *Essays in International Finance*, no. 61 (Princeton: Princeton University Press).

Kindleberger, Charles P. (1973). *The World in Depression, 1929–1939* (Berkeley: University of California Press).

Lindert, Peter H. (1969). 'Key Currencies and Gold, 1900–1913.' *Essays in International Finance*, vol. 24 (Princeton: Princeton University Press).

Micossi, Stefano and Fabrizio Saccomanni (1981). 'The Substitution Account: The Problem, the Techniques, and the Politics.' *Banca Nazionale del Lavoro Quarterly Review*, vol. 137 (November-December), pp. 171–178.

Papaioannau, Elias and Richard Portes (2008). *Costs and Benefits of Running an International Currency.* European Economy, Economic Papers No. 348, November. European Commission, Brussels. <ec.europa.eu/economy_finance/ publications/publication_summary13484_en.htm> (August 2010).

Portes, Richard and Hélène Rey (1997). 'The Emergence of the Euro as an International Currency.' *Economic Policy*, vol. 13, no. 26, pp. 305–343.

Setser, Brad (2009). 'Who Bought All the Treasuries the U.S. Issued in 2008? And Who Will Be the Big Buyers in 2009?' *Follow the Money* (blog), Council on Foreign Relations, 26 February. <blogs.cfr.org/setser/2009/02/26/who-bought-all-the-treasuries-the-us-issued-in-2008-and-who-will-be-the-big-buyers-in-2009/> (August 2010).

Zhou Xiaochuan (2009). *Reform the International Monetary System.* 23 March. Bank for International Settlements. <www.bis.org/review/r090402c.pdf> (August 2010).

Chapter 15

The Role of International Money

Juan Carlos Martinez Oliva

The Old and the New Bretton Woods

One of the most striking features of today's global economy is the persistence of large payment imbalances between the United States and its creditor countries, and the apparent inadequacy of the international monetary system to promote a smooth adjustment. The world crisis has highlighted the fact that the current international monetary situation seems incapable of providing the necessary adjustment mechanism when imbalances are large and persistent. The huge size of capital markets makes financing payment imbalances much easier than in the past, and the small range of exchange rate movements is not helpful in correcting large-sized current account deficits. This situation has reached a stalemate, in view of the aim of the United States to preserve the privilege coming from its role of key currency country, while China aims to maintain its competitive advantage in the trade field and possibly avoid substantial capital losses in its dollar-denominated securities.

Before the outbreak of the 2007–09 financial turmoil such a situation did not seem a source of concern to those who viewed the current international monetary and financial system as a revived Bretton Woods system (Dooley et al. 2003). The parallel with the 1960s seemed to suggest that the old periphery, namely Europe and Japan, had been replaced by a new periphery, the emerging market economies of Asia and Latin America, with the U.S. playing the role of the core country that enjoys the privilege of issuing the main reserve currency and displays a tendency to live beyond its means. The old periphery had dismantled capital and foreign exchange controls, and was worried about the sustainability of U.S. current account deficits and foreign debt.[1] The new periphery, by contrast, seemed to care mostly about exporting to the U.S., maintained extensive capital and foreign exchange controls, and accumulated growing stocks of U.S. short-term liabilities. While, according to the Bretton Woods II view, such a situation might have continued for quite some time; according to others, there was a serious risk that the system

---

1 Notably, relations between Europe and the United States were dominated by growing disagreement on the distribution of the financial burden of military commitments related to Cold War. Political misunderstandings may thus been be included among the main causes of the failure of the Bretton Woods system (see James and Martinez Oliva 2009).

might soon collapse (see, for example, Eichengreen and O'Rourke 2010; Roubini and Setser 2005). In particular, it seemed that the new periphery had less incentive than the old one to cooperate in a multilateral framework intended to preserve the international monetary system. Moreover, while under the Bretton Woods regime there were no other currencies that might credibly replace the U.S. dollar, in the current world things had changed radically, with the euro representing a suitable alternative. Lastly, in the 1960s the U.S. was committed to converting dollars into gold at a fixed price, a commitment that no longer exists.

The world crisis has raised the case for a global rethinking of the current international financial architecture by showing that the build-up of large surpluses by emerging market economies has increased the interdependence of different areas of the globe and therefore the scope for coordination. The collapse of confidence that hit the system of financial intermediation in the U.S. and Europe threatened the stability of a system that allowed China and other emerging markets to experience a strong export-led growth backed by American and European demand for their products. While the U.S. has displayed a clear tendency to live beyond its means, China has benefited from pegging to the dollar, and keeping its peg unchanged as the dollar fell from 2002 to 2005.

China's Policy Dilemma

The question of whether Asian economies artificially hold down their currencies in order to protect their export-led growth has been much discussed in past years. The idea that China keeps the renminbi artificially cheap, thus giving Chinese exporters an unfair advantage over their competitors emerged some time ago in the political debate as an argument in favour of the introduction of tariffs on Chinese products in the United States.[2] Some scholars have found that the real exchange rate effects on trade flows are relatively small; they therefore challenge the idea that exchange policy alone would be sufficient to reduce the Chinese trade surplus (Cheung et al. 2008; Frankel 2008; Lafrance 2008).

The level of reserves held by China has risen dramatically since 2003. Year after year it has financed growing shares of U.S. current account deficits. While in 2000 foreign monetary authorities accumulated $43 billion in dollar reserves against a U.S. deficit of $417 billion, in 2006 the accumulation of dollar reserves reached $440 billion against a U.S. deficit of $811 billion, a figure that might perhaps understate the true extent of central bank financing of U.S. current account deficits.[3] China's reserves grew at an average annual rate of 11 percent

---

2   See, in particular, the Schumer-Graham bill announced in February 2005 and withdrawn in September 2006.

3   Such an understatement is due to the fact that central banks sometimes use anonymous transactions in their foreign exchange market interventions.

between 1995 and mid 2007, with a sharp acceleration after 2003.[4] As a result, the Chinese share of world international reserves rose from 5.3 percent in 1995 to 26.4 percent in 2007, and reached a level of $2,399 trillion at the end of 2009, up from $1946 trillion a year earlier. In spite of concerns about the future of the dollar, which accounts for about two thirds of China's overall reserves, Chinese authorities continued to increase their dollar assets.

This situation raises several problems. The level of reserves accumulated by large emerging markets is such that any shift in the composition of their reserve holdings might dangerously affect market expectations. There are nonetheless different ways to look at reserve accumulation by emerging economies. On the one hand, they can be viewed as the result of misallocation; on the other, they might reflect an increasing propensity by financially underdeveloped countries to choose the U.S. as a financial intermediary to allocate their large stock of savings. The saving rate has increased in so-called developing Asia from 33 percent in the 1990s to more than 42 percent in 2006. This pattern can be seen as a response to the unavailability of public insurance schemes for the old and the sick, and the rapidly increasing cost of education. In China, notably, the share of consumption on total income has fallen in recent years as income increased. High public and private savings together produce a huge amount of capital in search of a safe shelter.

For China things might get harder to handle in the future. Arguably, such an enormous amount of reserves involves serious challenges, among which are the market instability deriving from shifts in composition; increasing limits to the ability to sterilize with the consequence of inflationary pressures, as shown by China's recent experience; the search for diversification, which entails the risks associated with shifting from safer U.S. treasury bills to riskier private investment; and the search for alternative ways to manage assets, such as the sovereign wealth funds, which, by trying to acquire stakes in strategically relevant national companies in western countries, are raising growing concerns of political manipulation.

To address this problem Michael Bordo and Harold James (2008) have suggested that in the context of a broader reform of the governance of the International Monetary Fund (IMF), a special role might be attributed to the institution in reserve management. The fundamental aim of the new 'asset department' would be to generate satisfactory and stable returns that would make the reserve assets financially more rewarding and actually less risky. Another possible use of the new resources might be helping stem speculative attacks on the currency, in situations where the fundamental position may be judged sound, by acting as a lender of last resort and lending against collateral at pre-crisis interest rates.

---

4   At the end of 2002, Chinese reserves were $286 billion; two years later they more than doubled to $610 billion; two years later they almost doubled again to $1066 billion; during the first half of 2007 they rose by more than $300 billion.

The Case for International Monetary Reform

There is a widespread feeling that a new international monetary framework is needed to address the persisting imbalance in payments between the U.S. and the emerging market economies, particularly China. While a radical reform of the international monetary system might be seen as the most appropriate response in principle, such an option should be considered carefully, given the difficulty of achieving the necessary endorsement by the main actors. For example, Robert Mundell's (2005) proposal of a redesigned international monetary system that would result in a single world currency appears more like a captivating intellectual exercise than a realistic policy option. Due to reasons that are perhaps more ideological than practical, there is still a strong reluctance to accept the idea of replacing national reserve currencies with something else (Saccomanni 2008). The idea that bad domestic policies may affect other countries via spillover effects is nonetheless very popular today—in the aftermath of the 2007–09 financial crisis—than it was few years ago, thus reviving a debate that has been particularly deep in the past. The feeling that U.S. policies in the post-war years might have been damaging for the rest of the world inspired Keynes's early attempt to launch bancor as an alternative to U.S. dollar, the French attempt to introduce the collective reserve unit, and the IMF's attempt to create a substitution account (Micossi and Saccomanni 1981). The same feeling provided the driving force toward European monetary integration.

Many observers today, such as Henry H. Fowler who was U.S. treasury secretary in the 1960s, believe that 'providing reserves and exchanges for the whole world is too much for one country and one currency to bear' and seem persuaded that the dollar age is close to the end (IMF 2001b). This is nonetheless an assumption that should be considered very carefully. If simple extrapolations of past trends are considered, then the outlook does not appear particularly encouraging. In the absence of a credible plan for medium-term fiscal consolidation, and with two thirds of U.S. securities held by non-residents, the risk of a refinancing crisis might rapidly accelerate the decline of the dollar standard. U.S. creditor countries are increasingly concerned that the trend to monetization of fiscal deficits might eventually involve an inflation risk and erode the value of the U.S. currency.

However, in spite of the growing doubts about the future of the dollar as a reserve asset, foreign central banks holdings of U.S. treasury bills have continued to increase in recent times. Growth recovery of U.S. economy is already in place, led by a consistent set of policies, and this will probably back the dollar. The U.S. authorities seem particularly determined to preserve the dollar's role, as it appears in a number of recent statements.[5] In the longer term, another factor that might play a role is

---

5   For example, on 24 March 2009, U.S. president Barack Obama (2009) stated: 'The dollar is extraordinarily strong right now. And the reason the dollar is strong right now is because investors consider the United States the strongest economy in the world, with the most stable political system in the world'.

the balance of soft power. The growing interest of the current U.S. administration in the merits of soft power might shift the emphasis of U.S. foreign policy from military and strategic considerations to foreign assistance, economic development, institution building and the rule of law, good governance, basic services for the people, and more.[6] A growing investment in this direction by the U.S., together with a credible improvement of economic fundamentals, might positively enhance the reputation of the dollar, foster overall stability, and help maintain the *status quo*. The Marshall Plan, consistent with the Truman doctrine and one of its most brilliant achievements, is a case of how the increase of soft power contributed to reinforce U.S. hegemony in Europe, and the dollar's international role.

Pietro Alessandrini and Michele Fratianni (2009b; 2009a) have put forward a proposal that envisages a totally new international monetary system based on a supernational bank money issued by an international clearing union against short-term domestic assets provided by the U.S. Federal Reserve System and the European Central Bank. The international money would coexist alongside national currencies, allowing for a gradual implementation of the new setting. As in Keynes's original proposal, an international agency would determine the size of countries' quotas, the size and time length of overdrafts, and the coordination of economic policies. The basic rationale is that an agreement among key currency countries would not suffice to generate the necessary adjustment mechanism to correct external imbalances. Looking back, the authors argue that in the gold exchange standard, chosen at Bretton Woods, the asymmetry deriving from the dual role of the dollar as both a national and international currency proved to be unstable in the long run. The dollar standard that followed the discontinuation of dollar-gold convertibility increased the asymmetry, since the core country continued to operate with an even softer external constraint while enjoying the supplementary benefit of being released from the gold convertibility obligation.

While Alessandrini and Fratianni claim that a clearing system based on a supernational bank money would represent a relevant step forward from the special drawing rights (SDR) system, it could be argued that a difference exists between a system that extends credit, up to a given amount, to members in a debtor position *vis-à-vis* the clearing union and one that distributes tokens (the SDR), which can be used by member countries for the same purpose is more conceptual than practical. Indeed, the difference lies in the operational framework, and in this respect, admittedly, the current SDR system is impaired by rules that severely limit its use as a pivotal component of the international monetary system. Among them is one clause related to the existence of a long-term global need to supplement existing reserve assets, as required by the IMF's Articles of Agreement for a general allocation or a cancellation to take place. The intrinsic ambiguity of the concept of 'long-term global need' has often been a source of disagreement among

---

6   Defence secretary Robert Gates (2007) advocated as much in a speech on 26 November 2007, when he said that U.S. counterterrorism efforts require not just combat operations, but a broader range of economic development and diplomacy.

member countries on the existence of such a need, as well as on the advisability of using an extraordinary unconditional source of financing rather than ordinary conditional resources. Another major limitation of SDR is represented by the complex procedures for allocation and cancellation. They require an executive board proposal to be submitted to the board of governors for final approval with a majority of 85 percent of quotas (IMF 2001a).

It is not surprising, therefore, that the proposal by Zhou Xiaochuan (2009), the governor of the People's Bank of China, to give SDR a greater role as a perspective supranational reserve currency involves a radical rethinking of its functioning. In a similar vein, on the occasion of an IMF Conference on the Future of SDR in 1996, the deputy governor of the People's Bank of China, Zhu Xiaohua (1996), had already advocated an enhanced role of SDR, while suggesting that the extent to which the SDR could contribute to the monetary system depended on the quality and quantity of future improvements to its mechanism.

Given the above considerations, it is clear that the world financial crisis raises the case for a global rethinking of the current international financial architecture. The bold and long-sighted contribution of Pietro Alessandrini and Michele Fratianni in Chapter 14 can be viewed as a very helpful contribution to that end.

Lessons from the Past

Even if the 'imaginative and ambitious' scheme elaborated by Keynes—as described by Lionel Robbins (1971)—was vetoed by the United States at Bretton Woods, it still found a successful implementation in the European Payments Union (EPU), an arrangement for payments settlement among European countries between 1950 and 1958. Here, each country's foreign position with other European countries was reported monthly to the Bank for International Settlements (BIS) in Basel, and the offsetting claim cleared. The balances of countries were consolidated, and the resulting individual creditor or debtor positions with regard to the EPU were financed with credits up to a given threshold and settled in dollars or gold when exceeding the quota of each country. A progressive settlement rule was established, involving decreasing credits and increasing gold payments as the deficit grew. A managing board handled the ordinary business and the special situations occurring when a member came close to exhaust its quota. The board could provide policy recommendations, with the help of independent financial experts, provide special credits and quota extensions, and report to the ministerial council of the Organisation for European Economic Co-operation (OEEC) (Kaplan and Schleiminger 1989; Martinez Oliva and Stefani 2000).

The EPU was an experiment whose success was favoured by a number of factors, notably countries that had committed expressly to cooperate in exchange for their participation in the benefits of the Marshall Plan and that shared a need to reactivate trade and payments, in the face of a dramatic foreign reserve shortage. The process was supervised and politically enforced by the United States, which had provided the initial capital endowment to the EPU. Member countries' cooperative attitude was encouraged by the hope of eventually achieving currency convertibility. They were politically tied together by common objectives and mutual obligations set by the Treaty of Brussels of 1948 and by the North Atlantic Treaty of 1949. Last but not least, the EPU was regarded as a temporary device, to be dismissed once currency convertibility was achieved.

Clearly, the situation today is very different. One wonders whether there are conditions that might help reaching the needed consensus on a smooth transition toward a lasting arrangement based on a supernational bank money and an international clearing union. Given the payoff for the two main actors, Chinese authorities would most likely be interested in endorsing a reform in that direction, as it would offer a major opportunity to protect and diversify China's international reserves and reinforce the country's role in the international monetary system. Arguably, China's enormous reserves involve serious challenges. It is clearly in China's interest to try to diversify its reserve portfolio while avoiding anything disruptive to the world economic order in general, and to the dollar in particular. A proposal to introduce an international clearing union might be an optimal response to that need. Indeed, in its annual financial stability report, issued in July 2009, the People's Bank of China stated that it would push to overhaul the international currency system to make it more diversified and reasonable and reduce over reliance on the current reserve currencies.

On the U.S. side things appear more problematic. The views of Ben Bernanke (2007), chair of the U.S. Federal Reserve, show that U.S. monetary authorities are firm and consistent in supporting the concept that the dollar remain the dominant currency. Indeed, it is hard to see why U.S. authorities should embrace a reform that would erode the dollar's international standing and limit the country's ability to borrow from the international financial markets at a reduced cost as it has done for many decades. In this light, one wonders whether a constructive debate on the design of new rules for the international monetary system may be started at this stage, taking into account the representation of the main economic actors in the international arena within groups or institutions. Reaching a consensus on international monetary reform may prove to be very long, and require a great deal of flexibility and perseverance.

Conclusion

The world financial crisis has raised the case for a global rethinking of the current international financial architecture. The issue of reforming the international monetary system in a direction consistent with the need to cope with today's world challenges has become particularly pressing in the wake of recent financial disorders. The international financial institutions have proven weak. The main international actor has been the G7, where the Asian emerging economies have no representation. The original Bretton Woods system has evolved in a way that entails serious problems of medium-term sustainability. The overall perception is that the exchange rate of the dollar *vis-à-vis* the renminbi is no longer consistent with trade balance equilibrium between the U.S. and China. The current international monetary architecture seems incapable of providing the necessary adjustment mechanism when imbalances are large and persistent. The unprecedented dimension of capital markets makes financing payment unbalances much easier than in the past, while the small range of exchange rate movements is not helpful in correcting large-sized current account deficits. This situation persists due to the U.S. aim to preserve the privilege coming from its role of key currency country, while creditors are interested in maintaining their competitive advantage in the trade field and possibly avoiding substantial capital losses in their dollar-denominated securities.

The consequences require some action to be taken. Starting a constructive debate on the design of new rules for the international monetary system may be helpful at this stage, taking into account the representation of the main economic actors in the international arena within groups or institutions, and displaying a good deal of flexibility and perseverance. Experience shows that the success of an international monetary arrangement may heavily depend on the existence of common goals and on the size of payoffs for the countries involved. This last condition, in particular, may prove crucial to the goal of reaching the necessary consensus.

References

Alessandrini, Pietro and Michele Fratianni (2009a). 'Keynes and International Cooperation.' In J.C. Martinez Oliva and H. James, eds., *International Cooperation Across the Atlantic* (Frankfurt: Adelmann).

Alessandrini, Pietro and Michele Fratianni (2009b). 'Resurrecting Keynes to Stabilize the International Monetary System.' *Open Economies Review*, vol. 20, no. 3, pp. 339–358. <www.springerlink.com/content/dn56083066127818> (August 2010).

Bernanke, Ben S. (2007). 'Global Imbalances: Recent Developments and Prospects.' 11 September, Bundesbank Lecture, Berlin. <www.federalreserve.gov/newsevents/speech/bernanke20070911a.htm> (August 2010).

Bordo, Michael D. and Harold James (2008). *The Past and Future of IMF Reform: A Proposal.* 30 November (mimeo).

Cheung, Yin-Wong, Menzie D. Chinn, and Eiji Fujii (2008). 'China's Current Account and the Exchange Rate.' In R. Feenstra and S.-J. Wei, eds., *China's Growing Role in World Trade* (Chicago: University of Chicago Press) <www.nber.org/books_in_progress/china07> (August 2010).

Dooley, Michael P., David Folkerts-Landau, and Peter Garber (2003). *An Essay on the Revived Bretton Woods System.* <www.nber.org/papers/w9971> (August 2010).

Eichengreen, Barry J. and Kevin H. O'Rourke (2010). 'What Do the New Data Tell Us?' 8 March, VoxEU. <www.voxeu.org/index.php?q=node/3421> (August 2010).

Frankel, Jeffrey A. (2008). 'Comment on "China's Current Account and Exchange Rate," by Yin-Wong Cheung, Menzie Chinn and Eiji Fujii.' In R. Feenstra and S.-J. Wei, eds., *China's Growing Role in World Trade* (Chicago: University of Chicago Press) <www.nber.org/books_in_progress/china07> (August 2010).

Gates, Robert (2007). 'Landon Lecture.' 26 November, Remarks delivered at Kansas State University, Manhattan, Kansas. <www.defenselink.mil/speeches/speech.aspx?speechid=1199> (August 2010).

International Monetary Fund (2001a). *Financial Organization and Operations of the IMF.* No. 45, 6th ed. International Monetary Fund, Washington DC. <www.imf.org/external/pubs/ft/pam/pam45/pdf/pam45.pdf> (August 2010).

International Monetary Fund (2001b). 'The Dollar Glut.' Money Matters: An IMF Exhibit—The Importance of Global Cooperation, System in Crisis (1959–1971). <www.imf.org/external/np/exr/center/mm/eng/mm_sc_03.htm> (August 2010).

James, Harold and Juan Carlos Martinez Oliva (2009). *International Cooperation across the Atlantic* (Frankfurt: Adelmann).

Kaplan, Jacob J. and Gunther Schleiminger (1989). *European Payments Union: Financial Diplomacy in the 1950s* (Oxford: Clarendon Press).

Lafrance, Robert (2008). *China's Exchange Rate Policy: A Survey of the Literature.* Bank of Canada, Ottawa. <www.bankofcanada.ca/fr/res/dp/2008/dp08-5.pdf> (August 2010).

Martinez Oliva, Juan Carlos and Maria Lucia Stefani (2000). 'Dal Piano Marshall all'Unione europea dei pagamenti. Alle origini dell'integrazione economica europea.' In F. Cotula, ed., *Stabilità e sviluppo negli anni Cinquanta. L'Italia nel contesto internazionale* (Rome: Banca d'Italia).

Micossi, Stefano and Fabrizio Saccomanni (1981). 'The Substitution Account: The Problem, the Techniques, and the Politics.' *Banca Nazionale del Lavoro Quarterly Review*, vol. 137 (November-December), pp. 171–178.

Mundell, Robert A. (2005). 'The Case for a World Currency.' *Journal of Policy Modeling*, vol. 27, no. 4, pp. 465–475.

Obama, Barack (2009). 'News Conference by the President.' 24 March, White House. <www.whitehouse.gov/the-press-office/news-conference-president-3-24-2009> (August 2010).

Robbins, Lionel (1971). *Autobiography of an Economist* (London: Macmillan).

Roubini, Nouriel and Brad Setser (2005). *Will the Bretton Woods 2 Regime Unravel Soon? The Risk of a Hard Landing in 2005–2006.* Paper prepared for the 'Revived Bretton Woods System: A New Paradigm for Asian Development?' Federal Reserve Bank of San Francisco and University of California at Berkeley, San Francisco, 4 February. <www.frbsf.org/economics/conferences/0502/Roubini.pdf> (August 2010).

Saccomanni, Fabrizio (2008). 'Managing International Financial Instability.' 11 December, Remarks at a meeting of the Peterson Institute for International Economics, Washington DC. <www.bis.org/review/r081217c.pdf> (August 2010).

Xiaohua, Zhu (1996). 'The Potential Role of the SDR in Improving the Reserve System.' In M. Mussa, J. Boughton, and P. Isard, eds., *The Future of the SDR in Light of Changes in the International Financial System* (Washington DC: International Monetary Fund).

Zhou Xiaochuan (2009). *Reform the International Monetary System.* 23 March. Bank for International Settlements. <www.bis.org/review/r090402c.pdf> (August 2010).

Chapter 16

Asymmetries in the
International Monetary System

Domenico Lombardi[1]

In the future, the U.S. balance of payments should no longer be, as it has in the past, a major source of growth in world reserves.

William McChesney Martin

The current international monetary system exhibits deep-seated sources of instability that, in the absence of corrective measures, may affect the long-run sustainability of the financial globalization that has occurred since 1980. Beyond the classic deflationary bias documented by Keynes long ago, the wave of financial globalization of late has deepened the divide between those countries that are issuers of hard currencies and those that are not.

The 2007–09 financial crisis further highlighted the asymmetries embedded in the current system, whereby the central banks of the United States and the euro area played a key role in propping up their economies by injecting unlimited amounts of liquidity, while non-hard currency issuers relied either on their massive foreign exchange reserves or on financial support from the International Monetary Fund (IMF) to shield their economies from the transmission of the financial crisis.

Meanwhile, the scale and severity of the crisis drove the attention of world leaders, policy makers and analysts to the policy responses needed to put the global economy on a recovery path. In so doing, it narrowed the scope of the debate over the long-term systemic determinants of a stable international monetary system that, to some extent, had surfaced throughout the earlier part of the decade in relation to the large global imbalances and their effects on the current global reserve system.

This chapter first reviews the historical foundations of the current international monetary system, highlighting early attempts to analyse and control its potential sources of instability. It then elaborates on the increasing sources of asymmetries exhibited by the monetary system in the recent decades. It ends with an assessment of options for reforms based on recent proposals.

---

1 The author gratefully acknowledges various exchanges with Kemal Derviş and Jose Antonio Ocampo on the issues covered in this chapter.

Early Plans for the Post-War International Monetary System

The inherent flaws in the international monetary system stem from the fact that it does nothing to ensure that balance-of-payment surpluses and deficits will compensate each other without negatively affecting the global economy. In his preparatory work for the Bretton Woods conference in 1944, Keynes underscored that in the global monetary system there exists a fundamental asymmetry running against deficit countries, which in turn spurs a global deflationary bias: in the face of insufficient financing, the adjustment that deficit countries must achieve to balance their external accounts will not be matched by expansionary policies in surplus countries, as the latter are not under equal pressure to adjust.

Foreshadowing Bretton Woods

This awareness of the intrinsic asymmetry in the international monetary system prompted Keynes to elaborate his reform proposals. Prior to his better known plan of the early 1940s for an international currency union, in the concluding chapter of his Treatise on Money, which may be regarded in some respects as the plan's first draft, Keynes has already included a supernational bank and advanced such concepts as an international reserve unit, national borrowing quotas, and world price-level stability with full employment (Keynes [1930] 1971, [1943] 1969).

With the end of World War I, Keynes focused on the problem of unemployment in the United Kingdom. In his view, it was a direct consequence of an inadequate level of investment caused by excessively high interest rates. At the same time, he was acutely aware that if the United Kingdom's monetary authorities dared intervene in open market operations to reduce the level of interest rates, given the gold standard and fixed foreign exchange rates, the lower interest rates *vis-à-vis* the rest of the world would have brought about an outflow of gold. To counteract such an outcome, some form of international cooperation was required, which Keynes included in his proposed supernational bank, whose membership would be reserved to central banks.

In Keynes's vision, the national monies of the central banks belonging to the supernational bank would be purchasable and encashable, in the bank's own money on the same terms as gold. Eventually the national monies would become encashable only in supernational bank money, ensuring that the latter would assume the role of international standard of first instance, with gold—into which bank money would then be encashable—serving as the ultimate standard. The supernational bank would regulate terms of credit to central banks through both the bank rate and the discount quota. These would be largely determined by consultations and joint action with and between the central banks, whose senior officials would be asked to discuss their respective credit policies at monthly meetings of the board of the supernational bank and to respect to the extent possible the credit lines jointly endorsed. In addition, the bank would have discretionary power to conduct open market operations, by buying or selling securities on its own accord.

The commonalities between this plan and the more in-depth plan for an international clearing union drafted by Keynes in 1942 are well known. Both plans called for the settlement of net international balances by bookkeeping entries as opposed to gold transfers. Both would make available to the individual nations vast new international reserves. Both would allow member countries to run up fairly large debit balances without being obliged, as under the gold standard, to put their domestic economies in order. As with the supernational bank plan, Keynes's clearing union proposal provided for the discretionary borrowing rights of the various national central banks to be limited by discount quotas and for the supernational bank to engage in open market sales of securities in any country where domestic inflation appeared to be out of line with the rest of the world. In the clearing union plan, Keynes also recommended quota limitations on the drawing rights of the member countries. He was nevertheless convinced of the willingness and ability of the various central banks and governments to engage in sensible domestic monetary and fiscal policies, as witnessed by the provision in both of his plans for sufficient international reserves to allow any given nation to pursue, within very considerable limits, whatever domestic monetary and investment policies it saw fit (Horsefield 1969a).

In Keynes's vision of international cooperation, a fundamental premise was that creditor as well as debtor countries should assume responsibility for balance-of-payment adjustments. This symmetric aspect of the international monetary system was to be elaborated more clearly in his later plan for an international clearing union.

Keynes's efforts to establish an international framework to support the long-run stability of the global economy overlapped with those of Harry White of the U.S. Treasury. In a draft dated March 1942, White conceived the international bank, later to become the World Bank, that would make loans partly in the currency of the borrowing country and partly in its own notes (Oliver 1975). These notes would be non-interest-bearing and redeemable in gold, on demand by any member government. The bank would maintain at all times a gold reserve of at least 50 percent, and its note-issuing power would be limited to 100 percent of the par value of the obligations to the bank of all member governments. Repayment and interest payments on the loans would be in local currency, to the extent that local currency was borrowed and in international bank notes or gold for the difference.

The most innovative feature of this plan was that the proposed international bank could issue non-interest-bearing notes. It was White's intention that these notes should, like gold, serve as an international reserve and a medium of exchange. Had White also proposed that the notes should serve as monetary reserves for the various member nations and that the international bank should regulate the supply of these notes in the interest of stability of the world price level, his proposal would have resembled Keynes's 1930 plan for a supernational bank. In White's plan, the international bank notes were a counterpart to the bancor overdrafts of Keynes's clearing union proposal and were not unlike the special drawing rights (SDRs) now available to member governments of the IMF. The most important difference between the two plans was that White's international bank notes would not have been issued at the discretion of borrowing countries as readily as bancor overdrafts, nor would they have financed general balance-of-payment deficits as do SDRs. They would have been issued only to finance reconstruction or development projects approved by the bank.

White made it clear that his proposed international bank notes would be used primarily to increase the loanable funds at the bank's disposal. According to White, the notes were to be as good as gold, and, thus, member states were to be as willing to accept and hold them as they were to accept and hold gold or SDRs today.[2] In the end, this particular feature was eliminated from the international bank proposal as the war drew to a close and as discussions in Washington on the post-war economic order turned increasingly political.

Preparing for Bretton Woods

In efforts to shape the post-World War II international monetary system, two competing visions soon materialized: the U.S. Treasury plan—as elaborated by Harry White—was to be more restrictive than Keynes's clearing union plan, as it was meant to finance only temporary balance-of-payment disequilibria and with considerably greater discretion than the automaticity of drawings implied in Keynes's plan. While Keynes was hoping for an institution that would act on the basis of pre-agreed rules, White wanted an institution with substantial discretion in the way it would manage the international monetary system.

In Keynes's ([1941] 1973) own words: 'The *essence* of the scheme is ... the extension to the international field of the essential principles of *banking* by which, when one chap wants to leave his resources idle, those resources are not therefore withdrawn from circulation but are made available to another chap who is prepared to use them—and to make this possible without the former losing his liquidity and his right to employ his own resources as soon as he chooses to do so'. Thus, the new entity would keep banking accounts for central banks along the same lines as central banks keep accounts for commercial banks. The accounts would be denominated in an international currency (bancor) of (adjustable) value in terms of gold. Keynes's plan differed from regular banking in that his institution would charge an interest rate on both debit and credit balances, thereby stimulating adjustment in both surplus and deficit countries. The clearing union would ask any member with a substantial debit balance to take corrective action, but this would not include deflationary policies through monetary measures along the lines of the automaticity of the gold standard (Horsefield 1969a).

Keynes insisted that the drawing rights in his clearing union were not intended to finance long-term investment: 'It should be emphasised that the purpose of the

---

2   If this feature had been included in the final design of the World Bank as agreed upon at the Bretton Woods conference, the World Bank's lending capacity would have been many times the initial paid-in capital.

overdrafts of bancor permitted by the Clearing Union is, not to facilitate long-term, or even medium-term, credits to be made by debtor countries which cannot afford them, but to allow time and a breathing space for adjustments and for averaging one period with another to all member States alike, whether in the long run they are well-placed to develop a forward international loan policy or whether their prospects of profitable new development in excess of their own resources justifies them in long-term borrowing' (Horsefield 1969b). But the U.S. believed that in this way too much of the burden of balance-of-payment adjustment might fall on the surplus country or countries. It feared that the UK plan might simply enable some countries to finance substantial current account deficits of a semi-permanent nature with no real obligation to restore external equilibrium, thus forcing inflation upon a surplus nation (like the U.S., at the time) (Viner 1943).[3]

As it turned out, White's plan shaped to a greater extent what turned out to be the IMF. He envisioned a body that would stabilize foreign exchange rates, encourage the flow of productive capital, help correct the distribution of gold among countries, reduce the necessity and use of foreign exchange controls, eliminate multiple currency practices and bilateral clearing arrangements, reduce barriers to foreign trade, and, finally, promote more efficient and less expensive clearings of international exchange transactions.

In the White plan, furthermore, any member could purchase the currency of any other member upon the fulfilment of specific conditions: the currency requested was to meet an adverse balance-of-payments shock with respect to the country issuing the requested currency, the purchase would not exceed the amount contributed by the member, and the relevant exchange rate would be defined by the IMF. If a country wanted to make a larger purchase of foreign currency, it needed first to secure 80 percent of the members' votes, accept the condition to undertake corrective measures as recommended by the IMF, and agree to repay the purchase within the time limit set by the IMF.

What most profoundly separated the Keynes and White plans, then, was that the Keynes plan allowed debtor or deficit countries to run up substantial debit balances without the express approval of the clearing union, while White's plan made it more difficult for debtor or deficit countries to obtain international credits arbitrarily from the IMF. In other words, while Keynes emphasized national economic sovereignty, White thought it better to codify the rules of governmental behaviour in international monetary and investment matters and therefore wanted any new international organization to scrutinize every transaction meticulously.

---

3   This line of reasoning was similar to that expressed by Americans and Europeans concerning the issue of SDRs by the IMF in the 1970s, although their respective positions had reversed.

After Bretton Woods

From its inception in 1946 through the first three decades of its existence, the IMF was the cornerstone of a rule-based system of exchange rates. The economic order envisaged by the Bretton Woods founders was designed to spur international trade and growth by ensuring that all countries had a convertible currency and that the exchange rate system as a whole was stable. Thus, the international monetary system evolved into the Bretton Woods exchange rate system whereby each currency—but one—would be pegged to the U.S. dollar and the latter to gold (the gold exchange standard).

The aim was to set up a system that could offer a reasonable anchor of stability, as the gold standard had a few decades before, but without the same significant shortcomings. The painful cost faced by the UK in the 1920s in terms of deflationary pressures was very much on Keynes's mind. White had great appreciation for gold as a medium of exchange but was wary of relying on it as the international monetary anchor. Moreover, he was well aware that, for an open international trade system to come into being after the end of the war, gold would need to be redistributed from the U.S. to the rest of the global economy.[4] As a result, the ensuing gold-dollar feature of the Bretton Woods system, acknowledging the inelasticity of gold supplies, relied on the U.S. currency to provide for the increase in international reserves, as required by the envisaged steady expansion of international trade.

On a broader level, the U.S. was committed to shaping an international monetary system that would guarantee monetary policy stability, following the turmoil that the country had experienced through the Great Depression. In contrast, the British were aiming to create an international monetary system that would offer more freedom of action in conducting their monetary policies, following the painful strictures endured by the Bank of England in the 1920s when it found itself unable to tailor monetary policy to the economy's needs in the face of gold standard constraints. Thus, the ensuing gold exchange standard of Bretton Woods was thought to be a pragmatic alternative to the gold standard, meeting as it did both the American desire for pegged exchange rates to promote the recovery of international trade and the British desire to pursue the exchange rate adjustments needed to accommodate policies aimed at sustaining its balance of payments (Eichengreen 2007). After a country was admitted into the IMF's membership, the country's exchange rate would become subject to IMF scrutiny and could only be altered in accordance with the rules upheld by the IMF. Exchange rates were the anchors for ensuring international economic cooperation. Every member of the IMF committed to a par value system—a fixed but alterable exchange rate—that did not impose restrictions on current payments and transfers.

---

4   The U.S. share of gold roughly doubled from 35 percent to 70 percent from the mid 1930s to the mid 1940s, as the country accepted gold contributions in return for its war efforts.

With the collapse of the Bretton Woods system in the early 1970s, the IMF was no longer required to apply rules to any country wishing to alter its exchange rate. The major exchange rates were now freely floating and, as a consequence, the role of the IMF in the international monetary system in general and its capacity for exchange rate surveillance changed. After the fixed parities system was abandoned, the IMF's Interim Committee met in Jamaica in 1976 to begin amending the IMF's Articles of Agreement. The result was the Second Amendment of 1978 which set up the framework for the IMF's modern surveillance function. The new framework reflected the preference for a flexible regime that would foster adjustment through regular consultations but still allow individual countries themselves to create the conditions for attaining domestic macroeconomic objectives. That is, exchange rates stopped being the anchor for international monetary cooperation; rather, the IMF became the new, institutional anchor of the post-Bretton Woods system (see Saccomanni 2008).

The IMF's new role was achieved by strengthening the obligations of the membership. The most important of such obligations are those found in the amended Article IV of the IMF's Articles of Agreement, regulating the IMF's new surveillance mandate. Article IV implies a commitment on the part of each member country to adhere to a code of conduct on exchange rate policies, as well as on domestic economic and financial policies. At the same time, it mandates to the IMF the responsibility of monitoring each member's adherence to the code. Specifically, Section 1(i) stipulates the cooperative behaviour required of a member country in formulating its own economic policies so as to contribute to an 'orderly economic growth with reasonable price stability' (IMF 2009b). Section 3 establishes the role of the IMF as the overseer of the international monetary system and outlines the obligations that each member must fulfil and for which the IMF must verify compliance. In particular, the IMF is charged with the task of exercising 'firm surveillance over the exchange rate policies of members' in order to ensure the effective operation of the international monetary system. Each member must provide the information necessary for the IMF to discharge its task and must consult with the IMF whenever asked to do so.

An asymmetry has been observed in the current mandate for IMF surveillance between the obligations of each member country and the IMF's lack of effective instruments for their enforcement (Lombardi and Woods 2008). While member countries are required to abide by a code of conduct, the articles do not give the IMF the tools necessary to enforce the code's implementation. This is in direct contrast with the IMF's role in the Bretton Woods fixed exchange rate system, whereby the IMF had to validate the exchange rate parity of a member country with the U.S. dollar. Furthermore, whereas a member's economic policies resulted in an unsustainable external position, the need to protect the exchange rate parity in the Bretton Woods system put additional pressure on the member to comply with IMF prescriptions that went hand in hand with balance-of-payment financial support. In the post-Bretton Woods era, this same pressure applies only to (potential) borrowing members, that is, the developing economies. It does not typically apply to advanced economies or members determined not to turn to the IMF for balance-of-payment support. By this time, the IMF is no longer regarded as a credit union, where all members were deemed equally likely to apply for temporary balance-of-payment support to uphold the fixed exchange rate system. There comes to be a distinction among the membership between creditors and (potential) borrowers, approximately reflecting that between industrial and developing countries (Lombardi and Woods 2007).

Asymmetries in the International Monetary System

With the end of World War II and the steady expansion of the world economy in the decades that followed, an expanded stock of international reserves was required to smooth balances of payments and insulate economies from shocks to their international accounts. This could be accumulated only in the form of dollars, and, as a result, the stock of dollars held outside the United States in the form of liquid balances was growing relative to the stock of monetary gold and, in particular, relative to the stock of monetary gold held by the U.S. authorities. It was only a matter of time before concerns emerged about whether the U.S. could continue to stabilize the relative price of the two assets (Eichengreen 2007). The gradual accumulation of dollars made possible by U.S. expansive policies is precisely what led to the abandonment of the gold-exchange standard in the early 1970s.

By adopting the dollar—a national currency—as the international reserve currency, Bretton Woods had created its own internal instability, captured by the so-called Triffin dilemma in accordance with the work of the Princeton economist of the same name (Triffin 1961, 1968). There must be a current account deficit in the U.S. in order for other countries to build up net dollar assets; however, U.S. deficits weaken confidence in the dollar as a reserve currency, which means that adjustments may be necessary to restore credibility—or reverse dollar depreciation—although this would only intensify the system's deflationary bias.

Thanks to such embedded asymmetries in the international monetary system, the U.S., with its central position in the global reserve system, developed a completely independent monetary policy. It represents yet another way in which the U.S. authorities enjoy international seigniorage through the use of the dollar as the world reserve asset. The country's technical ability to insulate its monetary base as a result of the dollar reserve currency status depends on a worldwide perception that U.S. treasury bills are the world economy's safest assets. This implies that the determinants of U.S. interest rates are fairly independent of the exchange rate of the U.S. dollar against other currencies; this goes against the usual assumptions of open macroeconomic models, whereby runs on currencies are typically connected to upward pressures on domestic interest rates, as evidenced by the experience of most countries facing balance-of-payment crises (Derviş 2010).

The only major constraint on the U.S. in running an independent monetary policy was the possibility early on that other countries might transform their dollar reserves into gold. However, this constraint was eliminated at the start of the 1970s, as the system moved from the gold exchange standard to a fiduciary dollar standard. Insofar as the U.S. does not consider the actual or possible weakening of its currency a condition to be rectified, the implication resulting from the absence of any constraint whatsoever on U.S. monetary policy is that, in contrast to Keynes's classic views of the deflationary bias in the global reserve system, in certain periods a fiduciary dollar standard can indeed exhibit the opposite phenomenon: an inflationary bias (Derviş 2010).

An additional source of asymmetry of the current international monetary system is the fact that it is inequitable. The demand for foreign exchange reserves leaves developing countries no choice but to transfer resources to the countries issuing those reserve currencies—a case of reverse aid (United Nations 2001). In the financial and capital market liberalization of recent decades, this particular asymmetry has become even more pronounced due to pressures exerted by strongly procyclical flows that developing countries must confront in world financial markets, which ultimately limit the countries' ability to adopt countercyclical macroeconomic policies.

In the case of a country with a hard currency, the monetary authority in effect represents a source of precautionary finance by means of the rediscounting and other facilities it makes available. A good example of this is the European Central Bank: it has put large amounts of liquidity at the disposal of the banking system but does not face the danger of a collapse in the (external) price of the euro. This does not hold true in emerging market economies. Their national currencies are not reserve assets in the international economy, so the supply cannot be remarkably increased lest the currencies face a severe decline in value. As a result, there has been an enormous accumulation of foreign exchange reserves on the part of developing countries attempting to 'insure' themselves against capital flow reversals. This adds to the more traditional 'precautionary' demand for reserves in commodity-exporting countries against commodity price volatility (Derviş 2009; Ocampo 2009).

Counter to expectations, the increased exchange rate flexibility since 1980 has not led to decreased demand for reserves in developing countries. On the contrary, developing countries amassed more reserves than ever before. Both the 1994 Mexican crisis and the 1997–99 Asian crisis after it showed developing countries that sudden reversals in capital flows could be far more destabilizing than fluctuations in current account transactions. Moreover, the demand for reserves increased owing to financial sector crises, which triggered balance-of-payment crises. Sudden changes in exchange rates have traditionally meant capital losses for banks with currency mismatches on their balance sheets and, consequently, large recapitalization needs. Central banks with strong reserve positions are better able to assist governments in recapitalizing banks, since the reserves represent a source of strength on the consolidated public sector balance sheet and allow governments greater flexibility and better access to capital markets. In other words, countries unable to issue large amounts of currency without witnessing a collapse in its value must hold fast to hard currency reserves, regardless of whether they have a floating exchange rate (Derviş 2009).

A strong current account is seen as one of the factors that has positive effects on growth because it reduces the dependence on the volatility associated with capital flows. If, however, this were to become the general thinking of developing countries, it might lead to a significant breakdown in the global trading system. This self-protection motive forces countries to absorb net capital flows in the form of additional foreign exchange reserves, which is costly and contrary to the rationale for capital flows in the first place, namely to transfer resources from rich to poorer countries. A further implication is that the additional rationale for capital account liberalization—to diversify risk—is clearly insufficient, as countries would, regardless, feel as if they need the additional self-protection of larger foreign exchange reserves (Perry 2009).

Clearly, were a large group of developing countries to follow this route, it would generate a current account surplus and an additional demand for safe assets. This would have contractionary effects on the world economy unless matched by current account deficits and the supply of those assets by industrial countries. Self-protection is both a costly form of insurance for individual countries and a source of instability for the global economy. What is needed, rather, is a solution to the demand triggers for self-protection, specifically the strongly procyclical capital and trade flows and the lack of adequate supply of collective insurance against balance-of-payment crises (Ocampo 2009).

Inequities in the international monetary system are certainly nothing new. But from the 1990s onward, their presence has been increasingly felt, as developing country economies have pursued trade and domestic financial liberalization, and capital account liberalization brings with them the associated risks. For potential creditors, procyclicality is merely a response to the risks involved in lending to developing countries; these risks, however, are not independent of the countries' positions in the global economy or, more importantly, in the global reserve system. This is a fundamental asymmetry in the current system.

Since 2000, the accumulation of global imbalances has prompted renewed demand for a substantial change in the international reserve system. If SDRs were created regularly and allocated to countries as reserves, there would be less need to create reserves through a U.S. balance-of-payment deficit, and the desire for reserves would not then bring global payments imbalances. If the recent allocations were supplemented periodically by further allocations, the current dollar-based international reserve system could gradually be replaced by a system in which the SDR would be a key global reserve asset (Derviş 2010; Ocampo 2009).

Governing Asymmetries in the International Monetary System

Strengthening Special Drawing Rights

Prompted by the need for strengthening the reserve asset position of developing country economies, the G20 endorsed a general allocation of SDRs equivalent to $250 billion, which became effective on 28 August 2009.[5] Created by the IMF in 1969, the SDR is an international reserve asset designed to supplement member countries' official reserves. Its value is based on a basket of four key international currencies: the euro, the yen, the pound sterling, and the U.S. dollar. SDRs can be exchanged for freely usable currencies and the IMF acts as a broker between members and prescribed holders to ensure that SDRs can be exchanged in the absence of a settlement system. SDRs are costless assets. However, if a member's SDR holdings rise above its allocation, it earns interest on the excess; conversely, if it holds fewer SDRs than allocated, it pays interest on the shortfall. In other words, SDRs provide the option of acceding to a loan without maturity, whose cost is indexed to money-market interest rates.

In the context of the 2007–09 financial crisis, the provision of the potential credit contained in SDR holdings was intended to provide support for liquidity-constrained countries through unconditional financing, by limiting the need for adjustment and allowing greater scope for countercyclical policies (IMF 2009c). The broader aim was to alleviate the concerns of those countries that might be induced to increase their reserve assets in response to the systemic uncertainty stemming from a crisis by managing their exchange rates so as to generate a large trade surplus. If such policies were to be followed by several countries at once, the global trading system, and worldwide economic activity along with it, would experience a serious downfall (Truman 2009).

Yet because SDRs are an artificial unit of account with limited scope for use within the existing agreed parameters, the head of the Chinese central bank proposed a significant overhaul aimed at enhancing the role of the SDR (Zhou Xiaochuan 2009). Building on the notion of a truly global fiduciary currency, Zhou Xiaochuan's proposals aimed to establish a settlement system between the SDR and other currencies; actively promote the use of SDRs in international trade, commodity pricing, investment and corporate bookkeeping; and create financial assets denominated in SDRs. SDRs would thus be key in reducing the fluctuations of asset prices denominated in national currencies and, more broadly, in creating a supranational reserve currency that removes the inherent instability of the

---

5 The allocation was designed to provide liquidity to the global economic system by supplementing the IMF members' foreign exchange reserves. Separately, the Fourth Amendment to the IMF Articles of Agreement provided for a special one-time allocation of SDRs, which was made effective on 9 September 2009. The total of SDRs created under the special allocation would amount to SDR 21.5 billion (about $33 billion).

international monetary system embedded in the use of a single-nation credit-based currency.

By proposing the increased adoption of SDRs in commercial and financial transactions, Zhou's proposal would have undermined the role of the dollar as the main international means of payment. It would have made the SDR a full-fledged supernational currency. It is relevant that the Chinese proposal was based upon the notion of the IMF as the overseer of the international monetary system and a truly supernational institution, as witnessed by the suggestion that part of member countries' reserves be entrusted to the centralized management of the IMF, as a way to deter speculation and to stabilize financial markets.

Subsequently, the United Nations Commission of Experts of the President of the UN General Assembly on Reforms of the International Monetary and Financial System (2009) advocated a greatly expanded role of the SDR through regular or cyclically adjusted emissions as a better way to deal with international economic risks facing countries that are not issuers of hard currencies. Such emissions would provide developing countries with a more stable source of funding and would counteract the inequity bias embedded in the current international reserve system. That said, even in such a reformed system, the existing rules still limit the extent to which SDRs are interchangeable with hard currency liabilities indexed to money market interest rates.

Strengthening the Institutional Anchor: Reforming the IMF

The unprecedented shock facing the global economy in 2007–09 brought about a rapid increase in IMF financing, admittedly from historically low levels. This happened against the backdrop of the IMF's own substantially declining financial resources, in relation to various global economy metrics, since the last general increase in member quotas in 1998.

The mobilization of unprecedented resources by the G20 leaders aimed to ensure that the IMF could comfortably meet potential demand from member countries, while bolstering public confidence that international spillovers could be adequately managed. Because a general quota increase might require time, IMF resources were supplemented by official borrowing. The latter included direct bilateral lines of credit, issuance of notes, and the expansion of existing credit arrangements within the so-called New Arrangements to Borrow (NAB).[6] However, unless these resources are permanently endowed to the IMF through a quota increase, in the medium term its role as a stable provider of precautionary reserves and emergency finance is unclear, despite recent best efforts.

---

6   In the past, official borrowing was activated to fund the oil facilities in 1974–75, the supplementary financing facility in 1979–81, and, later, the enlarged access policy of 1981–86. Borrowing peaked in the mid 1980s, but played its most important role in relation to the size of the IMF in the late 1970s, when borrowing financed over 60 percent of IMF credit and represented almost 30 percent of total quotas.

In the context of a deepening worldwide crisis increasingly threatening the stability of the world economy, days before the G20 London Summit in April 2009—where a rapid and substantial increase in the IMF's lending capacity would be agreed on—the IMF announced a significant overhaul to its lending framework. In an effort to provide collective insurance through its own facilities, the IMF established a flexible credit line (FCL), granting uncapped resources to countries with a sound track record of policy implementation. In an unprecedented move, three countries—Mexico, Poland, and Colombia—requested IMF precautionary assistance under the FCL terms. Access limits to IMF resources under the other facilities were doubled.[7] The unused Supplemental Reserve Facility and the Compensatory Financing Facility were dropped. Conditionality was simplified by scrapping structural performance criteria in favour of greater reliance on program reviews and *ex ante* policy measures.[8]

All these reforms aiming at greater institutional effectiveness occurred in an environment of no substantial governance reform.[9] Several contributions underscored that the asymmetric distribution of the voting power in the institution's decision making did not reflect the current international economic order. The triangular interaction between the distribution of voting power, the majority rules adopted in the institution's decision making and the composition of

---

7   Non-concessional loan access limits for countries were doubled, with the new annual and cumulative access limits for IMF resources being 200 percent and 600 percent of quota, respectively. These higher limits aimed to give countries confidence that adequate resources would be accessible to them to meet their financing needs. Access above these limits would continue to be provided on a case-by-case basis under the so-called exceptional access procedures.

8   In parallel, the IMF stepped up its concessional lending framework for low-income countries. Besides doubling concessional lending access limits, the IMF capacity was increased to up to $17 billion through 2014, including up to $8 billion over the next two years, from an annual concessional lending capacity of roughly $6 billion in 2008. This exceeded the G20's call at the London Summit to double concessional lending. Thanks to the mobilization of additional resources, including from sales of IMF gold, the IMF would grant interest relief, with zero payments on outstanding concessional loans through the end of 2011, to sustain low-income countries while they cope with the crisis. Moreover, interest rates would regularly be reviewed so as to preserve the concessionality of the resources loaned to poor countries. Finally, facilities for low-income countries were overhauled with the aim of better meeting the needs of low-income countries and the crisis challenges they are coping with.

9   Meanwhile, several reviews have been conducted inside the IMF itself (Independent Evaluation Office of the IMF 2008); in the so-called G20 process, where IMF reform was been the focus of a dedicated working group (G20 2009); and through other initiatives fostered by independent institutions, non-governmental organizations, and scholars (Lombardi 2008). The IMF held consultations with the 'fourth pillar' (made up of academia, think tanks, and civil society organizations) on the IMF's own governance reform process, which produced a report (Lombardi 2009).

the executive board, are key in understanding the sources of the current bias in the IMF's governance (Lombardi 2009).

The distribution of voting power shapes the allocation of board chairs and thus the dynamics and tone of the institution's decision making. Another source of asymmetry in decision making is the majority rule, which means that a simple majority of votes is needed for most decisions. The election of the managing director by only a simple majority provides the legal underpinning to allow a few members to steer the whole selection process. Even when super majorities are required, far from protecting the less powerful members they typically result in providing a single country, namely the U.S., with a blocking veto over decisions.

These biases in the IMF's own governance, besides creating a sense of disengagement in the members left as policy takers, generate a significant asymmetry, insofar as a minority of members (with a majority of votes) makes decisions applicable to the broad membership. That same minority may, however, unilaterally exempt itself from compliance due to the control it exerts over the institution's decision making. In the redesign of the post-crisis international financial architecture, where the IMF is asked to strengthen surveillance on the international economic and financial system, this creates a great source of tension.

What Comes Next?

As the 2007–09 financial crisis unfolded, the IMF gained significantly in prominence. By discussing IMF issues at G20 summits, for the first time in history, government leaders took on a task they traditionally mandated to their respective finance ministers. What this means in the long run for the role of the IMF in the international monetary system is unclear. Two scenarios can be envisaged.

In the first, member countries would use this opportunity to address the greatest challenge that the IMF has faced since the end of the Bretton Woods era in the 1970s, when its membership withdrew political capital from the institution, making it ineffective as a forum for multilateral discussions. That shift in authority away from the IMF and back to member countries was a defining feature of the new IMF role that emerged after the demise of the Bretton Woods system, whereby national policy makers claimed for themselves absolute discretion in setting their economic policies (Lombardi and Woods 2008).

To counteract this shift and its effect on the IMF, member countries would have to be willing to delegate to the institution some sovereignty over their economic policies, so as to make the IMF a true solution-finding forum. So far, however, the IMF's own ministerial committee, the International Monetary and Financial Committee (IMFC), has played a marginal role in the reform process. This has renewed calls from officials, analysts, and civil society organizations for the activation of Schedule D of the IMF's Articles of Agreement, concerning the establishment of a decision-making ministerial council (see Derviş 2010).

While this would give greater political impetus to IMF decision making, under this scenario its role cannot be merely subordinate to that of the G20. Ideally, the G20 finance ministers could be dissolved into the IMF's ministerial council, as suggested by Mervyn King (2010), governor of the Bank of England. However, history suggests that member countries want to retain flexibility by having their own interministerial forums in which to discuss economic issues of common concern, in addition to multilateral forums. As a result, the relationship between the new ministerial council and the G20 may be one of coexistence, the contours of which will have to be defined as experience is gathered.

In the second scenario, the G20 would indeed become the global steering committee, with the IMF serving as an executive arm (despite the existence of a ministerial council), as it is highly regarded for its fast, competent implementation capacity. Its political capital, however, would still be provided by entities outside the institution. This perhaps more realistic scenario is in line with the history of the recent decades and with the new policy coordination framework agreed by the G20 in 2009, which commits their members to a mutual assessment of their economic policies drawing on the IMF's analytical expertise (IMF 2009d). Both scenarios, however, hinge on the IMF as the international agency for overseeing the international monetary system. The former does so by providing the institution with greater political capital and legitimacy, the latter by assigning to it a role of implementing agency.

Consistent with both interpretations is the renewed interest in the IMF shown by the G20 countries, which significantly stepped up the IMF's lending capacity in order to build confidence that the financial crisis would not spill over, unchecked, to emerging market and other developing countries. However, under the first scenario, such enhanced lending capacity would be geared toward underpinning the institution's main role of provider of 'the machinery for consultation and collaboration on international monetary problems', as stated by Article I(i) of the IMF's Articles of Agreement (IMF 2009a). Under the second scenario, more simply, the lending capacity would underpin IMF support for medium- and small-sized members when hit by a crisis, upon their request. The scope and nature of the next institutional reforms will determine what role the membership intends to attribute to the IMF.

References

Derviş, Kemal (2009). 'Perspectives on Better Global Governance.' *Today's Zaman*, 17 March. <www.todayszaman.com/tz-web/detaylar. do?load=detay&link=169782> (August 2010).

Derviş, Kemal (2010). *Precautionary Resources and Long-Term Development Finance: The Financial Role of the Bretton Woods Institutions after the Crisis* 4th annual Richard H. Sabot Lecture, 11 June. Center for Global Development. <www.cgdev.org/content/publications/detail/1423582> (August 2010).

Eichengreen, Barry J. (2007). *Global Imbalances and the Lessons of Bretton Woods* (Boston: MIT Press).

G20 (2009). 'G20 Working Group 3: Reform of the IMF.' 4 March, Final Report. <www.g20.utoronto.ca/docs/wg3-imfreform.pdf> (August 2010).

Horsefield, J. Keith (1969a). *The International Monetary Fund, 1945–1965: Twenty Years of International Monetary Cooperation* Vol. I: Chronicle (Washington DC: International Monetary Fund).

Horsefield, J. Keith (1969b). *The International Monetary Fund, 1945–1965: Twenty Years of International Monetary Cooperation* Vol. III: Documents (Washington DC: International Monetary Fund).

Independent Evaluation Office of the International Monetary Fund (2008). *Governance of the IMF: An Evaluation.* International Monetary Fund, Washington DC. <www.ieo-imf.org/eval/complete/eval_05212008.html> (August 2010).

International Monetary Fund (2009a). 'Article I: Purposes.' Articles of Agreement. <www.imf.org/external/pubs/ft/aa/aa01.htm> (August 2010).

International Monetary Fund (2009b). 'Article IV: Obligations Regarding Exchange Agreements.' Articles of Agreement. <www.imf.org/external/pubs/ft/aa/aa04.htm> (August 2010).

International Monetary Fund (2009c). *Guidance Note for Fund Staff on the Treatment and Use of SDR Allocations.* 28 August. International Monetary Fund, Washington DC. <www.imf.org/external/np/pp/eng/2009/082809.pdf> (August 2010).

International Monetary Fund (2009d). *The G20 Mutual Assessment Process and the Role of the Fund.* 2 December. International Monetary Fund, Washington DC. <www.imf.org/external/np/pp/eng/2009/120209a.pdf> (August 2010).

Keynes, John Maynard ([1930] 1971). 'A Treatise on Money.' In *The Collected Writings of John Maynard Keynes*, Vol. VI (London: Macmillan).

Keynes, John Maynard ([1941] 1973). 'Proposal for an International Currency Union, Letter to Montagu Norman, 19 December 1941.' In *The Collected Writings of John Maynard Keynes,* Vol. XXV: Activities, 1940–1944 (London: Macmillan).

Keynes, John Maynard ([1943] 1969). 'Proposals for an International Clearing Union.' In J.K. Horsefield, ed., *The International Monetary Fund 1945–1965,* Vol. III: Documents (Washington DC: International Monetary Fund).

King, Mervyn (2010). 'Speech at the University of Exeter.' 19 January. <www.bankofengland.co.uk/publications/speeches/2010/speech419.pdf> (August 2010).

Lombardi, Domenico (2008). 'Bringing Balance to the IMF Reform Debate.' *World Economics*, vol. 9, no. 4, pp. 13–26.

Lombardi, Domenico (2009). *Report to the IMF Managing Director on the Civil Society (Fourth Pillar) Consultations with the IMF on Reform of IMF Governance.* International Monetary Fund, Washington DC.

Lombardi, Domenico and Ngaire Woods (2007). *The Political Economy of IMF Surveillance.* Working Paper No. 17. Centre for International Governance Innovation, Waterloo, ON. <www.cigionline.org/publications/2007/2/political-economy-imf-surveillance> (August 2010).

Lombardi, Domenico and Ngaire Woods (2008). 'The Politics of Influence: An Analysis of IMF Surveillance.' *Review of International Political Economy,* vol. 15, no. 5, pp. 711–739.

Ocampo, José Antonio (2009). 'Reforming the Global Reserve System.' In S. Griffith-Jones, J.A. Ocampo, and J. Stiglitz, eds., *Time for a Visible Hand: The Lessons from the 2008 World Financial Crisis* (New York: Oxford University Press).

Oliver, Robert (1975). *International Economic Co-operation and the World Bank* (London: Macmillan).

Perry, Guillermo (2009). *Beyond Lending: How Multilateral Banks Can Help Developing Countries Manage Volatility* (Washington DC: Center for Global Development).

Saccomanni, Fabrizio (2008). 'Managing International Financial Instability.' 11 December, Remarks at a meeting of the Peterson Institute for International Economics, Washington DC. <www.bis.org/review/r081217c.pdf> (August 2010).

Triffin, Robert (1961). *Gold and the Dollar Crisis: The Future of Convertability* rev. ed. (New Haven: Yale University Press).

Triffin, Robert (1968). *Our International Monetary System: Yesterday, Today, and Tomorrow* (New York: Random House).

Truman, Edwin M. (2009). 'Message for the G20: SDR Are Your Best Answer.' 6 March, A commentary in the VoxEU Debate on the Global Crisis: Development and the Crisis, VoxEU. <www.voxeu.org/index.php?q=node/3208> (August 2010).

United Nations (2001). *Report of the High-Level Panel on Financing for Development.* Ernesto Zedillo, chair. United Nations, New York. <www.un.org/reports/financing/full_report.pdf> (August 2010).

United Nations Commission of Experts on Reforms of the International Monetary and Financial System (2009). *Recommendations.* A/63/XXX. Draft, 19 March. United Nations, New York. <www.un.org/ga/president/63/letters/recommendationExperts200309.pdf> (August 2010).

Viner, Jacob (1943). 'Two Plans for International Monetary Stabilization.' *Yale Review,* vol. 37, no. 1, pp. 77–107.

Zhou Xiaochuan (2009). *Reform the International Monetary System.* 23 March. Bank for International Settlements. <www.bis.org/review/r090402c.pdf> (August 2010).

PART VII
From G8 to G20

Chapter 17

Reconciling the Gs: The G8, the G5, and the G20 in a World of Crisis

Andrew F. Cooper and Andrew Schrumm

The era of the traditional G8 summit configuration appears to be coming to an end. The shockwaves of the 2007–09 financial crisis exposed both a significant shift in global economic power and a weakness of governance mechanisms to respond and correct. Influence and authority in world affairs are slipping away from traditional poles in the industrialized North, requiring a new power-sharing arrangement with the major economies in the global South. Pre-crisis suspicions of the inability of institutions established in a different era—such as the G8—to broker solutions in this new political and economic environment were reinforced. Mercifully, a much wider recognition quickly emerged at the outset of financial collapse of the need for authentic global solutions to such complex and far-reaching problems.

In addition to the G8's well-examined flaws concerning legitimacy as a global steering committee are its increasingly accentuated problems of efficiency of delivery in functional areas. When the financial tsunami hit in autumn 2008, it was thus the G20—elevated to the leaders' level—that moved to the pivotal position of crisis management, not the G8. This phenomenon bolstered the notion that the major challenges presented to global governance could no longer be addressed without the equal participation of, and buy-in from, the emerging powers. The move to the G20, however, has revealed the risks of duplication or competition in the concurrent operation of the various Gs—the G8, the G5, and the G20—and the need to reconcile their mandates, agendas, and practices. This chapter thus has two core objectives. The first is to examine more closely the deficiencies of the G8 configuration and strategies employed to mitigate them. The second is to examine whether, due to its vulnerabilities, the G8 will be permanently eclipsed by the G20 or other bodies that better represent the current global economic order. It argues that, while the G8 has considerable accumulated strengths, the financial crisis has accentuated its structural flaws and prompted a reconfiguration of informal global leadership for the 21st century.

The G8's Double Challenge

The longstanding structural criticism of the G8 has been its inability to escape a serious double challenge of legitimacy and efficiency. The greatest source of weakness—as well, paradoxically, of its strength in terms of club cohesion—is its self-selected (and unelected) status. To China, India, and most other outsiders, it is precisely this feature that demarks the G8 as an illegitimate body in contrast to the universal form of multilateralism via the United Nations system (with all its formalism).

On top of the legitimacy issue is the build-up of the G8's efficiency gap. The G8 was meant to function as a body coordinating the practices of its own membership. As Robert Putnam (1988) and others described a long time ago, this role was performed in a dual fashion: with a keen eye on both the one big G8 table and on the individual domestic tables back at home.[1] It has been a role that all the members have had a huge stake in performing. In terms of managing the affairs of the rising powers, however, the G8 has little credibility. The G8 could not simply dictate in order to affect change. It had to engage with the 'upstarts' in the system outside the club.

What has transformed these tensions over a democratic deficit into a structural crisis has been the increased inability of the G8 to deliver effectively on an issue-specific basis. On many of its traditional economic concerns, the G8 has shown itself to be stronger with words than with deeds. On currency revaluation, in particular, the G8 has focused great attention on exhorting action from China, but has had little or no impact. The same can be seen in declarations on foreign policy and security issues, with firm statements on the Middle East but no tangible results. At the same time, the G8 has continued to expand its agenda in areas of global governance. It has been in these non-traditional areas, however, that many of its perceived and celebrated successes have come. Influence and progress on social and development issues, such as debt relief for Africa and global health campaigns, have overshadowed the G8's core economic and security efforts.

Still, rather than subduing criticism, these successes actually increase the normative need and procedural momentum for G8 reform. While evident even in the early operations of the G20, the global economy can no longer be managed (or globalization reshaped) without the active participation of the major emerging powers (Cooper 2007). When extended to the social and development arena, this governance gap is magnified. China, India, and Brazil—each regional economic and political hubs—have extended their own functional reach in these domains to share resources and knowledge among developing countries while at the same time boosting trade linkages. As these trends continue, can leaving them out of the G process be seen as ethical or even practical?

From this perspective, the concept of a G20 at the leaders' level as the nucleus of global governance has a number of attractions. To begin with, a leaders' G20 has an innovative quality that allows it to transcend many if not all of the G8's

---

1   The G8 began with only six members present at Rambouillet in 1975, when France, the United States, the United Kingdom, Germany, Italy, and Japan. Canada attended the next meeting and the group became known as the G7 until 1998, when Russia was invited to the summit table. For the purposes of this chapter, however, the term 'G8' is used throughout.

deficiencies (Carin and Thakur 2008). The very essence of the G20 configuration is to go beyond the tightly defined membership limits of the G8 and engage a wider set of countries in truly global debates. In particular, it includes the Group of Five of countries (China, India, Brazil, South Africa, and Mexico) that met in parallel fashion to the G8 from 2007 to 2009 to enhance South-South dialogue at the leaders' level. Moreover, the G20 is premised on an extension of the equality of membership, where each country has the same authority and responsibility. Operating on the basis of this principle comes into tension with the concept of outreach or 'variable geometry' as advocated by the defenders of the G8 concert in place.

The second feature that adds weight to the progressive credentials of the G20 initiative is its global and interregional dimensions. In terms of concert plurilateralism, it is precisely the informality of the crucial top-down case—the G8—that produces the club-like atmosphere of the summit. Although tested by disagreements on a wide number of issues (most divisive, perhaps, on the Iraq war), the glue that has held this forum together has been a shared mindset concerning basic rules and processes concerning liberal democracy, individual liberty, and the rule of law.

Expanding membership of the G8 to a group of highly 'unlike' states is thus an idea that is both ambitious and risky. At the instrumental level, the logic is unassailable from a reformist (albeit not transformational) perspective to absorb major emerging powers such as China, India, Brazil, and others from the South into the longstanding club with all its informal rules, patterns of socialization, and voice and participation opportunities. This integrative motivation is tied up in turn with the high level of anxiety about the future global order not only from the peripheral actors but also at the core of the global system. From an institutional point of view, it is clear that if these emerging and emergent powers are not brought in and accommodated, they could concentrate their activities on other clubs that operate outside the G8 domain, such as the Shanghai Cooperation Organisation (SCO) and the India-Brazil-South Africa (IBSA) Dialogue Forum, or that compete with the G8 with respect to international rule making, such as the rise of the summit of the BRICs—Brazil, Russia, India, and China.

The G20 from Concept to Reality

Given the nature of the G8's double challenge, advocates of a G20 at the leaders' level have not been surprised that the concept has become reality (Carin and Thakur 2008). Studying the G20 closely since 2003, experts at The Centre for International Governance Innovation (CIGI) had asserted that a G20 would only come about through a major structural crisis that reverberated through the entire global system. Many issues that could have provoked such a meeting were deflected to other forums, whether the meeting of 40 health ministers during the avian influenza outbreak or the activities of the Major Economies Forum on Energy and Climate (MEF). However, the financial tsunami of 2008 finally triggered a G20 at the leaders' level, just as the Asian financial crisis of 1997–99 had triggered the original machinery of finance ministers and central bank governors. If unanticipated, the crisis played to the G20's established functional strengths in coordination (see Helleiner and Pagliari 2008).

The theme of legitimacy was well rehearsed during this early phase of institutional change. Paul Martin (2009), the formal head of the G20 finance at its establishment, picked up on this topic in his campaign for reform: 'Whatever form the renewed global financial architecture ultimately takes, all countries must "buy into it" and take ownership. Only then will the framework have legitimacy.' But the development of this theme was left to academics, who privileged the legitimacy concept (see Bergsten 2004; Porter 2000; Sohn 2008). The early academic literature, however, missed an appreciation of the forward-looking vision driving the G20 finance initiative. With symbolism came a deep concern with efficiency. What should not be overlooked were the ways this orientation went well beyond 'managing' the fallout from the immediate crisis of 1997–99 to a concern with innovative policy entrepreneurship. At the core of the novel quality of the G20 finance was the institutional design of the forum. Up to that point the post-1945 financial architecture had been almost exclusively the preserve of the industrialized countries of the North. The International Monetary Fund (IMF) and the G8 were central pivots to this system, with the G8 expanding its role most dramatically after the Mexican peso crisis. However, there were many other important parts to this system as well, including the Group of Ten (G10) central bank governors.

The establishment of the G20 finance forum set a precedent by opening up membership on a procedural basis to the global South. Not only did a large group of countries from the South—from all quadrants of the globe—participate in the G20, but these countries also gained some significant ownership of the forum. The informal culture of the G20 provided countries from the South with a sense of 'we-ness'. The order and distribution by which countries from the global South took on the hosting function (India in 2002, Mexico in 2003, China in 2005, South Africa in 2007, Brazil in 2008, and Korea in 2010) showed that the G8 was willing to share in this instrument of power. This was, perhaps, a signal of the uniqueness of the G20: it was about improving the global financial system, as well as specifically bringing in the major emerging powers as part of a rearranged system, and more generally into the structure of globalization.

To highlight the point that the G20 was not just a narrow, technical forum, the G20 ministerial meeting in Montreal in 2000 focused on the opportunities and challenges to globalization (Hajnal 2007, 154). The equity rationale was compelling. Acting on the wider purview of the 'Montreal consensus' from the 2000 meeting, the G20 expanded its range of interest to encompass promotion of the UN Millennium Development Goals (MDGs). But the main argument, which also prompted a call for an extension to a leaders' summit, was based on instrumental necessity. As Angel Gurría (2005, 63), secretary general of the

Organisation for Economic Co-operation and Development (OECD) and former Mexican finance and foreign minister, put it bluntly, 'the different forums that deal with globalization are not working'.

Reinforcing the visionary aspect—as opposed to simply a sense of pragmatism—about the push to bring in the emerging powers from the South was the appreciation that these countries had other options beyond the ones offered through the G20. It was not simply a case of 'allowing' a country in. A G20 had to offer something to China, India, and others that they could not find elsewhere—they had to want to join the club.

This question of buy-in from the global South was not clearly defined. China had invested in its reputation as a universalistic-orientated actor, consistent with its role as a privileged member of the Permanent Five (P5) of the United Nations Security Council (UNSC) and as a country that valued the role of Bretton Woods institutions in China's modernization since the 1980s. Therefore, entering more restrictive club systems, especially those offered by the G8, involved considerable problems. Externally there were abundant reputational sensitivities about China eroding its solidarity with the rest of the global South. Internally there were concerns that China—by joining forums such as the G20—was making itself susceptible to criticism about its domestic policies.

The ability to establish the G20 finance starkly demonstrated how much progress had been made on both sides. And with the Asian crisis—and alternative initiatives such Japan's proposed Asian monetary fund (which China opposed)—the incentives for China being brought into the G20 'big tent' gained momentum. Since the start, China has actively participated in all G20 meetings—including successfully hosting the October 2005 finance ministerial. The success of the G20 in building trust and connections between the G8 countries and China—along with the other big emerging countries of the global South—needs to be acknowledged (see Chin 2008).

Still, the visionary component of the G20 does not end with the mechanisms inherent to that forum. While the substantive details of the G20 meetings deserve attention—preventive technical sharing on codes and standards in transparency and financial sector policy—the forum's catalytic quality elevates it to a higher stratum. In the face of global economic catastrophe, the G20 became the natural site for leaders' level crisis management not only for its capability of technical regulation but because of its representative North-South membership.

Constraints on the G20

At its inception, the prime task of the G20 finance was inevitably that of seeking solutions to vulnerabilities in the financial system. Yet, in the aftermath of the September 11 terror attacks, the agenda shifted toward security-oriented priorities. The 2002 ministerial in New Delhi accelerated the fight against the financing of terrorism, while the 2003 meeting in Morelia, Mexico, focused on global poverty as a root cause of terrorism. Another current that swept through the G20 was the recognition that as the financial issues it sought to address were global in nature, so too were many issues on the G8 agenda. Terrorism, climate change, energy security, and health governance were among issues that could not be effectively addressed if left only to the G8—the traditional 'steering committee' of industrialized countries.

Viewed through this positive lens, it is easy to suggest that the G20 at the leaders' level constitutes a mechanism ready to seize the moment, turning a structural dilemma into institutional innovation and creative initiatives. The initial set of G20 summits—Washington in November 2008, London in April 2009, and Pittsburgh in September 2009—sent a sharp message that world leaders preferred hanging together through collective efforts rather than hanging separately through instinctive but short-sighted unilateral efforts. With its solid association via the G20 finance machinery and the IMF—another institution that revitalized itself in a time of crisis—the G20 boasts not only technical capabilities but is also favourably positioned as a catalyst for wider technical and institutional reform.

Yet for all of these positive attributes, some constraints remain before the G20 at the leaders' level can emerge as the summit of summits. The G20 as a hub of global policy making and governance is premised on the assumption that leaders (as opposed to finance ministers) will maintain their focus on the solutions as well as the problems associated with the financial crisis. As already recognized, most of these remedies are highly technical, whether dealing with a college of supervisors, implementing the accords set out by the Basel Committee on Banking Supervision (BCBS), responding to securities regulation, or crafting central bank legislation. A core challenge will be whether this agenda combines the right ingredients necessary to maintain the commitment of all G20 leaders (already two leaders did not attend the 2010 Toronto Summit, for domestic political reasons, and one did not attend the 2010 Seoul Summit, for health reasons). The London Summit banked in part on the magnetism of its host United Kingdom prime minister Gordon Brown, while the Pittsburgh Summit offered many G20 leaders the first opportunity to visit U.S. president Barack Obama on his home soil. But as the G20 begins to complete its primary tasks, economic order overcomes chaos, and the unifying threat of crisis subsides, there is the risk that a sense of G20 fatigue could emerge.

The G20 summit is not free from critique, particularly of its representational claims or its performance quality. As a replica of the G20 finance forum, the G20 leaders' format and membership have the merit of convenience (see Woods 2009). Argentina and Turkey were included in the G20 finance largely because of their position as debtor countries, but this rationale no longer stands up well. Perhaps alternative criteria, including the inter-civilizational dimension, should be added (for example, promoting Turkey but not Argentina). The G20 also privileges Saudi Arabia as a wealthy Arab country, as opposed to others with greater claims of diplomatic representation, most notably Egypt.

The issue of European overrepresentation continues to be sensitive. After more than 10 years of euro currency consolidation, the European Union still lacks an international strategy or a common position in multilateral forums, yet it occupies a plurality of G8 seats. French president Nicolas Sarkozy may be lauded for his diplomatic skills in adding Spanish and Dutch appearances at the G20 Washington meeting, along with the presence of the four European G8 members and the European Commission president. However, this persistent imbalance has created a backlash, prominently from the African Union (AU) for equal or fair representation, and has renewed calls from the global South for IMF quota and voice reforms to address disproportionate European weight (Subacchi and Helleiner 2009). The move by leaders at the Pittsburgh Summit to call for similar reforms, of reallocating up to 5 percent of voting shares to the emerging economies, can be seen as diverting open confrontation on the issue.

Another critique is whether the G20 can catalyse change beyond its immediate economic mandate. From its initial meetings, achievements came in the blend of old and new winners in this institutional evolution. The IMF, which appeared to be nearing obsolescence before the crisis, rebounded robustly with greatly enhanced lending capacity. By the infusion of bilateral government loans into the IMF's quasi credit line (the New Arrangements to Borrow [NAB]), the IMF's issuing of bonds denominated in its special drawing rights (SDR) currency, the selling parts of its gold reserves, and expediting a general increase in its members' quotas, the IMF was reinvigorated. However, with this renewed mandate, the IMF faces the challenge of meeting the needs of countries combating financial difficulties in turbulent economic times. Its task, however, is different now from the financial crises of the 1970s, 1980s, and 1990s. Today it is the emerging market economies and oil-producing states that have the surplus capital to shore up international financial liquidity. Yet these capital-surplus members are not interested in the IMF, because they view it as a reflection of the outdated economic power of the Europeans and Americans (Momani 2009, 40). If the G20, as the hub of global economic governance, is to change institutional processes and perceptions, it will take time and persistence. One positive development toward this end, coming largely out of the shadows, was the Financial Stability Board (FSB), which was expanded both in functions and in membership, and provided the emerging powers with greater oversight on more issues.

The leaders' personal engagement combined with the momentum of the G20 offers the prospect of a multi-element grand bargain that has implications for a fundamental redesign of the international organizations responsible for the global economy. Akin to the critical junctures of the Great War and the World War II, the financial crisis provided an opportunity to think and act on an ambitious scale. At its core, this vision must be directed not only to get the international economic organizations to work more effectively on an individual basis, but also to do so in an interconnected fashion. As evident in the 2007–09 crisis, monetary policy affects trade and investment flows and trade policy affects macroeconomic policy.

The G20 has distinguished itself as a crisis committee but its record and legacy are still to be played for. In its initial meetings, it faced tests that covered both systemic and institutional dimensions. All the momentum it has built up can be eroded if the implementation stage is not delivered in a timely and substantive fashion. Leaders are not always comfortable with details and their attention can wander back to domestic needs and interests. Sherpas and other officials have become overburdened with a myriad of meetings, and the possibility of the reduced effectiveness arising from a multiplicity of forums must be recognized and addressed. Since the Pittsburgh Summit, the G20 has been measured by a different measuring stick. Having declared itself the 'premier forum of international economic cooperation,' it has become institutionalized with obligations and expectations.

Indeed some observers view the G20 as a *status quo* institution and not a reformist one—precisely because it has not triggered new momentum toward true reform of the UN or international financial institutions (IFIs). This view is held most strongly in a country such as Japan, which sees itself a 'loser' with the rise of China in the G20 while unable to move into the UNSC itself. As leading Japanese commentator Kazuo Ogoura (2009) asks, 'if the tip of the balance of economic power requires a change in economic dialogue, is it not more important to change the pattern of the international political structure?' Others see the consolidation of decision making in the G20 as a threat to multilateralism, calling for a 'G192' through the UN General Assembly (Hilary 2009). Although there is a self-serving component in any specific idea for extended piece of reform (from those with the reward of enhanced status), it does not reduce the importance of the catalytic issue. The ancillary question is whether any reform initiatives—including those pertaining to the G20—will simply reinforce club diplomacy. Talk of a 'G2' of the U.S. and China, or a new concert of nations, simply reinforces this point.

Any notion of the G20 as part of networked diplomacy by contrast must be sharply nuanced with the emphasis being on networking between leaders and their personal advisors. This image may help the technical efficiency but will reduce the legitimacy. This gap is most widely associated with civil society. But the gap extends to other domains as well, most notably the lack of participation in the G20 activities by parliaments. The call by Colin Bradford (2003), made as part of the project to create the leaders' G20, has still not been heeded: 'Parliamentarians are more directly accountable to the public than executive administration officials … But parliaments around the world have been less engaged in "foreign affairs" issues than in domestic issues.'

Despite these constraints, the G20 format enjoys clear advantages over the established G8 format, particularly evident in the wake of the G8's 2009 L'Aquila Summit, where the Italian hosts stretched notions of variable geometry. The G20 process takes the positive features developed through G8 summitry—the personal engagement of leaders, detailed preparation by sherpas—but expands it to provide equal status for big emergent states from the global South. Moreover, the putative deficiencies can be managed by some further refinement. One way forward is to institutionalize the process beyond a hosting rotation, by developing a rotational G20 secretariat or informal management group that shares organizational duties equally among all members. Another, bolder, step is to pare the G20 down to a more manageable G13 or G14, with strong participation from the major emerging powers, which French president Nicolas Sarkozy has historically advocated.

Dilemmas of Variable Geometry

As explored throughout this chapter, the ascendancy of the G20 has called into question the future of the G8 as the central node of global governance. On the face of it, the G8 has increasing difficulty justifying itself as the 'likeminded' group— due to the presence in its ranks of Russia—particularly in a time of economic crisis with all of its global ramifications. Yet some G8 leaders maintain serious reservations about any form of 'big bang' membership expansion along the lines of a permanent G20 leaders' forum that would replace the traditional club. In 2009, Italy, one of the most resistant countries to membership reform, chaired the G8. The stop-gap solution offered by the Italians was a form of variable geometry as an attempt to minimize the deficiencies and maximize the comparative advantages of this summit process *vis-à-vis* the G20.

The 2009 G8 L'Aquila Summit will be remembered for clustering different leaders and heads of international organizations who were invited for topic-specific discussions of issues such as trade, climate, food, and aid. The first day was reserved exclusively for the G8 leaders, their discussions focused on the world economy and their declaration offered a near carbon copy of the G20 London Summit communiqué. On the morning of the second day, the G5 countries were added to the mix, with final reporting on the structure and key topics of the Heiligendamm Dialogue Process (HDP). Significantly, in another break from the G20 formula, Egypt was added to these discussions. In the afternoon, the second leaders' level meeting of the MEF was convened on climate and energy (Schrumm 2009). On the third and final day, the summit table was expanded even further to include a group of African leaders to discuss collaborative food security initiatives and new aid relationships. In a sharp differentiation from the G20's summits at the time, the president of the AU was also invited. This form of participation circumvented the dilemma of selecting African representation beyond South Africa and now Egypt. It also signalled that Africa would not be forgotten by the G8 during the financial crisis.

Over the course of the summit, the Italians welcomed the leaders of Algeria, Angola, Australia, Brazil, China, Denmark (as chair of the UN's Copenhagen conference on climate change), Egypt, Ethiopia (as chair of New Partnership for Africa's Development [NEPAD]), India, Indonesia, Korea, Libya (as AU chair), Mexico, Netherlands, Nigeria, Senegal, South Africa, Spain, Sweden (as EU chair), and Turkey. They also invited the institutional heads of the AU, the European Commission, the Food and Agriculture Organization, the International Energy

Agency, the International Fund for Agriculture and Development, the International Labour Organization, the IMF, the OECD, the World Food Programme, the UN, the World Bank, and the World Trade Organization.

While this approach tempered expectations for straight-up reform while allowing for inclusion of the key non-G8 countries, the practice of variable geometry cannot be sustained over the long term. Thomas Wright (2009, 179) argues that effective reform of global institutions should include 'the states most relevant to a particular set of problems, whether it is arms control, climate change, or the global economy'. Yet in the informal G8 process, it inserts a new layer of complication, sustaining the 'who's in, who's out' mentality and underlining the outreach dimension so rejected by the emerging powers. In trying to avoid the question of conditions for membership, variable geometry muddles any constructive discussion and creates problems of inclusivity by putting labels on these various formats (Davis and Schrumm 2009). By definitional standards, some countries straddle various categories: Russia may be in the G8 but has been a leader in the BRICs group, and Mexico may be in the G5 but it is an active member of the OECD. By advancing different country groupings for issue-specific discussions, variable geometry creates numerous overlapping structural dilemmas. More importantly, instead of creating a mechanism to address the G8's deficiencies of representation and effectiveness, variable geometry emphasizes the club's inability to create and deliver global solutions on its own.

The Heiligendamm Process as a Middle Path

The G8's HDP offered some possibility of opening up a middle path for initiating change in the international system. In terms of intensity, it shifted the onus from a grand or big bang approach—transforming the global structure at the apex of authority—to a more diplomatic incremental process (see Cooper and Antkiewicz 2008). In terms of membership, it balanced the claims of China as the largest and most challenging emerging power with those of the rest of the G5 as additional (if uneven) emerging powers and robust democracies.

This process, it must be acknowledged, was overshadowed and indeed overtaken by the rise of the G20—where the G5 and G8 have equal status—and other impromptu calls for G8 enlargement. Nonetheless the theme of both incrementalism and a targeted membership remained built into its declarations. An excellent illustration of this perspective comes out in one of the frequent references to G8 reform made by France's Sarkozy (2007):

> The G8 must continue its slow transformation, which got off to a good start with the Heiligendamm Process. The dialogue conducted during recent summits with the top leaders of China, India, Brazil, Mexico and South Africa should be institutionalized and scheduled for an entire day. The G8 can't meet for two

days and the G13 for just two hours. That doesn't seem fitting, given the power of these five emerging countries. I hope that bit by bit, the G8 becomes the G13.

While enlargement may not have been on the formal agenda at the 2007 G8 Heiligendamm Summit, the major milestone of that summit was the deliberation on the future relationship between the world's most industrialized countries and key emerging countries. In recognition of their stature as major economic and diplomatic players, China, India, Brazil, South Africa, and Mexico were invited to participate in a structured forum for ongoing dialogue with the G8 countries over the following two years. The HDP was established to focus on four topics: the promotion of innovation, the enhancement of free investment and corporate social responsibility, common responsibilities in respect to African development, and knowledge exchange on technologies to fight climate change (G8 2007).

By the time of the 2009 G8 summit in L'Aquila—the official end-date of the HDP—the use of a low-key approach had produced a number of significant results in bridging the gaps between the G8 and the G5. Prompted by the global economic crisis, the need for cooperation among key countries was reinforced. The functional emphasis of the HDP allowed confidence to be built in an understated but sustained fashion (Leininger 2009). Rather than immediately fading away in the shadows of the G20, the HDP was extended for another two-year period with final reporting at its 2011 G8 summit in France. Renamed the 'Heiligendamm-L'Aquila Process' (HAP), its issue-based mandate was reinforced and structure reconfigured to be a dialogue among equal parties. If not a transformative outcome, the continuation of the Heiligendamm process offered ongoing, substantive dialogue among the major economies on important issues while at the same time providing for careful reflection on the long-term G8/G20 structural questions.

Despite overlapping membership and policy areas, the HDP/HAP tried to coexist with the G20 leaders' forum. After much posturing, by early 2010, the HAP signalled that the G8-G5 dialogue would revolve around development cooperation and related topics of food security and energy efficiency standards. While the G20 had the advantage of a wider array of countries involved, the G5 made up the dominant core both in economic and diplomatic terms. As such, it had some built-in advantages if the Gs become competitive rather than cooperative. The ability of the G20 to operate as a crisis committee provided it with strengths. However, it remains unwieldy, particularly after the addition of extra European countries at both the Washington and London meetings.

To highlight the early success of the Heiligendamm process is not to underestimate the challenges. Pressures increased over its second two-year cycle concerning delivery, especially as the HAP turned its attention to producing an interim report for Canada's 2010 G8 Muskoka Summit on possible common responses in sensitive issue areas, such as a new multilateral framework for accountability.[2] The desire to provide forward-looking and tangible results, while strengthening mutual understanding, increased the degree of difficulty in balancing this initiative alongside the G20's efforts to stabilize the world economy. Meanwhile, however, the spectacle of summitry continued. While the quick turn-around from London to L'Aquila to Pittsburgh allowed prompt follow-up on the core agenda items, the timing also strained the attention and energies of leaders, sherpas, and officials to carefully develop policy and appreciate the current shift in economic power.

In the past, structural reorderings have featured emerging powers claiming new powers of authority and voice in massive convulsions of the international system. Yet even with the degree of coercion attached to these decisive breaks with the *status quo*, huge amounts of uncertainty remained about the new order in terms of its institutional make-up and rules of the game. The 'regulative and allocative principles of the global system', in the words of Ian Clark (1991, 10), remained marked—and marred—by ambiguity, fragility, and the need for reassurance. Accentuated by its voluntary, diplomatic, and ad hoc or incremental nature, the Heiligendamm process reflected a high degree of contestation as even a partial resettlement to a new order—if not a new system of global governance. Space may have been allowed for an innovative form of engagement between the members of the old pivotal club of the North and the new elite of powers emerging from the South, yet questions remained whether incentives exist for those countries to promote an enlarged club system.

The Gs as Collaborators (Not Competitors)

As the nature of their relationship plays out, some element of tension among the G8, the G5, and the G20 is inevitable. Will the G8 be weakened by giving the core components of its traditional economic mandate over to the G20? Or does this create a better division of labour so both can coexist by concentrating on different topics? How does the level playing field of the G20 affect G5 unity? Will these Southern leaders embrace greater global responsibilities?

If the G8 can embrace the latter, it may strengthen its claim to global leadership (Kirton 2009). Where the G20 materialized in reaction to the economic crisis, both are autonomous bodies that each offer a 'distinctive agenda and global public goods'. The G20 can fill a gap on issues abandoned by the G8, such as financial stability, fiscal and monetary stimulus, financial regulation and supervision, and trade and investment liberalization, allowing the G8 to refine its processes and focus on social issues such as African development, climate change, health, energy,

---

2 By the time of the G8 Muskoka Summit, however, HAP participants were devoting their energies to the G8 and G20, and a further extension of the process seemed unlikely. While in the lead-up to the G20 Seoul Summit, development cooperation was identified as a future area for G20 leadership, further nullifying the HAP as a middle path.

and education, as well as critical political issues such as nuclear nonproliferation, security, and democratization. With leadership in these areas, the G8 is able to reinforce the image of club like-mindedness.

With the advent of the G20 as the premier forum for economic governance, the G8 cannot grab back credibility on the economic agenda. Its efforts to build clustered coalitions on social issues through variable geometry have demonstrated the G8's inability to act alone effectively. In the future, the G8 will have to regain some of the legitimacy associated with the G20—due to its more representative membership—and signal that it is ready to provide a comprehensive vision for 21st-century policy making and global governance (Cooper 2009). The preparations for the 2010 G8 Muskoka Summit indicated this type of strategy, offering small steps toward renewing confidence in the club of industrialized countries. Muskoka's theme of accountability—where likeminded members work to comply with commitments—appears to be a key part of this effort. Functionally, this will play out on the G8's approach to the MDGs, particularly with regard to maternal, newborn, and child health.

With the big emerging powers gaining the status of equal partners in the G20, the G8 has found it difficult to go back to traditional modes of outreach with the G5. For the first time since the 2005 Gleneagles Summit, the G8 leaders did not meet with their G5 counterparts at Muskoka. In a similar sense, leaders of China, Brazil, India, South Africa, and Mexico can boost the G8 through continued support of the HAP, despite its asymmetrical foundations, and develop stronger policy dialogue on international development cooperation.

Maintaining the *status quo* remains an option, but the risks attached to a deepening of G8 exclusivity must be appreciated as well. Without some complementary mode of reform in sync with the G20—whether via an exact replica in membership or through a G13 or G14—the G8 (or more accurately a G7, without Russia) will be relegated to a caucus. Again it may possess some strengths on security issues, but it will provoke a response by the G5 to reinforce membership in other clubs, whether the BRICs, IBSA, the SCO, or other new configurations. Instead of integration, this approach is likely to spark fragmentation.

The other option, arguably more constructive for global governance, also has negative consequences for the G8. This scenario would see the G20 emerge as the undisputed summit of summits. Having proven its legitimacy and effectiveness as an economic crisis committee, the G20 would widen its mandate from its technical and financial orientation to a forward-looking sociopolitical and economic agenda. This approach appeared to be the preference of the 2010 G20 Korean chair, which convened a presidential committee that, among other things, developed outreach strategies on both the issues and consultation to prepare for the Seoul Summit. Korea's efforts to further institutionalize the G20 supported its substantive agenda on development cooperation and public-private financing options.

In part, the future of the G8 configuration rests on the performance of the G20 and its ability to transcend established criticisms of the G process. While still in its early days, the G20 appears to be making the grade. As the sense of urgency provided by the crisis wanes, however, it will need to find new ways to sustain its momentum and cohesion. The G8 will likely live on in some modified form beyond 2011, as a caucus or streamlined forum, due to its accumulated strengths and historical ties. While the global economic crisis may have amplified the G8's double challenge, it may also have provided avenues for resilient reform.

References

Bergsten, C. Fred (2004). 'The G20 and the World Economy.' 4 March. <www.iie. com/publications/papers/paper.cfm?ResearchID=196> (December 2009).

Bradford Jr., Colin I. (2003). *Anticipating the Future: A Political Agenda for Global Economic Governance.* Brookings Institution, Washington DC. <www. brookings.edu/gs/bradford_anticipating.pdf> (August 2010).

Carin, Barry and Ramesh Thakur (2008). *Global Governance for a Global Age: The Role of Leaders in Breaking Global Deadlocks.* CIGI Policy Brief No. 7. Centre for International Governance Innovation. <www.cigionline.org/ publications/2008/11/global-governance-global-age-role-leaders-breaking-global-deadlocks> (August 2010).

Chin, Gregory T. (2008). 'China's Evolving G8 Engagement: Complex Interests and Multiple Identities in Global Governance Reform.' In A.F. Cooper and A. Antkiewicz, eds., *Emerging Powers and Global Governance: Lessons from the Heiligendamm Process* (Waterloo: Wilfrid Laurier University Press).

Clark, Ian (1991). *The Post-Cold War Order: The Spoils of Peace* (Oxford: Oxford University Press).

Cooper, Andrew F. (2007). *The Logic of the B(R)ICSAM Model for G8 Reform.* CIGI Policy Brief No. 1. Centre for International Governance Innovation, Waterloo ON. <www.cigionline.org/publications/2007/5/logic-bricsam-model-g8-reform> (August 2010).

Cooper, Andrew F. (2009). 'Down But Not Out.' In J.J. Kirton and M. Koch, eds., *The G8 2009: From La Maddalena to L'Aquila* (London: Newsdesk Publications).

Cooper, Andrew F. and Agata Antkiewicz, eds. (2008). *Emerging Powers in Global Governance: Lessons from the Heiligendamm Process* (Waterloo: Wilfrid Laurier University Press).

Davis, Ruth and Andrew Schrumm (2009). *Is the G8's Variable Geometry Sustainable?* Commentary, 14 July. Chatham House, London. <www. chathamhouse.org.uk/media/comment/g8_sustainable> (August 2010).

G8 (2007). 'Growth and Responsibility in the World Economy.' 7 June, Heiligendamm. <www.g8.utoronto.ca/summit/2007heiligendamm/g8-2007-economy.html> (August 2010).

Gurría, Angel (2005). 'A Leaders' 20 Summit?' In J. English, R. Thakur, and A.F. Cooper, eds., *Reforming from the Top: A Leaders' 20 Summit*, pp. 63–71 (Tokyo: United Nations University Press).

Hajnal, Peter I. (2007). *The G8 System and the G20: Evolution, Role, and Documentation* (Aldershot: Ashgate).

Helleiner, Eric and Stefano Pagliari (2008). *Towards the G20 Summit: From Financial Crisis to International Regulatory Reform.* CIGI Policy Brief No. 9. Centre for International Governance Innovation. <www.cigionline. org/publications/2008/11/towards-g20-summit-financial-crisis-international-regulatory-reform> (August 2010).

Hilary, John (2009). 'End the G8 Charade: We Need a G192.' *Guardian,* 6 July. <www.guardian.co.uk/commentisfree/2009/jul/06/g8-g20-g192> (August 2010).

Kirton, John J. (2009). 'Coexistence, Co-operation, Competition: G Summits.' *Aspenia,* no. 43-44 <www.g20.utoronto.ca/biblio/kirton-aspenia-2009.pdf> (March 2010).

Leininger, Julia (2009). *Think Big! Future Prospects of the International Summit Architecture: The G20, G8, G5, and the Heiligendamm Process.* Discussion Paper 6/2009. German Development Institute, Bonn. <www.die-gdi.de/CMS-Homepage/openwebcms3.nsf/(ynDK_contentByKey)/ANES-7SUGZM/ $FILE/DP 6.2009.pdf> (August 2010).

Martin, Paul (2009). *The International Financial Architecture: The Rule of Law.* Remarks prepared for the Conference of the Canadian Institute for Advanced Legal Studies, 12 July. Cambridge.

Momani, Bessma (2009). 'Facilitating Global Lending and Vital Reforms.' In A.F. Cooper and D. Schwanen, eds., *Flashpoints for the Pittsburgh Summit* (Waterloo: Centre for International Governance Innovation) <www.cigionline. org/publications/2009/9/flashpoints-pittburgh-summit> (August 2010).

Ogoura, Kazuo (2009). 'Whither G7, G8, or G20.' *Japan Times,* 26 May. <search. japantimes.co.jp/cgi-bin/eo20090526ko.html> (August 2010).

Porter, Tony (2000). 'The G7, the Financial Stability Forum, the G20, and the Politics of International Financial Regulation.' Paper presented at the annual convention of the International Studies Association. Los Angeles. <www. g8.utoronto.ca/g20/biblio/porter-isa-2000.pdf> (December 2009).

Putnam, Robert (1988). 'Diplomacy and Domestic Politics: The Logic of Two-Level Games.' *International Organization,* vol. 42, no. 3, pp. 427–460.

Sarkozy, Nicolas (2007). 'Fifteenth Ambassadors' Conference: Speech by M. Nicolas Sarkozy, president of the Republic.' 27 August, Paris. <pmv4.premier-ministre.gouv.fr/pm_article.php3?id_article=57109> (August 2010).

Schrumm, Andrew (2009). 'Energy Cooperation and Competition in Global Governance Reform.' Paper presented at the workshop on 'Emerging Powers and Global Governance Reform', Shanghai, 14 August.

Sohn, Injoo (2008). 'Asian Financial Cooperation: The Problem of Legitimacy in Global Financial Governance.' *China Quarterly,* vol. 194, pp. 309–326. <japanfocus.org/data/sohn.chi.fin_1654.pdf> (August 2010).

Subacchi, Paola and Eric Helleiner (2009). *From London to L'Aquila: Building a Bridge between the G20 and the G8.* Briefing Paper. Chatham House and the

Centre for International Governance Innovation. <www.chathamhouse.org.uk/files/14254_0609ch_cigi.pdf> (August 2010).

Woods, Ngaire (2009). 'The G20 Summit: Saving Globalisation ... Again?' *World Today*, vol. 65, no. 4. <www.chathamhouse.org.uk/publications/twt/archive/view/-/id/1883/> (August 2010).

Wright, Thomas (2009). 'Toward Effective Multilateralism: Why Bigger May Not Be Better.' *Washington Quarterly*, vol. 32, no. 3, pp. 163–180. <www.twq.com/09july/docs/09jul_Wright.pdf> (August 2010).

Chapter 18

The G8, the G20, and Civil Society

Hugo Dobson

At first glance, the impact of civil society on meetings of presidents and prime ministers orchestrated by bureaucrats might seem unlikely to amount to much. However, the role of civil society and its interaction with the various mechanisms of global governance and the G8 summit process specifically have been topics of popular debate and scholarly enquiry for several years now. This has been driven to a large extent by the success with which a number of civil society groups and non-governmental organizations (NGOs) have managed to penetrate the summit process and become recognized as important stakeholders in the process. The most notable and cited case is the Jubilee 2000 campaign and its successor, the Drop the Debt campaign. The campaign reached a peak of popular exposure at the 2005 Gleneagles Summit as a result of a march in Edinburgh with more than 200 000 protestors on the weekend before the leaders met, the Live 8 series of concerts held around the globe, and the access that the two public faces of the campaign—Bob Geldof and Bono—had to the host, United Kingdom prime minister Tony Blair, and the other G8 leaders (Cooper 2007). In addition, a number of 'uncivil' elements of civil society have targeted the G8 summit over the years reaching their own apogee of media attention at the 2001 Genoa Summit, which resulted in 230 injuries, 280 arrests, and the death of one protestor. Six years later at the 2007 Heiligendamm Summit protests once again peaked with tens of thousands of protestors clashing with German security forces; and in 2010, the demonstrations at the G8 Muskoka and G20 Toronto summits resulted in the largest group arrest in Canadian history.

These developments are not simply isolated, recent events. Rather, they are part of a historical process of interaction between the G8 and civil society. Peter Hajnal (2007, 103–116) has traced this process back to the original summit of the G7 at the château in Rambouillet in November 1975, and has categorized the evolving relationship into a series of phases. Initially, between 1975 and 1980, limited interaction existed between both camps, largely due to mutual ignorance. Thereafter, as the G7's agenda expanded between 1981 and 1994, civil society began to pay attention. This attention was particularly manifest in the creation of alternative summits. Between 1995 and 1997, the G7 began to return the compliment and recognized civil society both in terms of references in summit documentation, with NGOs mentioned for the first time in G8 statements at the 1995 Halifax Summit, and concrete engagement. Finally, from 1998 onward, civil society became better organized and more influential, even established, within the G8 summit process.

This chapter builds upon Hajnal's analysis by focussing on recent events, especially in light of the November 2008 creation of the G20 at the leaders' level while the G8 continues to meet. The G20 was originally a mechanism born of the Asian financial crisis of the late 1990s by which finance ministers met in 1999 for the first time under the vision of former Canadian prime minister Paul Martin (Kirton 2001). This mechanism was upgraded to the leaders' level in light of the financial crises and global recession of 2008. So far it has met in Washington on 14–15 November 2008, subsequently in London on 2 April 2009, in Pittsburgh on 24–25 September, in Toronto on 26–27 June 2010, and in Seoul on 11–12 November 2010 (Kirton and Koch 2009a, 2009b, 2009c, 2010a, 2010b). As of 2011, it will begin meeting once annually. The G8 met in Japan from 7 to 9 July 2008, a year later in Italy from 8 to 10 July 2009, and a year later in Canada on 25 to 26 June 2010. In between these three regular summits in the cycle of G8 summitry, the newly created G20 met in Washington, London, and Pittsburgh, with the Toronto Summit immediately following the G8's Muskoka Summit in 2010. As a result of this dual, and as yet murky, division of labour (Subacchi 2009; Subacchi and Helleiner 2009), these two mechanisms of global governance held five summits in the space of two years. Certainly the reasons and impetus for the creation of these groups are real and important, but what is left is 'a disorderly scrum of bodies fighting for turf', as once was said about the G7 (Economist 2004). Five summits in such a short time offer both a new target and considerable challenge for civil society activities in the most appropriate and effective use of resources. In this context, an article published on the web edition of *The Economist* on 2 April 2009 (after the first day of the G20 London Summit had concluded) traced the decline of anti-capitalist protests (Economist 2009a). The 1999 ministerial meeting of the World Trade Organization (WTO) at Seattle attracted 100 000 protestors, resulted in 520 arrests and damage to property and business of $13 million. A few years later, the 2001 G8 Genoa Summit saw 250 000 protesters, over 280 arrests, over 230 injured, $20 million in damage and the death of Carlo Giuliani. With the 2009 London Summit, only 4000 protestors gathered in the City of London on the day of the summit (although an additional 35 000 participated in a march before the summit) and smashed bank windows. The 2008 G20 Washington Summit had attracted limited and peaceful protest. Thus, in contrast to a decade of more high-profile protest going back to the WTO Seattle meeting and although civil society was once touted as a numeric addition to the alphanumeric mechanisms of global governance, it would appear possible that civil society activities might continue this decline not only in terms of the 'uncivil' civil society groups but also with regard to the more established organizations. This chapter will explore whether claims of the decline and death of civil society are greatly exaggerated by focusing on five summits. It concludes they are.

The G8 Toyako-Hokkaido Summit

The G8 Toyako-Hokkaido Summit was the fifth time for Japan to host the summit and the second time that it had been held outside of Tokyo.[1] Civil society activity was organized under the umbrella of the 2008 Japan G8 Summit NGO Forum. It was formed in January 2007 under the chair of Hoshino Masako and embraced over 120 NGOs. Building on previous developments before and during the 2000 Okinawa Summit, such as direct dialogue between the Japanese prime minister and civil society representatives of large-scale protest the weekend before the summit and providing a workspace for NGOs, a number of initiatives were introduced ahead of the 2008 summit.[2] Dialogue between the government and civil society was encouraged, with the prime minister's sherpa, Kono Masaharu, meeting with the forum on 19 February and again with the other sherpas on 24 April (Hajnal 2008). Furthermore, Prime Minister Fukuda Yasuo met with some of the NGO Forum representatives on 18 June for a 90-minute meeting, which was valued highly by a number of NGO members. During the summit itself, a number of civil society groups and NGOs were able to access the media centre but were given their dedicated space geographically separated from the media. NGO media centres were also established in Sapporo with the support of the local government.

Apart from the official summit proceedings, other events took place. These included a G8 Youth Summit on 11 to 15 March and a meeting within the Africa Partnership Forum from 7 to 8 April (Hajnal 2008). A Junior 8 (J8) Summit was held from 1 to 10 July in Chitose near Sapporo for the fourth time in summit history. It was hosted by the United Nations Children's Fund (UNICEF) and the Japanese Ministry of Foreign Affairs, and culminated in the delivery of a message

---

1 Previous summits held in Japan were the 1979, 1986, and 1993 G7 summits all in Tokyo and the 2000 G8 Summit held in Okinawa.

2 Other attempts at engagement with civil society at the 2000 Okinawa Summit included the following: the creation of the post of director general for civil society participation; the Japanese sherpa Nogami Yoshiji met with representatives of several NGOs such as Save the Children, Christian Aid, and Amnesty International; Prime Minister Mori Yoshiro met with the representatives of a number of NGOs calling for the cancellation of African debt, action on infectious diseases, and a reduction in the U.S. military presence in Okinawa and was handed by Jubilee 2000 a petition of more than 17 million signatures calling for debt cancellation (Hajnal 2002, 217); NGOs were involved in the follow-up to the summit including the creation of two taskforces to address the digital divide and renewable energy and a programme to combat infectious diseases; and—probably the most tangible action taken by the Japanese government—a workspace was constructed for 44 NGOs and 300 activists offering computers, telephones, and photocopiers during the summit. This was symbolic in that it was the first time for the host nation to create a physical space for NGOs to conduct their operations (Dobson 2004, 122–131). This was welcomed by some: 'I think the Japanese government made an effort to make this space for the NGOs and the chance to meet Prime Minister [Mori Yoshiro]. The equipment is great and people here are very helpful' (Japan Times 2000).

to the leaders. In addition, a University Summit from 29 June to 1 July at Hokkaido University brought together university presidents, deans, and rectors from 35 universities across the globe. A summit of world religious leaders was held from 2 to 3 July in Sapporo. Local groups advocating the Russian return of the Northern Territories and the resolution of the issue of kidnappings of Japanese citizens by North Korean agents (*racchi jiken*) were also active in using the summit to highlight their cause (Seaton 2008). Finally, and in parallel with the actual summit, an alternative summit was held in a suburb of Sapporo while the leaders met at the Windsor Hotel by the shores of Lake Toya.

In addition to these activities, some of which have an established tradition within the G8 summit process, new civil society-organized summits took place. An indigenous peoples' summit was held from 1 to 4 July, a month after the Japanese Diet passed the 'Resolution calling for the Recognition of the Ainu People as an Indigenous People of Japan' on 6 June, thereby granting the Ainu people such status for the first time, with the hosting of the G8 summit as a motivating factor for the Japanese government. As has been argued:

> As such, the G8 Summit made possible a critical moment—a moment for articulating agency—whereby a new generation of grassroots Ainu leaders were able to launch new initiatives, by harnessing the wave of international attention focused on Hokkaido in early July to articulate a new politics of Ainu indigeneity, which this time had received the imprimatur of Japanese officialdom (Lewallen 2008).

Moreover, a one-day symposium entitled 'Peace, Reconciliation, and Civil Society' was held on 9 July, the final day of the main summit, based on the question of 'what can citizens do to create peaceful future relations among the peoples of the world, while also recognizing historical responsibility?' (Zablonski and Seaton 2008). Thus, an active diary of events was in place and provided a considerable 'head of steam' for follow-up activities.

In contrast to this high level of activity, the low level of protest at the Toyako-Hokkaido Summit was notable. There was a demonstration held in the centre of Sapporo on the Saturday (5 July) before the summit began, but it only attracted 5 000 protestors (according to the most optimistic estimates), was heavily policed (in total 21 000 police, 16 000 from outside of Hokkaido, were mobilized to police the summit), and caused minimum disruption with only a handful of arrests. Cultural stereotypes that play down the importance and opportunities for protest in Japan do not explain the low numbers of demonstrations as previous G7 and G8 summits held in Japan had attracted extreme protests, including a mortar attack on the venue at which the leaders were meeting at the 1986 Tokyo Summit (Dobson 2004, 63–69). Philip Seaton captures the damp squib that the summit protests turned out to be:

Demonstrators had been kept a safe distance from the summit venue in campsites in the villages of Sobetsu and Toyoura. The demonstrators were not helped by inclement weather that left them bedraggled in their tents. Their soggy marches (where protesters were almost outnumbered by police) were covered on local television news, but on the first day of the summit a group of foreign demonstrators found their way out of the campsite blocked by police in riot gear. NHK followed the story of one student protestor, Sueoka Tomoyuki, who had traveled to Hokkaido from Kyoto to register his concerns about globalization. But while the small contingent of around 1,000 protesters had their moment in the local (and for an even shorter time national) spotlight, they were outnumbered and out muscled by the police. With no major disturbances around the summit venue, there was relatively little coverage of the anti-G8 and anti-globalization protests (Seaton 2008).

After the summit:

On 20–22 September, there was a meeting of representatives of many of the citizens groups that had organized events to coincide with the summit. Only a few dozen people attended, creating the impression that Hokkaido, like the rest of the world, moved on fairly quickly after the party was over. Then on 3–4 October, an exhibition was held at the Former Hokkaido Government Building (Aka Renga, 'Red Brick'). There were far more people queuing to taste one of the dishes on the summit dinner menu and buy organic vegetables from the stalls visited by the leaders' spouses on the second full day of the summit than there were people visiting the photo exhibition of the main summit (Seaton 2008).

The G20 Washington Summit

Four months after the G8 met in Japan, the first G20 leaders summit was held in Washington DC to address the worsening global economic and financial recession. Despite the touted importance of the meeting and the innovation demonstrated in creating this mechanism and attempting to bring the relevant leaders around the table, civil society activity was limited at best. On the civil side, it could be seen to have failed to build upon the momentum created in Japan. On the 'uncivil' side, there was little protest or disruption. In fact, the numbers were in the 'hundreds' and the mood was festive and peaceful (BBC 2008).

This is not to say that civil society was wholly absent from the event. Ahead of the summit, G20 leaders were the target of civil society campaigns. According to a report in *The Observer*, 'more than 600 civil society groups from over 100 countries have signed a petition calling for a wider range of countries to be involved, under the auspices of the United Nations' (Stewart 2008). The same report quoted Nick Dearden, director of the Jubilee Debt Campaign, saying 'our worry at the moment is that this will simply be a resuscitation of the existing system'. In the specific case of the UK, a coalition of 24 UK trade unions, charities, environmental, and religious groups wrote to Prime Minister Gordon Brown ahead of the summit stressing that:

> The current economic system has created great inequalities of wealth and power which are not only morally unjust, but also economically and environmentally inefficient and unsustainable. Tackling poverty and inequality is an essential part of recovering from this crisis …
>
> At the heart of the new approach should be a recognition that effective government action is needed to manage economies sustainably, and that past approaches have failed. The current structures and policies actively restrict the ability of governments to do what is needed to serve the public interest, and must be changed (Jubilee Debt Campaign 2008).

In addition, some civil society groups expressed concern about the issue of representation at the summit and the marginalization of the South. Finally, as possibly the first official interaction between the G20 and civil society, the G20-created task forces were charged with engaging 'in multi-stakeholder "downreach" with civil society experts, but only on a functional, epistemic community model, rather than a fully democratic one' (Kirton and Guebert 2009, 14).

The G20 London Summit

The venue for the second meeting of the G20 leaders was the ExCeL centre in East London's Docklands, although the focus for protest was the City of London and the Bank of England. In the run-up to the summit, there was a range of civil society activities. A meeting of G20 business leaders in collaboration with the Confederation of British Industry was held on 18 March to stress the need to avoid protectionism and relay this message to the G20 leaders. The International Trade Union Confederation called on the G20 governments to address issues such as climate change, job creation, and the nationalization of the banks.

Immediately before the summit on Saturday 28 March, the weekend ahead of the actual summit, 35 000 people participated in the 'Put People First' march in Hyde Park in central London, stressing 'jobs, justice and climate'. This served as an umbrella for more than 120 groups and organizations including Christian Aid, Oxfam, the Trades Union Congress, and the Campaign for Nuclear Disarmament.

On the less civil side of protest, the G20 London Summit was overshadowed partly by initial scaremongering of the media and police regarding the extent of possible violent protests breaking out among the 4 000 protestors during the summit itself. The phrase 'summer of rage' arose in much of the less rigorous reportage. A more balanced view depicted the scene as follows:

Anti-capitalists are billing it as 'Financial Fools' Day' and climate-change worriers are gearing up to protest against 'fossil fools'. For London's police, charged with protecting world leaders at the G20 summit and quelling the crowds who are massing to rail at them, April 1st is going to be a long day.

Police are expecting an 'unprecedented' coalition of protesters to gather in the city's financial district the day before the summit, to demonstrate against everything from Iraq to subprime mortgages. Groups last seen in the 1990s are thought to be unfurling their banners again, to take advantage of a force that is already stretched (Economist 2009b).

G20 Meltdown was one of the main groups organizing protests during the actual summit. Its attention focused on the war in Iraq, globalization, human rights, climate change, and so on. The mood was intended to be carnivalesque using the four horsemen of the apocalypse.

In total 10 000 officers were deployed (along with journalists probably outnumbering the protestors) in an operation that cost more than \$10 million. But a return to the anti-globalization protests of the kind seen at Seattle never materialized. Instead, reportage on the day noted the festive and peaceful nature of the protests. However, in the days that followed two examples of police brutality emerged. The first and more salient case was the death of Ian Tomlinson, who was hit with a baton and then pushed to the ground. He later died. Tomlinson was not protesting but returning home from his job as a newspaper seller. Ironically, it was an American fund manager who filmed the incriminating footage of the police assault that led to Tomlinson's heart attack. The second was an incident in which a female protestor was struck by police the day after Tomlinson died. Both cases emerged as a result of protestors filming the incidents (Economist 2009d). One outcome was the questioning and review of police tactics in handling these kind of political protests and their counterproductive use of the technique of corralling (or 'kettling') protestors for hours (BBC 2009b).

The G8 L'Aquila Summit

Peter Hajnal and Jenilee Guebert (2009) have documented a range of civil society activities that took place in the run-up to the hastily rearranged L'Aquila Summit of July 2009.[3] Like the previous year's G8 summit, these included meetings that embraced various stakeholders from governmental to intergovernmental to nongovernmental, and academic to religious to think tank experts. They included the Global Health Forum held in Rome on 13 February 2009, the G8 Youth Summit held in Bocconi

---

3   Originally the 2009 Italian-hosted summit was to be held in La Maddalena in Sardinia, but Italian prime minister Silvio Berlusconi decided to shift the venue to the earthquake-hit region of Abruzzo in April 2009, two months before the summit began on 8 July.

University in Milan from 15 to 19 March, and the Civil G8 Dialogue in Rome from 4 to 5 May that facilitated direct access for a number of NGOs (258 delegates in total) to the leaders' sherpas with a view to arranging a meeting during the summit itself (the mayor of Rome stressed the need for governments 'to listen to the voice of civil society—in the shape of associations representing public opinion— before taking action') (ANSA 2009). A religious leaders' meeting hosted by Pope Benedict XVI in Rome from 16 to 17 June included discussion of the G8's themes and a trip to L'Aquila with the goal of communicating a religious view of the issues discussed at the summit to the G8 leaders. This was the fourth time for these faith leaders to meet ahead of the G8 (Hajnal and Guebert 2009).

In addition, G8 Farmers Unions met in Rome on 19 March to discuss food security, hunger, and climate change and tap into the G8 agricultural ministerial meeting in April and the leaders' meeting in July. Heads of business organizations met in Cagliari from 23 to 24 April. The University Summit was held for the fifth time, in May at Valentino Castle in Turin. It brought together 40 university leaders from 19 countries, although thousands of students targeted the event for violent protests leading to injuries on both sides. Catholic bishops from the G8 countries wrote to their respective leaders urging them to increase contributions in official development assistance (ODA) and work towards the Millennium Development Goals (MDGs). Scientists from the G13 released a joint statement in June proposing a number of measures on climate change. A J8 summit was held in Rome from 5 to 12 July immediately ahead of and during the summit itself. The Global Call to Action Against Poverty (GCAP) organized a typically effective poster and internet campaign. Civil society organizations and NGOs had access to the media village in L'Aquila, in contrast to the previous year's summit where they had been located separately from the journalists.

Despite the declared intentions at the 2008 summit, no indigenous peoples' summit was held. The Indigenous Peoples' Global Summit on Climate Change was held in Alaska in April 2009 with the focus placed more on the UN than the G8. An alternative summit, named Gsott8, was held immediately before the actual summit in the original choice of venue of Sardinia.

As regards celebrity diplomacy, according to the *Irish Times*:

> Summit host Italian prime minister Silvio Berlusconi was given a torrid time when Bob Geldof had a private meeting with him in the government's Palazzo Chigi over the weekend. Questioning the prime minister's 'credibility' and his right 'to lead the G8', Geldof complained bitterly that Italy has thus far delivered on only 3 per cent of the aid promised to developing countries by Mr Berlusconi four years ago. According to the editor of La Stampa, Mario Calabresi, who was present for the meeting, the prime minister apologised, saying that 'we made a mistake'.
>
> Geldof found an unlikely ally in Pope Benedict XVI who called on the G8 leaders 'to maintain and boost development aid, not in spite of the crisis but precisely because this is one of the main solutions to it'. The pope went on to say

that he hoped the 'voice of Africa' and of developing nations would be heard at L'Aquila (Agnew 2009).

As regards more uncivil elements, 'No Global' was one group planning a naval siege on La Maddalena when the summit was to be held there. The Italian authorities also arrested a number of protestors in June, a month before the summit, accusing them of having left-wing connections and planning terrorist activities (BBC 2009a). Ahead of the summit, *The Irish Times* reported that

> in what many saw as a G8 curtain-raiser, 13,000 demonstrators protesting against a US military base in the northern town of Vicenza clashed briefly with police on Saturday. Protests planned in L'Aquila are expected to pass off peacefully (Agnew 2009).

An anti-capitalist protest took place on the Saturday before the summit opened, when 4 000 protestors congregated under the banner "The G8 Is the Earthquake, We Are All Citizens of L'Aquila". The mood was peaceful. On the first day of the summit, according to Associated Press (2009b):

> Environmentalists broke into power stations across Italy and shed their clothes in downtown Rome on Wednesday as world leaders discussed a new deal to combat global warming.
>
> Dozens of activists from 18 countries scaled smokestacks and occupied four Italian coal-fired power plants, hanging banners that called on the Group of Eight summit in central Italy to take the lead in fighting climate change, Greenpeace said.
>
> Italian energy giant Enel, which owns three of the plants, said production had not been disrupted by the protests ...
>
> In Rome, activists from charity group Oxfam International put on masks of world leaders and dressed up as chefs, stirring a mock Earth in a pot representing the planet's rising temperature.
>
> On the historic Spanish Steps, environmentalists stripped half-naked in front of tourists and unfurled a banner calling on leaders to 'Keep climate cool'.
>
> Police briefly detained two women, a French citizen and an American, as well as a Greek man ...
>
> The climate change stunts came a day after anti-globalization groups in the capital blocked roads and rail tracks and clashed with police in violent protests against the G8. Nearly 40 activists were detained.

Five days later, on 11 July, after the summit had concluded, *The Irish Times* reported that:

Greenpeace activists on inflatable boats yesterday painted a coal ship in Civitavecchia, near Rome, with the message 'G8: FAILED' at the end of a week of protests in Italy and elsewhere calling on world leaders to set a more ambitious agenda (McDonald 2009).

As regards more local concerns during the summit, 'Yes, We Camp' was the parody of the Obama catchphrase in his 2008 electoral campaign. In addition, 'a group of women made homeless by the earthquake ... staged a protest with banners describing themselves as "Last Ladies"' (Squires 2009):

A group of 'last ladies' chanted, 'Michelle, come to our tents, the women of Abruzzo await you in their underwear.' One held a sign reading, 'A stroll in the centre for the first ladies, for the women of Aquila only tents and cement' (Popham 2009).

The *Financial Times* also reported that:

NGOs and the committees are worried about the security enforced on those who live in the camps. According to Enrico [one of the founders of Comitato 3e32]: 'Constitutional rights of information, meeting and expression have been taken away from us. We cannot form assemblies in the camps and are banned from distributing pamphlets' (Segreti 2009).

Celebrity diplomacy reared its head again when George Clooney and Bill Murray toured L'Aquila, opening a cinema for survivors of the L'Aquila earthquake left homeless.

The G20 Pittsburgh Summit

The third meeting of the G20 leaders took place at the environmentally sustainable David L. Lawrence Convention Center in Pittsburgh. Pittsburgh was chosen as the venue in May 2009 after considerable lobbying from the city with the goal of showcasing its economic and social transformation, in the words of U.S. president Barack Obama, 'transformed itself from the city of steel to a centre for high-tech innovation—including green technology, education and training, and research and development' (reported in the Economist 2009c).

Civil society activities were planned by the Bail Out the People movement, the Thomas Merton Center, and the Pittsburgh Organizing Committee in a way that stressed the local as well as the global focus in protest—a theme that has emerged in the review of recent civil society activity sketched above. In addition, an unofficial media centre was established with the support of the U.S. Climate Action Network and in collaboration with the World Wildlife Fund, Oxfam, the Environmental Defense Fund, and the TckTckTck campaign for a deal on climate change. The venue was the August Wilson Center for African American Culture, which provided a central location for a series of press conferences.

Pittsburgh braced itself for protests from the more uncivil elements of civil society, with the G20 London Summit still fresh in the collective memory and the fear that protests would detract attention from the success story of Pittsburgh's transformation. Ahead of the summit, the Pittsburgh G20 Resistance Project called for disruption of the meeting through a mass march, targeted businesses such as Starbucks and McDonald's, and urged a 'peoples' uprising'. In response, requests from hundreds of protestors to camp in the city's botanical gardens, in whose Phipps Conservatory the G20 leaders dined on the first night of the summit, were rejected by the local courts ahead of the summit. The city's police force was reinforced by bussing in police forces from New York, Virginia, and Kentucky and placing national guard troops and the coastguard on alert. There were even unfounded rumours circulating that prisoners were to be released in order to accommodate the anticipated number of arrests.

During the summit itself, all was calm within the area cordoned off around the convention centre. However, not far from this restricted area, there were reports of riot police using sirens, tear gas, and rubber bullets to deal with thousands of protestors, resulting in skirmishes and road blocks on the first day and evening of the summit. Reaction from one protestor drew a link with policing techniques at previous summits:

> This kind of force has been used as an option of first resort by cops (at summits) in Italy, London and now Pittsburgh ... We have managed to create a pretty big disturbance without destroying any property (Reuters 2009).

The second day of the summit saw a self-proclaimed and police-authorized 'peoples' march' to protest against the 'war on terror' and the G20's response to climate change and poverty. This event was attended by 10 000 people and was peacefully concluded in contrast to the previous day's events (Nichols and Barnes 2009). In total, 83 people were arrested during the summit and $50 000 of damage was caused (Associated Press 2009a). In summary, one editorial dubbed the protests as 'lacklustre' and opined that:

> At the time of writing, the protests in Pittsburgh, host city to this year's G20, don't seem to be reaching the peak we saw at the 'Battle of Seattle' in 1999. Even the lowest estimates put that crowd at more than 40 000, all there to decry the evils of globalisation.
>
> Ten years on, after the worst financial collapse in living memory, the G20 seems a far less controversial affair (Rushe 2009).

Furthermore, much of the protest was seen to be 'unfocused' and constitute 'a shopping-list of grievances that did not necessarily gel very well together' (Deveson 2009).

Conclusion

As Hajnal (2007) has pointed out, because the G8 summit process itself is intended to be informal it follows that its relations with civil society are informal. Thus, the trajectory of interaction between the two is never going to be steady and unidirectional. Rather, it will wax and wane. The 2004 Sea Island Summit was a blip in terms of the development of G8–civil society relations in that little engagement took place. However, the fact that this summit was followed by Gleneagles demonstrates the difference a leader can make. Nevertheless there has been a degree of institutionalization over the years. A number of civil society activities suggest that although civil society may never formally be added to the alphanumeric groupings of global governance, it will continue to have a presence. In this light, the predictions of the decline of civil society activity made by *The Economist* are overstated. Admittedly, the intention of *The Economist* was to focus on 'uncivil' elements of civil society. However, by including or failing to distinguish the civil elements, it provided a blinkered view of the range of civil society activities surrounding summit meetings such as the G8 and G20. As demonstrated above, the majority of events are peaceful and do not generate media headlines.

One question that emerges is whether the multilayered and regular schedule of civil society activities that has developed around the G8 can or should be transferred to the G20, especially at a time where the division of labour between the G8 and G20 is unclear? One of the central strengths of effective campaigns like Jubilee 2000 and the Drop the Debt campaign and GCAP's work is a good knowledge of the workings of the G8, wide consultation processes, and an ability to use the media to attain a high profile for an issue (Hajnal 2007). As a result, when civil society and the G8 have engaged with each other, epitomized by the 2005 Gleneagles Summit, cooperation has resulted in mutual benefits, public engagement, and understanding, and, ultimately, legitimacy. In all probability the broad range of issues that are on the agendas of both groupings ensure that a wide number will be attracted to the G8 and G20. But can a similarly productive relationship be created with the G20? Have civil society groups tethered their wagons to the G8 horse, or will a two-track process emerge? And how will they manage the resulting demands on their resources? Despite having held five summits in two years, these processes are still being developed.

So, although it is still too early to tell, these questions should be kept in mind alongside the pressing agenda items of both Gs as the annual schedule of global governance continues to fill up. So far in the short history of G20–civil society interaction, uncivil elements have been the focus (London, Pittsburgh, Toronto) or there has not been much attention at all (Washington). At the G20 summit in Korea on 11–12 November 2010, despite the tradition of sometimes violent protest that exists there, the mood was predominantly calm. However, alongside protest and demonstrations, future summits have the opportunity to encourage engagement and dialogue, alternative summits, and civil society participation in summit task forces and working groups. The G20's early tendency to host summits in urban centres might certainly create problems for protest and policing. Nonetheless, not running away to remote corners of the globe could place the G20 in a position to create a dialogue with civil society that mirrors and even surpasses that of the G8.

References

Agnew, Paddy (2009). 'Pope and Geldof Have Say in Run-Up to G8.' *Irish Times*, 6 July.

ANSA (2009). 'Rome Mayor Promises Meeting for Civil Society and G8 Leaders.' 4 May.

Associated Press (2009a). 'Boisterous Protesters March at G20 Summit.' 25 September. <www.msnbc.msn.com/id/33017820/ns/us_news-life> (August 2010).

Associated Press (2009b). 'Environmentalists Protest G8 Summit.' 8 July. <www.cbsnews.com/stories/2009/07/08/politics/main5145167.shtml> (August 2010).

BBC (2008). 'Hundreds in G20 Protest.' 16 November. <news.bbc.co.uk/1/hi/world/americas/7731875.stm> (August 2010).

BBC (2009a). 'Italy Arrests G8 Attack Suspects.' 11 June. <news.bbc.co.uk/1/hi/world/europe/8095033.stm> (August 2010).

BBC (2009b). 'Police Criticised over G20 Cordon.' 6 August. <news.bbc.co.uk/1/hi/uk/8187343.stm> (August 2010).

Cooper, Andrew F. (2007). *Celebrity Diplomacy* (Boulder: Paradigm Publishers).

Deveson, Max (2009). 'Summit Protesters Lack Focus.' *BBC*, 26 September. <news.bbc.co.uk/2/hi/business/8276035.stm> (August 2010).

Dobson, Hugo (2004). *Japan and the G7/8, 1975–2002* (London: RoutledgeCurzon).

Economist (2004). 'G-Force.' 7 October. <www.economist.com/node/3262467> (August 2010).

Economist (2009a). 'Beating the System, More Gently.' 2 April. <www.economist.com/node/13402777> (August 2010).

Economist (2009b). 'Brace Yourselves: What Police Can Expect from Protesters, and Vice Versa.' 26 March. <www.economist.com/node/13381980> (August 2010).

Economist (2009c). 'Lessons for the G20.' 17 September. <www.economist.com/node/14460542> (August 2010).

Economist (2009d). 'The Camera Is Mightier Than the Sword.' 16 April. <www.economist.com/node/13497460> (August 2010).

Hajnal, Peter I. (2002). 'Partners or Adversaries? The G7/8 Encounters Civil Society.' In J.J. Kirton and J. Takase, eds., *New Directions in Global Political Governance: The G8 and International Order in the Twenty-First Century*, pp. 191–208 (Aldershot: Ashgate).

Hajnal, Peter I. (2007). *The G8 System and the G20: Evolution, Role, and Documentation* (Aldershot: Ashgate).

Hajnal, Peter I. (2008). 'Meaningful Relations: The G8 and Civil Society.' In J.J. Kirton and M. Koch, eds., *The G8: Hokkaido Toyako Summit 2008* (London: Newsdesk Publications).

Hajnal, Peter I. and Jenilee Guebert (2009). 'A Civil Society.' In J.J. Kirton and M. Koch, eds., *The G8: From La Maddalena to L'Aquila* (London: Newsdesk Publications).

Japan Times (2000). 'NGOs Divided Over How to Get Message Across.' 22 July. <search.japantimes.co.jp/cgi-bin/nn20000722e1.html> (August 2010).

Jubilee Debt Campaign (2008). 'Prime Minister Urged to Radically Rewrite Global Financial Rules.' 14 November. <www.jubileedebtcampaign.org.uk/download.php?id=777> (August 2010).

Kirton, John J. (2001). 'The G20: Representativeness, Effectiveness, and Leadership in Global Governance.' In J.J. Kirton, J.P. Daniels, and A. Freytag, eds., *Guiding Global Order: G8 Governance in the Twenty-First Century*, pp. 143–172 (Aldershot: Ashgate).

Kirton, John J. and Jenilee Guebert (2009). *A Summit of Substantial Success: The Performance of the G20 in Washington in 2008.* 7 March. <www.g20.utoronto.ca/biblio/g20-2008-performance.pdf> (August 2010).

Kirton, John J. and Madeline Koch, eds. (2009a). *The G8 2009: From La Maddalena to L'Aquila* (London: Newsdesk Publications).

Kirton, John J. and Madeline Koch, eds. (2009b). *The G20 London Summit: Growth, Stability, Jobs* (London: Newsdesk Publications).

Kirton, John J. and Madeline Koch, eds. (2009c). *The G20 Pittsburgh Summit 2009* (London: Newsdesk Publications).

Kirton, John J. and Madeline Koch, eds. (2010a). *G8 & G20: The 2010 Canadian Summits* (London: Newsdesk Publications).

Kirton, John J. and Madeline Koch, eds. (2010b). *The G20 Seoul Summit 2010: Shared Growth Beyond Crisis* (London: Newsdesk Publications).

Lewallen, Ann-Elise (2008). 'Indigenous at Last! Ainu Grassroots Organizing and the Indigenous Peoples Summit in Ainu Mosir.' *Asia-Pacific Journal: Japan Focus*, vol. 48 (November). <japanfocus.org/-ann_elise_lewallen/2971> (August 2010).

McDonald, Frank (2009). 'Environmentalists Angry at Perceived Failure.' *Irish Times*, 11 July.

Nichols, Michelle and Jonathan Barnes (2009). 'Protesters March Against G20 in Pittsburgh.' *Reuters*, 25 September. <www.reuters.com/article/idUSTRE58N65020090925> (August 2010).

Popham, Peter (2009). '"Yes We Camp": Protests Greet Wives in Quake Zone.' *Independent*, 10 July. <www.independent.co.uk/news/world/politics/yes-we-camp-protests-greet-wives-in-quake-zone-1740226.html> (August 2010).

Reuters (2009). 'Police Use Pepper Gas to Disperse G20 Protesters.' *Financial Times*, 25 September.

Rushe, Dominic (2009). 'Reagan Made Us What We Are.' *Sunday Times*, 27 September.

Seaton, Philip (2008). 'The G8 Summit as "Local Event" in the Hokkaido Media.' *Asia-Pacific Journal: Japan Focus*, vol. 48 (November). <japanfocus.org/-Philip_Seaton/2972> (August 2010).

Segreti, Giulia (2009). 'Glare of Publicity Sheds Light on Plight of Tent Dwellers.' *Financial Times*, 10 July.

Squires, Nick (2009). 'Dislike That Made Bruni Delay Her Entrance.' *Daily Telegraph*, 10 July.

Stewart, Healther (2008). 'Developing World Demands a Voice at Global Finance Summit.' *Observer*, 2 November.

Subacchi, Paola (2009). 'G20 and the G8: G Force.' *World Today*, vol. 65, no. 8/9, pp. 32–33. <www.chathamhouse.org.uk/files/14419_wt080932.pdf> (August 2010).

Subacchi, Paola and Eric Helleiner (2009). *From London to L'Aquila: Building a Bridge between the G20 and the G8*. Briefing Paper. Chatham House and the Centre for International Governance Innovation. <www.chathamhouse.org.uk/files/14254_0609ch_cigi.pdf> (August 2010).

Zablonski, Lukasz and Philip Seaton (2008). 'The Hokkaido Summit as a Springboard for Grassroots Initiatives: The "Peace, Reconciliation and Civil Society" Symposium.' *Asia-Pacific Journal: Japan Focus*, vol. 48 (November). <www.japanfocus.org/-Lukasz-Zablonski/2973> (August 2010).

Chapter 19

The G8 and the G20: Rejuvenated by the Crisis

Giorgio La Malfa

A Rejuvenated G8 in 2009

In recent years, G8 summits have increasingly lost their appeal both to their participants and to the media. Only young protestors seem to believe that important decisions are taken there, and that it is therefore necessary to try to disrupt them. Media reports cover the meetings routinely, while concentrating on the numbers and forms of the protests and on police reactions to them. G8 summits have tended increasingly to be—and to be considered as—'non-events'. The question has been not if, but how long they can survive.

The world economic crisis, at least for a time, had a rejuvenating effect on the G8 as well as effecting other international gatherings such as the more recent G20 summits. When it became clear that, although originating in the United States, the economic turmoil was rapidly spreading everywhere, and involving both banking and financial institutions and the real economy, the role of international meetings as forums for international deliberation and decision making was rehabilitated. Governments were eager to show that they were facing up to the challenge (even if it was not at all clear, especially when the crisis erupted, what was really happening and why). Meetings at the highest level would indicate that they were actively engaged in finding solutions. This gave impetus to the G20, but it also injected new energy into the preparations for the G8. In this sense the 2009 L'Aquila G8 was successful beyond all expectations, as attested to by the comments of its participants. Perhaps one can detect a sense of relief in these utterances insofar as previous experiences had been largely disappointing. But how far will this effect help the G8 survive in the medium term?

Part of L'Aquila's success was due to Italy's concept of changing the format of the meeting. Following an initial session of the eight, an assorted number of countries from Asia, Latin America, and Africa and representatives of various international organizations were asked to take part in the deliberations. To extend the invitation to the G8 summit to a number of countries whose economic and political relevance could no longer be ignored indicated a way forward. Whether this 2009 experience paved the way to the formal enlargement of the G8 and, perhaps, to its merging with the G20 remains, however, an open question.

Indeed, such an outcome, while possible, does not appear imminent. Yet it will be necessary, in the coming years, to tackle the question of the best format for these kinds of meetings. The eight members of the group no longer represent, as they did in the past, the largest part of the world's gross domestic product (GDP). Nor do they form, as the G7 did at the time of the Soviet Union, a sort of 'sacred' union of the most important democratic countries in Europe, America, and Asia. There is now a truly multipolar world both in economic and military-political affairs. In this sense a wider membership would be more representative of the world as it is today.

However, two caveats are in order. The first is that the larger the number of participating countries, the more difficult it is to take important, yet unstructured, decisions. A small group of countries meeting informally may arrive at substantive agreements on common policies without the need to be very precise on the formulation of what has been decided: the follow-up may be left to further consultations at lower echelons of government. No large group of countries will be able to operate in this fashion. To prevent the risk of being unable to agree on common conclusions, they will need either extensive preparations by their sherpas, which would water down any substantive agreement, or rules for decision making, which would be hard to reach in a forum not based on a full international treaty. Thus, while more superficially appealing, abandoning the G8 and putting in its place a larger and more representative body would by no means guarantee substantive decisions.

The other caveat is that after a departure from the present format of seven plus one, it would be very difficult to agree on which countries would be in and which would be left out of this larger format. The obvious criterion of GDP would not be particularly helpful, insofar as it would be contentious to define a cut-off limit for participation. There is also a problem of geographical representation, in the sense that a strict GDP criterion would probably lead to an underrepresentation of Africa, which would be politically unwise, once the decision to enlarge the G8 to move to a more representative forum is taken.

From this it follows that the early demise of the G8 is somewhat improbable. It is likely that the 'variable geometry' adopted by Italy for the 2009 meeting will be replicated and perhaps become the norm in the coming years. It does not seem probable that the G8 will formally merge into the G20 in the near future. Only time will tell which of these formats will emerge as the meaningful forum for consultations among the most powerful countries in the world.

Assessing the Results of L'Aquila

The question is, apart from the general sense of relief about the way L'Aquila developed, what can be said about its results. From the point of view of the summit's deliberations and conclusions, the assessment is fragmented. The final communiqué included, as usual, a number of general political statements about terrorism, nonproliferation of nuclear weapons, the Middle East, and the like, which did not seem to break new ground. There were, however, important points of agreements arrived at in two areas and some interesting developments in the way in which economic problems were looked at.

One such concrete decision was on aid for Africa. The leaders' declaration reads:

> For Africa, this will include increasing, together with other donors ODA [official development assistance] by US$25 billion a year by 2010, compared to 2004. The OECD-DAC [Development Assistance Committee of the Organisation for Economic Co-operation and Development] estimated that the combined commitments of G8 and other donors would increase overall ODA by around $50 billion a year by 2010 compared to 2004. We will continue to provide debt relief according to the Enhanced HIPC [heavily indebted poor country] initiative, the Multilateral Debt Relief Initiative and the Paris Club's Evian Approach (G8 2009).

These are hardly staggering figures. But the commitment is a concrete step in confronting the plight of the region that has not shared the benefits of the higher growth brought by globalization. It also allows proper verification of implementation for future G8 meetings.

The other important achievement is an agreement in principle on carbon dioxide emissions and the targets that were to be set at the post-Kyoto Copenhagen conference held in December 2009. The G8 declaration reads:

> We reconfirm our strong commitment to the UNFCCC [United Nations Framework Convention on Climate Change] negotiations and to the successful conclusion of a global, wide-ranging and ambitious post-2012 agreement in Copenhagen, involving all countries, consistent with the principle of common but differentiated responsibilities and respective capabilities. In this context we also welcome the constructive contribution of the Major Economies Forum on Energy and Climate to support a successful outcome in Copenhagen. We call upon all Parties to the UNFCCC and to its Kyoto Protocol to ensure that the negotiations under both the Convention and the Protocol result in a coherent and environmentally effective global agreement (G8 2009).

Although this text is still at the level of general statements of intentions and far from precise undertakings by the major polluters, the novelty at L'Aquila was the U.S. position. It became evident that the Obama administration—at its first G8 summit—was determined to move forward in an area where traditionally the United States was unwilling to commit itself to proper action. Although the participation of India and China in an agreement was still very much in doubt, they now recognized that the problem exists. Perhaps L'Aquila helped prepare the ground for potential positive outcomes at the Copenhagen conference.

The Economic Crisis

The careful wording of the declaration at L'Aquila indicated that, while agreeing on the general framework and direction of present economic policies, the G8 leaders did not engage in a full discussion of the nature, causes, and possible long-term solutions of the economic crisis. In particular, they managed to get around two thorny issues on which there were wide and unreconciled differences of opinion among the participants. The first is a serious reassessment of the view that has largely prevailed in past years that markets are generally efficient and can be trusted to deliver best results when state interference is reduced to a minimum. The other issue is the problem of the continuing imbalance of the U.S. balance of payments and its long-term consequences on the international system and the ways to deal with it.

On the policies to be adopted to confront the crisis, the leaders' declaration, after noting some signs of stabilization in the world economy, stated that

> as our measures reach their full effect on economic activity and contribute to improving confidence and expectations ... the economic situation remains uncertain and significant risks remain to economic and financial stability. We will take, individually and collectively, the necessary steps to return the global economy to a strong, stable and sustainable growth path, including continuing to provide macroeconomic stimulus consistent with price stability and medium-term fiscal sustainability, and addressing liquidity and capital needs of banks and taking all necessary actions to ensure the soundness of systemically important institutions (G8 2009)

There are in this passage two references to the role of governments in economic policy. One is an explicit pledge to 'continuing to provide macroeconomic stimulus' to return the global economy to a strong and stable growth path. The other is a more carefully worded reference to a pledge to take the necessary steps to insure 'the soundness of systemically important institutions'. The declaration recognizes an enhanced role for public supervision of financial institutions to insure

> consistency between accounting and prudential standards and setting up adequate tools to address procyclicality, as well as ensuring a comprehensive oversight of all systemically significant entities and activities. We commit to vigorously pursue the work necessary to ensure global financial stability and an international level playing field, including on compensation structures, definition of capital and the appropriate incentives for risk management of securitisation, accounting and prudential standards, regulation and oversight of systemically important hedge funds, standardisation and resilience of OTC derivative markets, establishment of central clearing counterparties for these products, and regulation and transparency of credit rating agencies (G8 2009).

The wording indicates that, at last, the crisis had substantially weakened the strict allegiance to the idea that unregulated markets are the most effective way to promote growth and that government intervention is generally unneeded, if not positively harmful—a notion that has been the centrepiece of the world's economic philosophy for the last 30 years or so. It would have been very difficult to maintain a strict *laissez-faire* attitude in the face of so much havoc generated by unrestricted competition in the banking and financial sectors and the risk of an economic downturn of unfathomable proportions. The question, however, is that, whereas governments have been made wiser by the crisis, most academic thinking in economics still seems unable and unwilling to distance itself from the received doctrines of the recent past.

Eighty years ago, in the midst of the great crisis of 1930s, the change in policies was heralded by Keynes's (1936) *General Theory of Employment, Interest, and Money*, which undid the theoretical underpinnings of the prevailing conventional wisdom. 'I believe to be writing a book on economic theory', Keynes ([1936] 1973) wrote in a letter to George Bernard Shaw, 'which will largely revolutionise—not, I suppose, at once but in the course of the next 10 years—the way the world thinks about economic problems'. Nothing comparable to the impact of Keynes's great treatise is in sight today. The pages of financial newspapers in the United States and in Great Britain still show the predominance of the conventional wisdom, which holds that excesses of various types were mostly responsible for the crisis and that the normal functioning of markets will by itself provide the cure. Until governments hear these unrepentant voices, they will move as hesitantly as they have so far.

In the U.S., Barack Obama's economic advisors come mostly from academic institutions where the clarion call of *laissez-faire* economics is less adhered to. But the situation in Europe is much less promising. There academia, the European institutions, the European Central Bank (ECB) and most of the governments remain in the traditional mould. The L'Aquila G8 did confirm the sad reality of the absence of a clear European voice and the inability of the representatives of the European Union (namely the chair of the European Commission and the president of the European Council) to formulate a meaningful common policy. The well-known weakness of European institutions deprives an area of 500 million inhabitants, with a GDP comparable to the U.S., of its voice. This is a serious problem within the problem.

The Dollar Crisis

Lurking beyond the current economic crisis are the huge imbalances in world trade, balance of payments, and the pile-up of financial debts of some countries facing the accumulation of assets in other countries. The L'Aquila Summit had very little to say about this problem. The leaders' conclusions reads:

> We emphasize the need for an enhanced global framework for financial regulation and supervision, promoting consistency between accounting and prudential standards and setting up adequate tools to address procyclicality,

as well as ensuring a comprehensive oversight of all systemically significant entities and activities. We commit to vigorously pursue the work necessary to ensure global financial stability and an international level playing field, including on compensation structures, definition of capital and the appropriate incentives for risk management of securitisation, accounting and prudential standards, regulation and oversight of systemically important hedge funds, standardisation and resilience of OTC [over-the-counter] derivative markets, establishment of central clearing counterparties for these products, and regulation and transparency of credit rating agencies (G8 2009).

While formally correct, this statement hardly indicates a determination to take the necessary corrective actions to tackle the problem effectively.

Most observers now agree that the U.S. balance of payments deficit is untenable insofar as it leads to an accumulation of American financial liabilities especially by China. It is also obvious that, lacking any corrective action, sooner or later a sudden collapse of the dollar will be a distinct possibility. A drastic reduction of the exchange rate for the dollar *vis-à-vis* other major currencies would have momentous consequences both in the financial sector and in the real economy. The world might find it very difficult to extricate itself from such a situation. As for Europe, a strong dollar devaluation with respect to the euro would affect European exports and contribute to deepening the already serious economic downturn the major European economies suffer from.

The only possibility of preventing this scenario is a decision by the U.S. to put its house in order through a progressive combination of tighter economic policies at home and a moderate (and controlled) reduction of the external value of the dollar. This course of action would imply that the U.S. should reconsider the financial size of its stimulus package. Other countries should step in instead, providing the necessary stimulus to the world's economic recovery. Here there is a contradiction: the rest of the world, while expressing concern for the U.S. balance of payments position, relies heavily on the stimulus provided by U.S. economic policies. While that concern is frequently expressed, no country or group of countries seems willing to step in to replace the U.S. recovery plan with one of its own.

Together with a more moderate economic policy stance of the U.S., a progressive revaluation of China's renminbi is needed to alleviate the American balance of payments problem. Neither China nor the U.S. appears particularly keen to embark on these policies. The balance of payments surplus, fed by an abnormally low level of the renminbi, serves the political aims of the Chinese leadership in many ways. It allows an active policy of penetration in Asia and Africa and gives China a privileged status with respect to the United States. This is a situation China does not seem ready to give up.

The U.S. is not particularly keen to have its internal policies put under scrutiny in an international forum. Nor is it willing to accept the idea that it no longer enjoys, as it did for most of the post-war period, a degree of freedom greater than everybody else. The world is probably witnessing—as Allan Meltzer (2008) put it—the 'end of the American century'. But the process will be long and complicated.

An exclusive U.S.-China dialogue poses a problem for the rest of the world. It would be much better if a truly multipolar world were to emerge from the crisis, possibly assisted by some forum for discussion and deliberation born out of the present G8-plus. The solutions emerging from such forums might be more balanced and more forward looking. Europe is the main candidate to take part in the U.S.-China dialogue and to enlarge it to take into account of the problems in a balanced way. It is again unfortunate that Europe, which could play a significant role as one of the major economic and financial centres of the world, is not able to speak with one authoritative voice. If Europe is a victim of an exclusive U.S.-China dialogue, it will be solely a consequence of its inability to look seriously at the problems and to decide it must move forward into a fully fledged economic and political union. The ECB has played an important role in the actions taken to cope with the financial crisis. The lack of an economic as well as political counterpart to the monetary union condemns Europe to irrelevance. This is in the interest of neither the European countries nor of the world at large.

Canada, as the host of the 2010 G8 Muskoka Summit, would have been well advised to put the question of a correction of the current imbalances squarely on the table as one of the crucial tests for leadership in the multipolar world of tomorrow.

At the L'Aquila Summit, there was mild optimism that the UN's Copenhagen conference might make some progress. But this was not to be. The meeting in Copenhagen was largely unsuccessful: there were too many voices and the gulf between the G8 countries and the new protagonists of today's economic development—China, India, Brazil, and the other emerging economies—was too large. Yet there remains the impression that, even if the positions are far apart, there is a growing awareness in all quarters of the existence of the problem and the need to address it. Thus, in a sense, a measure of optimism remains justified.

As to the economic problems, however, there is no sign of a willingness to tackle in a cooperative way the balance-of-payment adjustment problem. Moreover, the U.S. tends to develop a one-to-one relationship with China. This is not the best format for facing the problems of balance of payment imbalances. To proceed in this direction appears as a recipe for continuing disorder.

References

G8 (2009). 'Responsible Leadership for a Sustainable Future.' 8 July, L'Aquila Summit.   <www.g8.utoronto.ca/summit/2009laquila/2009-declaration.html> (August 2010).

Keynes, John Maynard (1936). *General Theory of Employment, Interest, and Money*. Vol. 9, 4th ed. (London: Macmillan).

Keynes, John Maynard ([1936] 1973). 'Letter to George Bernard Shaw.' In D. Moggeridge, ed., *Collected Writings of John Maynard Keynes,* Vol. XIV (London: Macmillan).

Meltzer, Allan H. (2008). 'End of the "American Century".' *World Economics,* vol. 9, no. 4, pp. 1–12.

Chapter 20

The Contribution of the G8's 2009 L'Aquila Summit

John J. Kirton

On 8–10 July 2009, the leaders of the world's most powerful market democracies assembled at the recently selected, earthquake-scarred site of L'Aquila in central Italy for their 35th annual G8 summit (Kirton 2009c; Kirton and Koch 2009). Italian prime minister Silvio Berlusconi was at his seventh summit, as the only G8 leader to host it for a third time. He welcomed U.S. president Barack Obama and Japanese prime minister Taro Aso to their first summit, British prime minister Gordon Brown and Russian president Dimitri Medvedev to their second, French president Nicolas Sarkozy to his third, German chancellor Angela Merkel and Canadian prime minister Stephen Harper to their fourth, and European Commission president José Manuel Barroso to his fifth.

For the fifth straight year the G8 heads invited their colleagues from the Group of Five (G5) emerging powers of China, India, Brazil, Mexico, and South Africa. They added the leaders of Australia, Indonesia and Korea from democratic Asia, as well as Denmark for the second summit meeting of the Major Economies Forum on Energy and Climate ([MEF], formerly the Major Economies Members). Among the other numerous guests were the leaders of Angola, Egypt, Ethiopia, Libya, Nigeria, and Senegal from Africa, Italy's fellow Europeans from the Netherlands and Spain, Turkey, and the heads of several multilateral organizations relevant to the summit's work.

Immediately after the summit ended, there arose the familiar debate about what it had achieved and why. One school argued that little or nothing had been achieved, because the G8 no longer included the world's real rising powers, confined those rising powers to second class status with only partial participation, was being superseded by the new G20 summit club, and lacked the presence of Chinese president Hu Jintao (Travers 2009; Smith 2009; Persichilli 2009; Nikkei Weekly 2009; Barry and Raum 2009; Australian Financial Review 2009). Some felt it failed to produce needed decisions on stimulus, climate change, and G8 expansion, or even made things worse by solidifying the deep North-South divisions on climate change (Peiser 2009).

A second school saw substantial success on selected subjects, due largely to the leadership of America's Barack Obama at his first G8 summit, with a strong second from America's reliable ally Japan (South China Morning Post 2009; Financial Times 2009; Dinmore and Segreti 2009; Asahi Shimbun 2009). One achievement was the L'Aquila Food Security Initiative (AFSI), should the $20 billion the G8 mobilized for this purpose be made available. Another was nuclear non-proliferation and disarmament, driven by Obama's bold vision of ridding the world of nuclear weapons, his promise to hold a nuclear security summit in Washington the following spring, and the hope that America would join all its G8 partners by ratifying the Comprehensive Test Ban Treaty.

A third school saw more comprehensive success, covering trade, climate, summit architecture and food. Such success came due to the arrival of Obama's American leadership, the greater participation of emerging and developing countries and multilateral organizations and the rival G20's large size, cumbersome character, lack of flexibility, and ineffectiveness to date (Cerretelli 2009; Xinhua 2009; Business Standard 2009; Asahi Shimbun 2009).

A more systematic analysis shows that the L'Aquila G8 was a summit of solid success, across most dimensions of global governance on most of the major issues it addressed in the economic, global and political-security domains (Kirton 2009a). It featured substantial achievements on climate, trade, and G8 architecture, followed by solid advances on democracy in Iran, food security, and even the economy and finance. Its advances were propelled by surrounding shocks from the financial, economic, food, and nuclear proliferation crises, the failure of the established multilateral organizations to cope on their own, the intensified inclusion of emerging powers in the summit, and the common democratic values activated by the election in Iran. Yet success also required the personal commitment and skill of two popular, prominent political leaders—Silvio Berlusconi hosting his third summit and Barack Obama attending his first—to produce leader-like advances, even in the absence of Hu Jintao, who had been politically hijacked by domestic insurrection at home.

The Summit Challenges

At L'Aquila, G8 leaders confronted unusually large global challenges. The first was the worst financial and economic crisis since the Great Depression of the 1930s and the deep recession that still had all the G8 members and much of the world in its grip. G8 leaders were called, after a long absence, to address seriously the subjects of financial regulation and reform, macroeconomic management, and trade. They had to nurture the economic 'green shoots' finally appearing in G8 economies into a reliable recovery, without unleashing unsustainable fiscal deficits, government debts, tax burdens, or the inflationary spirals they had conquered at such cost in the 1980s. They also needed to attack the trade, investment, and financial protectionism then spreading, and promote further liberalization, notably by trying to conclude the badly overdue Doha Development Agenda negotiations that had been launched at the World Trade Organization (WTO) soon after Italy had hosted its last summit in 2001.

The second challenge was climate change. The incoming scientific evidence showed that this problem, of potentially existential dimensions for some countries and conceivably even human life on the planet itself, was more ominous and urgent than the most recent report of the Intergovernmental Panel on Climate Change (IPCC) in 2007 had said. With the 1997 Kyoto Protocol to the United Nations Convention on Climate Change (UNFCCC) a clear failure, and with the UN system still deadlocked in the lead-up to its December Copenhagen conference to devise a successor, the G8 and its MEF partners had to identify the key principles upon which a new, now effective regime could be based. They could do so by building on the agreement at the 2008 G8 Toyako-Hokkaido Summit in Japan, which called for all established and emerging countries to control their carbon and for 'bottom up' sectoral approaches.

The third challenge was development, as the economic crisis harmed the poorest the most. They and others were afflicted by shortages of affordable, accessible, and safe energy, food, and water, even as natural disasters and health epidemics such as H1N1 'swine influenza' added to their heavy burden. The G8 would be hard pressed to meet its many past commitments to give access to treatment to everyone with HIV/AIDS, cut tuberculosis and malaria in half, and eliminate polio by 2010. The global community would be equally hard pressed to deliver its Millennium Development Goals (MDGs) by their due date of 2015, unless G8 leaders and their powerful partners at L'Aquila ambitiously took the lead.

The fourth challenge came in the realm of political security, from new threats of nuclear proliferation and new hopes for democratization, both arising in nearby Iran. The G8 also needed to help the UN grapple with nuclear proliferation in North Korea and elsewhere as well as with regional conflicts and high seas piracy, especially in nearby Somalia, so close to the oil tanker routes from the Persian Gulf. It also had to lead in promoting democracy and combating terrorism in the Middle East, Afghanistan, Pakistan, and other afflicted states.

The fifth overarching challenge was to create effective global governance for a world that increasingly shared a single fate. The G8 needed to have itself and the new G20 summit deliver their many bold promises on financial stability, economic growth, trade, investment, development, international financial system reform, and climate change. The G8 would thus be asked to reform itself to improve its accountability and to mobilize the power and potential of the world's rapidly rising G5 powers. As both groups got to work in L'Aquila, they looked forward to the Canadian-hosted summit in Muskoka, Ontario, the following June and prepared to launch a new round of G8-plus summitry in France in 2011.

Italy's Summit Strategy

Key Concepts, Themes, and Agenda

In designing the summit, the Italian hosts adopted both a long-term and a short-term perspective. They identified several key concepts to guide and explain their work.

Italy's long-term goal was evident in the points it prepared for discussion with its partners to start the preparatory process in December 2008. The central goal was to ensure that the G8 could contribute to creating a system of global governance that was open, innovative, inclusive, and sustainable. This meant promoting, in the face of the unprecedented economic crisis, an economy that was open for trade and investment and remained innovative and capable of creating and using ideas, in order to help the most vulnerable and confront the challenges of the environment and climate change.

It also required the inclusion of emerging economies as full players in new formats, such as the G8 Plus Five (that is, the G8 and the G5), the MEF, the G20, and other clubs. It was clear from the start that the G20 summit would address financial issues, while the G8 Plus Five would deal with the world economy and other international challenges. In this context the G8 remained a club of countries that shared core values and principles and were prepared to take responsibility for solving the most pressing global challenges of the day. They would do so by working inclusively, involving key players, and leading by example.

Italy saw the G8 as a group of countries willing to lead on a broad set of issues. These included traditionally structural ones such as development, microeconomic policies, social policies, the environment, climate change, and political security. Italy believed the G20 had been very successful in tackling major challenges and crises. It looked forward to receiving reports from those monitoring members' compliance with commitments by the G8, in order to improve implementation.

Italy's short-terms goals began with tackling the global financial and economic crisis at hand. It worked with Britain, which held the chair of the G20, to ensure that the G20's London Summit in April 2009 would produce a meaningful package and strategies for the world economy, investment, environment, climate change, and development. The two chairs of the G8 and G20 cooperated closely, with the G20 taking the lead on financial issues and the G8 on structural ones.

On the road to L'Aquila, Italy assembled a very broad agenda. Its coherence would be achieved not by highlighting a few priorities or themes, but by focusing on several key concepts—rules, vulnerability, accountability, and inclusiveness.

On rules, Italy sought to bring ethics back into economic behaviour by devising standards for global markets. The goal was to restore confidence by reaffirming and rendering more effective the key principles of propriety and transparency. To make peer review effective, Italy worked with the Organisation for Economic Co-operation and Development (OECD), which was the custodian of these principles, and a number of its committees. Italy hoped to have concrete results at L'Aquila.

On vulnerability there were two dimensions. The first, within G8 societies, was to 'put people first,' which Italy took as a conviction rather than a simple slogan. There was thus great attention to the social and human dimensions of the crisis. This concern was forwarded through a G8 meeting with trade unions and the involvement of the International Labour Organization (ILO). It would be raised at the summit itself. The second dimension was the vulnerability of the least developed countries and the resulting need for more effective development policies. The G8 would thus reaffirm its commitments on the volume and quality of official development assistance (ODA) and devise ways to promote the mobilization of all possible resources, in keeping with the consensus of the 2002 UN International Conference on Financing for Development at Monterrey.

On accountability, there was a willingness from G8 countries to put this at centre of the summit, starting with the development issues. L'Aquila would thus devise a system to identify G8 commitments and monitor progress in their implementation. It would produce the first accountability reports, on education, food, water, health, and peace and security. Italy also sought to have the summit launch a more systematic process of accountability to be realized over the following year.

On inclusiveness, Italy sought from the start to involve emerging economies on far more than the usual outreach basis including in every G8 ministerial meeting leading up to the summit. They were also involved in the preparation of documents. A joint statement on some of the most pressing issues would be issued on the second day of the summit itself.

Summit Participants, Process, and Organization

In designing the summit process, Italy knew that the G8 was simultaneously facing one of the worst crises in modern times, witnessing the emergence of new players and formats, and welcoming a new U.S. president who had aroused very high expectations.

Italy thus arranged a three-day summit that would be very dense in its agenda and participants. The summit would start with the standard session on the world economy, followed by sessions on global issues featuring development and climate change. It would end with an evening session on political issues, including regional crises, nuclear proliferation, and terrorism. For the second time there would be a parallel G5 summit taking place in nearby earthquake-ravaged Coppito during the G8's first day.

On development two separate results were planned. One was a message on the importance of accountability for the commitments made by G8 governments on the volume and effectiveness of aid. Italy hoped to set in motion a process to monitor implementation better, starting with understanding the contents of the commitments, as these were not always clear. The G8 members needed to clarify their meaning among themselves. L'Aquila would see the delivery of five thematic reports: on education, health, food security, water and sanitation, and peace and security, including corruption.

Italy was the first to put on the table a proposal to increase accountability. Canada and America built on this proposal and submitted a new, more ambitious one. Italy insisted that in order to be serious, the G8 needed to move beyond different countries reporting data on implementation in different ways. Italy thus wanted to work closely with the OECD's Development Assistance Committee (DAC) to assess how the G8 was progressing in meeting different objectives.

Implementation had been difficult for some countries—including Italy. But given the delays in meeting the commitments made at the 2005 Gleneagles Summit, there was a determination to respect those commitments. Experts, including those in Italy's foreign and economy ministries, worked on how Italy could catch up. Italy saw a strong message coming from the L'Aquila Summit on the willingness to fulfil these commitments and thus to reach the Gleneagles goals.

The second result on development would be the message that while ODA was very important, it had to be made more effective. Aid effectiveness would be a summit priority. Aid required working on trade, with the summit seeking to unblock the Doha negotiations. Development also required working on investment. The time was not yet right for another multilateral agreement on investment. But, with emerging economies becoming major investors abroad, conditions were more favourable than they were when the OECD last tried to implement such an agreement in the late 1990s. Development also required working on reducing the costs of remittances by improving transparency.

For the summit's second day, Italy invited five emerging economies to join the G8 as equals. They would join not just for one session, to discuss the Heiligendamm Dialogue Process (HDP), but for a full day of substantive discussions, including the proper approach to globalization (Cooper and Antkiewicz 2008). In the morning sessions the G8, the G5, and Egypt would discuss the HDP and adopt its concluding report. The leaders would note that the HDP had produced concrete results on investment, innovation, energy security, and international development, and that it had surpassed the expectations at its outset in 2007. In some areas, in fact, there had been substantive progress. In other, more difficult areas, common ground was now emerging, after two years, among the 13 countries and their leaders. In the morning session on that second day, the G8, the G5, and Egypt, along with some international organizations such as the UN, the OECD, and the international financial institutions, would also discuss economic issues.

The afternoon would be devoted to the MEF session on climate change and energy. Co-chaired by Obama and Berlusconi, the meeting would try to find a common approach to the UN's Copenhagen conference. Italy had high expectations for an important outcome. From the start, it was understood that L'Aquila must produce more than Hokkaido had the year before. Substantive progress was anticipated, with Copenhagen only four months away.

The third day at the summit would have the traditional outreach to Africa that had started in 2001 when the five African leaders of the New Plan for Africa's Development (NEPAD) had first attended. The issues to be addressed would, for the first time, be prepared with the personal representatives of the African leaders. The agenda would focus on the impact of the crisis on the continent and how the G8 could work with Africa to minimize these effects. There would then be an innovative session, devoted to the specific topic of food security, involving all the leaders and the heads of international organizations participating at L'Aquila. The Italian presidency put this issue at the core of the agenda. In the lead-up it organized the first ever G8 ministerial meeting for agriculture, and invited all these partners in an effort to develop joint positions. The overall result was an ever expanding summit format, with a variable geometry as the subject at hand required.

The Preparatory Process

Putting this strategic plan into action involved a dense web of meetings of the G8 leaders' personal representatives or sherpas and of G8 ministers: for finance on 13–14 February in Rome, 24 April in Washington DC, and 12–13 June in Lecce; for labour on 29–31 March in Rome; for agriculture, for the first time, on 18–20 April in Treviso; for environment on 22–24 April in Siracusa; for energy on 24–25 May in Rome; for justice and home affairs on 29–30 May in Rome; for development on 11–12 June in Rome; and for foreign affairs on 25–27 June in Trieste. At the senior official level there were many G8-centred groups at work. The most notable was the structured exchange of the HDP on investment, innovation, development, and energy.

The L'Aquila Summit would be the first G8 summit since the G20 leaders had first met in Washington in November 2008 and then in London in April 2009, but before their next summit in Pittsburgh in September 2009. The advent of G20 summitry now needed the G8 and G20 to define the relationship between these two central clubs for global governance (Berlusconi 2009; Kirton 2009b).

In confronting these challenges, the G8 was boosted by its respectable record of compliance with its key commitments from last year's summit. Finance and climate led the list of promises kept (G8 Research Group 2009).

The Summit

The L'Aquila Summit opened on Wednesday 8 July, at 13:00, when the leaders of the G8 (including the EU) met alone. Over a working lunch, they dealt with the world economy. Then they had a session on global issues, focused on climate and energy. On day two, Thursday 9 July, the leaders of the G8 gathered with those of the G5 and Egypt starting at 10:00 to discuss global issues and development policies, as well as the HDP. They were joined by the heads of the International Energy Agency (IEA), the ILO, the International Monetary Fund (IMF), the OECD, the UN, the World Bank, and the WTO for a working lunch to discuss 'future sources of growth'. After lunch the G8, G5, and Egypt were joined by Australia, Denmark, Indonesia, and Korea for the MEF session on climate change and energy. Berlusconi hosted a large number of guests for dinner, including the 17 MEF members, along with leaders of Algeria, Angola, Ethiopia, Libya, the Netherlands, Nigeria, Senegal, Spain, Turkey, and the heads of the African Union (AU), the IEA, the ILO, the IMF, the OECD, the UN, the World Bank, the

WTO, the Food and Agriculture Organization (FAO), the International Fund for Agriculture and Development, and the World Food Programme.

Performance by Key Governance Dimensions

Overall Performance

In the end, the G8's 2009 L'Aquila Summit was a solid success. It earned a grade of B, slightly above the long-term G8 summit average of B–, if a little below the previous summit's performance of B+. L'Aquila's success was led by its B+ achievements on climate, trade, and G8 architecture, followed by B on democracy in Iran and a B– on food security and the economy and finance (see Appendix 20.1). L'Aquila thus largely lived up to the potential it had promised through its preparatory process, as it met current global conditions on the summit's eve (Kirton 2009a).

This judgement of a solid success was supported by the high degree of satisfaction expressed by the leaders of its members and guests. It was also sustained by the evidence from L'Aquila's performance on the six major dimensions of governance appropriate to plurilateral summit-level institutions such as the G8, the G8 plus G5, the MEF, and even the 40 assembled on L'Aquila's final day (see Appendices 20.2 and 20.3).

Domestic Political Management

On the first dimension of domestic political management, the summit worked well at home for its host. The G8 leaders themselves were full of compliments for Italy and other members, as recorded in the collective documents they released (see Appendix 21.3). Italy's media coverage was dominated by the summit's activities and achievements and by Berlusconi himself, rather than stories of the summit's physical disorganization and its host's social life as featured by a few foreign media before the summit's start. Berlusconi also successfully used the summit as a local fundraiser to mobilize money from his G8 partners to rebuild the earthquake-ravaged town where the summit was held.

Immediately after the summit, a public opinion poll of Italians showed, according to Italian foreign minister Franco Frattini, that 75 percent 'appreciated and believed the results of the G8 summit to be important' (ANSA 2009). Their appreciation for the organization of the summit rated near '10–9.2' on a scale of 10, and Berlusconi's popularity rose to 68.4 percent.

Deliberation

L'Aquila's deliberative performance was somewhat above average. The addition of a working session on the first afternoon gave G8 leaders more time together at the summit table than they had had at recent summits. Housing them in residences on the summit's military college grounds maximized the time they (and their delegations) had for spontaneous encounters. U.S. president Barack Obama and Canadian prime minister Stephen Harper took full advantage of this proximity and flexibility, taking a long walk together before the summit's delayed 'family photo' finally took place.

The summit in its various numerical configurations issued 10 documents in all, a number in keeping with the 21st-century norm. At 31 167 words, these documents contained the second highest total in summit history, exceeded only by George Bush's Sea Island Summit in 2004.

Direction Setting

The summit produced a solid performance in setting new principles and normative directions based on the G8's core mission of promoting open democracy and individual liberty in the world. The 62 direct expressions of these values in those documents were in line with the long-term summit average, although well below that of recent years. Not surprisingly, a large majority of these references to democratic and human rights values came in the four documents issued on the first day, when the all-democratic, popularly elected G8 leaders met alone.

Decision Making

L'Aquila's decisional performance, as measured by the clear, future-oriented commitments or rules it created, was strong. Its 254 commitments were the fourth highest number in summit history and consistent with the 21st-century norm. The $21.1 billion it mobilized in new money, including $20 billion for the AFSI, was well above average, dwarfed only by the 2005 Gleneagles Summit. L'Aquila's stress on fulfilling past commitments indirectly added a much larger sum, assuming these promises would be met on time.

Delivery

However, the summit's likelihood of delivering its 2541 commitments within the year before the next summit was somewhat less strong. While the new process for monitoring accountability was expected to help with delivery, L'Aquila's commitments contained rather few of the catalysts shown to raise compliance. The number of references to core international organizations, which help compliance, was exceeded by references to other international organizations, which lower compliance (Kirton 2006; Kirton et al. 2010). Nonetheless, the documents contained robust priority placement and references to a one-year timetable, both of which have boosted compliance in the past. Here the presence at the summit of the many multilateral organizations, which each had to be recognized in the communiqué, may have damaged compliance, especially if the G8 communiqué references were used as ammunition in their subsequent competition for scarce resources and turf.

Development of Global Governance

In developing global governance, L'Aquila's performance was strong. The G8 and its partners repeatedly referred to the G8 summit that would be held in France in 2011. This implied that an eight-year cycle of summitry would start again for a club that would continue to have a long life. They also made extensive reference to the G20 summit, including at least 15 specific references to the G20 in the various communiqués. The summit leaders pledged to implement the London decisions swiftly and to use the Pittsburgh Summit proactively to help get the Doha trade negotiations done and approve the 'Lecce Framework Common Principles and Standards for Propriety, Integrity, and Transparency' of a global rule of law for firms (see G7 Finance Ministers 2009). They clearly signalled that, given the still struggling global economy, they should stay focused on stimulus for 'as long as needed', leaving sustainability and exit strategies as a medium-term concern. They promised that reforms of financial regulations would be implemented swiftly, to ensure a level playing field. To repair the financial system, they declared 'it is crucial to deal decisively with distressed assets and to recapitalize viable financial institutions', using 'common principles' and an 'objective and transparent valuation' (G8 2009b). They also promised to avoid competitive currency devaluation and addressed global reserve currencies and reform of the international financial institutions. They indicated that Pittsburgh would have an expanded agenda, dealing more with climate change and perhaps even, on the margins, political-security concerns, notably nuclear proliferation in Iran. Beyond the Pittsburgh Summit, Obama spoke of holding a summit on nuclear disarmament in Washington in the new year. The G8 thus did much to define a cooperative, mutually reinforcing relationship between these two key summit forums and give the new G20 summit the support and leadership it needed to work (Kirton 2009b).

The G8 also gave much support and guidance to multilateral organizations as well as some to institutions of its own. Its references to and reliance on its own G8-centred bodies were highest in the areas of climate and energy and of counterterrorism, while on non-proliferation and political security issues the summit depended heavily on the multilateral organizations. It did less well in reaching out to civil society organizations or to public-private partnerships.

Performance by Key Issues

A detailed look at the summit's achievements on its key issues confirms this finding that L'Aquila was a summit of solid success.

Climate Change

The G8 made several ambitious commitments on climate change during the first day of negotiations, when its members met alone. All G8 members agreed that all major carbon producers must control their carbon in the 'beyond Kyoto' regime. They further agreed to a cap of two degrees Celsius in additional global warming beyond the levels of the pre-industrial age. Here they importantly said they would follow the science, and implicitly agreed to act at any time to secure as much as it took to stay below the two degrees or what the evolving science said. They also reiterated now as a goal the Toyako-Hokkaido target of a 50 percent world reduction of greenhouse gas emissions, with an 80 percent or greater reduction for developed states. This was a category they left undefined but one that could conceivably include all existing and future members of the OECD, including Mexico and Korea. Anyone could calculate how much the G8 expected developing countries to do. They called for more specific targets in the form of short- and medium-term goals. They urged all the MEF members to adopt quantifiable goals for emissions reductions by a specified year. They stressed that poverty eradication and climate change mitigation were linked and agreed on the importance of green growth plans for developing countries. They strongly supported the creation of a post-Kyoto climate regime at the Copenhagen conference in December 2009. They endorsed action on land degradation and forest destruction and degradation.

The leaders also linked climate and the economy in their green recovery plan. They agreed to work toward a greener economy and declared that the global recession would not affect their climate change mitigation. They called for continued work on lowering tariffs on goods aiding climate change mitigation through the WTO. They stressed the importance of the free market for mitigating climate change globally, and agreed that efforts such as carbon cap and trade systems and taxation were appropriate.

There was also extensive discussion on technology related to climate change. The leaders called for accelerated investment in green technology and better diffusion, deployment, and cooperation with developing states. They reiterated their Toyako-Hokkaido initiative to launch 20 carbon capture and storage projects by 2010 with increased investment and collaboration with developing nations, the IEA, and the Carbon Sequestration Leadership Forum. They agreed that nuclear energy was an important part of the green energy mix.

The leaders further agreed that even with current and increased mitigation measures, the world would nonetheless experience seriously adverse effects of climate change. They thus agreed to discuss adaptation at Copenhagen. Beyond this, they promised to provide funding for adaptation—of an unspecified amount— and work closely with developing countries to create national adaptation plans.

The MEF reiterated many of the agreements made by the G8. The leader of China, the world's top greenhouse gas emitter, was absent, which may have had a negative effect on the outcome of the talks. The MEF did agree to a cap of two degrees Celsius and pledged to reduce greenhouse gas emissions meaningfully from business as usual trajectories in the mid term. It did not, however, set any quantifiable targets or timelines for emissions reductions either globally or among its members. It agreed to negotiate more concrete targets and timetables at Copenhagen. However, emerging and developing countries had been promised assistance in the form of freer trade, financial support, technology deployment and development, and capacity building from the G8 countries the day before.

The MEF reiterated the importance of adaptation, with a focus on helping the world's poorest, who would be most affected by climate change. It launched a global partnership for low-carbon, climate-friendly technology. It stressed the need for transparency and predictability of investment in green technology. It agreed to work to double public sector investment in low-carbon technology by 2015 as a soft medium-term target and timetable, and, in the very short term, to establish national technology roadmaps and action plans by 15 November 2009.

Taken together, the G8 and the MEM clearly affirmed for the first time the revolutionary principle that all major carbon-producing powers must control their carbon and reduce their emissions in the new climate control regime (Kirton and Boyce 2009). They agreed that the world's temperature must never exceed more than two degrees Celsius beyond pre-industrial levels. The G8, including the long resistant U.S. and Russia, agreed that the world must reduce its emissions by 50 percent by 2050 and that the developed world would lead by cutting theirs by 80 percent by then. Talks covered forests and land degradation and energy efficiency for building and cars. The G8 made a marginally stronger, if still seriously inadequate, statement on the advantage of nuclear power as part of the energy mix. The MEF endorsed the limit of two degrees Celsius, implying that its emerging powers—now the world's leading emitters—would control their carbon emissions as well. In the months following the summit, China signalled for the first time that its emissions would peak in 2080, while Indonesia promised to reduce its by 40 percent by 2030.

There were some shortcomings. The G8's short- and medium-term goals and country targets were largely unspecified. No single baseline year for reductions was set. No time was set for when greenhouse gas emissions should peak and subsequently start to decline. The G8's enhanced emphasis on carbon capture and sequestration was seriously overblown. The emerging economies only promised to specify their long-term targets soon and did not agree to a global reduction of 50 percent by 2050 right away.

Trade and Investment

On trade, both the G8 and the G5 agreed to complete the long overdue Doha Development Agenda's negotiations for multilateral trade liberalization by the end of 2010. To give credibility to the commitment, they agreed to skip the intermediate stage of defining modalities and move straight to the end game of specifying the actual reductions they would exchange. They also abandoned the existing mini-ministerial forums that had failed. They asked their own trade ministers to meet before the G20 summit in Pittsburgh, scheduled for 24–25 September 2009, at which time the leaders themselves would have another chance to act.

G8 Architecture

On G8 architecture, the G8 strengthened its internal operations and external credibility by putting in place the first serious process of accountability. It focused on identifying the meaning of the many commitments made by the G8 leaders collectively at L'Aquila and at previous summits and their compliance with those commitments. The G8 and G5 extended their official-level structured dialogue among the G8 and G5 members as equals by lengthening its operation for two years and renaming it the Heiligendamm L'Aquila Process (HAP). They broadened its mandate to include any subject and to allow other countries to join on a case-by-case basis. They agreed that this increased inclusiveness would take place at 'all levels'. Many widespread references to the G20 in the communiqués issued by the G8 and others at L'Aquila showed that leaders wanted the G20 to reinforce rather than compete with the G8, and that the G8 would continue to be the sole source of leadership within and for the wider G20. Above all, the G8 alone and with the G5 repeatedly agreed in writing that the G8 summit would take place in France in 2011. With France the traditional kick-off of the eight-year cycle of G8 summits, this gave a clear signal that even with the new G20 summit, the old G8 would continue.

Democracy

On democracy, the central issue was Iran. The questionable results of the Iranian presidential election of 12 June and resulting protests and repression had placed Iranian democracy and respect of human rights at the heart of the G8 agenda (Feinberg and Kirton 2009). On the eve of the summit, in a move reminiscent of the 1979 American embassy hostage taking, Tehran had arrested eight local staff members from the British embassy and had imprisoned a French teacher on espionage charges. With these actions and the violent crackdown against the internal outcry in Iran for true democratic elections, Iran provided a challenge tailor made for the democratically devoted G8.

The G8 responded swiftly. On the eve of the L'Aquila Summit, Berlusconi suggested that the G8 was moving in the direction of endorsing or imposing sanctions. The EU members signalled they might withdraw their ambassadors from Tehran. Condemnations also came from the UN and the United Nations Educational, Social, and Cultural Organization (UNESCO). Angela Merkel compared Iran's leaders with communist East Germany's Stasi. The statement issued by Franco Frattini, chair of the G8 foreign ministers meeting, on 27 June offered a long and detailed list of places where G8 leaders could act to further democracy, human rights, and the rule of law. By the start of the summit, Iran had released the local British embassy employees.

On 8 July, the G8 dedicated much of its first working dinner to Iran. The resulting G8 political communiqué started with the subject of democracy in Iran, stated that the G8 (2009a) remained 'seriously concerned' and affirmed the values of democracy, rule of law, civil and political rights, and press freedom. It highlighted the sanctity of embassies and their staff. The leaders also agreed to direct diplomatic negotiations on nuclear proliferation between Iran and the sextet of China, France, Germany, Russia, the UK, and the U.S. as well as other G8 members. The G8 promised to monitor the progress made in the talks and 'take stock' in September at the G8 foreign ministers meeting on the opening of the United Nations General Assembly. Implicitly, it would also take stock of Iran's anti-democratic repression.

The G8 abstained from recommending or referring to sanctions on Iran, perhaps as a reward to Iran for freeing the embassy hostages. Progress, already underway, seemed to strengthen as the French teacher was allowed to speak to the French ambassador early on the summit's second day. The unanimous call on the Iranian government to resolve its problems through democratic dialogue was the first time the G8 had ever issued a statement to that effect. The G8's readiness to engage in direct negotiations with Iran with regard to its nuclear programme, itself significant, was further reinforced by the two-month deadline imposed on the negotiations. The G8 (2009a) bluntly added that it 'condemn[ed] the declarations of President Ahmadinejad denying the Holocaust'. It thus reaffirmed the 2007 Heiligendamm Summit statement on the issue, but, for the first time, singled out Iran's leader by name (G8 2007).

Food and Agriculture

On food security, long scheduled to be the summit's concluding deliverable, the results were respectable, if a little lower than what expectations had become. The anticipated new funding, to be declared as agreed in the summit statement, was only expressed as a welcome to those who had contributed to a goal of mobilizing $20 billion over three years. Similarly general and elusive were the passages on increasing the percentage of ODA for development, igniting a new green revolution, and defining rules for those who would buy agricultural assets abroad. The specified links of agriculture to trade were appropriately substantial. But those to climate and health were fragile indeed.

Economy and Finance

On the economy and finance, the G8 added more value than the past several summits had done. It sent a strong, clear signal to stay the course on stimulus, with both the G8 and the G5 saying so in a unified voice. On domestic financial regulation the G8 declared that the priority was to disclose and dispose of the bad assets that the big banks, largely in Europe, still had. The G8 and G5 also promised to prevent competitive currency devaluation, reducing the chances that this nightmare from the 1930s would return in real form.

Other Issues

Elsewhere there were several disappointments. Little of serious substance was done on health, relative to recent summits and to the last one hosted by Berlusconi in Genoa in 2001 (Kirton and Guebert 2009). Moreover, on none of the key issues did the summit secure a grade in the A range. This was consistent with its character as a summit with a comprehensive agenda that it advanced as a convoy against the broad range of global challenges, rather than a focused summit making major advances on a few key fronts.

Causes of Summit Performance

This pattern of performance is adequately explained by the concert equality model of G8 governance, especially when a few adjustments and enhancements are made.

Shock-Activated Neo-Vulnerability

The first cause of L'Aquila's solid success was intense shock-activated vulnerability, especially that which exposed the new vulnerability of all major countries to processes arising from non-state or even non-human sources. By the first half of 2009 severe financial system seizure had spread from America to Europe, leaving only the financial systems of Japan and Canada intact. The speed, spread, scope, scale, and severity of the financial crisis and its spillover into the real economies of most developed and now many emerging and developing economies had created the worst economic conditions since the Great Depression. As financial stability and economic growth were directly relevant to most of the G8 agenda and members' core interests and values, the crisis provided a strong incentive to cooperate on all agenda items, save the political-security ones.

This shock-activated vulnerability accounted for the summit's overall success and its above-average performance on finance, economics, and trade. It accounts less well for the summit's standout success on climate change, where there had been no climate shocks and where the climate-finance links were not considered as strong.

A further shock came from the natural disaster of the L'Aquila earthquake, so visible around the site of the summit. As the G8 leaders toured the ruins, they had an emotional first-hand encounter with the deadly and destructive consequences of the shock-activated, non-state neo-vulnerability they all potentially faced. They could see and feel how they were standing together to compete with nature, rather than standing alone to compete among themselves.

Multilateral Organizational Failure

The second cause of the summit's solid success was the failure of the established multilateral organizations to respond adequately to the global crises and challenges at hand. To combat the proliferating financial crisis the under-resourced, and only marginally reformed, IMF had to depend on the G20 London Summit in April to raise $1.1 trillion for development and stimulus, and to hasten the voice and vote reform that the G20 finance ministers had started a few years before. The WTO's Doha Development Agenda still depended on the high-level political push that only the G8 leaders and their G5 partners could give. The UN conference at Copenhagen in December depended on the G8 and MEF bridging divides that the UN's Kyoto protocol regime had intensified. And the 2010 review conference of the Nuclear Non-Proliferation Treaty similarly needed G8 action to have any chance of success. Even on food security, the FAO's recent summit had not been enough.

This failure of the UN system generated the need for the G8 to bring the heads of so many multilateral organizations to the G8 summit, and for their decision to come so eagerly. They clearly regarded the G8 as a globally representative and legitimate forum, as reinforced by their own presence. Yet G8 success also depended on the G8 finding the formula for the expanded plurilateral, institutionalized summitry in the form of the G8 plus G5, the MEF, and the G20.

Predominant Equalizing Capability

The third cause of solid success was the strong equalization of capability between the established and emerging economies and among countries within the G7. First-ranked America saw its economy contract at a seasonally adjusted annualized rate of 6.3 percent in the fourth quarter of 2008 and a further 6.1 percent in the first quarter of 2009. The contractions for second-ranked Japan were estimated in late April 2009 at 3.1 percent for the year ending in March and, by the IMF, at 6.2 percent for 2009. For third-ranked Germany, the late April estimate was for a contraction of 5.4 percent in 2009. For the 27-country EU as a whole 2009 offered a 4 percent drop. Canada had been late to enter the recession, but the Bank of Canada predicted that Canada's economy would contract by more than 7 percent annualized in the first quarter of 2009, the biggest fall on record.

In sharp contrast, the strongest large emerging market, China, where growth had fallen to almost zero in the fourth quarter of 2008, predicted growth of at least 6.1 percent in the first quarter of 2009, with signs that it would accelerate even more. India, too, seemed likely to maintain growth above 5 percent during this Great Recession, even though this was a major retreat from earlier levels.

The only partial offset to these changes in the real economy lay in the area of exchange rates. A flight to safety, or survival for those who needed to repatriate capital to cover losses in their American home, gave the U.S. dollar a temporary boost. Yet the overall long trend of a declining dollar soon resumed.

Common Democratic Principles

The fourth cause of solid success was the common commitment of G8 and G5 members to political stability and political openness in various ways. This was seen most clearly on the first day, when the G8 acted decisively on its own against Iran. But the democratic caucus and consensus were reinforced in the larger group on days two and three, by the fact that China's Hu chose not to attend the summit and by the use of the MEF, which added the democratic Asian powers of Australia, Indonesia, and Korea to the G8 and G5. Italy's addition of non-democratic Egypt slightly offset these thrusts.

More immediately, the G8 was concerned about the economically devastated democracies in the many new and prospective Eastern and Central European countries that had recently joined the EU, and were thus now represented in the G8. The newer democracies of Indonesia and Korea as well as Mexico, which was afflicted by drug wars, aroused similar concerns. The unifying fear was that economic distress would breed social unrest, political extremism, and authoritarianism, as it had in Europe and Japan in the 1930s. China had strong reasons to fear an intensification of its social instability, even if it did not share a democratic ideal as the ultimate goal, for Hu's absence was due to an insurrection in Xinjiang, Indeed, when added to the recent upset in Tibet, Xinjiang aroused the spectre that China could lose one third of its territory should the separatist forces succeed.

Political Control, Capital, Commitment, and Continuity

The fifth cause of solid success came from the adequate political control, capital, conviction, and continuity of the G8 leaders at home and abroad. Much leadership came from Obama, who had similar summit experience from the G20 London Summit in April, control of both houses of Congress, a fresh electoral mandate, and enormous popularity at home and abroad. Similarly, summit host Berlusconi was, uniquely in G8 history, hosting his third summit, with strong popularity and political control at home. His populist touch was seen in his much acclaimed last-minute decision to move the summit to ruins of L'Aquila, and to use the event to help with the task of reconstruction after the earthquake.

Constricted, Controlled Participation

The sixth cause of solid success was the still controlled, if increasingly less constricted, participation at the summit. By beginning on day one, the G8 was able to act alone on core issues such as Iran and set the broader strategy to secure advances on key issues such as climate change. The G8 had by now considerable experience in dealing with the G5 at the leaders' level and in the official-level HDP. The bond was intensified by housing the leaders and delegations in Spartan military barracks within walking distance of one another. As the only time the G8 had ever been held at the devastated site of a recent national disaster, leaders could see directly the nature of damage brought by ecological shocks, if they did not act together against climate change.

Conclusion

At the summit's end, Silvio Berlusconi, as chief architect and host of L'Aquila, could credibly claim credit for the event and his own role therein. The summit achieved enough in enough areas to make its convoy-like approach adequate, especially as the compelling challenge of climate change was where the most progress was made. Furthermore, the innovative format of ever expanding summit participation—from G8 to G8 plus G5 to MEF with 17 members to 'G40' over three days—proved to be a subject-driven formula that worked. L'Aquila thus bode well for the success of the 2010 G8 summit in Muskoka, Canada, and for more inclusive global governance, based on the continuing G8 core, in the years ahead (Harper 2009; Kirton 2009c).

References

ANSA (2009). 'Public Opinion on G8 Positive, Frattini.' 15 July.

Asahi Shimbun (2009). 'G8 Nuclear Statement.' Editorial. *International Herald Tribune/Ashahi*, 11 July.

Australian Financial Review (2009). 'Europe-centric G8 Has Outlived Its Usefulness.' Editorial. 11 July.

Barry, Colleen and Tom Raum (2009). 'Lackluster G8 Summit Brings Fresh Pressure for Expanding Too-Exclusive World Leaders' "Club".' *Associated Press*, 10 July.

Berlusconi, Silvio (2009). 'From La Maddalena to L'Aquila.' In J.J. Kirton and M. Koch, eds., *G8 2009: From La Maddalena to L'Aquila* (London: Newsdesk Publications).

Business Standard (2009). 'Time for a G11: The G8 Summit in Italy Has Turned Out to Be…' Editorial. 12 July.

Cerretelli, Adriana (2009). 'First Rehearsals for "World Governance".' [Prime prove di «governance planetaria».] Commentary. BBC Monitoring European text of report by Italian newspaper Il Sole-24 Ore website, 14 July. *Il Sole 24 Ore*, 11 July.

Cooper, Andrew F. and Agata Antkiewicz, eds. (2008). *Emerging Powers in Global Governance: Lessons from the Heiligendamm Process* (Waterloo: Wilfrid Laurier University Press).

Dinmore, Guy and Giulia Segreti (2009). 'Leaders Pledge $20bn for Food Security.' *Financial Times*, 11 July.

Feinberg, Julie and John J. Kirton (2009). 'G8 2009 Summit Performance: Promoting Democracy in Iran.' 9 July. <www.g8.utoronto.ca/evaluations/2009laquila/feinberg090709.html> (August 2010).

Financial Times (2009). 'Food Security Is G8 Chance of Relevance.' Editorial. 10 July.

G7 Finance Ministers (2009). 'The Lecce Framework: Common Principles and Standards for Propriety, Integrity, and Transparency.' 13 June, Lecce, Italy. <www.g8.utoronto.ca/finance/fm090613.htm#framework> (August 2010).

G8 (2007). 'Chair's Summary.' 8 June, Heiligendamm. <www.g8.utoronto.ca/summit/2007heiligendamm/g8-2007-summary.html> (August 2010).

G8 (2009a). 'Political Issues.' 8 July, L'Aquila, Italy. <www.g8.utoronto.ca/summit/2009laquila/2009-political.html> (August 2010).

G8 (2009b). 'Responsible Leadership for a Sustainable Future.' 8 July, L'Aquila Summit.   <www.g8.utoronto.ca/summit/2009laquila/2009-declaration.html> (August 2010).

G8 Research Group (2009). '2008 Hokkaido-Toyako G8 Summit Final Compliance Report.' <www.g8.utoronto.ca/evaluations/2008compliance-final/index.html> (August 2010).

Harper, Stephen (2009). 'The 2010 Muskoka Summit.' In J.J. Kirton and M. Koch, eds., *G8 2009: From La Maddalena to L'Aquila* (London: Newsdesk Publications).

Kirton, John J. (2006). 'Explaining Compliance with G8 Finance Commitments: Agency, Institutionalization, and Structure.' *Open Economies Review*, vol. 17, no. 4, pp. 459–475.

Kirton, John J. (2009a). 'A Summit of Sound Success: Prospects for the G8 at L'Aquila 2009.' 6 July. <www.g8.utoronto.ca/evaluations/2009laquila/2009prospects090706.html> (August 2010).

Kirton, John J. (2009b). 'Coexistence, Co-operation, Competition: G Summits.' *Aspenia*, no. 43–44, <www.g20.utoronto.ca/biblio/kirton-aspenia-2009.pdf> (August 2010).

Kirton, John J. (2009c). 'Prospects for the 2009 L'Aquila Summit.' In J.J. Kirton and M. Koch, eds., *G8 2009: From La Maddalena to L'Aquila* (London: Newsdesk Publications).

Kirton, John J. and Madeline Boyce (2009). *The G8's Climate Change Performance.* G8 Research Group. <www.g8.utoronto.ca/evaluations/g8climateperformance.pdf> (August 2010).

Kirton, John J. and Jenilee Guebert (2009). *Health Accountability: The G8's Compliance Record from 1975 to 2009.* 28 December. G8 Research Group. <www.g8.utoronto.ca/scholar/kirton-guebert-health-091228.pdf> (August 2010).

Kirton, John J. and Madeline Koch, eds. (2009). *The G8 2009: From La Maddalena to L'Aquila* (London: Newsdesk Publications).

Kirton, John J., Marina Larionova, and Paolo Savona, eds. (2010). *Making Global Economic Governance: Hard and Soft Law Institutions in a Crowded World* (Farnham: Ashgate).

Nikkei Weekly (2009). 'G8 Summit Sees Historic Shift.' 13 July.

Peiser, Benny (2009). 'G8 Stalemate Shows It's Time for Climate Cool-Down.' *Financial Post*, 11 July.

Persichilli, Angelo (2009). 'G8 Unable to Keep Up with World's Problems.' *Toronto Star*, 12 July.

Smith, Gordon (2009). 'Time to Get With It, G8 Admit "Second Class" Guests.' *Globe and Mail*, 14 July.

South China Morning Post (2009). 'G8 Food Fund the Right Step, If Promises Are Kept.' Editorial. 12 July.

Travers, James (2009). 'G8 Losing Lustre as Canada's Turn Nears.' *Toronto Star*, 11 July.

Xinhua (2009). 'News Analysis: G8 Summit Features Evolution of Global Governance.' 15 July.

Appendix 20.1   The achievements of the G8's L'Aquila summit 2009

Issue	Score	Factors contributing to success
Climate	B+	'all in', 2 degrees, 50/80 percent by 2050
Trade	B+	Doha, investment
Architecture	B+	accountability, Heiligendamm Dialogue Process, G20, new cycle
Democracy	B	Iran
Food	B–	$20 billion goal
Economy and finance	B–	stimulus, banking, currency devaluation
Average	B	

Appendix 20.2   G8 performance from 1975 to 2009

Year	Grade[a]	Domestic Political Management[b]		Deliberative			Directional[c]	Deci-sional	Delivery[d]	Development of Global Governance[e]	Attendees[f]	
		% Mem	Ave # Refs	# Days	# Statements	# of Words	# Refs to Core Values	# Cmts	Compliance	# Bodies	Min/Off	# Par C/IO
1975	A–	33%	0.33	3	1	1129	5	14	57.1	0/1	4/6	0/0
1976	D	33%	1.00	2	1	1624	0	7	08.9	0/0	7	0/0
1977	B–	50%	1.50	2	6	2669	0	29	08.4	0/1	8	0/0
1978	A	75%	3.25	2	2	2999	0	35	36.3	0/0	8	0/0
1979	B+	67%	3.33	2	2	2102	0	34	82.3	1/2	8	0/0
1980	C+	20%	0.40	2	5	3996	3	55	07.6	0/1	8	0/0
1981	C	50%	3.75	2	3	3165	0	40	26.6	1/0	8	0/0
1982	C	75%	1.75	3	2	1796	0	23	84.0	0/3	9	0/0
1983	B	60%	3.00	3	2	2156	7	38	–10.9	0/0	8	0/0
1984	C–	25%	0.50	3	5	3261	0	31	48.8	1/0	8	0/0
1985	E	33%	1.00	3	2	3127	1	24	01.0	0/2	8	0/0
1986	B+	80%	4.40	3	4	3582	1	39	58.3	1/1	9	0/0
1987	D	25%	6.00	3	7	5064	0	53	93.3	0/2	9	0/0
1988	C–	25%	0.50	3	3	4872	0	27	–47.8	0/0	8	0/0
1989	B+	50%	1.00	3	11	7125	1	61	07.8	0/1	8	0/0
1990	D	33%	0.67	3	3	7601	10	78	–14.0	0/3	8	0/0
1991	B–	20%	2.80	3	3	8099	8	53	00.0	0/0	9	1/0
1992	D	33%	1.33	3	4	7528	5	41	64.0	1/1	8	0/0
1993	C+	33%	1.00	3	2	3398	2	29	75.0	0/2	8	1/0
1994	C	40%	1.80	3	2	4123	5	53	100.0	1/0	8	1/0
1995	B+	25%	0.25	3	3	7250	0	78	100.0	2/2	8	1/0
1996	B	40%	0.40	3	5	15 289	6	128	41.0	0/3	8	1/4
1997	C–	40%	0.40	3	4	12 994	6	145	12.8	1/3	9	1/0
1998	B+	60%	1.00	3	4	6092	5	73	31.8	0/0	9	0/0
1999	B+	80%	1.60	3	4	10 019	4	46	38.2	1/5	9	0/0
2000	B	25%	9.50	3	5	13 596	6	105	81.4	0/4	9	4/3

Year												
2001	B	40%	1.20	3	7	6214	3	58	55.0	1/2	9	0
2002	B+	17%	0.17	2	18	11 959	10	187	35.0	1/8	10	0
2003	C	75%	1.25	3	14	16 889	17	206	65.8	0/5	10	12/5
2004	C+	33%	0.67	3	16	38 517	11	245	54.0	0/15	10	12/0
2005	A-	50%	0.50	3	15	22 286	29	212	65.0	0/5	9	11/6
2006		25%	0.25	3	8	30 695	256	317	47.0	0/4	10	5/9
2007		75%	1.25	3	6	25 857	651	329	51.0	0/4	9	9/9
2008	B+	33%	1.33	3	10	16 842	NA	296	48.0	1/4	9	15/6
2009	B	NA	NA	3	10	31 167	62	254	NA	NA	NA	28/10
Total				98	206	345 082	1,105	3,369		13/92	289	74/43
Ave. all	B-	43%	1.74	2.8	5				41.35	0.38/2.71	8.5	2.17/1.26
Av. cycle 1	B-	47%	1.94	2.1	2.9	2 526	1.1	29	32.46	0.14/0.71	7.43	0/0
Av. cycle 2	C-	46%	2.45	3	3.3	3 408	1.3	34	32.39	0.29/1.14	8.43	0/0
Av. cycle 3	C+	33%	1.26	3	4	6 446	4.4	56	47.54	0.58/1.29	8.14	0.57/0
Av. cycle 4	B	43%	2.04	2.9	6.7	10 880	5.7	106	42.17	0.58/3.57	9.00	0.86/1.00
Av. cycle 5	B-	49%	0.88	3	12.5	25 181	177	255.67	56.56	0.17/6.16	9.50	10.67/6.0

Notes: NA = not available. [a] Grades up to and including 2005 are given by Nicholas Bayne; from 2006 on are given by John Kirton, using a different framework and method [b] Domestic Political Management: % Mem is the percentage of measured G8 countries that referred to the G7/8 at least once that year in their national policy addresses. Ave # Refs = the average number of references for the measured countries. [c] Directional: number of references in the communiqué's chapeau or chair's summary to the G8's core values of democracy, social advance, and individual liberty. [d] Delivery: Compliance scores from 1990 to 1995 measure compliance with commitments selected by Ella Kokotsis. Compliance scores from 1996 to 2008 measure compliance with G8 Research Group's selected commitments. [e] Development of Global Governance: Bodies Min/Off is the number of new G7/8-centred institutions created at the ministerial (min) and official (off) level at or by the summit, or during the hosting year, at least in the form of having one meeting take place. The first number represents ministerials created; the second number represents official-level bodies created. [f] Attendees refers to the number of leaders of full members, including those representing the European Community, and the number of invited participants of countries and international organizations at the G8 leaders' session. Russia started as a participant in 1991 and became a full member in 1998. In 1975, the G4 met without Japan and Italy; later that year the G6 met. C = Countries; IO = International Organizations. The first number represents non-G8 participating countries; the second number represents participating international organizations.

Appendix 20.3 Summit performance for 2009

Documents	Date of Release	DPM Number of Members	CCC	Deliberation Words	Direction Setting DP	Decision Making CMT	MOM Old	MOM New	Delivery Compliance Catalysts Total	CIO (+)	OIO (−)	PP (+)	1YT (+)	Development of Global Governance G8 Bodies	MO	CSO	PPP
Responsible Leadership for a Sustainable Future	8 July	9	0	16 250	19	173	$462 billion	$1.2 billion	45	15	19	24	27	20	110	3	6
Political Issues	8 July	9	8	3160	13	18	0	0	−2	0	2	0	0	3	18	1	1
L'Aquila Statement on Non-Proliferation	8 July	9	11	1992	1	7	0	0	4	2	0	0	2	1	20	0	0
G8 Declaration on Counter Terrorism	8 July	9	0	1367	9	4	0	0	0	0	0	1	0	6	5	1	0
Joint Declaration: Promoting the Global Agenda	9 July	15	0	2035	4	26	0	0	0	2	4	5	2	3	12	0	1
Declaration of the Leaders of the Major Economies Forum on Energy and Climate	9 July	17	0	1086	2	9	0	0	5	1	0	1	4	2	0	0	3
A Stronger G8–Africa Partnership on Water and Sanitation	10 July	18	1	513	1	6	0	0	2	1	0	1	1	0	2	0	1
L'Aquila Joint Statement on Global Food Security	10 July	40	NA	1835	2	11	0	$20 bn	−1	1	3	2	1	NA	NA	NA	NA
Chair Summary of the G8–Africa Session at the G8	10 July	NA	NA	566	2	0	0	0	0	0	0	0	0	NA	NA	NA	NA
L'Aquila Summit Chair's Summary	10 July	NA	NA	2363	9	0	0	0	0	0	0	0	0	NA	NA	NA	NA
Total		20		31 167	62	254	$462 bn	$21.2 bn	65	22	28	34	37	35	167	5	12

Notes: DPM = domestic political management; CC = communiqué compliment; ST = statement; DP = democratic principle; CMT = commitment; MOM = money mobilized; CIO = core international organization; OIO = other international organization; PP = priority placement; 1YT = one-year timetable; G8 = G8 body; MO = multilateral organization; CSO = civil society organization; PPP = public-private partnership.

PART VIII
Conclusion

Chapter 21

Conclusion and Recommendations

John J. Kirton

Taken together, the analyses in this volume offer considerable consensus on several key issues but an ongoing debate, and the resulting need for further research and reflection, on many more. This blend of consensus, debate, and resulting recommendations arises in regard to all elements of the analytical framework— the financial and economic crisis, its consequences, the capabilities of the actors it affected, their policy responses, the innovations in these responses, governance at the international level, and recommendations for policy and institutional reform.

Crisis

The crisis is widely seen as having erupted with the collapse and nationalization of British bank Northern Rock in 17 September 2007, reaching a new height with the collapse of American investment bank Lehman Brothers on 15 September 2008, and abating by the autumn of 2009 with the return of growth in gross domestic product (GDP) in all leading economies save for the United Kingdom, even if American bank failures, unemployment, and mortgage defaults continued to increase.

In regard to the catalysts and causes of this global crisis, there is a consistent consensus in this book, although individual authors emphasize different parts of the causal chain. All agree that it was catalysed by the collapse of commercial and investment banks, flowing from their lack of the liquidity required to cover a sudden loss of confidence in their ability to meet their obligations. The ultimate cause, for Naoki Tanaka, was the policy choice of American authorities in response to the Great Depression and then the victory of World War II, to encourage widespread home ownership and consumer lending on a broader scale, with high consumption and low savings as a result. As Robert Fauver emphasizes, under the Clinton administration this priority was reinforced by policy changes and pressure from the administration, Congress, and Freddie Mac and Fannie Mae to lend on ever easier terms to ever more borrowers with an ever more limited ability to pay. Essential reinforcement, most agree, came from persistently lower interest rate policies by the U.S. Federal Reserve in response to the dot.com bubble that burst in 2000 and the terrorist attacks of 11 September 2001, as well as from the widespread adoption of the originate-to-distribute (OTD) model and securitization, for mortgages and other assets.

Several other factors were important: the willingness of European institutions to acquire and adopt such American-initiated financial products; public emphasis on the housing sector in Britain, Ireland, and Spain; the emphasis on export-led growth in Germany, Japan and above all China; a reliance on low-cost labour and imported capital on Europe's periphery; and the international imbalances and exchange rate misalignments that flourished as a result. Libero Monteforte adds the adoption of a 'new economy' paradigm, poor financial practices and supervision, and international imbalances, as well as the Clinton administration's decision to bail out the hedge fund Long-Term Capital Management (LTCM) in 1998 and the subsequent moral hazard. Carlo Bollino highlights the rise of world oil prices to historic nominal levels and European regulations requiring climate change control, both of which increased investment demands on industry as well as costs. Raffaele Galano focuses on the fundamentals of interconnected networks and information asymmetries, as well as a climate of financial euphoria and deregulation. In all, despite the tendency of some politicians, notably France's president Nicolas Sarkozy, to point to Wall Street in New York City as the cause of the crisis, all authors agree that there is enough blame to go around on a much wider scale. Indeed, the causes were global, involving many firms, national governments, and inadequate international institutions, spanning many countries and regions of the world.

There is a similar consensus on the depth and duration of the crisis. Most contributors see the 2007–09 crisis and its 'Great Recession' as unprecedented in severity since at least the Wall Street stock market crash in October 1929 and the Great Depression that ended only with the outbreak of World War II in September 1939. Yet for Fauver, the 2007–09 crisis was only the worst since the financial shocks and recession of the 1970s, catalysed by the oil shocks in 1973 and 1979. And others note it was merely the long-delayed, and hence more virulent, crisis flowing from poor policy choices in the preceding decades, and no worse in its depth, duration or character than the many that have afflicted the world before and will again. Drawing on work by Charles Kindleberger (1978), Bollino notes that such crises have come an average of every nine years since 1622. And indeed the 2007–09 came nine years after the last one in 1997–99.

However normal the 2007–09 crisis may have been from this standpoint, there was a highly sharp and severe downturn. As Fauver notes, global equity markets lost more than 50 percent, or $31 000 billion of market capitalization in one year, with similarly large decreases in average net worth and national GDP. And while most agree that it was a short-lived crisis, coming to an end with the resumption of growth for most countries by the end of 2009, few feel that the earlier *status quo* had been restored—or would be soon.

The contagious course of the crisis stood out for the speed and the scope of the spread across sectors, regions, and countries. What started as a financial crisis soon reached the real economy, and spread from the United States and the United Kingdom to all over the world. The conduits were the close interconnections between the financial systems of New York and London, the absence of a global regulatory framework for investment funds to contain the spread, and the dependence of so many economies on exports to a U.S. with sharply declining demand. Galano notes that the contraction of trade was particularly important for Latin America, led by Mexico and Brazil. Gregory Chin charts the wide array of economic channels through which the crisis came to the emerging economies, with only the foreign aid channel still in some doubt.

With regard to the comprehension the actors had of the character and course of the crisis, the consensus is that it was low, and indeed remains rather low. Several authors note how surprising the onset of the crisis was. Monteforte attributes the widespread surprise and misunderstanding to its exceptional size and the inability of standard econometric models to include the deep parameters of risk aversion that lay at its core. He notes that uncertainty continues about the type of crisis. This suggests that the global financial system and economy have become a complex adaptive system that the old linear models could not capture. Yet the fact that William White of the Bank for International Settlements (BIS) and a few private sector economists saw it coming suggests that early warning systems are possible, even if the inner working of the crisis remain poorly understood.

Consequences

There is a general consensus about the consequences of the crisis, across regions and countries, in the economic and political realms, over the short, medium, and longer terms. In the economic realm, in the short term, the crisis was felt first in the financial system and then in the real economy, with the dynamics in one sphere intensifying those in the other one. As risk aversion increased, business confidence, investment, and consumer demand plummeted, and household saving increased. The financial crisis reduced banks capital and reserves and household savings.

As Fauver notes, U.S. growth and average net worth plummeted, with particularly strong costs for pre-retirement baby boomers and the newly retired. In Japan, where the financial system concentrated risks in banks' loan assets, the consequences were not home grown but imported. As Tanaka says, as early as May 2008 the market capitalization of companies exporting to China began a massive correction. In October 2008 Japanese firms drastically reduced inventory in anticipation of the worldwide final durable demand being reduced by half. In export-dependent Europe, the decline in U.S. demand first hit the manufacturing sector hard, especially in Germany, while countries with large financial sectors or financial sectors—the UK, Spain, Ireland, and Austria— were also hit hard, along with Turkey and Russia outside the European Union. Inflows of foreign capital quickly dried up in Eastern Europe. Banks and securities markets in countries with less developed financial systems, such as— some would say—Italy, were less affected by the crisis but still felt its effects.

In the short term, as Chin emphasizes and Victoria Panova and Raffaele Galano confirm, the crisis had a very different impact among Brazil, Russia, India, and China (BRICs). China, with its closed financial system and the reforms it took in response to the 1997–98 crisis, suffered the least, with only a short and mild slowdown in growth, exports, and employment, and with growth resuming by March 2009. China thus was on course to overtake Japan as the world's second largest economy, and Germany as the world's largest exporter, by 2010. Russia suffered the most among the BRICs and the G8, as incoming foreign direct investment (FDI) dried up, even if the high inflation rate declined. India and Brazil stood in the middle. The latter's exports and government revenues shrank, as did capital exports to Latin America and consumer credit there as a whole.

While Diéry Seck portrays sub-Saharan Africa as highly vulnerable to the crisis, George von Furstenberg reports that the region's GDP declined only mildly at a rate slightly above the contraction in global output but far less compared to the members of the Organisation for Economic Co-operation and Development (OECD). Moreover, African countries with oil or commodities to export did well, and the lack of integration between African and global financial markets helped too.

Another short-term effect came in the realm of ideas. As Subacchi notes, the finance ministers of Germany and Italy blamed Anglo-Saxon-style capitalism for the crisis China started resisting Anglo-American management and models. More broadly, the basics of financial market and macroeconomic theory were cast into doubt within the Anglo-American world itself.

It remained unclear how fast and far the recovery would take hold in the medium term or longer. Bollino notes that most predicted a quick, V-shaped recovery, as in recessions past. But Paola Subacchi argues that Europe would suffer for a very long time. Rising public indebtedness would likely endure well past the next decade in advanced economies from a pre-crisis average of 70 percent debt-to-GDP ratio to 90 percent in the five years after 2009, with more for the U.S., Japan, Italy, and Ireland. Most agree that rising long-term debt, the upward path of long-term bond rates, inflationary pressure, and the strained ability of government to obtain financing would make the recovery long and slow. Indeed, output may not return to its pre-crisis level but may remain permanently below, especially in Europe and Japan with their low population growth. Paolo Savona and Chiara Oldani see global imbalances, instability, and challenges to the dollar standard increasing as well. The implications for official development assistance (ODA) for the developing world remain unknown.

In the geopolitical sphere, most contributors judge the impacts of the crisis to be significant. The dominant view, following former Brazilian president Ignacio Lula da Silva, is that the crisis has made the G7 and the BRICs more equal (Zakaria 2008). Panova concludes that the BRICs can now challenge the G7: by 2050 the four countries will be among six largest economies in the world. Led by Jim O'Neill of Goldman Sachs, some see China's growth intensifying to the point where it will overtake the U.S. economically and the BRICs will overtake the G7 in 20 years. Galano, citing Goldman Sachs, similarly says that in 2040 China, India and Brazil will overtake the EU countries and in 2043 China will surpass the United States. Chin cautions that there is no consensus on the impact of the crisis on the BRICs' continuing rise in the world, with some seeing it stalling. Indeed, long-term forecasts are hard to make, as those who were optimistic about a booming Japan in the 1980s know all too well. But Chin concludes that the crisis could bring a significant qualitative shift in the global order, and Panova confidently concludes that Russia too will soon resume its rise. However, as Galano emphasizes, the different interests and positions among the BRICs make it unlikely that they will become a single bloc to challenge or lead the rest. A new bloc-versus-bloc bipolarity, reminiscent of the Cold War, is thus unlikely to emerge.

Within the major polities, the budget cuts, fiscal stimulus, and rising unemployment brought by the crisis could strain social cohesion and intergenerational solidarity. But they could lead citizens to rely more on the state. And thus far the crisis had led none of the newer democracies to relax or reverse course, in any way reminiscent of Germany during the interwar years.

Capabilities

The responses of the individual regions and countries to the crisis and its consequences depend importantly on the capabilities each can bring to bear. Here there is a strong consensus on the capabilities and resources that the BRIC countries had at the time of the crisis, in size, surplus or surge capacity, and resilience. This strength was substantially a result of the lessons they learned from the previous global financial crisis of 1997–99, which had afflicted them the most and the established G7 powers the least.

Within the developed world, most countries beyond the United States and Canada had been, in contrast, hampered by declining populations, poor productivity growth, and a reliance on labour-intensive industries (as in Spain). In sharp contrast to many G7 powers, the BRICs started the crisis with strong macroeconomic fundamentals. As Galano notes, in 2007 the BRICs held more than 40 percent of international reserves, while China, Russia, three Gulf states, and Singapore held 42 percent of global savings. Among the established powers, only Japan stood out, as China, Japan, and Russia had the largest foreign exchange reserves.

Among the BRICs China led with high reserves, room for policy easing, a high savings rate and low leverage, and a low level of foreign debt relative to its large foreign currency reserves. Indian banks had strong balance sheets, were well capitalized and regulated, and sported capital adequacy ratios well above Basel norms, with the result that none had to be rescued by the state.

Beyond these big two, since 2003 Brazil's economy had grown at an annual average of 5 percent. It derived considerable strength from its reforms over the previous decade, its Real Plan strengthening external accounts and controlling inflation, its commodity boom, and its expanding middle class with buying power. Reinforcement came from inside the BRICs as commodity demand from China and India let Brazil build large foreign exchange reserves. As Galano documents, between 2003 and 2007 Latin America as a whole had boomed as never before, with rising raw material prices, trade, remittance inflows, low interest and inflation rates, exchange rate stability, low financial volatility, balanced public accounts, and accumulating international reserves.

In the decade before the crisis, as Panova charts, Russia enjoyed the strongest sustained growth in its history, with GDP rising almost seven fold in nominal U.S. dollars—more than any other major country. Large capital inflows helped Russia's international reserves reach almost $600 billion. Sustained fiscal surpluses almost ended its public debt, and foreign assets reached 13 percent of GDP by the end of 2008. Russia, which had defaulted in August 1998, had built up large foreign exchange reserves from its large oil and commodities exports, which were soon in demand once again by the second half of 2009.

Seck shows in sub-Saharan Africa countries started with no crippling external debt, but they had low human development performance, were increasingly losing ground to other regions, and were disadvantaged by highly landlocked transportation, low life expectancy, and high dependence on volatile commodity exports. In contrast, von Furstenberg emphasizes the large amount of ODA that Africa has received, the good growth it enjoyed prior to the crisis, the abundant oil and commodities exports of some African countries, and the relative insulation of sub-Saharan African financial systems from those in the developed world.

In the critical and related realm of resilience and invulnerability, the BRICs also did best. China's lack of mature integrated financial markets protected it from the Anglo-American meltdown. The country had a latent trade capacity by going down the technological scale to export to Asian neighbours when markets in the G7 dried up. China, like Brazil, had a state-controlled economy that allowed government to direct credit to the sectors where it was needed most. Brazil's growing manufacturing and service sectors alongside its booming commodities gave it a resilience that others lacked, notably a country dependent on energy exports such as Russia. But even as Russia also suffered from a declining population, as Panova notes, expatriates felt safe and wanted to stay, while its undervalued stock market and companies offered other underlying strengths.

Response

With this configuration of capabilities, national governments, international institutions and firms responded swiftly, comprehensively, and on a massive scale, in several standard ways. The dominant response came in fiscal stimulus, monetary stimulus, and direct financial support, reinforced in a second stage by domestic financial regulatory reform.

Fiscal stimulus was led by the U.S., first with the Troubled Asset Relief Program (TARP) designed to purchase banks' toxic assets, then with a second fiscal stimulus of $787 billion from Barack Obama's *American Recovery and Reinvestment Act* passed on 17 February 2009, and, finally, from an expansionary budget. Japan quickly passed three stimulus bills, once again relying on new public works to increase the number of jobs. Europe was slower to stimulate, but for 2009 Germany budgeted a deficit of 3.3 percent of GDP, France 8.75 percent, Italy almost 6 percent, and Spain 2.8 percent. On 10 November 2008, China announced a seemingly large fiscal stimulus of $586 billion, consisting largely of subsidized credit and aimed at encouraging growth and domestic consumption in 10 areas. The U.S. and Chinese stimulus plans were larger than Europe's, especially as Germany was reluctant to see its deficit rise as an election loomed. But the combined fiscal stimulus in 2009 represented about 10 percent of global GDP. The stimulus was spent largely on traditional infrastructure projects, tax reductions, and subsidies. Outside the G7, Russia's April 2009 budget produced stimulus focused on education, health, and pensions. Brazil, too, used macroeconomic stimulus and sought expanded international cooperation.

In monetary policy, the U.S., Japan, and China relied heavily on a rapid drop to very low levels of policy interest rates, with China relying on credit rationing as well. Despite an ill-timed rise from the European Central Bank (ECB) at the outset of the crisis, monetary policy interest rates were soon reduced to near zero almost everywhere. As Subacchi notes, from the collapse of Lehman Brothers in mid September 2008 to March 2009, the Bank of England cut its interest rate by 450 basis points. While the ECB lagged with a rate still 1 percent higher, its subsequent cut to 1 percent was the lowest since the euro had been created. Savona and Oldani note that central banks moved swiftly to supply any amount of monetary base to cover the drastic reduction in the velocity of money. In China, India, and Latin America central banks also used monetary policy easing. As Galano details, the latter employed international reserves as well to stabilize exchange rates and export credit, lowering compulsory reserves and public banks for credit.

Direct financial support also came, starting with Britain's nationalization of Northern Rock in September 2007—the first British bank to fail since the 19th century save for Barings in 1995. The Netherlands, Belgium, and Switzerland also soon supported their troubled banks. In the U.S. the Federal Reserve continuously injected liquidity into markets. Ireland and Greece guaranteed all domestic deposits. When the credit crunch hit in August 2007, the ECB led by injecting and emergency £4.8 billion into the euro area's money markets. From 2007 to 2009 $2 trillion was spent to support financial institutions through capital injections, guarantees, or partial nationalizations. G8 countries together spent trillions of dollars in direct rescue plans for financial institutions and other firms. The European Bank for Reconstruction and Development (EBRD) also gave direct support to Eastern European countries and Iceland. Elsewhere Brazil's central bank injected $100 billion into the banking system and gave special financing through state banks for the agricultural and industrial sectors.

Financial reform in the U.S. came as the administration sought a complete overhaul of financial market regulations and a consolidation of oversight into a single agency. The Securities Exchange Commission (SEC) imposed a central clearinghouse for over-the-counter (OTC) transactions, such as credit default swaps. Europe moved more rapidly, for example when the European Commission and parliament created a working group in July 2007 to explore the causes of the crisis. In February 2009 the de Larosière report recommended a new regulatory structure, stronger and more coordinated supervision, more effective crisis management, and 31 improvements in the global financial architecture. It emphasized the weakness of Basel II capital requirements, the procyclicality of its rules, the weak link from shadow banking systems, poor credit rating practices, and the need for more simplified and standardized OTC transactions. However, in contrast to the U.S., Europe had not put these recommendations into practice by mid May. At the firm level, Japanese firms shifted to focused on the research-intensive environmental and clean energy sector.

While there is considerable consensus on the content of key policy responses, there is more debate about their appropriateness and adequacy. Most contributors to this volume approve of the rapid rediscovery, new respectability and deployment of Keynesian monetary and policy stimulus, and the speed at which action was taken, at least relative to the days of the Great Depression. But Fauver concludes that only time will tell if the unprecedented stimulus in the U.S., Japan, and China will work. Bollino considers Europe's response to have been poor, due to poor learning, indecisiveness over strategy, and the absence of a common or even coordinated fiscal policy to align with its monetary one. Subacchi sees similar defects. Monteforte disapproves of the ease with which the EU abandoned its previous consensus to control members' deficit and debt limits. He highlights the difficulty of matching fiscal stimulus with ever changing growth forecasts and getting the added spending into the real economy in a timely way. He also notes that governments proclaimed gross figures rather than net ones, with some such as the automotive industry benefiting disproportionately from the spending surge. The Greek crisis seemed to confirm these concerns.

Savona and Oldani point out that Europe's stimulus was late and thus larger than needed, as well as poorly coordinated, due to differing structural constraints in EU members' economies and the lack of will to use and strengthen its institutions. They single out Britain and France and, to a lesser extent, Italy for trying to save themselves at Europe's expense. They argue that Europe was less effective as a result. Bollino criticizes the ECB's decision to raise interest rates at the worst time in July 2008.

Most contributors approve of the reduction of monetary policy interest rates to nearly zero. However, they worry about the medium- and long-term inflationary effects, the need for exit strategies to be clearly recognized, and the likelihood that resulting global imbalances and free but asymmetric exchange rate regimes will cause problems in the years to come.

In the realm of financial regulation, Monteforte notes that regulatory reform in Europe was undertaken without a proper analysis of its structural effects. Savona and Oldani add that the U.S. and the SEC moved to regulate the OTC market without understanding what credit derivatives really were.

Innovation

In the face of a crisis of such historic challenges, the authors in this volume see relatively little innovation in the instruments, ideas, and institutions. Much of the innovation that did come is judged to have been less for the better than potentially or actually for the worse. Nor was did the greatest innovation come in those countries suffering the worst consequences. As it was the very lack of earlier financial innovation that helped many countries escape the worst consequences of the financial crisis, there was a diminished incentive for such innovation and an increased desire to move back to basic 'balance sheet banking' in the years ahead. In all, national governments and international institutions everywhere seemed to have failed the test, wasting the opportunity for innovation created by the crisis.

In the realm of instruments, innovation came as much in scale as in design. In the U.S. TARP was used to inject capital into banks through direct injections rather than to buy troubled assets, and the stimulus package was historic in its size and back-end loading. Japan's supplemental budget emphasized energy credits and its firms moved to invest in green research and development. The Bank of England created a monetary base unprecedented in its 340-year life, in part through quantitative easing. Ireland and Greece guaranteed all bank deposits. From Europe and the U.S. came direct financial support to endangered sectors, detailed regulations during peacetime on how much firms could pay their senior staff and car scrappage schemes.

In the emerging economies, in 2008 Russia adopted a growth strategy for 2020 focused on innovation and creativity, with less reliance on energy exports and overseas borrowing. Its budget had a three-year horizon for the first time and introduced the new concept of a non–oil-and-gas balance. China, with no historical experience in stimulating demand, produced a major fiscal stimulus. The crisis moved it to a new growth strategy based not on exports but on industrial upgrading and technological innovation. The Reserve Bank of India created a rupee-dollar swap facility for Indian banks. In Brazil Lula established a sovereign wealth fund of $6.4 billion. China and Brazil drew up sectoral development plans.

In the realm of ideas, the crisis discredited the efficient market hypothesis in favour of behavioural finance theory. It also ended the EU's orthodox monetary and fiscal policies and the underlying principle of intergenerational equity. In monetary affairs, the European elite suggested the use of the euro as a global reserve currency, while BRIC members wanted their national currencies used in the special drawing right (SDR) created by the International Monetary Fund (IMF). EU economic commissioner Joaquín Almunia rejected the proposal of Zhou Xiaochuan, governor of Bank of China, for a larger use of SDRs and the coordinated management of international reserves at the IMF. The concept of a supernational money was supported only by Kazakhstan within the intergovernmental Shanghai Cooperation Organisation (SCO), which also includes China, Kyrgyzstan, Russia, Tajikistan, and Uzbekistan.

In the realm of global governance, an early proposal for a TARP-like plan in the EU was quickly rejected. Europe's needed new paradigm for individual talent, new human capital, lean state regulation, and a new energy and climate regime was not in sight, nor was the proposal set out in the de Larosière report for a European Systemic Risk Council (ESRC) and a European System of Financial Supervision (ESFS). The G8 at the 2009 L'Aquila Summit pointed out the urgent need for a common legal standard for financial markets and players, but no such standard materialized. Despite bold declarations from French president Nicolas Sarkozy and others, there was no real sign that the concept of sovereignty itself was under serious assault.

In the realm of institutions, the new allocation of SDR 250 million by the G20 leaders at their London Summit in April 2009 was an important short-term step but not a long-term solution. The IMF still lacked a uniform exchange rate regime or single global monetary standard. More modestly, however, the IMF invented new standby arrangements and a flexible credit line. Iceland became the first western country to be bailed out by the IMF since 1976, followed by Greece in 2010, aided by the EU, and, at the end of the year, Ireland. The crisis helped give emerging countries the promise of greater voice and vote in the IMF, the World Bank, and the BIS. The BIS increased the number of permanent member countries in its Basel Committee on Banking Supervision (BCBS), adding some emerging countries as well as the BRICs. The new Financial Stability Board (FSB) was formed from the Financial Stability Forum, with broader membership. Most broadly, the BRIC meeting in Yekaterinburg in 2009 showed the emergence of a new group that could challenge the G7.

Yet there remains real doubt about the effectiveness of these innovations in preventing future crises and in putting a better global economy in place. Massive fiscal and monetary easing could lead banks to take on risky assets and thus pose medium-term problems, and allow an accumulation of global imbalances and asymmetric exchange rate regimes and reserves. The massive interest rate reductions and quantitative easing by central banks posed an inflationary threat. The unprecedented accumulation of debt as a result of large-scale fiscal stimulus pointed to rising long-term bond rates, inflation, and difficulties in government financing. And there were no signs that any serious smart, coordinated exit strategies were being designed or put into effect.

Governance

In regard to the changes in global governance catalysed by the crisis, much uncertainty prevails and consensus remains elusive. There is a common conviction that, despite the unprecedented, 1930s-like character of the crisis and the responses, the ideas and institutions of global governance have not yet been transformed in any way comparable to the creation of the Bretton

Woods architecture in 1944 (Ikenberry 2001; Ruggie 1983). Nor has the crisis seriously challenged, let alone replaced, such fundamental conceptual pillars of the global order as state sovereignty and a market economy unsubordinated to any supernational source of authority that could end the structural anarchy and market instability of old. Rather, it has led more modestly to stronger powers, resources, and reforms for the old institutions, notably the IMF and the EU. It did catalyse the creation of several new, innovative plurilateral institutions, notably the G20 and BRIC summits and the FSB. It also re-energized the expanding G7/8 system, especially in the finance and economic domain. But how well the newly invented and newly reinvigorated institutions are designed and operated—and how they will come together to overcome their institutional rivalries, deliver effectively, and thus create a new generation of global governance—remain a matter of great debate and doubt (Fratianni et al. 2005; Kirton et al. 2010).

The International Monetary Fund

The greatest area of agreement is about the advances made, and those still needed, in the IMF—the pillar of the existing system. The crisis revived the IMF, which had had its relative resources and powers over its members reduced since 1971, by restoring its prominence, capabilities, and even the process of institutional reform. As Giorgio La Malfa notes, it also had a place for all the oil-exporting countries and emerging markets with the needed resources. Juan Carlos Martinez Oliva adds that the crisis also created an agreement that a new international monetary order was needed, and that the IMF would have a central place within it, as the Chinese proposal for a new monetary standard showed. The current system, Domenico Lombardi notes, contains a deep instability that may affect the globalization the world has enjoyed since the 1980s.

Yet most conclude that the IMF, while moving in the right direction, failed in many ways. It ignored the key issues of asymmetric exchange rates, global imbalances, and the need for a different monetary standard beyond the U.S. dollar. It also did not operate an adequate global warning system, nor did it find a way to scrutinize and adjust the policies of all its members, including those in the G7, including, above all, a sovereignty-sensitive United States. There was also little actual change in the asymmetric quota and voting power, the rules for majority decision making, the composition of the IMF's executive board, and the selection of the managing director, although significant progress had been made by the end of 2010. Moreover, in the crisis the IMF's International Monetary and Financial Committee played only a marginal role.

The Multilateral System

Other pillars of the 1940s multilateral firmament failed as well. The World Bank needed the G20's London Summit to raise the resources on which the developing world—including sub-Saharan Africa—depends. United Nations agencies have high ratios of operating costs to disbursements, as von Furstenberg notes, and the United Nations Development Programme (UNDP) spends more on its administrative budget than it gives in aid. John Kirton emphasizes how the failure of many multilateral organizations, including the World Trade Organization (WTO), the International Labour Organization (ILO), and the Food and Agriculture Organization (FAO), helped lead the G8 to its achievements at its L'Aquila Summit in 2009. In contrast, the BIS, which predicted the crisis and gave emerging countries permanent membership in its BCBS, is seen as performing and reforming well. So is the FSB, having welcomed new emerging members.

The Other Contenders

There is also a combined acknowledgement that regional, functional, or plurilateral contenders have thus far failed to show that they are essential elements, or relevant components or competitors of any new order that might be formed. The EU comes in for particularly harsh criticism for its failure to take common decisions, to issue directives to secure financial regulatory reform, to broaden its macroeconomic surveillance and rules beyond fiscal deficits, and to create a common fiscal policy to match its monetary one. The BRICs held their first summit on 16 June 2009 at Yekaterinburg, and called for more transparency and democracy and a greater role for them in the international financial institutions, showing they could challenge the G7. But natural unity among the BRIC countries remains limited, as not all members share a colonial history or even membership in the WTO. Andrew Cooper and Andrew Schrumm also suggest that other new institutions, such as the SCO and the India–Brazil–South Africa (IBSA) Dialogue Forum could emerge as challenges. But few other authors note how they did or might. And La Malfa notes that the still unborn G2 of the U.S. and China is unlikely to be acceptable to the rest of the world, or effective.

The Group of Twenty

The most promising contender to serve as the platform for a new generation of global governance is the new G20 summit-centred system (Bradford Jr. and Lim 2010; Kirton and Koch 2009a, 2009c; Kirton and Alexandroff 2010). It sprung into life at the leaders' level in November 2008, mobilized major new money at its second summit in April 2009, and proclaimed it would become the primary permanent centre of global economic governance less than a year later at its third summit in Pittsburgh in September 2009. Yet there remains disagreement about how well the G20 has been designed and has dealt with the crisis, and how well it will be able to deal with central issues in the emerging post-crisis world.

Several authors see the G20 as promising in both its design and early performance. Cooper and Schrumm view it as the nucleus of informal global governance thanks to its innovative quality, equality of membership, and diversity of perspectives; it also has support from the G20 forum of finance ministers and central bank governors. The latter included emerging powers from all quadrants of the globe as equals as a response to the global financial crisis of 1997–99 and to the broader challenges brought by globalization (Kirton and Koch 2009b; Kirton 2010). If the G20 extends further beyond its economic agenda, it could produce a multidimensional grand bargain that bring a new order as a whole, in the same way the World War II 'after victory' moment did (Ikenberry 2001). Others add that the G20 strengthened the position of Brazil and other emerging economies, pushed a new financial order with a greater role for emerging countries, had leaders directly discuss monetary matters and IMF reform, and put the IMF back at centre stage.

However, Cooper and Schrumm note that relying on the G20 is risky, due to its diverse membership, ever expanding European participation, narrow agenda, lack of legitimacy compared to the UN's 'G192', and the exclusion of legislators. Hugo Dobson adds that the G20's connection with civil society has been confined to the uncivil parts. Others add that the G20 has displayed disunity and delay in its response to the crisis, has done increasingly little to strengthen financial regulation and supervision, and offers no guarantee of making and implementing the substantive decisions that the G8 also has not.

The Group of Eight

An even more vigorous debate surrounds the well-established G8, with its expanding array of participants at its annual summits and in its ministerial and official-level forums. Cooper and Schrumm assert that the era of the G8 is coming to an end, as the crisis highlighted the failures of efficiency as well as legitimacy in a club that confines rising powers to second class status and fails to deliver on the economic, global, and security issues where it claims the leading role. Bollino adds that the G8 cannot generate a common policy that meets the different needs of the U.S. and Europe, beyond issuing a communiqué with vacuous words. Other defects include the failure of the 2008 Toyako-Hokkaido Summit to address the financial crisis explicitly, the inadequate representation of emerging Asian economies, the erosion of democratic commonality in a club that now includes Russia, the downside of the variable geometry formula used at L'Aquila, the endorsement at L'Aquila rather than improvement of what the G20 had done at London a few months before, and L'Aquila's failure to address global imbalances seriously or inspire Europe to speak with a single voice.

However, La Malfa argues that L'Aquila revived the G8, endorsing the need for global standards for than merely European ones and supporting the Lecce Framework—a body of common principles and standards regarding the conduct of international business and finance set out by the G8 finance ministers at their June 2009 meeting. Sara Savastano concludes that the G8 backed the needed countercyclical policies. Kirton, too, sees L'Aquila as a summit of solid success, across the economic, Transnational, and security domains, with accomplishments in climate, trade, G8 architecture and accountability, democracy in Iran, and food security. This was due in part to an experienced host and a variable geometry formula that functioned. L'Aquila was properly designed to be open innovative, inclusive, sustainable, and accountable. It succeeded, leading G8 leaders to decide to meet again in France in 2011 and, as Cooper and Schrumm note, extend and expand the renamed Heiligendamm–L'Aquila Process (HAP).

In regard to the larger issue of legitimacy, Kirton notes that all the heads of the world's major multilateral organizations, representing everyone, considered the G8 sufficiently legitimate to come when they were called. Dobson details how the G8 has developed a dense network of supportive civil society, in contrast to a G20 which has little. And others emphasize how the G8 challenged the wisdom of the unregulated market, in a way that others did not.

Coherence in Global Governance

The greatest source of disagreement and doubt is over how these major international institutions will cooperate or compete to put a new global order in place, or at least adequately govern the existing one once the impact of the 2007–09 crisis is gone for good.

Panova argues that the crisis inspired all the major contenders—the G20, the G8, HAP, the BRICs, and the SCO—to action and to support a far-reaching reform of the global financial architecture, if not a supernational currency or any diminution of state sovereignty. Galano adds that the crisis showed that all these international institutions could play a useful role. Kirton sees the G8 at L'Aquila working in a supportive tandem with the London G20. The chair of each cooperated actively. The G8 communiqué made 15 direct references to the London Summit. The G8 gave support and leadership to the G20. And the L'Aquila G8 brought together the heads of most major multilateral organizations, succeeding where they themselves had failed.

In contrast, Dobson notes that the division of labour between the G8 and the G20 is unclear. He reports the view that a turf war could erupt. Cooper and Schrumm see some inevitable tension between the G20 and G8. Lombardi notes that the G20 can serve as a global steering committee that uses the IMF for implementation, but also that the IMF with a new ministerial council can take centre stage as it has the political capital and legitimacy that the G20 still lacks.

Recommendations

On the basis of these conclusions, many authors offer policy recommendations directed at several countries, regions, and international institutions. Those recommendations range from those feasible for the short term in regard to critical components through to those fundamental changes required over the long term for the global system as a whole. All are based on the conclusion that the existing responses, innovation, and governance have been inadequate to the scale of the crisis and the consequences it has brought. There is a general consistency in the direction, if not the details of the short- and medium-term measures, but a vigorous debate about the bigger proposals for international institutional redesign.

At the country level, Tanaka suggests that Japan adopt a strategy with specific targets, for enhancing the role of labour, agriculture supply, medical care, other services, environmental production, and innovative production. A comprehensive chain of reforms to enhance Japan's role in Asia would give highest priority to environmental protection and resource conservation and, in the medium to long term, supply-side retraining and life-long education, capital equipment, research, and the creation of a coalition of the willing for a low-carbon society.

Many recommendations are directed at the EU, to have it serve as a stronger, more unified actor in global financial and economic affairs. In regard to financial regulation, the European Commission and parliament should legislate into existence the key recommendations of the de Larosière report to establish new bodies for financial supervision and ensure that issuers of securitized products retain some portion of them for a meaningful time. On banking it should segregate financial businesses, contain liquidity risk, limit the size of deposit insurance to avoid moral hazard, and prevent free riding on the public guarantee. It should make any derivative in the global financial system that is collateralized, and not just the credit default types of contracts, pass through a central clearinghouse. Its regulations should cover all counterparties. Subacchi says Europe urgently needs more policy coordination, as well as a timely, clear, credible response to sovereign debt crises such as Greece's and a plan for fiscal consolidation backed by structural policies, and public support and domestic fairness. Europe also needs stronger EU fiscal and economic surveillance of its members and smarter criteria for the admission of new states.

In terms of macroeconomics policy, the EU should monitor national economic performance more comprehensively to highlight the potential for instability. Bollino suggests it produce binding principles and rules for intergenerational solidarity in fiscal policy, and consider inflation as an exit strategy as well. The EU should press for a revalued Chinese renminbi, new rules for foreign exchange management, and a new global monetary standard, as China's central bank governor has suggested.

With regard to emerging economies, Galano recommends short-term policies that ensure social cohesion in economically difficult times. For developing countries more broadly, Savastano suggests countercyclical policies and increased financial flows from developed countries for this purpose. She also calls for safety nets to protect the poor and vulnerable, open markets in trade, and G8 investment in education, health, and infrastructure, and also more monitoring and impact evaluation on the part of international organizations involved in development. For developing sub-Saharan Africa in particular, Seck offers a comprehensive slate of institutional and international development reform, for which von Furstenberg provides a comprehensive critique.

A further set of recommendations are directed at the international monetary system with the IMF at its institutional core. Lombardi focuses on IMF reform, suggesting that the IMF provide members with collective insurance against payment crises instead of their current reliance on accumulating large national exchange reserves. He further recommends the regular creation of SDRs that are allocated to countries as reserves, so that the SDR would gradually become key global reserve asset, as advocated by the UN Commission of Experts on Reforms of the International Monetary and Financial System. Moreover, resources should be permanently endowed to the IMF through a quota increase.

Pietro Alessandrini and Michele Fratianni recommend that a restricted group of key countries, led by the U.S. Federal Reserve and the ECB, create a supernational bank money within a clearing union to stabilize the international monetary system, It would become supernational money for central banks. Martinez Oliva agrees that that the IMF should have a greater role in reserve management and that the proposal to create a supernational bank money is needed and feasible given China's interest; however, because it is not in the interests of the U.S., he doubts it can be created.

A more vigorous debate arises in regard to the role and design of the new G20-centred system, and its relationship with the older G8. Cooper and Schrumm see the G20 summit as the future winner. They endorse the proposal that it should have a legislative companion, suggest it develop a rotational G20 secretariat or informal management group that shares duties equally among all members, and consider paring down its membership from 20 to 14 or 13. Dobson argues that the G20 should follow the G8 in developing the civil society institutions and involvement that mirror and even surpass the G8 ones. In contrast, La Malfa sees the 2009 L'Aquila Summit as reviving the G8 as an effective global economic governor and recommend that it take up the big issue of global imbalances. Kirton shares this favourable view of the G8's 2009 performance and the future potential to which it points.

References

Bradford Jr., Colin I. and Wonhyuk Lim, eds. (2010). *Toward the Consolidation of the G20: From Crisis Committee to Global Steering Committee* (Seoul and Washington DC: Korea Development Institute and Brookings Institution).

Fratianni, Michele, Paolo Savona, and John J. Kirton, eds. (2005). *New Perspectives on Global Governance: Why America Needs the G8* (Aldershot: Ashgate).

Ikenberry, G. John (2001). *After Victory: Institutions, Strategic Restraint, and the Rebuilding of Order after Major Wars* (Princeton: Princeton University Press).

Kindleberger, Charles P. (1978). *Manias, Panics, and Crashes: A History of Financial Crises.* 5th ed. (Hoboken: John Wiley and Sons).

Kirton, John J. (2010). 'The G20's Global Governance Network.' In A.S. Alexandroff and A.F. Cooper, eds., *Rising States, Rising Institutions: Can the World Be Governed?* (Washington DC: Brookings Institution).

Kirton, John J. and Alan S. Alexandroff (2010). 'The "Great Recession" and the Emergence of the G20 Leaders' Summits.' In A.S. Alexandroff and A.F. Cooper, eds., *Rising States, Rising Institutions: Can the World Be Governed?* (Washington DC: Brookings Institution).

Kirton, John J. and Madeline Koch, eds. (2009a). *The G8 2009: From La Maddalena to L'Aquila* (London: Newsdesk Publications).

Kirton, John J. and Madeline Koch, eds. (2009b). *The G20 London Summit: Growth, Stability, Jobs* (London: Newsdesk Publications).

Kirton, John J. and Madeline Koch, eds. (2009c). *The G20 Pittsburgh Summit 2009* (London: Newsdesk Publications).

Kirton, John J., Marina Larionova, and Paolo Savona, eds. (2010). *Making Global Economic Governance: Hard and Soft Law Institutions in a Crowded World* (Farnham: Ashgate).

Ruggie, John G. (1983). 'International Regimes, Transactions, and Change: Embedded Liberalism in the Postwar Economic Order.' In S.D. Krasner, ed., *International Regimes*, pp. 195–232 (Ithaca: Cornell University Press).

Zakaria, Fareed (2008). *The Post-American World* (New York: W.W. Norton).

Index

Global Finance Series

Full series list